# THE
# ROCK
# ALBUM

# THE
# ROCK
# ALBUM

## MAXIM JAKUBOWSKI

Frederick Muller Limited
London

First published in Great Britain 1983 by
Frederick Muller Limited, Dataday House,
London, SW19 7JZ.

British Library Cataloguing in Publication
Data
Jakubowski, Maxim
  The rock album.
  1
  1. Music, Popular (Songs, etc.) —
  Periodicals
  I. Title
  780'.42'05      ML3545

  ISBN 0–584–11045–6

Printed in Great Britain by
Butler & Tanner Ltd, Frome and London

**Maxim Jakubowski** was the creator of
the successful *Rock Yearbook*, now in its
third year. He is the author of *The Wit and
Wisdom of Rock and Roll* and writes for
the leading British music weekly, the *New
Musical Express*. A publisher, he is also
known for his fantasy fiction.

# Introduction

Few people would question the fact that rock music has somehow become the foremost sound of the latter half of our twentieth century. Itself the complex, bastard offspring of country and western, hillbilly, blues and other influences, rock has since splintered into a myriad of categories and sub-genres: rock 'n' roll proper, progressive rock, punk, new wave, fusion rock, country, outlaw music, reggae, soul, disco, funk, electro-pop and so on.

The record industry as we know it has been forged by the advent of rock and, despite difficult times, still caters extensively to the public's varied tastes. There are undeniably too many records (and, even more so, many bad records) being released and it has become increasingly difficult for the average buyer to keep up with the flow of 'product' landing each week in the record stores' racks. Most retail outlets in England and America no longer have in-store listening facilities and it's often a source of puzzlement to many who try and rely on reviews in specialist music papers to get even a basic idea of the sound or type of a particular new performer or band on record.

Which is where this book comes in.

In 1980, I conceived *The Rock Yearbook* (published by Virgin Books in the UK, Delilah/Grove Press and in later years St Martin's Press in the USA) as an entertaining, heavily illustrated annual almanac providing a complete souvenir of the past year in the field of rock and popular music. One of the most popular features in this volume was an extended album review section covering all the major records released on 33 $\frac{1}{3}$rd in the UK and the USA during the twelve months covered in the book. The majority of the capsule reviews were written by me (under an assortment of pen-names to conceal my natural megalomania) with the principal contributors to the *Yearbook* each supplying a few in their specialist areas. To avoid a bland, boring consensus of opinion, our policy was very much to offer idiosyncratic, personal views of the records which in many cases did in fact differ strongly from the generally accepted view. After I left the originating publishing house, my successors there changed this album review section into a more selective one covering a smaller percentage of the year's releases; furthermore, the concept of personalised reviews was dropped and replaced by the device of comparing excerpts from already existing reviews published in an assortment of newspapers and magazines. Being a sucker for writers with a strong personality, I decided, here we go again,

that this is where *The Rock Album* should come in.

On the one hand, *The Rock Album* contains not just a selection but reviews virtually *all* the rock albums released in the UK and the USA (with some selective Canadian and European albums). This proved a formidable task; pinpointing releases by the major companies was no problem, but locating what precisely has been published by small, sometimes regional labels out in, possibly, Poughkeepsie or Milford-On-Sea who only made one album this year in a limited pressing of, say, 100 copies (half of which were bought at a special discount by the lead singer's grandma) possibly eluded me on occasions. This, I regret and hope that in years to come, such small independent companies will recognise my quandary, manifest themselves and make my task easier (I can be contacted – and will review anything I am sent – through this book's publishers).

On the other hand, I have continued to make these capsule reviews a very personal affair indeed, betraying my sometimes unusual tastes, my twisted sense of humour and my assorted prejudices. Compare opinions on records you already own or performers you idolise and you will soon find out if you usually agree or disagree with me on rock music, the meaning of life and the gender of angels. Should you perchance scream on every occasion I do a nasty on a group you like, this can still be a useful book: avoid the records I recommend and systematically hunt down those I damn.

Why me? Why Maxim Jakubowski?

Well, the book was my idea and someone had to write it who would not be driven into double-reinforced insanity at the prospect of spending most of the year listening to rock music and who wouldn't mind becoming the prime target for hate mail (music fans can be very touchy, you know). Who the hell am I and why do I think I should foist my opinions upon thousands of innocent readers? Well, I see myself as an average music lover (and an above-average collector, needless to say). A strong classical and folk music buff until the age of sixteen, I only came to rock (which makes it sound like a vocation) when Bob Dylan went electric, thus missing out to a large extent on the early days of the Sun label, Presley and other pioneers. I still have an unfortunate blind spot when it comes to Presley, whom I've always disliked most intensely (there goes half of my potential readership. . .). The Beatles came and conquered and I was hooked for ever on the sound of the elec-

tric guitar. Mind you, it's the electric bass guitar which I truly love; if I could play an instrument, that's the one I'd practice in front of my mirror while listening to my hair turning grey, striking macho poses and seeing my growing children ask me with doubt in their eyes whether I really saw the Fab Four perform live at the Paris Olympia. But, alas, I never did learn to play an instrument or read music when I was younger and took up the acoustic typewriter instead. . . . You should hear my end of line bell, though, it's really quite striking in an asthmatic and tintinnabulating way!

I certainly don't see myself as a full-time critic of music. In fact, my occasional contributions to *New Musical Express* are usually about books and science fiction.

The main idea behind these reviews is to be informative, so that the reader might rapidly identify under what category any given record falls, be it reggae, lethal heavy metal, punk, country, etc. . . . Then, once you have become accustomed to my Mister Average views, you will quickly recognise what you are likely to enjoy and might have missed out on.

This first volume of *The Rock Album* covers 1982 releases and while the majority of the albums covered are still available in shops – many should already be in the bargain racks, thus making your buying spree less onerous. Hopefully, year after year, *The Rock Album* will build up into an invaluable consumer reference guide of use to impulse buyers, vinyl freaks, record retailers, record buyers, the curious and fans of music and will be a *fun* book to leaf through years or months after the fact.

Don't read this book in one go, it's not a novel. Take your time, pick out a few reviews at random, choke in despair on my obscene judgements, then wonder, 'Oh, what does he say about those incredible albums I have by the Newsky Prospekt or the Phosphorus War?' and check out the entries with a sting of anticipation ringing through your ears or other relevant parts of your body. Flit from one review to the other. Keep it handy on your shelves and plunge back into it at regular intervals. It might not work wonders for your health but it will certainly harm your wallet by making you buy more records than you should! Which doesn't mean I'm an undercover agent for the record industry, but every record sold increases the chances for new musicians to get recording contracts and that's where the future of music must lie.

Recent developments in the music industry have seen a sharp increase in the output of EPs or mini-albums and a trend towards cassette-only releases (particularly by the enterprising New York REACH OUT INTERNATIONAL label). As this project was primarily meant to cover album releases (almost 2,000 in 1982!) I have been obliged to adopt a conservative approach here: there is only a small selection of the more representative EPs in the book and there are *no* cassette-only reviews. Possibly next year, time, contacts and finance allowing. Similarly, I have avoided listing most past hits compilations, especially TV-advertised ones not available in record stores.

To speed up publication of the book, the reviews were written (and delivered to the publishers for instant typesetting) on a quarterly basis, which explains the volume's lay-out and occasional lack of reference earlier on to later events such as, for example, the break-up of the Jam or Squeeze. When two labels are listed, this indicates that the record was released by different companies in the UK and the USA (in that order). Certain 1981 records are also listed where the album was only released in one or the other country in 1982. *The Rock Album*'s other charms and quirks are mostly self-evident.

This is the part where I have to thank all the people who helped. It might be quite boring for you, the reader, out there in the great unknown beyond this typewriter and turntable but there's not for you to reason why. So, a warm kiss and/or a vote of thanks to Sheri Safran, Antony White, Katie Cohen, Moira O'Donnell, Richard Laws, Colin Lewis and Emily White. Press Officers and record companies' staff without whom, as the saying goes are too numerous to mention, but particularly helpful were Berni Kilmartin (Chrysalis), Iain McNay (Cherry Red), Mike Hales (A&M), Kit Buckler (CBS), Colin Bell (Phonogram), Julian Henry (Albion), Rob Partridge and Neil Storey (Island), Sue Humphries (MCA), Brian Southall and his merry bunch at EMI. Sorry, folks, when the review is a bad one.

Star-billing, naturally, to my wife Dolorès and junior pop fans Adam and Natasha who suffered a vinyl invasion, a loss of family life and thousands of dubious noises percolating through the walls of my study throughout the whole year, and provided me with so much more than just moral support.

*Maxim Jakubowski*

## A

### THE ACT
**Too Late at Twenty** (Hannibal)
Sound melodic pop by new British band, but the songs by Nick Laird-Clowes albeit sweetly pleasant, lack originality and display a pervasive range of diverse influences (Costello, Parker, Joe Jackson). Breezy but forgettable; their next album is worth looking out for, though. Produced by Joe Boyd and John Wood.

### ADC BAND
**Roll With the Punches** (Cotilion)
Detroit-based US soul group with three lead vocalists. Decent party music. Produced by Bill Curtis, Gerry Thomas and the group.

### AFRAID OF MICE
**Afraid of Mice** (Charisma)

First album by new British group. Enthusiastic outing by vocalist Philip Franz Jones cannot help conceal the rather boring songs with many pretentions of modernity. Anonymous but professional and oh so very middle-of-the-road with a strong voice but music that just lacks the right commitment and goes through motions seen (or rather heard) a hundred times before. Produced by Tony Visconti.

### AFTER THE FIRE
**Batteries Not Included** (CBS)
Safe, middle-of-the-road rock and roll from a British band of some experience and limited success. This is their third album and although it doesn't suffer from some of the religious pomp of previous efforts, it does nothing to elevate the group from the second division of the music business. Easy listening, what else can one say?

### AIR CONDITION
**Namyslowski** (Affinity)
Interesting jazz-funk from a Polish group. Although a trifle old-fashioned, you can tap your toes to it without breaking too much sweat. Poland is, in fact, a hot-bed for jazz and, despite the current political juncture, it does appear that the strains of fusion rock are making place for a quirky dose of funk, English-style. Produced by Zbigniew Namyslowski.

### ALABAMA
**Mountain Music** (RCA)
Huge in America and going nowhere fast everywhere else, this Southern band are in the tradition of the original Allman Brothers Band and uphold a rich tradition of musical virtuosity which combines blues and country in satisfying proportions. This time around, there are pleasant strains of the late-lamented Creedence Clearwater Revival on the upbeat numbers and, elsewhere, a mellow tone (including a lullabye!) but overall the group just seems to lack that little something extra, a spark of personality that would make it a truly original outfit. Title track and CCR's 'Green River' are the best tracks. Produced by Harold Shedd and the group.

### ALTERED IMAGES
**Happy Birthday** (Epic)

| | |
|---|---|
| Intro Happy Birthday | Happy Birthday |
| Love and Kisses | Midnight |
| Real Toys | A Days Wait |
| Idols | Leave Me Alone |
| Legionnaire | Insects |
| Faithless | Outro Happy Birthday |
| Beckoning Strings | |

Already a major success in Britain in the winter, the first Altered Images album was only released early in 1982 in the USA. The title track of this album by a very young Scottish group achieved number one status in the UK charts. The music is a refreshing mixture of poppish whimsy with an infectious beat which owes a lot to the archetypal British new wave sound (particularly Siouxsie and the Banshees, one of whom produced the record). However, it's Clare Grogan's little girl swoops and swoons in her high-pitched voice which, after an initial period of disbelief

and possibly irritation, wins you over. The tunes range from happy, insoucient pop ditties to sometimes more sombre and atmospheric pieces but the general effect is refreshingly innovative and attractive. Produced by Steve Severin (title track by Martin Rushent).

### ANGEL CITY
**Night Attack** (Epic)
Mild-mannered Australian heavy metal band with nothing like the power of their compatriots AC/DC. Tepid riff wars. Produced by Ed Thacker, John Brewster and Rick Brewster.

### ANVIL
**Hard'n Heavy** (Attic)
With a name like Anvil, you expect heavy metal mayhem and that's just what you get. This time around it's from Canada and the liner notes indicate with a stupendous lack of originality that you should 'play it loud'. The lead singer is called Lips and all the tunes sound much the same to me, submerged as they are in manic sturm and drang. Unusual cover of the Rolling Stones' 'Paint It Black'. For addicts only.

### APACHE
**Apache** (Atlantic)
Heavy American rock of the thirteen to the dozen variety. The most memorable thing about this record was that it was co-produced by the usually better-advised Ahmet Ertegun, who should, as the saying goes, have known better than to add a children's choir to 'Please Don't Stop the Music'. We all remember what W. C. Fields said about children and dogs, don't we? Apache don't and this is no slur on the Indian nation.

## CARMINE APPICE
**Carmine Appice** (Riva/Pasha)
A solo album by a drummer . . . which says it all I fear. Has any such effort ever made the grade in the past? No, sir. Appice, late of Vanilla Fudge, KGB, Beck, Bogert & Appice and now dutifully employed by Rod Stewart, gives his vocal chords an outing on self-penned songs and covers of rock classics. Must have been authorized by young Rod as a necessary tax-loss for his record label. Produced by Richard Podolor.

## ASIA
**Asia** (Geffen)
Asia is: Geoffrey Downes (Keyboards, Vocals), Steve Howe (Guitars, Vocals), Carl Palmer (Drums, Percussion), John Wetton (Lead Vocals, Bass). Asia is: the first genuine super-group of the 1980s. You know, a Supergroup, an assemblage of well-known musicians who have been big, but really big, man, in previous groups, preferably of the late '60s or early '70s. Asia is: an album that rapidly made it to the top of the US LP charts, bearing witness to sales in the hundreds of thousands of units. The pedigree is perfect; ex-Buggles, Yes, ELP, Family, King Crimson, etc. . . . The music is slick, polished, professional rock, with a swing, a beat and a calculated touch of classical pomp. In brief, Asia is: just what the big record companies think the public want. Old-fashioned music that bears little relation to today's state of rock. But it sells, so who am I to criticise the ringing bells of the cash registers of consumerland? Produced by Mike Stone.

## THE ASSOCIATES
**Fourth Drawer Down** (Situation 2)
A two-man Scottish group, The Associates released one of the finest albums of 1980 'The Affectionate Punch' which I described in *The Rock Yearbook* as 'often

reminiscent in its romantic, operatic bleakness of the David Bowie of 'Station to Station'.' Since then, they have released a continuous batch of singles which didn't score in the British charts despite flattering reviews. This album, originally released in Germany, collects all these singles and B-sides and therefore does not truly constitute a new Associates album (see 'Sulk' in Part Two). The influence of Bowie has faded from the melodies of the songs, but Billy Mackenzie's strong, passionate voice still reminds one of the Thin White Duke. These are quirky, unpredictable songs which take some getting used to but are ultimately most rewarding: 'Tell Me Easter's on Friday'. 'A Girl Named Property', 'White Car in Germany'; impenetrable, intriguing lyrics and a flamboyant, deceitfully melodramatic delivery make this an album to go back to time and again to discover further pleasures. Produced by the group.

## ASWAD
**A New Chapter of Dub** (Island)
One of the best reggae albums of the year, carefully dosing traditional dub values and clever, but unobtrusive, experimentation. Full of fire and commitment, combining advanced studio techniques with impeccable playing. Produced by Michael Campbell and the group.

## ATLANTIC STARR
**Brilliance** (A&M)
Quality soul-cum-funk with a healthy touch of disco dance paraphernalia. Lead vocalist Sharon Bryant powers the superlative 'Circles' while Wayne Lewis takes the honours on 'Sexy Dancer'. Produced by James Anthony Carmichael.

## THE ATTRIX
**Procession** (Scoff)
Overdue debut album by young Irish

group. Recorded over a period of two years and using various producers, the LP never coalesces into a whole and remains patchy throughout . Odd mixture of pop and gloom with quirky discordances. Should improve if given another chance. Produced by Midge Ure, Philip Chevron and Jim Leekie.

## MIKE AULDRIDGE
**Eight-String Swing** (Sugar Hill)
Virtuoso dobro instrumentals by a master of the genre. A satisfying mixture of folk, bluegrass and even jazz (an idiosyncratic version of Duke Ellington's 'Caravan'). Produced by Mike Auldridge.

# B

## LOU ANN BARTON
**Old Enough** (Asylum)
First album by an American big white hope. Comparisons are already being made with Janis Joplin as Barton is clearly capable of switching from raucous barrelhouse rockers to tender blues or country ballads. Careful production has in fact avoided a surfeit of her live boogie-woogie repertoire by giving her a number of more contemporary songs (Marshall Crenshaw's 'Brand New Lover', Allen Toussaint's 'It's Raining') to balance her innovative interpretations of golden oldies ('Maybe'). A highly promising debut by a lady who's going to be big. Produced by Jerry Wexler and Glenn Frey.

## THE B-52'S
**Mesopotamia** (Island/Warners)

| | |
|---|---|
| Loveland | Cake |
| Deep Sleep | Throw That Beat |
| Mesopotamia | in the Garbage |
| | Can |
| | Nip It in the Bud |

The B-52's first two albums displayed a tacky form of chic that betrayed more than

BILLY MACKENZIE: THE ASSOCIATES

a hint of calculation. But you could dance to clever rhythms while smiling at the obviously twee lyrics about 'Planet Clare' or 'Rock Lobster'. Their new effort is a profound disappointment, as well as a step in the wrong direction. Using David Byrne of Talking Heads as producer for this abbreviated set, described as a mini-album, shows the group taking itself too seriously and indulging in a spurious dance-as-art posture that never really makes it.

## BIRTHDAY PARTY/LYDIA LUNCH
**Drunk on the Pope's Blood/The Agony is the Ecstasy** (4AD)
An unusual combination this, with two performers sharing opposite sides of an album. The Birthday Party are an intense avant-garde Australian group whose first album revealed strong Captain Beefheart ('Safe-as-Milk' period) influences while Lydia Lunch is a shrieking madonna of the New York experimental scene, whose vinyl output has been most varied and never uninteresting. Both sets here were recorded live at the London Venue and bear witness to what the performers were at in November 1981. The results are somewhat incoherent with neither performers attaining the strengths of previous studio recordings, although both hint at intriguing possibilities.

## BLACK FLAG
**Damaged** (Unicorn)
Los Angeles hard-core power punk. It's amusing how the intensity of UK punk soon deserted home shores and found itself transplanted not to the dark alleyways of New York, as one might logically have expected, but to the gutter-level clubs of California, betraying the sun and surf mental image we usually hold of the place. After X, here comes Black Flag and what amazes about this record is its sheer level of intensity. These are musicians who are angry, who vent their feelings with an uncommon force that makes listening an obligation. Sometimes samey, always loud. Punk certainly isn't dead yet.

## BLACK UHURU
**Tear it Up** (Island/Mango)
A live collection from the reggae band now ready to take on the international recognition of the late Bob Marley. Recorded on the occasion of a European tour, the trio are here accompanied by the Taxi Allstars. Produced by Alex Sadkin and Godwin Logie.

## BLAH BLAH BLAH
**Blah Blah Blah** (Trans Universal)
Unremarkable self-released album by a synthesiser band who had a track on last year's 'Some Bizarre' compilation.

BLACK UHURU

## THE BLASTERS
**The Blasters** (F-Beat/Slash)
Polished revivalist rock and roll from new US band. A rightful blend of R&B, soul and rockabilly. Singer Phil Alvin delivers gutsy versions of 'Marie, Marie', 'Highway 61', 'I Love You So'. American music in the best tradition.

## FRANKIE BLEU
**Who's Foolin' Who?** (Unicorn)
Standard writer-performer's sensitive first album mixes ballads with up-tempo numbers. Won't set the world on fire, but some might like it. Produced by Joe Chemay.

## MICHAEL BLOOMFIELD
**Cruisin' for a Bruisin'** (Sonet/Takoma)
A last album from the revered blues guitarist. Rough production and voice but a decent souvenir nonetheless. Produced by Norman Dayron.

## MICHAEL BLOOMFIELD
**Living in the Fast Lane** (BBJ)
A sampling of quality blues guitar from reasonably recent sessions prior to Bloomfield's death. Produced by Norman Dayron.

## ANGELA BOFILL
**Something About You** (Arista)
Third album from an American singer with strong jazz and blues roots. Polished production sees her tackle soulful middle-of-the-road numbers in an attempt at gaining a wider public. Better on uptempo numbers. Produced by Narada Michael Walden.

## MARC BOLAN & T. REX
**Across the Airwaves** (Cube)
Yet another Bolan compilation from the vinyl vaults, compiled this time around by his fan club and including some original BBC radio sessions. Many stalwarts: 'Jeepster', 'Hot Love', 'Ride a White Swan'.

MARC BOLAN

## THE BONGOS
**Drums Along the Hudson** (PVC)
15 dance-pop tracks by a young Hoboken band. Pleasant but generally innocuous (includes all the songs on the British-released 'Time and the River'). Produced by Ken Thomas, Mark Abel and the group.

## THE BONGOS
**Time and the River** (Fetish)
Mini-album of nice songs by nice guys with a barrelful of classic pop influences.

## KARLA BONOFF
**Wild Heart of the Young** (CBS/Columbia)

| | |
|---|---|
| Personally | Gonna Be Mine |
| Please Be The One | Wild Heart of the Young |
| I Don't Want To Miss You | It Just Takes One Dream |
| Even If | |
| Just Walk Away | |

Third, long-awaited, album by an outstanding West Coast writer/performer many of whose earlier songs had been covered (blandly) by Linda Ronstadt. There is always a sharp poignancy of romantic despair in Karla Bonoff's songs but, this time, it has been tempered by an injection of rhythm and blues, particularly in the orchestrations, which doesn't always suit her confidential style. The album is never less than pleasant but suffers from blandness and, dare I say it, a lack of commitment in the emotional stakes as if she were just going through the motions. Can do better; will do better. Produced by Kenny Edwards.

## THE BOOMTOWN RATS
**V Deep** (Mercury/Columbia)
It's easy to say now that I was never very impressed by the Boomtown Rats, even in the early days when they were scoring hits in Britain with alarming regularity. Though always full of pep and candour, their songs smacked of crafty manipulation and never truly ingested the influences of whoever else had a commercial style (Sparks, Seger, Springsteen. . .). Geldof's hour of glory has come and we are now left with an established band still desperately trying to carve out an original musical persona. This album veers with wild abandon from one style of music to another without ever settling for a mood. It's clever, it's slick, but ultimately it's ever so vacuous, even when espousing Caribbean rhythms in 'House on Fire', the only hit to make it from the album. Produced by Tony Visconti and the group.

DAVID BOWIE

## DAVID BOWIE
**Baal** (RCA)

| | |
|---|---|
| Baal's Hymn | Ballad of the Adventurers |
| Remembering Marie A | The Drowned Girl |
| | The Dirty Song |

Released in the UK as an EP and in the USA as a mini-album, 'Baal' is the soundtrack for the Bertolt Brecht play which Bowie performed in the title role on British television. Bowie's voice surprisingly moulds itself around the Weill and

Brechtian-like music by Dominic Muldowney and appropriates the style as if he had always sung that way. Theatrical but immensely powerful, these songs demonstrate Bowie's chameleon-like facility at adopting a European 'chanteur' style as he did, years ago, when interpreting some songs by Jacques Brel. It's not pop by a long way, but fascinates and seduces. Produced by Tony Visconti and David Bowie.

## DAVID BOWIE
**Christiane F. – Original Soundtrack** (RCA)
As Bowie is steering clear from recording studios this year, we must make do with film and teleplay soundtracks. This is the background music for a notorious German film about a teenage drug addict in Berlin (in which Bowie appears briefly in a concert sequence). Includes 'Heroes' (in English and German), 'TVC-15', 'Warszawa', 'Station to Station' and many other Bowie recordings of the same period. Produced by Bowie and Tony Visconti

## GLENN BRANCA
**The Ascension** (99)
New York experimentalist with a rock guitar and bass line-up. Original, demanding but never less than fascinating.

## LAURA BRANIGAN
**Branigan** (Atlantic)
Powerful new American female rocker with debut LP. Her material could be better but she is definitely a name to watch. Produced by Jack White.

## THE BREAKFAST BAND
**Dolphin Ride** (Breakfast Music)
Debut album for London band in a jazz mould. An ambitious outing with an assortment of ethnic dance numbers. Skilled and lively. The album was cut using the ½-speed mastering technique and pressed under classical-type conditions to ensure quality of sound. Produced by the band.

## BRIAN BRIGGS
**Combat Zone** (Avatar/Bearsville)
Mainstream rock by an expert musician who produces (under his true name) and plays guitars, keyboards, percussion and sings. Bright pop songs which, however, leave no lasting impression on my memory. Produced by John Holbrook.

## GARY BROOKER
**Lead Me to the Water** (Mercury)
Solo album by the leading personality in Procul Harum. The voice and the melodies are instantly recognisable but the final result is not memorable. The musicianship is irreproachable (Phil Collins, Eric Clapton, Henry Spinetti, Albert Lee, George Harrison, Mel Collins and Chris Stainton are amongst the friends backing Brooker) but there is a pervading sense of dullness that surrounds the whole procedure. There was often a poignancy (mitigated by pretentiousness) that coloured the songs of Procul Harum post-'Whiter Shade of Pale'; here, Brooker invokes little emotion. Produced by Gary Brooker.

## BROTHERHOOD OF BREATH
**Yes Please** (In & Out)
British jazz band, now based in France; with an enviable pedigree, a mellow outing on the borderlines of funk. Superlative musicianship (Chris McGregor, Harry Beckett, John Tchicai, Mark Charing, etc. . . . .). Worth investigating.

## JACK BRUCE & ROBIN TROWER
**Truce** (Chrysalis)
Cream meets Jimi Hendrix for the nth time around! Predictable but perversely enjoyable blues workouts by veteran musicians with little new to offer, but great ways of doing so!

## BRUZER
**Round One** (Handshake)
Typical anonymous American radio rock. Produced by Bill Pfordresher.

## BUCKNER & GARCIA
**Pac-Man Fever** (Columbia)
New American duo with a right eye for catchy hooks. Commercial but unenter-

GARY BROOKER

prising. Video-game concept makes this a novelty album. Produced by Buckner and Garcia.

## JIMMY BUFFETT
**Somewhere Over China** (MCA)

Buffett's laid-back ditties with their perfume of sea spray and Florida beaches have never really broken through outside the USA. On this new album, he injects some emotion into his songs and seems to be catching up with reality. Best tracks are 'When Salome Plays the Drums' and 'It's Midnight and I'm Not Yet Famous'. Produced by Norbert Putnam.

## THE BUGGLES
**Adventures in Modern Recording** (Carrere)

The Buggles scored a massive hit with 'Video Killed the Radio Star' and then sort of faded away. This second album sees them treading commercial ground again, but the hooks and gimmicks are much less in evidence, replaced on some songs by a touch of pomp (courtesy of Yes?) and the magic seems to be lacking. Intelligent pop with pretensions to more (*viz.* borrowing 'Vermilion Sands' from SF writer J. G. Ballard). Produced by Trevor Horn. John Sinclair and Geoff Downes.

## CORNELIUS BUMPUS
**A Clear View** (Broadbeach)

Solo jazz and rhythm and blues outing by Doobie Brothers brother. Fluent saxophone and flute and occasional vocals. Average. Produced by Cornelius Bumpus and C. Randolph Nauert.

## THE BURRITO BROTHERS
**Sweet Sundown** (Curb)

From album to album, the Burrito Brothers have been shedding members of their original line-up with increasing regularity. Where they once pioneered electric country-rock, they are now just one of many exponents of this richly mined genre. This new album is slick and pleasant but will shift no mountains (or hills). For fans only. Produced by Michael Lloyd.

# C

## BOBBY CALDWELL
**Carry On** (Polydor)

R&B artist moves sideways to a more middle-of-the-road approach. Slick, smooth and silky but dull and lifeless. Produced by Bobby Caldwell.

## J. J. CALE
**Grasshopper** (Mercury/Shelter)

| | |
|---|---|
| City Girls | Drifter's Wife |
| Devil in Disguise | Don't Wait |
| One Step Ahead | A Thing Going |
| of the Blues | On |
| You Keep Me | Nobody But You |
| Hangin' On | Mississippi River |
| Downtown L. A. | Does Your |
| Can't Live Here | Mama Like to |
| Grasshopper | Reggae |
| | Dr. Jive |

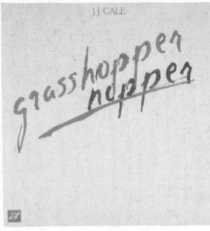

A new J. J. Cale album is like an old J. J. Cale album: an old friend with whom an hour-long conversation will offer quiet pleasures, never surprise and soon be forgotten. This one is no exception. Cale still slurs his vocals in his lazy, inimitable fashion while taking on a variety of musical styles which he reduced to his own common laid-back denominator. Steel drums dominate the title track, a rare innovation for Cale who, elsewhere, duets with paramour Christine Lakeland on a selection of blues, country, rock, R&B and even a soft reggae tune. Produced by Audie Ashworth and J. J. Cale.

## THE CALL
**The Call** (Mercury)

An innovative new American band. Assisted by the Band's Garth Hudson, The Call produce some memorable and lively rock. Lead vocalist Michael Been stands out as a particularly strong personality. The album soon landed in bargain racks but should be investigated as the band might

re-emerge again. Produced by Hugh Padgham.

## IRENE CARA
**Anyone Can See** (Network)

Solo debut for the singer/actress of *Fame*. Standard versions of old reliable showbiz toons like 'Reach Out, I'll Be There' and 'Anyone Can See'. A trifle histrionic but powerful voice. Produced by Ron Dante.

## CENTRAL LINE
**Breaking Point** (Mercury)

Veterans of the British dance floor gangs, Central Line have been slow in putting their music onto vinyl. This is their first album and the experience shows through. First-class songs ('Walking into Sunshine' was the major hit) which is a must for any party. Recommended.

## A CERTAIN RATIO
**Sextet** (Factory)

A disappointing release by a promising band. Once seen at the forefront of a British 'intellectual funk' revival, A Certain Ratio have here deserted their rhythms of dance and lapsed into funereal dirges more suited to a wake than a dance floor. New vocalist Martha Tilson sings in a sombre mood a variety of samey pieces, few of which really stand out, as did last year's 'Waterline'. Too much intelligence (and experimentation) spoils the bopping broth. Self-produced.

## PETER CETERA
**Peter Cetera** (Warners)

Solo album by Chicago (the band) member. Superfluous.

## BILL CHAMPLIN
**Runaway** (Elektra)

Solo outing by former Sons of Champlin founder and veteran session man. Versatile, slick and, ultimately, run-of-the-mill effort which adds little to the politics (and philosophy) of modern rock. Produced by David Foster.

## CHARLENE
**I've Never Been to Me** (Motown)

As *Billboard* puts it aptly, 'soft, mass appeal adult contemporary fare'. Smooth and sickly, but effective in its radio saturation aims I suppose. Produced by Ron Miller, Berry Gordy and Don Costa.

## THE CHEATERS
**Sweat It Out** (Revo)

Muddy, 'live' sound for a shot of rhythm and blues, British-style, from a struggling Manchester band. Raucous, rough and ready and startlingly unoriginal. It's all been heard before and done better by bands already long out of fashion. This won't strike any R&B revival. Produced by Neil Brockbank and Phil Ault.

### CHUBBY CHECKER
**The Change Has Come** (MCA)
The man whose invention of the Twist first got me on to a dance floor whilst at grammar school (the headmistress had youthful legs and figure, I recall – a very progressive school it was indeed) now tries a comeback with innocuous versions of more recent rock songs ('Under My Thumb', 'It's Only Rock and Roll'). A curiosity. Produced by Evan Pace.

### CHRON GEN
**Chronic Generation** (Secret)
Skinhead punk beat and thrash. Appreciated in some circles. Not mine. Produced by Rock Cassman and the group.

### THE CHURCH
**The Church** (Carrere/Capitol)
Neo-psychedelic Australian band with strongly-accented 12-string guitar sound. Very much in a '60s groove, but never too contrived, pleasant pop songs. Worth get-

ting at reduced prices. Produced by Chris Gilbey and Bob Clearmountain.

### THE CIMARONS
**Reggaebility** (Pickwick)
An established reggae band tackles a bevy of old-fashioned standards at the initiative of Paul McCartney (who owns all the copyrights involved). Awful idea and awful record. However if you wish to hear reggae versions of 'Mull of Kintyre', 'Arrivederci Roma', 'Pickin' a Chicken', 'Love Me Do' and others, you're quite welcome. Produced by Vic Keary and Sid Buckner.

### CLASSIX NOUVEAUX
**La Vérité** (Liberty)
Second album by British group sometimes seen as part of the short-lived new romantic movement. One track stands out by a long shot: 'Is It a Dream' – but the rest is sadly bland and instantly forgettable. Promises unfulfilled. Produced by Sal Solo, Colin Thurston and Mik Sweeney.

SAL SOLO: CLASSIX NOUVEAUX

### LINDA CLIFFORD
**I'll Keep On Loving You** (Capitol)
Quality soul album where Clifford is in good voice and ably assisted on some tracks by Luther Vandross. First-class dance music. 'Let it Ride', 'Ain't You Glad' and 'Build a Fire' stand out. Produced by Leo Graham and Michael Gore.

### DAVID ALLAN COE
**Rough Rider** (Columbia)
Once the epitome of the hard-rocking country 'outlaw' artists, David Allan Coe has never truly fulfilled his earlier promises. This album goes no way towards redeeming his status; it is one of his weakest. An uneven compendium of songs in conflicting styles and content. Produced by Billy Sherrill.

### NATALIE COLE
**Happy Love** (Capitol)
Lightweight soul by Nat 'King' Cole's daughter. Her silken voice is always a pleasure but she is let down by her choice of material. Only covers of Percy Sledge and Junior Walker's respective 'When A Man Loves A Woman' and 'These Eyes' catch the attention, although Smokey Robinson's producer, George Tobin, expertly papers over the cracks elsewhere. Can do better.

### JUDY COLLINS
**Times of our Lives** (Elektra)

Great
  Expectations
The Rest of
  Your Life
Grandaddy
It's Gonna Be
  One of Those
  Nights
Memory

Sun Son
Mama Mama
Drink A Round
  To Ireland
Angel On My
  Side
Don't Say
  Goodbye Love

After a series of disappointing albums nodding a touch too far in the direction of respectable show-biz, Judy Collins makes a partial comeback to the areas she has diligently pioneered. Although her interpretation of Andrew Lloyd Webber's theatrical 'Memory' scores an orchestral hit-to-the-heart and is possibly the stand-out track, Judy Collins has returned to her own, doom-laden, folk-tinged, compositions and these are the songs that linger on in the memory ('Mama Mama', 'Angel On My Side', 'Don't Say Goodbye Love'). Nice version of the McGarrigle sisters' 'Sun Son'. A welcome return for an unmistakable voice. Produced by Lewis Hahn and Judy Collins.

### PAUL COLLINS' BEAT
**The Kids are the Same** (Columbia)
Pleasant but unremarkable power pop by a polished West Coast band on its second album outing. Produced by Bruce Botnick.

### JESSI COLTER
**Ridin' Shotgun** (Capitol)
Jessi Colter has always been overshadowed by the success of her husband Waylon Jennings. This is a genuine pity as she has one of the most poignant voices in country music; she is also a fine songwriter. 'Ridin' Shotgun' sees her attempting more up-tempo songs in a possible change of direction; I feel, however, she is more at ease on slow, contemplative material, and the album never delivers. Produced by Randy Scruggs and Waylon Jennings.

### DAVID COVERDALE
**Northwind** (Purple)
A four-year-old solo effort by the one-time lead vocalist for Deep Purple. A patchy effort which hasn't improved with time.

### CREATION REBELS/THE NEW AGE STEPPERS
**Threat to Creation** (Cherry Red)
Ponderous dub cum would-be-reggae jam session by various secondary luminaries of the London new wave scene, including Keith Levine and Ari Up. Orchestrated and led by prolific producer Adrian Sherwood this assemblage starts nowhere and goes nowhere even faster.

### CRISPY AMBULANCE
**The Plateau Phase** (Factory Benelux)
Great group name. Puzzling music. Manchester band very much in the footsteps of Joy Division are let down by sub-standard vocals on a set of gloomy atmospheric pieces tinged with a jazzy, dislocated feel. Produced by Chris Nagle and the group.

### ANDRAE CROUCH
**Don't Give Up** (Warners)
Gospel songster with strong soul connections. Mass market material but tastefully done in the extreme. Still, after all, they've

got God (and Joe Sample) on their side, haven't they? Produced by Bill Maxwell and Andrae Crouch.

### CUDDLY TOYS
**Trials and Crosses** (Fresh)
Second album for a glam rock outfit, but with almost all new personnel. Singer Sean Purcell is the only survivor of the original line-up and dominates this redundant, pomp rock set which wallows in clichés and over-indulges in rampant pretentiousness. Avoid.

### HOLGER CZUKAY
**On the Way to the Peak of Normal** (EMI)

| | |
|---|---|
| Ode To Perfume | On The Way to the Peak of Normal |
| | Witche's Multiplication Table |
| | Two Bass Shuffle |
| | Hiss 'N' Listen |

Holger Czukay was the mainstay of legendary experimental German group Can, a band sadly in advance of the times, and his first album 'Movies' was an outstanding achievement by any standards (influencing the popular collaboration of last year between Brian Eno and David Byrne, amongst others). The new album has been a long time coming and at first lacks the immediacy of its predecessor. Czukay's music is like a succession of imaginary film soundtracks where the listener has to work hard to conjure up the relevant visual images to accompany the music. But, slowly, the pieces coalesce and Czukay's fascinating music takes over. For once, the abundance of studio technique does not stand in the way of emotional excellence. Indescribable but indispensable. Produced by Holger Czukay.

## D

### ROGER DALTREY
**Best Bits** (MCA)
American compilation of the best of Roger Daltrey's solo efforts. Outside the Who, Daltrey has never really convinced and the accumulation of bombastic tracks here gets tiresome in the extreme. Too ambitious. Various producers.

### THE CHARLIE DANIELS BAND
**Windows** (Epic)
Quality collection of new, and surprisingly varied, songs by the Southern fiddler and his versatile group. 'Still in Saigon' reveals depths to Daniels hitherto unseen and proves that the band is not, as previously assumed, irredeemably rooted in South of the Mason-Dixon Line country boogie improvisations. Produced by John Boylan.

### dB'S
**Repercussion** (Albion)
Second album for a New York band working in the golden tradition of Liverpool rock. The first effort was a genuine thing of beauty which was often reminiscent of the Beatles at their melodic best. 'Repercussion' is more patchy and a touch gloomier but Chris Stamey and Peter Holsapple's songs carry an infectious beat characteristic of pop at its best. A must if your heart is still in a late '60s time-warp and you've never really accepted punk and other developments. And who cares if such music is no longer in the prime of fashion. It will always survive. Produced by Scott Litt.

### JOHN DENVER
**Seasons of the Heart** (RCA)
John Denver has been out of the limelight for a few years now, which is not a bad thing after a severe bout of over-exposure. His new LP offers no surprises, with tasteful ballads and reflective songs, including a version of Jesse Winchester's 'Nothing But a Breeze'. The fans will buy it. Produced by John Denver and Barney Wyckoff.

### DEPECHE MODE
**Speak and Spell** (Mute/Sire)
American release for one of Britain's 1981 hit albums. A young group that came out of nowhere with a series of consummate pop anthems with strong electronic-synthesiser melodies and backbeats. The music is as fresh-faced as the musicians; instantly forgettable, bubbly whip. The hit singles are the prominent tracks: 'Just Can't Get Enough', 'New Life'. A lot of anodyne filler material. Manufactured pop if you like that sort of thing. Producer Daniel Miller.

## JIMMY DESTRI
### Heart on a Wall (Chrysalis)

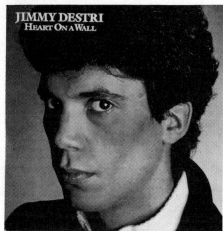

Solo effort by Blondie's keyboards player and, with Debbie Harry and Chris Stein, major songwriter. Group members help out here and there, but Destri has resisted the temptation of doing a Blondie Mark 2 album for male voice. His writing veers casually from fluent melodic rock to more sophisticated outings in a New York new wave mode (whence he came) reminiscent of John Cale at his best (in fact, Destri's voice is often very like Cale's). The result is patchy but rewarding. Solo albums by well-known group members have been a dubious exercise in the past; Jimmy Destri partly redeems the genre. Produced by Michael Kamen.

## BARBARA DICKSON
### All For a Song (Epic)
Folk singer turned popular entertainer in standard set. Predictable.

## AL DI MEOLA
### Electric Rendezvous (CBS/Columbia)
Fusion guitarist on a rock outing. Virtuoso pieces which display his awesome technique. Alternates between fiery electric pieces and softer, Spanish-tinged, acoustic ones. Jan Hammer takes a backstage seat on keyboards. Produced by Di Meola.

## DISLOCATION DANCE
### Music, Music, Music (New Hormones)
Heteroclit rock from Manchester? Dislocation Dance are a young band battling through their influences in search of a style. Snatches of jazz, reggae, pop and funk mingle to curious effect. A far from perfect album but worth a casual listen.

## DOC HOLLIDAY
### . . . Rides Again (A&M)
Despite the name, not a country and western laidback artist, but a fierce US heavy metal outfit from the Southern reaches. Loud grappling with rock clichés involving sex, drugs and other assorted joys. Produced by David Anderle.

## DOME
### Dome 3 (Dome)
Dome are Graham Lewis and Bruce Gilbert, once of arch-experimentalist British band Wire. It's still the same droning electronic minimalism. Aural wall fodder for electro-buffs only. Produced by Gilbert and Lewis.

## DOUG AND THE SLUGZ
### Wrap It! (RCA)
Canadian art-school rock. Often humorous pieces which satirise 1950s archetypal pop songs. The liner notes are also fun. Produced by Jim Vallance and Doug and the Slugz.

## LAMONT DOZIER
### Lamont (M&M)
Polished soul from a well-known writer of scores of Motown hits for many artists. Mid-tempo material. Produced by Lamont Dozier.

## THE DREGS
### Industry Standard (Arista)
Southern boogie. Until now a purely instrumental group, this offering innovates with two vocals by Patrick Simmons and Alex Ligerwood. Steve Howe also contributes fluent guest guitar on one track. The usual mixture of polished rock and jazz otherwise. Dependable. Produced by Steve Morse and Andy Offord.

## DR. HOOK
### Players in the Dark (Mercury/Casablanca)
Standard set for the ballad and jokes band. A bit of everything for the fans, but doesn't break any new ground. Produced by Ron Haffkine.

## GEORGE DUKE
### Dream On (Epic)
Highly polished soul set by an American musician who cannot break through to a crossover public, which many lesser artists have done somehow. The sound is right, the luck ain't. Produced by George Duke.

## DUKE JUPITER
### Duke Jupiter 1 (Coast to Coast)
Despite the somewhat misleading name, this is not a soul performer but a set of

DISLOCATION DANCE

average rock songs by a white band, off the New York bar and college circuit. Pleasant stuff, but will set no haystacks on fire today. Maybe tomorrow? Produced by Glen Kolotkin.

### IAN DURY AND THE BLOCKHEADS
**Juke Box Dury** (Stiff)
Stiff's Greatest Durys, for the American market. Compiles all the UK hits (which Dury has never really bettered since): 'Wake Up and Make Love to Me', 'Sex and Drugs and Rock 'n' roll', 'Reasons to be Cheerful', 'Hit Me with Your Rhythm Stick', etc. . . . The ideal introduction to this idiosyncratic and specifically British talent. Various producers.

# E

### CLINT EASTWOOD & GENERAL SAINT
**Two Bad DJ** (Greensleeves)
Lively set of reggae toasting by two of the leading disc jockey exponents of the genre, both of whom write their own music as opposed to verbal improvisations over other artists' music.

### JONATHAN EDWARDS
**Live!** (Chronic)
A live set by a writer-performer with country influences who has been out of the limelight for some time now, and appears to be without a major company recording contract. Pleasant background music with nice contributions by vocalist Cheryl Wheeler. Produced by Jonathan Edwards and Greg Morton.

### EEK-A-MOUSE
**Wa-Do-Dan** (Greensleeves)
Disco reggae by a dj toaster (real name Ripton Hylton) with verve and a surprisingly accessible humour.

### ELLI & JACNO
**Tout Va Sauter** (Celluloid)
Moderne musique from a French duo, earlier seen in the Stinky Toys proto-punk incarnation. Bouncy and optimistic electro-pop with jerky rhythms sustaining the girl-boy-synthesiser formula. Mild fun. Produced by Jacno.

### EYE TO EYE
**Eye to Eye** (Automatic/Warners)
The return of British writer and pianist Julian Marshall, once of the promising but short-lived Marshall Hain. This time, his female vocalist is Deborah Berg, whose voice and tones lack the strong immediacy of Kit Hain. Jazzy, tuneful songs minutely tailored for mass radio consumption but the overall effect is bland despite a clear,

IAN DURY AND THE BLOCKHEADS

first-class production by a Steely Dan stalwart. Credentials and taste in plenty but a dire lack of passion and commitment. Produced by Gary Katz.

# F

### TAV FALCO'S PANTHER BURNS
**Behind the Magnolia Curtain**
(Rough Trade)
If there's one thing the advent of punk has done, it's re-inject a solid dose of energy into that strangely old-fashioned area of rockabilly music. It's a paradoxical relationship but an invigorating one: the Clash borrow from Joe Ely's traditional country roots, the Stray Cats emerge from the ashes of an obscure NY punk formation and new rockabilly bands working in a deliberately primitive mould emerge with fire and emotion. Tav Falco's Panther Burns is one such band, paying homage to the earliest American rock traditions, mixing pop songs with Muddy Waters, Leadbelly and Junior Wells standards. The sound is rough and ready but the passion is all there. An anomaly of a record but a fascinating one. Produced by Panther Burns.

### THE FALL
**Hex Enduction Hour** (Kamera)
A maddeningly intense 60 minutes of music from one of the most uncompromising British groups. There are songs (although Mark E. Smith's voice is mixed so low that deciphering the lyrics becomes a strenuous aural exercise), snatches of tunes

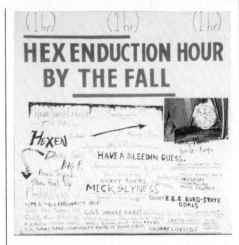

with non-recurring riffs and hooks bursting out at the seams, but the overall feeling is one long tapestry of sound, alternately joyful and despairing; an eerie painting of absorbing landscapes of the imagination hovering uncertainly between reality ('Who Makes the Nazis?') and a disturbed avatar of dreamland ('Iceland'). The Fall are a demanding group who demand total commitment from the listener, just like the old Velvet Underground or the early Captain Beefheart did. Just let yourself go with the flow. Produced by Richard Mazda and Mark E. Smith.

### FAMILY FODDER
**Greatest Hits** (Crammed)
An ironical title from an avant-garde group with a proud history of no hits whatsoever! This album collects some of this prolific group's singles releases together with tracks from their 'Monkey Banana Kitchen'

LP. Gallic singer Dominique vocalises a tongue-in-cheek art school fandango over quirky melodies by Alig. Family Fodder sometimes display the knowing innocence that is so lacking from a more accessible group like Altered Images and certainly deserve a similar public success. True originals.

### THE FAST
#### Leather Boys from the Asphalt Jungle (Decca)
One of the original New York punk bands, alongside Blondie, The Ramones and Talking Heads, The Fast are the group who didn't make it beyond the Lower East Side clubland. Interesting basic hard rock from the duo of Mikki Zone and Paul Zone. Produced by Mikki Zone.

### FAY RAY
#### Contact You (Warners/Elektra)
Welsh band with female vocalist Sheila McCartney (no relation) produced by Police mentor Nigel Gray. All the songs are by guitarist John Lovering. Honest, soothing pop, suffers from lack of drive and ambition, though.

### FELT
#### Crumbling the Antiseptic Beauty (Cherry Red)
New British talent keeps coming and coming, seemingly out of nowhere. Felt are a duo, Lawrence and Maurice Deebank and their music is hard to pinpoint. Mumbled, almost subliminal vocals knitted over a shimmering fabric of shining electric guitar work. Certainly mood music at its best without an electronic alibi. The band had

already broken up when the album was released so 'Crumbling the Antiseptic Beauty' will be a lone treasure, a seductive experiment in highly melodic, nay hypnotic, experimentation that deserves a large footnote in historical reference books. Anyone bored with the often all too predictable strictures of rock music should go out of his way to listen to and cherish this one.

### JAY FERGUSON
#### White Noise (Capitol)
Survivor music by a veteran of Spirit and Jo Jo Gunne. Solid, competent rock craftmanship; tunes written by the ever-worthy Jackie De Shannon and an interesting cover of the Beatles' 'I'm Down'. Produced by Michael Verdick and Jay Ferguson.

### BILLY FIELD
#### Bad Habits (CBS)
Gravel-voiced Field in turn recalls Louis Armstrong, Tom Waits and Leon Redbone. A major attraction in Australia, this is his first release beyond antipodean shores. Jazzy big band swing tunes. Appealing but takes some getting used to. A curio. Produced by Billy Field and Tom Price.

### ALVIN FIELDS
#### Special Delivery (A&M)
Big voice. Big sound. Small impact. Made in USA, radio fodder. Produced by Michael Zager.

### FINGERPRINTZ
#### Beat Noir (Virgin/Stiff)

Third LP from an eccentric British group who've never quite caught the public pulse in spite of superlative songwriting and memorable melodies. Moving away from the stalwart British pop tradition they had bravely been labouring in, Fingerprintz have adopted a strong dance stance following live success on the US club circuit. The results are patchy, but when the band are cooking they are truly superlative ('The Beat Escape'. 'The Chase', 'Going Going Gone'). One of many worthy bands who deserve better but alas seemed doomed to play support (they once backed Lene Lovich) until hell freezes over. There ain't no justice. Produced by Chris Kimsey.

### FLESHTONES
#### Roman Gods (IRS)

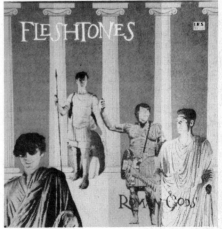

Garage rock rhythm and blues from a New York band. Infectious poppy sound in the good old footsteps of early '60s bands like the Easybeats or the Yardbirds. No innovations and a decided lack of innocence but gentle fun all around with minimal studio tricks to retain a live feel. Produced by Richard Mazda.

FELT

### THE FOUR TOPS
**Tonight** (Casablanca)
Old Motown vocal groups never die, they just fade away with a polite bow to the passing times and flow of styles and fashions. Sometimes, they get into the recording studio again and release sets that reek of consummate professionalism, like this new offering from The Four Tops, which stands up to past efforts but just doesn't grab you any longer. It's just that they're older . . . and so are you. For the memories.

### FRANKE AND THE KNOCKOUTS
**Below the Belt** (Millenium)
Second album for competent US power rockers. Produced by Peter Soley, Franke Previte and the Knockouts.

### MICHAEL FRANKS
**Objects of Desire** (Warners)
Competent jazz stylist seeks inroads with rock audience. The results are still as tediously bland despite contributions by a cast of thousands featuring Larry Carlton and Bonnie Raitt. A surfeit of taste makes Franks' new album tasteful but in no way tasty. Produced by Michael Colina and Ray Bardani.

### FULL MOON
**Full Moon** (Warners)
Session players at rest and play. Features Neil Larsen, Buzzy Feiten, David Sanborn, Bill Reichenbach, Chuck Findley, Jim Horn and others. A mix of rhythm and blues vocals with jazz-tinged instrumentals. Updated fusion music with a few nods to the pop audience. Music for over-30s (which I am – so it's not necessarily pejorative. . .). Produced by Tommy LiPuma.

### FUN BOY THREE
**Fun Boy Three** (Chrysalis)

| | |
|---|---|
| Sanctuary | Best of Luck |
| Way On Down | Mate |
| The Lunatics | T'Ain't What |
| Life in General | You Do |
| Faith, Hope and | The Telephone |
| Charity | Always Rings |
| Funrama 2 | I Don't Believe It |
| | Alone |

When Terry, Neville and Lynval left The Specials at the very heyday of the group's success, it was expected they would take a large share of the 2-Tone formation's natural exuberance with them. This is much in evidence in this fascinating debut album with a strong tribal feel and heavy reliance on vocals (with able support from the girls in Bananarama). It's dance music with a difference, flying off in all musical directions but somehow always landing on its feet. Having absorbed the lessons of New York-based rap, Fun Boy Three put it through a very English filter and come

FUN BOY THREE

up with a winner. Produced by Dave Jordan and the group.

### FUSE ONE
**Silk** (Polydor)
An all-star jazz/fusion session featuring Wynton Marsalis, Tom Browne, George Benson, Stanley Clarke, Stanley Turrentine, Eric Gale. Slick and relaxed but, ultimately, unmemorable. Produced by Creed Taylor.

# G

### JOHNNY G.
**Water Into Wine** (Beggars Banquet)
Johnny Gotting is one of Britain's great unsung musical eccentrics; surely the only musician to record a new, original version of 'Blue Suede Shoes' on every vinyl outing and still make it sound new! Also, for the second time running, this album co-

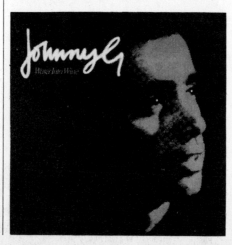

mes (in the UK) with an extra free one, featuring outtakes, rejected singles and other eclectic tunes he couldn't fit onto the album proper. A one-man band when performing in public, Johnny G. is a rhythm and blues addict who can nevertheless adopt other styles at the drop of a plectrum and his reggae version of (of all things) 'The Skye Boat Song' is a delight as is his low-key and almost unrecognisable treatment of King Crimson's bombastic '20th Century Schizoid Man'. The rock scene needs more individuals like Johnny G. A must. Produced by Bob Andrews.

### ROY GAINES
**Gainelining** (Red Lightnin')
Competent blues jamming from quality guitarist in studio trip with The Crusaders who inject a touch of soul to the proceedings.

### GAMMA
**3** (Elektra)
Melodic heavy rock from Ronnie Montrose-led band on their third album. Fluid and driving set with strong hooks and riffs galore. Produced by Ronnie Montrose.

### J. GEILS BAND
**Freeze-Fame** (EMI)

| | |
|---|---|
| Freeze-Frame | Flamethrower |
| Rage in the | River Blindness |
| Cage | Angel in Blue |
| Centerfold | Piss On the Wall |
| Do You | |
| Remem- | |
| ber When | |
| Insane, Insane | |
| Again | |

Some bands slog on, year after year, be-

THE J. GEILS BAND

*Freeze Frame*

fore giving up in despair at the lack of recognition that is their lot. Others persevere despite it all and, like the J. Geils Band with this album, suddenly strike gold. And not a day too early. After 11 years in the business as archetypal American good time R&B band, Geils and Peter Wolf's band are still firing away on all cylinders, no better or no worse than they've been before; but this time, courtesy of a fickle but faithful public, the hits came: 'Freeze-Frame', 'Centerfold'. This is first division rock at its best, with no messages to speak of, just an infectious beat and swinging rhythm of the eternal toe-tapping shuffle. Hideous sleeve though. . . . Produced by Seth Justman.

## GIBSON BROTHERS
**Quartier Latin** (Epic)
Polished salsa dance music with infectious harmonies. Produced by Daniel Vangarde.

## GIRL
**Wasted Youth** (Jet)
Second album for a routine glam cum heavy metal rock British group, fronted by Phil Lewis. Ponderous and repetitive although not without a manic, primitive energy. Produced by Nigel Thomas and the group.

## GLASS MOON
**Growing in the Dark** (Radio)
New group who still haven't shaken off all the blue-chip rock influences that any new formation should digest better (Who, Yes, Billy Joel, Elton John). Formula rock. Produced by John Pace and Raymond Silva.

## GLEAMING SPIRES
**Songs of the Spires** (Posh Boy)
An American duo formed by David Kendrick and Leslie Bohen, who have both previously worked with Sparks. The music is a similar blend of quirky, amusing electro-pop with witty, engaging lyrics. Might catch on, or then again it might not. A touch-and-go situation fame-wise. Produced by Steven Hague.

## GODDO
**Pretty Bad Boys** (Attic)
Well-established Canadian heavy-metal mayhem outfit on the usual loud, repetitive rampage. Sounds much the same to me, but the blitzkrieg experts in the British music press rate them highly and they have the staying power as this is already their fifth offering. Investigate at your own risk.

## GODLEY AND CREME
**Sneak Attack** (Mirage)
Released last year in the UK by Polydor as 'Ismism'. A definite return to form for the 10CC break-away duo back on the right side of the sales charts with compulsive, sneaky little pop tunes which penetrate your consciousness and then just won't go away. Godley and Creme are expert craftsmen and every song is manifestly a labour of love, switching from rock genre to style with unerring precision. The lyrics are as usual witty and penetrating, but it's the music that triumphs this time out. Outstanding tracks are 'Wedding Bells', 'Under Your Thumb' and 'The Party'. A classic platter. Produced by Godley and Creme.

## EDDY GRANT
**Live at Notting Hill** (Ice)
Soundtrack for a film of Eddy Grant's Notting Hill Carnival appearance. His two hits 'Walking on Sunshine' and 'Living on the Frontline' are both included here and this double-set provides an easy introduction to one of Britain's most popular and accessible reggae artists. Produced by Eddy Grant.

## TERRY GREGORY
**From the Heart** (Handshake)
Attractive country lady with a set leaning ever so slightly towards the borderlines of pop. Very slick and polished. In fact, would prove more appealing with a bit of roughness. Produced by Mark Sherrill.

## THE GUN CLUB
**Fire of Love** (Beggars Banquet/New Rose)

GUN CLUB

FIRE OF LOVE

EDDY GRANT

Mutant American swamp rock at its fiercest. Unlike The Cramps who worship at the shrine of rockabilly, The Gun Club are true modern exponents of the Delta sound of the old blues tradition. However what they do to it is quite amazing. Jeffrey Lee Pierce, lead singer and songwriter for the group, was a leading alternative journalist on the late *Slash* magazine and his critical roots are showing intelligently. The Gun Club's music gives a new meaning to the word aggression as the guitars shriek and devour the night in a vampire-like fashion. The only analogy I can dredge up is the steel guitar sound (courtesy of a young Ry Cooder) on Captain Beefheart's first couple of albums. A unique record which, I hope, will not prove to be a freak event as The Gun Club deserve long, and satanic, life. Produced by Chriss D. and Tito Larriva.

## ARLO GUTHRIE AND PETE SEEGER
**Precious Friend** (Warners)
Double live album of classic US folk songs and more modern compositions by two veterans of the scene. Both perform separately as well as together. No surprises; how could there be? Produced by John Pilla.

# H

## SAMMY HAGAR
**Standing Hampton** (Geffen)
Change of label for American rocker also sees him come under the guidance of Fleetwood Mac producer Keith Olsen. Decibel rock, loud and polished with a strong guitar-work emphasis. Melodies come through strongly and make this more palatable than the standard heavy metal set. Good version of the classic 'Piece of my Heart'.

## HAIRCUT ONE HUNDRED
**Pelican West** (Arista)

| | |
|---|---|
| Favourite Shirts | Fantastic Day |
| Love Plus One | Baked Bean |
| Lemon | Snow Girl |
| Firebrigade | Love's Got Me |
| Marine Boy | in Triangles |
| Milk Film | Surprise Me |
| Kingsize | Again |
| | Calling Captain |
| | Autumn |

Astonishingly youthful British band comes up with a winning combination of dance tracks on their first album, following hot in the footsteps of hit singles 'Favourite Shirts', 'Love Plus One' and 'Fantastic Day'. Irresistible hooks and harmonies make this one of the freshest sounds of the year. Singer Nick Heyward penned every single track and emerges as a major

musical hope in the pop composition stakes, proving himself a veritable master of lightweight, fizzy pop-funk. A refreshing dose of humour rushes through this record (*viz.* the cheeky use of the 'Pinball Wizard' intro on 'Marine Boy'), which reminds us that modern pop doesn't always have to be so gloomy. Produced by Bob Sargeant.

## CHARLIE HARPER
**Stolen Property** (Flicknife)
Disappointing solo outing by frontman for UK punk band the UK Subs. In a superfluous search for respectability he tackles a whole range of diverse songs like 'Louie Louie', 'Hoochie Coochie Man', 'Waiting for My Man', 'Femme Fatale', 'Hog for you Baby', making the album no more than a bizarre heteroclit assemblage of Velvet Underground, Bo Diddley and Chuck Berry cover versions. Unconvincing.

## HELIX
**White Lace and Black Leather** (H&S)
Routine power pop by Canadian group. Bar band swagger music.

## LEVON HELM
**Levon Helm** (Capitol)
A third solo album, after a long interval, for an ex-member of The Band. Solidly crafted songs in the American R&B tradition with the standard meaty Muscle Shoals session backing. Worthy but unoriginal. Ah, for the days when The Band were still playing together as a unit and Garth Hudson's organ and Jamie Robertson's guitar licks formed a better environment (and provided distinctive songs) for Levon Helm's mellow, distinctive voice! Produced by Jimmy Johnson and Barry Beckett.

## ROBYN HITCHCOCK
**Groovy Decay** (Albion)
Previously with British group The Soft Boys, this is Robyn Hitchcock's second solo album. An idiosyncratic personality often reminiscent of Syd Barrett, the

ROBYN HITCHCOCK

legendary early Pink Floyd acid casualty. Hitchcock pens quirky, offbeat songs in a very English manner. Determined to break away from the '60s innocence of his previous effort 'Black Snake Diamond', he attempts a diversification here with augmented backing and more varied material. It doesn't always come off, but when Hitchcock succeeds he's very good indeed. A true original. Produced by Steve Hillage.

## JOOLS HOLLAND AND THE MILLIONAIRES
### Jools Holland and the Millionaires
(A&M/IRS)
Ex-keyboards player for Squeeze, Jools Holland is now facing the limelight on his own. An engaging personality with a strong, burlesque sense of humour, he is at his best on rollicking barrelhouse piano tunes and pub sing-alongs. He is, however, less at ease on more traditional rock material. An interesting effort, though. Perky. Produced by Glyn Johns.

## HUANG CHUNG
### Huang Chung (Arista)
An English group in spite of the misleadingly Oriental name. Unusual line-up of drums, bass, sax and guitars with the occasional piano touches and Bowie vocal inflections. Predictable pop for prosaic people. Produced by Rhett Davies and Roger Bechirian.

## THE HUMAN LEAGUE
### Dare (Virgin/Epic)

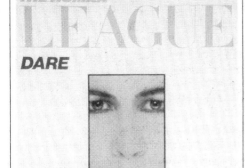

| The Things That | Get Carter |
| Dreams Are | I Am the Law |
| Made Of | Seconds |
| Open Your | Love Action |
| Heart | Don't You Want |
| The Sound of | Me |
| the Crowd | |
| Darkness | |
| Do or Die | |

A belated US 1982 release for the album that topped the British Xmas '81 charts.

Once a creditable cult electronic band, The Human League went through serious personnel upheavals and after a few medium-sized singles (included on the album – 'The Sound of the Crowd', 'Love Action') their new, polished incarnation has hit the jackpot as a sophisticated Abba avatar of the fashionable electro-pop set with the worldwide appeal of 'Don't You Want Me'. Memorable tunes and moods criss-cross this most accomplished and elegant of albums which truly deserves its astounding success. Singer Phil Oakey wields a surprisingly strong, crooning voice which interweaves lustily with the sparse electronic synthesiser backing. But the winning touch is the sudden female vocal descant which launches the hit song into a completely new dimension. Clever and calculating but catchy in the extreme. Produced by Martin Rushent.

## IDEAL
### Der Ernst des Lebens (WEA)
Which means 'The Seriousness of Life' in German, in case you were wondering. Modernist band with massed banks of synthesisers and female vocalist Annette Humpe; veer more towards heavy rock than synthesiser popiness. A touch of Blondie here and pyschedelia there. Interesting. Produced by Conny Plank.

## INSTANT FUNK
### Looks So Fine (Salsoul)
Production line soul with horns to the fore and vocals at the back of the mix. Competent if a touch predictable. Produced by Bunny Sigler and the group.

## IPPU-DO
### Radio Fantasy (Epic)
Multi-layered electronic ditties from Japanese group, includes version of the Zombies' 'Time of the Season'. Clever rather than toe-tapping stuff from this Yellow Magic Orchestra offshoot with a clear (slanted) eye on the Western market. Produced by Masami Tsuchiya.

## IRON MAIDEN
### The Number of the Beast (EMI/Capitol)
The nec plus ultra of contemporary heavy metal music, British streetwise division. Screaming vocals, screaming guitars and rip-roaring drums orchestrate a continuous symphony of mayhem in this frenzied turbo-charged collection which finds an increasing public. Sign of the times? For headbangers with medical insurance only. Produced by Martin Birch.

## J

## MILLIE JACKSON
### Live and Outrageous (Polygram/Spring)
Scatological soul rapping from a US singer who once enjoyed a healthy reputation in the R&B stakes. This is her second live album and again heavily emphasises her in-between talk, jokes, audience participation and response. The vulgarity is gratuitous to say the least, but there must be a market for it. The music's okay, the little of it there is, that is. Consider yourself warned: for adult ears only.

## JACNO
### Jacno (Celluloid)
Engaging, snappy electro-pop by French singer and writer. Gets better with every new spin. Never scales any heights, but always mildly pleasant in its absence of Anglo-US rock clichés. Produced by Jacno.

BRUCE DICKINSON: IRON MAIDEN

## THE JAM
**The Gift** (Polydor)

Happy Together
Ghosts
Precious
Just Who is the
  5 O'Clock Hero
"Trans-Global
  Express"

Running on the
  Spot
Circus
The Planner's
  Dreams Go
  Wrong
Carnation
Town Called
  Malice
The Gift

The Jam's music is as intense as ever, but their circle of social preoccupations seems to be narrowing even further, stranding them in a specifically British despairing no-man's-land where they are alienating their overseas appeal even more, in spite of the introduction of soul brass and hooks on some songs. There is no denying the commitment and intrinsic honesty of Paul Weller and his companions, but I do feel that their music is suffering. Once a clever Who-inspired band, The Jam see themselves now as social commentators. Music is the loser as earnestness sets in. This is their sixth album already, including various hit singles in the UK; although I'm very much in a minority, I must express strong reservations at The Jam's place in the rock hierarchy. Over-rated (start sending in those protest letters. . .). Produced by Peter Wilson and the group.

## CHAS JANKEL
**Questionnaire** (A&M)

A second solo outing for Ian Dury's musical mentor, this was released in the UK as 'Chasanova'. Effortless dance music in a chic, fizzy mood. Certainly lightweight but none the worse for wear, Jankel is a rare British example of soul not-made-in-USA and surprisingly potent and seductive it is. Perfect party music. Produced by Chas Jankel, Philip Bagenal and Pete Van Hooke.

## JAPAN
**Japan** (Epic)

A compilation of tracks from Japan's two albums released in Britain on Virgin ('The Art of Parties' and 'Visions of China'), destined for the US market where their much-earlier glam rock incarnation was unknown. Japan have since moved over to a sophisticated and superior form of art rock, finely chiselled atmospheric songs distinguished by David Sylvian's affected voice, too often reminiscent of Roxy Music's Bryan Ferry (but without the sad maturity, only the wimpishness). Clearly a band in search of its true voice, Japan veer here between moodiness and ethnic (generally oriental) feel. Certainly worth investigating although Japan are very much an acquired taste. Produced by Steve Nye, John Punter and the group.

## GARLAND JEFFREYS
**Rock and Roll Adult** (Epic)

Patchy live set from an unpredictable American artist who never seems to fit into any easy musical category. Supported by Graham Parker's old backing outfit The Rumour, Jeffreys moves quirkily from soul to imitation-Springsteen street rock, while embracing reggae, R&B and straight rock ('96 Tears'). Points for trying desperately hard, but back to the drawing board. Produced by Garland Jeffreys, Bob Clearmountain and Dick Wingate.

## WAYLON JENNINGS
**Black on Black** (RCA)

Country and western singers, particularly those of the so-called 'outlaw' branch of the field are amongst the most prolific recording artists in America and it is fast becoming impossible to keep in touch with the growing vinyl output of Willie Nelson and Waylon Jennings. This is Waylon's nth platter for the 1980s and it's no worse or no better than previous ones. Amiable melodies, deep velvet voice and accomplished backing. Nelson and wife Jessi Colter help out. The instrumentals are dandy. Produced by Chips Moman.

## JOAN JETT AND THE BLACKHEARTS
**I Love Rock n' Roll** (Epic/Boardwalk)

Tough girl rock in black leather attire. Joan Jett, once a forgotten and tarnished figure of the near past (The Runaways) makes a sudden recovery against all odds with a clean, simple, raucous formula of black and white rock and roll. No frills, just the real stuff, unladylike as it may be. Has already set the charts alight worldwide. The sort of record you don't talk about but experience. Produced by Ritchie Cordell and Kenny Laguna.

## THE JETS
**100% Cotton** (EMI)

Unexceptional rockabilly in a spirit of clean

22

fun by British band on second album outing. Produced by Stuart Colman.

### JOHNNY AND THE DISTRACTIONS
**Let It Rock** (A&M)
Hard melodic bar room blues and rock from new American band with lead vocalist imbued with sufficient whisky raspiness down his throat. Prosaic songs but energy to spare. Produced by David Kershenbaum.

### MATT JOHNSON
**Burning Blue Soul** (4AD)
Sixties hedonism in eighties coat of electronic colours = yet another stab at establishing psychedelia anew. Overlayed with gadgetry, which is a pity as Johnson, if he kept things simple, could have made a very decent debut album. As it stands, this is much too cluttered and confused . . . which might in fact be the idea!

### JON AND VANGELIS
**The Friends of Mr. Cairo** (Polydor)
Yes meets Chariots of Fire synthesiser flights. Wimp rock at its most extreme. For confirmed masochists only. Was very successful though, so draw your own conclusions as to this reviewer's feelings about art, commerce, the world, the universe and everything.

### GEORGE JONES
**Still the Same Old Me** (Epic)
Steel guitar, strings and heavenly choir punctuate this classy country album by a veteran of the genre. No surprises and a lot of schlock (including a duet with Jones' baby daughter Georgette!) Produced by Billy Sherrill.

### THE JONES GIRLS
**Get as Much Love as You Can** (Philadelphia)
Formula vocal group soul with disco touches. Comes in one ear, goes out the other. Leaves no lasting effect.

### JANIS JOPLIN
**Farewell Song** (CBS/Columbia)
They're digging zombies out of the vaults, again! Nine unreleased tracks by the inimitable Janis Joplin dating back from 1967–1970. The material has been culled from both studio and live work, some with Big Brother and the Holding Company. Adds little to the legend, but clean-up work by the producers has given a modern gloss to the recordings which follow Joplin from early days to maturity. All in all, could have been so much worse. Produced by Elliot Mazur, John Simon and Todd Rundgren.

### MICKEY JUPP
**Some People Can't Dance** (A&M)
High quality British bar boogie by a singer who's covered his fair share of floorboard, stages and recording studio carpeting. Good time music with a lively, infectious beat but lacking that something special that might promote Jupp into a higher division, let alone the Big Time. Produced by Mike Vernon.

# K

### CAROLE KING
**One to One** (Atlantic)
Carole King has faded fast since the dizzy days of 'Tapestry', but I'm sure her bank balance isn't complaining yet. She keeps on putting out gentle albums full of charm and care, but her music no longer connects with contemporary preoccupations. 'One to One' sees her in tougher, harder mood but the final result is still much too amiable and laid back. It's never less than professional but the slick backing and crystal-clear production do become tedious in the long end. Her fans will lap it up, though. Produced by Mark Hallman and Carole King.

### THE KINKS
**Give the People What They Want** (Arista)
Old groups never die, they just keep on haunting recording studios and playing US stadiums to capacity audiences. As Ray Davies sings on the album "Predictable – it's the word of the year". . . . The Kinks are going through the motions but their subject matter remains unchanged and strangely out of fashion, I fear. Witty, gentle rock. For Kinks completists and observers of the scene of yesteryear. Quite nice, though, admits MJ, betraying his age.

### KLEER
**Taste the Music** (Atlantic)
New York disco group closely patterned on Chic. Last year's thing. And, within those parameters, very ordinary at that.

### KOKOMO
**Kokomo** (CBS/Columbia)
One of British soul's big white hopes of the '70s makes a comeback with the producers of Champaign at the helm. The mixture as before, slick R&B with particularly strong vocal harmonies. Produced by Leo Graham and James Mack.

### THE KNACK
**Round Trip** (Capitol)
Third and final outing for the US band of 'My Sharona' fame. Mainstream pop of a highly calculated nature. This time, it didn't work for the punters and the band disbanded shortly afterwards. There is justice in this world, after all. Produced by Jack Douglas.

### KROKUS
**One Vice at a Time** (Arista)
Heavy metal sound barrage from Switzerland. Up to expectations. Produced by Tony Platt and the group.

KOKOMO

## FELA KUTI
**Original Sufferhead** (Arista)

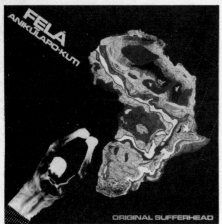

Second album released in the UK by the dissident Nigerian band leader, whose output is reputedly enormous at home. This set was recorded live in front of European audiences and offers an attractive amalgam of big band jazz with a zest of soul and African rhythms. Extended vocal improvisations, not dissimilar to Jamaican rapping, in a political vein put a strong anti-colonialist view forward with wit and verve. Produced by Fela Kuti.

# L

## PATTI LABELLE
**The Spirit's In It** (Philadelphia)
A diluted version of the group that once bore Patti's name. Polished smatterings of pop, soul and disco. Suffers from a lack of originality and homogeneity (various producers were involved). Dance floor fodder.

## BILL LaBOUNTY
**Bill LaBounty** (Curb)
Big sound ballads by big, very male, American voice. Not his first effort, although earlier ones made no impression; this one is not likely to, either. Bland, very bland. Produced by Russ Titelman.

## KIM LARSEN AND JUNGLEDREAMS
**Sitting on a Time Bomb** (Epic)
Swedish rock crooner tries to pass himself off as an authentic popster from the land of Coca Cola (tm) and surf music. Try again, Kim. Produced by Joe Delia.

## DAVID LASLEY
**Missing' Twenty Grand** (EMI)
Strong star backing (Pete Townshend, James Taylor, Bonnie Raitt, Luther Vandross) for session singer on his initial solo album of tasteful blue-eyed soul. Distinctive falsetto vocals and lush arrangements makes this a distinctive record which points to an interesting performer once Lasley has shed the many influences still apparent in his songs (Nyro, James Taylor). Worth looking out for. Produced by David Lasley, Willie Wilcox, Bill Schnee, Dave Iveland and Joe Wissert.

## THOMAS LEER
**Contradictions** (Cherry Red)
Electronic drones which might work as aural background for airports, lifts or supermarkets (*pace* Eno), but as a record this just bores and has few redeeming features. Aimless and clever. Oh, yes: arty is what they call it in circles of taste and distinction.

## LeROUX
**Last Safe Place** (RCA)
Fourth innings for Southern US band who lean towards a West Coast sound (cover of Buffalo Springfield's 'Rock 'n' Roll Woman') but never quite get it together. Patchy and, ultimately, disappointing album. Produced by Leon Medica.

## LEVEL 42
**The Early Tapes July-August 1980** (Polydor)
Polished tracks up from the vaults from a veteran British band who have scored a mild success on the dance circuit. Shows early promise but earlier versions of moderate hit singles don't quite justify this release so soon after their first album.

## LEVI AND THE ROCKATS
**The Louisiana Hayride** (Posh Boy)
A live performance dating back to 1979 for a British rockabilly revival group. Fuzzy production, hot energy and usual retrograde material. Produced by Tom Ayers.

## JONA LEWIE
**Heart Skips Beat** (Stiff)

Lewie is an amiable British eccentric singer/songwriter who scores the irregular left of the field, almost novelty hit in the UK but seems reluctant to approach the recording studio booth too often. This is only his second album in quite a few years (apart from a compilation on a past label). Modest, quirky tunes which only belong to him do tend to feel a bit samey in the long run, but there's no one quite like Jona Lewie. Worth a long detour. Includes 'Louise' and 'Stop the Cavalry'. Strong backing vocal by the neglected Stevie Lange on a few tracks. Various producers.

## HUEY LEWIS AND THE NEWS
**Picture This** (Chrysalis)

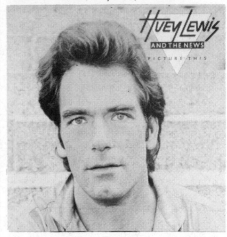

Bland rock from a San Francisco group with little connection with past California rock nobility. A minor hit in the US doesn't detract from the fact that this group are still an amalgam of undigested influences. Brass support by the Tower of Power. Produced by the group.

## RON LICHTENSTEIN
**Another Mile** (Grand Prix)
Surprising release from a record company that had so far only put out classical product. This is somewhat wimpish folk rock, often reminiscent of Cat Stevens at his more maudlin. Gentle and pleasant and tasteful and somniferous. Produced by Steve Markham.

## GORDON LIGHTFOOT
**Shadows** (Warners)
Albums by Gordon Lightfoot don't come as fast and furious as they used to but his prolixity paradoxically betrays the fact he has little left to say though he says it well, record after record. His voice remains as mellow and melancholic as ever on this set of slow, sad, intimate songs but he does seem to be going through the motions. Produced by Gordon Lightfoot and Ken Friesen.

## THE LIMIT
**High in the Mid '60s** (Flying Governor)
A Pennsylvania band still caught in a time-warp (as the record title cheerfully betrays) and skilfully recreating the spirit

of the British beat group invasion of the American shores and airwaves. Amusing. Produced by Pete Smoyer and Rick Levy.

## THE LINES
### Therapy (Fresh)
A debut album from a group formed as far back as 1977. Perfectionist monotony with rare hidden little riffs amongst the pensive, humdrum, atmospheric wallpaper. Very British contemporary, very self-conscious.

## VON LMO
### Future Language (Strazar)
American futurism by an 'artiste' who first destroyed his equipment with a chainsaw onstage. Derivative. Leave electro-pop to the British, Von (?) Lmo (?). Produced by Von Lmo, Diane Rose and Elliott Sewell.

## LOGIC SYSTEM
### Venus (EMI)
Electronic muzak made in Tokyo. Gives computers a bad name as rather boring. Features Hideki Matsutake, of Yellow Magic Orchestra connection. Produced by Toshi Endo and the group.

## LORA LOGIC
### Pedigree Charm (Rough Trade)
Dadaist rock by a survivor of punk pioneers X-Ray Spex. Lora Logic plays saxophone and sings in jazzy tones. Rather witty and danceable, although the little-girl-charm is laid on thick at times. Produced by Phil Legg and Lora Logic.

## ROY LONEY
### Rock and Roll Dance Party (War Bride)
Unadulterated party music by legendary San Francisco musician whose five minutes in the limelight (at least according to Warhol) have never come. Once in the Flamin' Groovies, Loney here delivers the set he always wanted to do and provides unambitious but infectious rock and rockabilly to move your body and brains. Produced by Roy Loney.

## THE LOOK
### The Look (MCA)
A creditable debut LP from a band until now seen as a one-and-a-half hit wonder. Pleasant melodic pop played simple and straight. Singer Johnny Whetstone has a most distinctive voice which contrasts with a strong organ-orientated sound. No innovations here, but a good 40 minutes of music. Worth hunting down in bargain bins.

## MIKE LOVE
### Looking Back with Love (Boardwalk)
Few solo efforts by members of the Beach Boys have yet to breach public consciousness in any serious manner (unless you count in-laws, as in American Spring, a delightful almost Brian Wilson solo album by proxy). This one will not change the situation. Bad. Produced by Jim Studer and Curt Becher.

## LOVERBOY
### Get Lucky (CBS/Columbia)
Lightweight heavy metal (!) by Canadian band which scored in a big way in the USA. Radio rock with a bite and a vengeance. The acceptable face of heavy metal, I suppose, insofar as the lyrics don't make you cringe and the riffs are hummable a few hours later without intense displeasure. Not perfect, but it'll do for now.

## NICK LOWE
### Nick the Knife (F-Beat/Columbia)

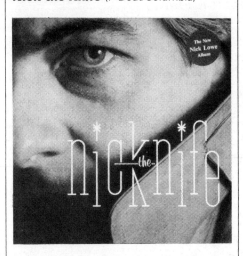

No-nonsense solo outing by the eponymous British producer cum singer cum writer cum husband of the delicious Carlene Carter. 'Queen of Sheba' is a favourite on this strong set of varied, imaginative and well-crafted songs. Lowe will never change the face of music but his enjoyment comes through on every track and that's a lot. Produced by Nick Lowe.

## LUDUS
### The Seduction (New Hormones)
Not quite an album but two 12-inch 45s. A mixture of Ludus old and new; intense, provocative rock in a punk mode. Takes some getting used to; harsh but ultimately redundant.

## SUSAN LYNCH
### Big Reward (Johnston)
In the Pat Benatar mould. New lady from LA with a big voice, looks and Phil Spector-sound backing, which she nevertheless manages to overcome. Promising. Let's wait for the next album to see if she can last the distance, though. Produced by Terry Melcher.

## MAGNUM
### Chase the Dragon (Jet)
Blueprint heavy metal with clichés instead of lyrics. Strictly for fans. The sort of record one can't even attempt to be witty about, as the target looms so large. Shame.

## PHIL MANZANERA
### Primitive Guitars (EG)

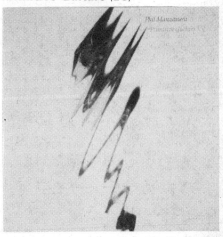

A dazzling collection of guitar-based instrumentals that forms an autobiography in music. Roxy Music's stalwart guitar player explores the ethnic styles and influences which make up his music. The tracks move from Spanish flamenco to South American rhythms to synthesiser atmospherics and Roxy-like tunes with effortless ease as Manzanera delivers the most truly personal in solo albums in a very long time. A compulsive must. Produced by Phil Manzanera.

## MARINE GIRLS
### Beach Party (Whaam)
Young British all-girl group with a strong line in idiosyncratic tunes and music. Sixteen songs project innocence, perversity, wit and wisdom in equal parts. The voices grate a bit, but if you let yourself go and accept the imperfections, this collection has something to please most listeners. A group that deserves a larger audience.

## RITA MARLEY
### Who Feels It Knows It (Greensleeves/Shanachie)
Bob Marley's widow with a strong offering of reggae. The Rastafarian religious dictums become rather existent, but if you close your mental ears to the lyrics, the music will quickly take a grip of your consciousness and the gentle beat and surprisingly varied line-ups will charm you. Produced by Rita Marley and Grub.

WYNTON MARSALIS

cratic delivery to catch one's fancy. Highly self-conscious and European but dizzily enjoyable. Produced by Jacno.

## WYNTON MARSALIS
**Wynton Marsalis** (CBS/Columbia)
19-year old New Orleans trumpet player in the Miles Davis tradition and jazz-fusion footsteps. A remarkably fluid debut with a strong sense of swing and joyous funk. A name to look out for. Produced by Herbie Hancock.

## MOON MARTIN
**Mystery Ticket** (Capitol)
Moon Martin's three previous albums each featured absolute gems and still regularly grace my turntable. This new one is a profound disappointment. His songwriting talent is as fresh and bountiful as ever, but producer Robert Palmer has spoiled the distinctive jangling-guitar

sound of Martin in an attempt to vary moods and tempo and, for me, this has taken the sheer magic away from the classic rock riffs and plaintive love-done-me-bad appeal of Moon Martin at his best. How I'd like to hear these songs again with a pared-down, simple, sparse instrumentation. . . . By any other standards, this is a good little album with some memorable songs ('X-Ray Vision', 'Dangerous Game', 'Aces With You') but, oh, if only. . . .

## STEVE MARTIN
**The Steve Martin Brothers** (Warners)
The American comedian and actor on a schizophrenic album: one side of comedy sketches and one side of flashy bluegrass toons. For Steve Martin completists only (and I know of at least one in London!).

## HANK B. MARVIN
**Words and Music** (Polydor)
Legendary pop guitarist with vocal solo album. Very much sixties pop; amiable but run-of-the-mill. Best track in fact features long guitar solo. Indulgent. Producer Peter F. Vince and Hank Marvin.

## MATHEMATIQUES MODERNES
**Les Visiteurs du Soir** (Celluloid)
French electro-pop duo in an attractive set that grows on you. A solid dance beat punctuated by tinny synthesiser hooks allow singer Edwige's distinctive arty tones to grab the songs and an idiosyn-

## MAXUS
**Maxus** (Warners)
Blueprint West Coast rock with all the usual session players. Another less than necessary album. Produced by Michael Omartian.

## MAZE
**Joy and Pain** (Capitol)
Although made in 1980 this album was only released in Britain in 1982, to capitalise on the group's first UK appearance. A strong, bopping set of hot soul with Frankie Beverley very much at the fore as producer, singer, writer and arranger. A touch of the Earth, Wind and Fire's doesn't come amiss. Eminently danceable.

## ELLEN McILWAINE
**Everybody Needs It** (Blind Pig)
Veteran blues guitarist, assisted here on bass by Jack Bruce with a competent album of fiery torch songs. Mixes fast rockers and slower blues songs. Produced by Ellen McIlwaine.

## JOHN McLAUGHLIN
**Belo Horizonte** (WEA)
Recorded in Paris with Katia Labeque, the celebrated young classical pianist, helping out, this is an essentially acoustic album for McLaughlin, once the reigning champion of speed-breaking electric fusion jazz guitar. Heavy synthesiser background over which McLaughlin embroiders Latin staccato melodies. Also features flamenco star Paco De Lucia on one track. A quiet but professional album. Produced by John McLaughlin.

## DON McLEAN
**Believers** (EMI)
A middle-of-the-road surrender with strings galore, schmaltzy arrangements and such chestnuts as 'Love Hurts' and 'Love Letters'. McLean once fooled listeners and critics with his soporific

'American Pie' and 'Vincent'. The mask is now down and he is seen as an insincere folkie with an eye for cabaret acceptance to keep his bank balance solid in his old days. Produced by Larry Butler.

## MECO
**Pop Goes the Movies** (Arista)
Vapid modernised treatment of a horde of movie themes from 'Zorba the Greek' to 'Goldfinger', not forgetting '20th Century Fox Trademark' (!). Produced by Meco Monardo, Tony Bongiovi and Lance Quinn.

## METHOD ACTORS
**Little Figures** (Armageddon)

Quirky minimalist duo from Athens, Georgia (also home to the B52s) with an idiosyncratic, wacky double album. This is intense, manic music with the power to disturb. David Gamble is a master percussionist while Vic Varney plays one-note guitar and delivers tortured songs in an odd squeal which veers fast from terror to dislocation. Utterly original, but maybe daunting at such length. E for Effort at the very least. For people who enjoy their music uncompromised.

## LOS MICROWAVES
**Life After Breakfast** (Posh Boy)
American intellectual art rock from the independent circuit. Electronic backgrounds and female vocalist provide an unusual combination. You can dance to the chanting. Produced by David Javelosa.

## MIGHTY DIAMONDS
**Changes** (Music Works)
Good reggae set by veteran genre band. Produced by Augustus 'Gussie' Clarke.

## MIGHTY DIAMONDS
**Indestructible** (Alligator)
Stalwart reggae trio with American release of album of standards, including Rita Marley's 'Hurting Inside'. Produced by Augustus 'Gussie' Clarke.

## MODERN LOVERS
**The Original Modern Lovers** (Bomp)
Rough but vital demo tracks by one of the groups that foreshadowed punk. Not to be confused with young Jonathan Richman's twee actual persona. Includes a couple of versions of the seminal 'Roadrunner', as well as songs which would surface again later when produced by John Cale ('Astral Plane', 'Egyptian Reggae'). Of historical interest only if you have the Modern Lovers one and only album. Produced by Kim Fowley.

## MODELS
**Local and/or General** (A&M)
Assembly line modern pop by Australian band. Instantly forgettable.

## MODERN ROMANCE
**Adventures in Clubland** (Atlantic)
Manicured young British band (including, this is important, a past rock critic) gives salsa a dusting and gives a new meaning to the British dance stance. Clever, calculated mix of worn rhythms given a semblance of modernity. You might call it cynical but the band certainly enjoyed a couple of months of glory before fading into temporary oblivion as I write these words. Will no doubt reappear soon with a polished new style and score again; they're too intelligent not too. Includes the obligatory hits 'Everybody Salsa' and 'Ay Ay Ay Moosey'. Produced by Norman Mighell, Geoffrey Deane and David Jaymes.

## MONDO ROCK
**Mondo Rock Chemistry** (Atlantic)
Identikit rock by yet another Australian band. Lack of any originality is a strong feature. Vocalist Ross Wilson comes via Daddy Cool. A typical example of an unnecessary record. Produced by Mark Moffatt.

## MELBA MOORE
**What a Woman Needs** (EMI)
Competent disco funk from black American songstress with adequate track record of moderate hits. Dance music and big sentimental ballads. Produced by Gene McFadden and John Whitehead.

## VAN MORRISON
**Beautiful Vision** (Mercury/Warners)

| | |
|---|---|
| Celtic Ray | Cleaning |
| Northern Muse | Windows |
| Dweller on the | Vanlose |
| Threshold | Stairway |
| Beautiful Vision | Aryan Mist |
| She Gives Me | Across the |
| Religion | Bridge Where |
| | Angels Dwell |
| | Scandinavia |

A personal confession: Van Morrison's

'Astral Weeks' is probably one of the three or four albums that I'll cherish forever and choose as a hypothetical desert island platter, while his London concert of summer 1973 was one of the most exhilarating experiences in live music I've ever experienced. When he's good, he's utterly fantastic and unique, and this is the fan in me speaking. When he's in middling form, he's still outstanding. This long digression is to admit that Morrison's recorded output has been decidely patchy and his evangelical leanings of recent years have left me increasingly frustrated. The nice thing to report is that 'Beautiful Visons' shows him on the right road back to transcendence, blending his newly-found devotion to faith with jazz and celtic influences into a satisfying whole. There is a quiet, spiritual grace in all these new tracks, alternatively swinging and deeply meditative, witness of an artist in full control of his talent. One of 1982's indispensable records. Favourite tracks: 'Dweller on the Threshold', 'She Gives me Religion' (in spite of the maudlin lyrics), 'Vanlose Stairway' and 'Scandinavia' (an instrumental first). Produced by Van Morrison.

## MORRISSEY MULLEN
**Life on the Wire** (Beggars Banquet)
Quality jazz funk with more than a passing nod to the dancing shoes from a duo with jazz, as opposed to pop, roots. Tight, disciplined and intelligent use of brass bravura with female vocals by Carol Kenyon. A worthy record. Produced by Chris Palmer.

## MOTHER GONG
**Robot Woman** (Butt)
The fantasy world of Gong lives on for another day. Come Year 2,000 and Grandfather Gong will, no doubt, still be present with weary, pixillated tunes of hippie paradise and ecological/nuclear warnings. A curiosity. Produced by Harry Williamson.

## MÖTLEY CRÜE
**Too Fast For Love** (Leathur)
High octane heavy metal from a new,

highly-lauded, glam rock outfit from yonder Yankee West Coast shores. Frenetic playing and knife-edge riffs and hooks. A most promising entry in the 100% rock 'n' roll stakes. Produced by the group.

## MOTORHEAD
**Iron Fist** (Bronze/Mercury)
Chart-topping LP by thunderhouse British heavy metal trio with a satanic drive and energy. Subtlety is not the word in the headbanging arena but Motorhead are amongst the most adept purveyors of the genre and this new album will do well with the massed fans scattered worldwide. Cool and efficient and commercial. Produced by Eddie Clark and Will Reid.

## THE MUFFINS
**185** (Random Radar)
Not to be confused with Martha and the Muffins (now sadly without the prettier Martha). Art school rock supreme by a new band who have apparently already disbanded. Experimental and dishevelled. Produced by Fred Frith.

## MICHAEL MURPHEY
**Michael Martin Murphey** (Liberty)
Sensitive US singer/songwriter in nth studio outing. Unremarkable and laid back. Produced by Jim Ed Norman.

# N

## NASMAK
**4Our Clicks** (Plurex)
Interesting album of pseudo-futuristic, gloomy atmospherics by a Dutch band, heavily in debt to British exponents of this peculiar, and often arrestingly effective, sub-genre. Nice keyboard textures and a light dancey feel.

## THE NECESSARIES
**Event Horizon** (Sire)
Urban American rock with a touch of the Talking Heads. Not quite hip-swivelling music but engaging modern rock with a deftness of touch that promises much for the future. A group to look out for.

## WILLIE NELSON
**Always on my Mind** (CBS/Columbia)
Sad assembly-line country and western platter. All too predictable with fiasco covers of 'Bridge Over Troubled Water' and 'A Whiter Shade of Pale'. Waylon Jennings guests. Produced by Chips Moman.

## COLIN NEWMAN
**Not To** (4AD)
Third solo album from a survivor of the Wire shipwreck. Colin Newman is slowly emerging as a cerebral poseur with an expert touch of the idiosyncrasies. Mildly

enjoyable modernist set, suffers from being too often subdued as if Newman wasn't always too sure how far his listeners would accept an injection of experimentation. Produced by Mike Thorne.

## NEW ORDER
**Movement** (Factory)

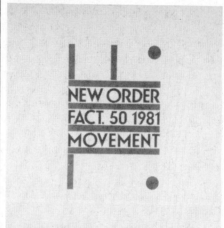

| | |
|---|---|
| Dreams Never End | ICB |
| Truth | The Him |
| Senses | Doubts Even Here |
| Chosen Time | Denial |

The long-awaited first album from the band that has quietly emerged from the sad ashes of Joy Division. Although they retain the gloom and doom laden atmospheric mood of Joy Division, New Order move beyond this restricted forbidden zone with a surprising hardness and rhythmic touch. Their forbidding aural paintings still weave a dark and brooding canvas but the musicianship is never less than outstanding. Truly music that reflects the dark ages we live in. These are not songs or tunes but bleached kodachromes of a reality that many would prefer to ignore. Produced by Martin Hannett.

## NEW YORK SKYY
**Skyyline** (Epic)
Derivative US disco done with pomp and circumstance. Tight, flashy and some-

times sophisticated. Produced by Randy Muller and Solomon Roberts Jr.

## NICODEMUS/TOYAN
**DJ Clash** (Greensleeves)
One for the regular reggae market, featuring two dj's rapping over the usual beat. Once you get used to the formula, it becomes quite witty and enjoyable. Produced by Henry 'JunJo' Lawes.

## NINE BELOW ZERO
**Third Degree** (A&M)
Third and final album from a British rhythm and blues outfit who, albeit smooth and sharp, never made the grade. This sees them trying to move away from their usual sound and nodding towards more mainstream rock and even reggae rhythms; but enthusiasm is not always enough. Produced by Simon Boswell.

## KLAUS NOMI
**Klaus Nomi** (RCA)
Weird music and weird appearance. Nomi is a mutant opera singer of sorts who indulges in coloratura renditions (treasons?) of rock and classic chestnuts. Curious but really appalling, once you get over the shock.

## ALDO NOVA
**Aldo Nova** (Portrait)
New Canadian heavy rocker who has already scored heavily in the American charts. Slick and professional. Not my own cup of tea, but there's no denying he's got class and guts in abundance. Produced by Aldo Nova.

## MICHAEL NYMAN
**Michael Nyman** (Sheet)
Trilling recorders and a pastoral feel for British minimalist in a lush, almost orchestral excursion. Five shorter and one longer piece feature the cream of British jazz, classical and experimental musicians. Enjoyable mood music with witty interjections and interruptions peppering the proceedings when you least expect them. Produced by Michael Nyman and David Cunningham.

# O

## OAK RIDGE BOYS
**Bobbie Sue** (MCA)
One more album by one more band. A mixture of accomplished country and western with a hard rock edge and flowing melodies and harmonies, but it doesn't amount to much in the end. Produced by Ron Chancey.

ORANGE JUICE

## OHIO PLAYERS
**Ouch** (Epic)
Disco/pop/soul/funk rides again . . . and again . . . and forever. Produced by Richard 'Dimples' Fields.

## MIKE OLDFIELD
**Five Miles High** (Virgin/Epic)
Having succumbed critically to a surfeit of saccharin macro instrumental tracks, virtuoso Oldfield turns, this time around, to a selection of shorter, almost light pop songs on side 2 ('Taurus II' another ponderous foray into respectable, redundant would-be symphonic panoramas wastes the first side of the album). Also, contrary to past efforts, Oldfield now works with a band, which adds a touch of immediacy to his lazy but tasteful melodies. Maggie Reilly shines on vocals. Not quite a come-back, as he's never really been away, but an enjoyable, unambitious record all the same. Produced by Mike Oldfield.

## SALLY OLDFIELD
**Playing in the Flames** (Bronze)
1967 lives again! Coy, whimsical folkish tunes by Mike Oldfield's sister who's been this way before in the excruciating SallyAngie. The girl should grow up. Fast. Avoid at all costs, this record softens brains. Produced by Sally Oldfield, Dave Davani and Laurie Jay.

## ONE WAY
**Who's Foolin' Who?** (MCA)
Soul group from Detroit with a striking ability to shift between fiery dance music and mellow, rich ballads. Title song was an American hit. Pleasant. Produced by ADK and Irene Perkins.

## ORANGE JUICE
**You Can't Hide Your Love Forever** (Polydor)
Another darling group of the British critics hits the dust. Edwyn Collins' mannered vocals grate on this anonymous collection of songs with indistinguishable melodies and murky production values. Back to Glasgow and the drawing board, kids, and learn to digest '60s influences before regurgitating them wholesale without improving on the originals. Produced by Adam Kidron.

## ORCHESTRAL MANOEUVRES IN THE DARK
**Architecture and Morality** (Dindisc/Epic)

Third album by the Liverpool duo who successfully managed to inject unusual warmth and feeling into electronic pop. They are in a subdued mood here, although the British punters happily accepted the two 'Joan of Arc' hit singles. In retrospect, the atmospherics dominate and the strong melodic hooks are not so much in evidence, betraying a certain staleness of inspiration. Or are OMD now taking themselves too seriously to get people onto the dance floor? The usual clean sleeve by Peter Saville. Produced by Mike Howlett, Richard Mainwaring and the group.

## VERNON OXFORD
**A Better Way of Life** (Mint)
Clean-cut, traditional country steel guitar in the hallowed footsteps of Hank Williams and Jimmie Rodgers. Carefully made in Nashville. Produced by Bob Ferguson.

# P

## THE PACE SETTERS
**Edikanfo** (EG)
Heavy on the percussion African big band. Jazz with an ethnic, almost out-fashioned slant which makes it all the more refreshing. Produced by Brian Eno.

## ROBERT PALMER
**Maybe It's Live** (Island)
No maybe about it. In fact, it's only half-live, one side of the album being devoted to new studio recordings including the outstanding, quirky 'Some Guys Have All the Luck'. The live side features a short resumé of Palmer's career ranging from blues-based material to his later collaborations with Gary Numan. Palmer has one of the most distinctive voices in the business and remains a constant innovator who should never be discounted. A much under-rated performer, this should commend him to a larger audience. Produced by Robert Palmer.

## GRAHAM PARKER
**Another Grey Area** (RCA/Arista)
A change of label for Parker works no magic as this album sees him stuck in an uncomfortable, bland groove. In the past, an outstanding vocalist and writer in a gritty R&B – according-to-Springsteen mould, Graham Parker is now caught between his roots and a desire to hit the radio audience between the eyes. The absence of his old backing group The Rumour, now replaced by competent but uncommitted US session players, only emphasises the half-hearted punch this record packs. A grey record, to say the least. Produced by Jack Douglas.

## PIGBAG
**Dr. Heckle and Mr. Jive** (Y)
Funk punk! A surprise hit instrumental homage to James Brown serves as an

appetiser for this versatile selection of fiery brass-based music by a young British band until now categorised dismissively in the punk bracket. Swing and whimsy co-exist well in a remarkable first album. Produced by Dick O'Dell and the group.

## PINSKI ZOO
**Introduce Me to the Doctor** (Despatch)
Experimental dance music from independent British band with a distinctive nod of the head to Coltrane, Albert Ayler, Ornette Coleman and other US free jazz prophets. Gets better with successive hearings, with a strong live feel.

## JEAN-LUC PONTY
**Mystical Adventures** (Atlantic)
Jazz violinist in a perfunctory shot at a cross-over market. Strong underpinnings of pop and funk mar the general quality of the playing. Produced by Jean-Luc Ponty and Arif Mardin.

## THE PRESSURE COMPANY
**Live in Sheffield** (Solidarity)
Pseudonymous live offerings by musicians from British electronic jugglers Cabaret Voltaire, released at a much reduced price in aid of the Polish union Solidarity. Improvised mood soundtrack for the times; the passion often shines through

JEAN-LUC PONTY

## DUDU PUKWANA
**Sounds Zila** (Jika)
A veteran of the London jazz and soul scene, Dudu Pukwana now fronts his own band, Zila. They perform big-band Afro-funk with a joyful, party mood and sprightly instrumental solos abound to pepper the proceedings. You can dance to it with your eyes safely closed.

## JIMMY PURSEY
**Alien Orphan** (Epic)
A second solo album by the frontman and mouth of Sham 69. Despairingly derivative and naïve in a wide-eyed manner, Pursey is now heavily influenced by his short contact with Peter Gabriel and radically breaks away from his punk chanting days. Heavy use of electronics and intruding sound effects make this an irritating and confused album which should have remained on the studio floor. Produced by James Pursey.

PINSKI ZOO

## PLANNING BY NUMBERS
**Planning By Numbers** (Beggars Banquet)
Imitation Gary Numan drone and inhumanity ditties on Numan's own label. Are they training a clone, for some unforeseen reason or as an insurance against young Gary perishing in a plane crash? Pretty dire, and that's almost a compliment. . . .

## PLAYER
**Spies of Life** (RCA)
As described quite accurately by an anonymous *Billboard* scribe: 'the soft heart of the pop mainstream.' Produced by Dennis Lambert, who also contributes an intrusive synthesiser sound to the polished rock and soul of the group.

## POCO
**Cowboys and Englishmen** (MCA)
Slick country meets pop by a band with experience. Adequate but in no way special or likely to promote Poco back to the higher leagues of the rock kingdom. Produced by Mike Flicker.

in Eric Random's guitar playing. More than just a curiosity.

## PRINCE JAMMY
**Destroys the Invaders** (Greensleeves)
Dull dub album with creditable credentials: Roots Radics backing, King Tubby mixing. But reggae and science fiction subject matter (even when bastardised by video) don't work. Produced by Prince Jammy.

## PRISM
**Small Change** (Capitol)
Canadian band with an uncertain mixture of genres: straight innocent pop, heavy rock, electronic keyboards. Never really convincing in any of the arbitrary categories. Another one for the bargain bins. Produced by Carter.

## MICHAEL PROPHET
**Michael Prophet** (Greensleeves)
Up-tempo reggae album with strong soul inclinations by a new, young singer. Produced by Henry 'Jungo' Lawes.

## QUARTERFLASH
**Quarterflash** (Geffen)
New band with strong similarities to the easy listening side of Fleetwood Mac, scored in a huge way with this debut album. Rindy Ross' vocals and polished saxophone playing made the single 'Harden My Heart' but most of the other songs on the album never attain the same, instantly recognisable sultry intensity and go round in slight, slick circles leading nowhere. An impressive band, but I fear not ready for an entire album of original material yet.

## BONNIE RAITT
**Green Light** (Warners)
Already on her eighth album, Bonnie Raitt has never achieved the recognition she

deserves as her recorded output pales beside her live performances. A fiesty performer of the blues and a virtuoso slide guitar player, she has never translated her energy onto vinyl. Here, an insistence on uptempo rock numbers with a lot more guitar work serves her well, but a generally uninspired choice of material lets her down. Nice, but won't make the earth move. Produced by Rob Fraboni.

## RANDOM HOLD
**Burn the Buildings** (RCA)
Interesting but overlooked album by a young British band with female vocalist Sue Raven. At times they sound like Talking Heads at a less frantic speed, at others they evoke some of the better electro-pop synthesiser outfits. A sameness of material prevents a decisive lift-off. Worth looking out for, though. Produced by Rikki Sylvan and the group.

## CHRIS REA
**Chris Rea** (Magnet/Columbia)
Fourth album (he does churn them out, doesn't he?) for assembly line British sensitive singer-songwriter. Bland and oh so tasty. Might one day reach the murky depths of Manilow division in the housewives' hearts but still has a way to go into further maudlin sentimentality. You guessed: I don't like Chris Rea. Produced by John Kelly and Chris Rea.

## THE RECORDS
**Music On Both Sides** (Virgin)

The Records are one of the great unsung groups of our time. Determinedly stuck in a late 1960s groove, they keep on, despite changes in line-up, crafting delicate, catchy songs full of melody and feeling and reap commercial oblivion as their reward with uncanny regularity! This is their third album and although patchy it has, as usual, moments of sheer magic (ah, the hook on 'Selfish Love', the harmonies on 'Imitation Jewellery'. . .). If the Beatles were still around and packed a strong rock punch, they would sound like 'The

Records. What else can I say? This is the ultimate in hummable pop. Investigate immediately if you've never heard The Records before. Produced by Will Birch.

## RED RIDER
**As Far as Siam** (EMI)
Faceless American rock. Comes and goes in a flash. Leaves no lasting effect.

## RED ROCKERS
**Condition Red** (415)
Political punk in a Clash style by strongly positive New Orleans band. Anthems rather than songs are much in evidence but the message is etched in words of rage (and clichés). The music rocks hard and furious. An unusual album from an American (independent) source, but where do they go from here once the manifesto has been made public? Produced by David Kahne.

## LOU REED
**The Blue Mask** (RCA)

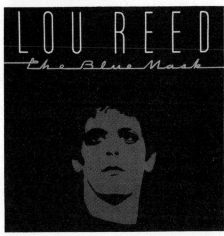

| | |
|---|---|
| My House | Average Guy |
| Women | The Heroine |
| Underneath the | Waves of Fear |
| Bottle | The Day John |
| The Gun | Kennedy Died |
| The Blue Mask | Heavenly Arms |

Just when so many had finally written him off, the mercurial Lou Reed returns with a stunning album which reminds us how often rock music can aspire to genuine art. With sparse, almost minimal instrumentation, Reed's new songs betray an acceptance of the smaller pleasures of life and a reflection on glories past and humility. These are miniature novels, low-key late-night confessions with an affecting accuracy and the nearest rock music has come to autobiography since . . . earlier Lou Reed albums. Lest it be thought that the whole package reeks of bleak introspection, one should also point out that Reed is also a master of irony and distanciation as he rhapsodises about the peace his wife has brought into his life or the

lurking presence of poet Delmore Schwartz in the house he now lives in. A must. Produced by Lou Reed and Sean Fullan.

## RIGGS
**Riggs** (Warners/Full Moon)
New hard rock American band from Tennessee, fronted by vocalist, guitar player and writer Jerry Riggs. This is their first album after a sneak preview on the top-heavy soundtrack of the 'Heavy Metal' animation movie. Dynamic and highly polished, but still lacking in that little touch of personality that might point to a glorious tomorrow beyond the clubs and bars. Guest appearance by Nicky Hopkins lends a bit of veteran class. Produced by Andy Johns and Marty Cohn.

## JIMMY RILEY
**Rydim Driven** (Taxi)
Pleasant reggae set from one of Jamaica's newer stars. Produced by Robbie Shakespeare and Sly Dunbar.

## SMOKEY ROBINSON
**Yes It's You Lady** (Motown)
As smooth and romantic as ever, Smokey Robinson hits the heart chords with his customary assurance. It's easy listening and strong on the saccharin sweetness, but Smokey's voice remains as velvety as ever. Quietly satisfying. Produced by George Tobin.

## THE RODS
**The Rods** (Arista)
Identikit US heavy metal with a bite in the heel and a hearty roar in the larynx. Not much else to say, really. Sorry.

## ROOTS RADICS
**Radical Dub Session** (Solid Groove)
Celebrated rhythm and backing band in a polished dub excursion.

## DIANA ROSS
**Diana's Duets** (Motown)
Now that Diana Ross has switched labels, her old company are dusting up past material to keep the register bills ringing. This one is not a bad idea, collecting Diana's past duets with a variety of other Motown soul nobilities: Lionel Ritchie, Marvin Gaye, the Four Tops, Stevie Wonder, even stretching the concept to include some Supremes and Temptations tracks. Various producers.

## PETER ROWAN
**The Walls of Time** (Sugar Hill)
A first-class country/folk/bluegrass album by an American artist who long ago moved away from the traps of hyped stardom to the simpler pleasures of his roots. Don't let the folk tag fool you, this is a vigorous electric album sometimes reminiscent of

when Fairport Convention and Steeleye Span first plugged in. Outstanding version of 'Plains of Waterloo'. Produced by Peter Rowan.

# S

## RIUICHI SAKAMOTO
### Left Handed Dream (Plexus/Alfa)
The output of the Yellow Magic Orchestra as a unit, solo performers, producers and general busybodies is admirable, and no doubt matches Japanese industrial productivity figures. This is another solo effort by Sakamoto who perhaps more than his colleagues seems capable of absorbing European avant-garde influences and blending them in with Japanese touches. This time he uses Adrian Belew of Talking Heads and King Crimson/David Bowie fame and the result sounds very much like Eno in more electronic/atmospheric days. Relaxing synth music with more than a touch of class. Produced by Robin Scott and Riuichi Sakamoto.

## NORMAN SALEET
### Here I Am (RCA)
Wallpaper ballads from the writer of Air Supply's hits. Well done but in a very minor key. Produced by Ted Glasser.

## SANDII AND THE SUNSETZ
### Heat Scale (Alfa)

Sculptural Japanese lady (with Spanish blood) in a sophisticated set of new wave rock, in the hallowed footsteps of Blondie. Very well done, but does pale against the original as it's all so earnest and devoid of humour. Probably works better live if photos of Sandii are to be believed. Produced by Haruomi Hosono.

## MICHAEL SCHENKER GROUP
### One Night at Budokan (Chrysalis)
One of the few live albums that captures the sweat, fire and debauchery of a full-flung heavy metal blitz. Recorded in Tokyo under optimum conditions, this double LP showcases Schenker's group (with Cozy Powell stoking the percussion machinery) in fourth gear.

## SCORPIONS
### Blackout (Harvest/Mercury)
German heavy metal war veterans on standard album outing. The same as last time and, no doubt, the same as next time. For the fans (and there are many). Produced by Dieter Dierks.

## TERRY SCOTT
### Terry Scott (Elektra)
Black singer and guitarist plays hard-core white music for the US radio audience. Well done but soon forgettable. This is no Jimi Hendrix. Produced by Hank Medress and Dave Appell.

## THE SCRATCH BAND
### Featuring Danny Flowers (MCA)
No longer are well-known members of big-name groups going solo, now comes the time of backing groups to do so. The Scratch Band are better known (?) for providing a soothing background to the mellifluous tones of Don Williams. Their outing is in a pop mode and is unmemorable. Produced by Garth Fundis and Don Williams.

## DAN SEALS
### Harbinger (Atlantic)
Crisp, sunny and somnolent middle-of-the-road American style ballads. Didn't even score there. Produced by Kyle Lehning.

## SECRET AFFAIR
### Business as Usual (I-Spy)
Third album from the band who, unsuccessfully, attempted to raise Mod from the grave some years back. Earnest urban music, with strong echoes of the Jam and the Who, but with a deft little dance feel from time to time. Ghastly kiddie chorus on 'Hide and Seek' is a killer, though.

## SHALAMAR
### Friends (Solar)
Soul trio on their first album for a new label find a prolonged lease of life. Snappy dance rhythms and subtle harmonies blend in well on generally mid-tempo material. Produced by Leon F. Sylvers.

## PETE SHELLEY
### Homosapien (Genetic/Arista)
Solo LP debut by former Buzzcocks front man. Surprisingly, this is a festival of electronics and synthesiser foolery, with Shelley's harsh but warm tones of yesteryear taking a back seat to a mechanistic, modern mood of alienation. Has its attractions and the title track lingers on, but the album

MICHAEL SCHENKER GROUP

SISTER SLEDGE

feels contrived. Produced by Martin Rushent and Pete Shelley.

## SHOOTING STAR
**Hang on for your Life** (Virgin)
Belated British release for Virgin's lone US signing on a second album outing. Hardcore rock with no distinctive features. A din.

## SIMON AND GARFUNKEL
**The Concert in Central Park**
(Geffen/Warners)
One for memory lane. A souvenir of the New York reunion of Paul Simon and Art Garfunkel which led to a more permanent renewed relationship. Impeccable sound quality for all the myriad hits and interesting interpretations of some of the songs they had previously recorded separately. Pleasant but, for a live recording, lacking in electricity. Tasteful in the extreme and sold millions. Produced by Simon, Garfunkel, Phil Ramone and Roy Halee.

## SIMPLE MINDS
**Celebration** (Arista)
Following the new lease of life a change of label has brought them in the UK, Arista recoup their outlay with the predictable, but highly enjoyable, compilation selecting the best of their previous three albums. Simple Minds are now at the forefront of British new wave music and this record shows the years of apprenticeship when their sound was rougher but no less catchy and attractive. Produced by John Leckie.

## SIMPLE MINDS
**Themes From Great Cities:**
**Definitive Collection 79–81** (Stiff)
A compilation of past British tracks for US electro-pop consumption. Produced by John Leckie.

## SINGERS AND PLAYERS
**Revenge of the Underdog** (Situation 2)
Studio reggae improvisations by an assortment of white and black musicians. Indulgent experimentation leading nowhere in particular. Redundant. Produced by Adrian Sherwood.

## SISTER SLEDGE
**The Sisters** (Atlantic/Cotillion)
Classy disco funk, but the gems here are the ballads with a lush remake of Smokey Robinson's 'My Guy' and an emotional 'Everybody's Friend'. Produced by the group.

## RICKY SKAGGS
**Waiting for the Sun to Shine** (Epic)
Guitarist and songwriter for Emmylou Harris now ventures out on his own. Unfortunately his voice is bland and lifeless and contrasts with the precise musicianship and delicately crafted songs in this clean but unmemorable Nashville production. Produced by Ricky Skaggs.

## SKYLINE
**Late To Work** (Flying Fish)
Acoustic East Coast folk quintet. Gentle, lilting tunes that seem to belong 20 years in the past. Produced by the group.

## SLAUGHTER AND THE DOGS
**Live at the Factory** (Thrush)
A corpse from the hard-core punk vaults. Surprising energy and commitment from a group who were almost buried at the time under critical assaults of the worst kind. A profane curiosity for future historians of the early days of the so-called British new wave.

## SLOW CHILDREN
**Slow Children** (Ensign)

Late US release for a new British-based group consisting of Pal Shazar on vocals and Andrew Chinich in counterpoint. A highly individualistic album of idiosyncratic songs in a modern mood. Grows on you fast like weeds in a water-swept garden and is, for me, one of the sleepers of the year and I'm already looking forward to their second album. Produced by Jules Shear and Stephen Hague.

## O. C. SMITH
**Love Changes** (South Bay)
A return to the combat zone by the man who sang 'Little Green Apples'. Soulful and mellow. Produced by H. B. Barnum.

## RUSSELL SMITH
**Russell Smith** (Capitol)
Easy-going country rock from a former member of the Amazing Rhythm Aces. Par for the course. Produced by Barry Beckett and Jimmy Johnson.

## MICHAEL SMOTHERMAN
**Michael Smotherman** (Epic)
Smooth, lukewarm pop crooner with a touch of the arrows in his poor, tormented heart. We've heard it all before, and much better done. Troubadour rock at its more tedious. Produced by Bill House, Michael Smotherman, Frank Rand and Larry Hamby.

## SNAKEFINGER
**Manual of Errors** (Ralph)
Third solo album for a British musician and guitarist now working in the USA and as-

sociated with arch-San Francisco experimentalists, the Residents. Spiky, disjointed pieces nearer to Zappa than Snakefinger's earlier outings. Disappointing. Produced by Eric Drew Feldman and Snakefinger.

## SOFT CELL
**Non-Stop Erotic Cabaret** (Some Bizzare/Sire)

| | |
|---|---|
| Frustration | Entertain Me |
| Tainted Love | Chips on my |
| Seedy Films |   Shoulder |
| Youth | Bedsitter |
| Sex Dwarf | Secret Life |
| | Say Hello, |
| |   Wave Goodbye |

1982 US release for hit British album of the previous winter. Unlikely tawdry, electro soul from the duo of Marc Almond and Dave Ball. A fascinating compendium of fascinations with the seedier side of life which somehow transmutes itself into infectious dance music. Strong and original, Almond's croonerish voice floats and undulates over Ball's fluid keyboard work. Although individual tracks ('Tainted Love') made it as singles, the album has an organic unity that is quite remarkable for such a new, and small, band. Recommended. Produced by Mike Thorne.

## SOUNDTRACK
**The Border** (MCA/Backstreet)
A highly subdued and mixed soundtrack for the Tony Richardson film starring Jack Nicholson. Possibly Cooder's least successful film collaboration. Atmospheric Mexican-influenced tunes with most of the guest performers faring better than Cooder: Sam 'The Sham' Samudio, John Hiatt, Freddy Fender. Rewarding in a low-key sort of way. Produced by Ry Cooder.

## SOUNDTRACK
**The Burning** (Charisma)
Rick Wakeman orchestrates this soundtrack for an already forgotten second rate horror film. Unmemorable. Produced by Rick Wakeman and Alan Brower.

SPANDAU BALLET

## SOUNDTRACK
**Death Wish II** (Swansong)
First recorded appearance by Jimmy Page since the drawn-out demise of Led Zeppelin is on this self-composed soundtrack for Michael Winner's Charles Bronson vehicle. Portentous, pomp guitar lift-offs which make little sense outside of the film's context and jar within. A sad failure. Produced by Jimmy Page.

## SOUNDTRACK
**Ragtime** (Elektra)
Following in family footsteps Randy Newman crafts an exquisite soundtrack for Milos Forman's film version of the esteemed Doctorow novel. In a deliberately classical mood and avoiding the obvious Scott Joplin rag temptations, Newman has captured both the essence of book and film and a loving, affectionate feel for the times they are set in. Only one vocal track, a lovely ballad sung by Jennifer Warnes, surfaces in the movie although the album does feature an extra song by Newman himself, in his usual inimitable style. A lovely album. Produced by Lenny Waronker and Russ Titelman.

## SOUNDTRACK
**Sharky's Machine** (Warners)
Ragbag compilation of hit songs for the Burt Reynolds film. Randy Crawford, Sarah Vaughn, Peggy Lee, Julie London, The Manhattan Transfers and others will probably enjoy the royalties but it's all rather undistinguished. Produced by Snuff Garrett.

## SOUNDTRACK
**Shock Treatment** (Warners)
Fizzy follow-up to 'The Rocky Horror Show' features quirky songs by Richard O'Brien with less of a satirical bent than the original set. Works with the film but not on its own.

## SPANDAU BALLET
**Diamond** (Chrysalis)
From limp futuristic thrashings to funk postures in the course of one album betrays Spandau Ballet's infatuation with fashion. This, their second album, confirms in my own eyes how contrived and manufactured the group are and no end of sales, hit singles or hype is likely to change my mind. Dishonest crap (and bad music). Produced by Richard James Burgess.

## SPIZZ
**Spizz History** (Rough Trade)
Back on an independent label after a brief affair with an international major, the band that changes names at the drop of a hat (Spizz Energy, Spizz Oil, etc. . .) offers a worthy selection of its past catalogue of art punk. A directionless set which is not devoid of humour (and two Star Trek parodies 'Captain Kirk' and 'Spock's Missing'). Raises a smile. Curious frolics.

## RICK SPRINGFIELD
**Success Hasn't Spoiled Me Yet** (RCA)
US sitcom star in continuation of surprisingly successful easy-listening singing career. Already on his third album,

Springfield offers a safe brew of sentimentality and knowing sexual innuendoes couched in a slick hard-edged rock. Big with teenagers and housewives. Produced by Keith Olsen.

## STEEL PULSE
**True Democracy** (Wiseman Doctrine/Elektra)
Reggae made in England (Birmingham) as opposed to the more common variety manufactured in the Kingston hit factories. Now on their own label, Steel Pulse have never compromised from a highly political stance and this energetic album remains in a similar rough groove, although a clever use of disco riffs opens up some numbers. Produced by Karl Patterson.

## STRAIGHT LINES
**Run for Cover** (Epic)
Run of the mill easy listening rock from a Canadian band in middling rocking form. Produced by Jeffrey Lesser.

## BARBRA STREISAND
**Love Songs** (CBS/Columbia)
Gone are the briefly-lived days when Her Highness Barbra flirted with the outer frontiers of rock. She has long since returned to a safe, easy-listening groove. New versions of old and more recent tracks, includes 'Memory', 'Don't Bring Me Flowers' and other popular tunes. Various producers.

## THE SUGARHILL GANG
**8th Wonder** (Sugarhill)
The *nec plus ultra* in street rap, New York style. A contagious collection of wordy hits by the utmost genre specialists. Perfect toe-tapping, hip-swivelling, body-stretching music. Includes 'Apache', '8th Wonder' and 'Showdown'. Produced by Sylvia Robinson.

## SUSAN
**The Girl Can't Help It** (Epic)
Naïve little girl voice and ever so saucy English lyrics in this first album released

in the West for leading Japanese pop singer. At first, it sounds refreshing but the overall sound soon becomes increasingly cloying. An acquired taste. Produced by Yukihiro Takahashi.

## KASIM SULTON
**Kasim** (EMI)
Innocuous solo outing for Todd Rundgren's Utopia's former bass player. The album features Sulton on all instruments and vocals on a hotch-potch of mainstream reasonably melodic pop. Produced by Bruce Fairbairn.

## SWOLLEN MONKEYS
**After Birth of the Cool** (Cachalot)
'A funny fiery collection of serious jazz honking, hopped-up ethnic boogie, and certifiably insane laughs' *(Melody Maker).* And I couldn't put it any better. A zany album of experimentation and improvisation which somehow remains great fun. Produced by Hal Willner.

## KEITH SYKES
**It Don't Hurt to Flirt** (Backstreet)
Memphis rocker on second album, with Rosanne Cash (for whom he has provided songs) on backing vocals. Sykes has a distinctive rock voice in a hundred and comes over most effectively on slower tempo material but too much of the album is devoted to ersatz rockabilly workouts which don't always do him justice. Worth looking out for, though; a name for the future. Produced by Jerene Sykes.

## SYREETA
**Set My Love in Motion** (Motown)
Below par album of saccharin ballads for Stevie Wonder's ex-wife and protegee. Has done and can do better.

---

# T

## YUKIHIRO TAKAHASHI
**Murdered by the Music** (Statik)
The second solo album of the Yellow Magic Orchestra's drummer, released two years later in the West by an enterprising independent label. This is a strong electro-pop excursion with heavy synthesiser reliance. Takahashi reveals a strong, but intelligently assimilated Bowie influence in both music and voice. Produced by Yukihiro Takahashi.

## YUKIHIRO TAKAHASHI
**Neuromantic** (Alfa)
Rapid British release for Takahashi's third solo album. Although still in a powerful electronic groove, this new effort opens up much more than previous attempts and blends a mix of European disco and dance rhythms with an Oriental texture and over-

all sound. Takahashi is aided by Roxy Music's Andy McKay and Phil Manzanera, as well as New Musik's Tony Mansfield on this highly accessible record. Produced by Yukihiro Takahashi.

## TALKING HEADS
**The Name of this Band is Talking Heads** (Sire)
An impeccable double live album which retraces the band's footsteps through time and covers their career chronologically from early days to last year's latest funk incarnation with a bevy of additional musicians. The evolution proves fascinating and the new, augmented sound on older songs is a genuine source of delight. Live albums (and double examples, at that) are rarely of interest outside a small circle of faithful fans, but Talking Heads prove a shining exception to the rule. Every track is worth mentioning, so just acquire the record, especially if you've collected the Heads' previous efforts. Produced by the group.

## TANK
**Filth Hounds of Hades** (Kamaflage)
With a title like that (and such a military moniker) how could it not be a species of heavy metal-itis? Which it is. Full stop.

## THE TEARDROP EXPLODES
**Wilder** (Mercury)

Wide-eyed and naïve Julian Cope's second effort in his earnest bid to become the Jim Morrison Mark 2 of the new psychedelia. The British critics who once lauded Teardrop Explodes are already deserting the band as fast as rats fleeing a sinking craft and Cope seems to have already overstayed his welcome. Which I feel he never really deserved. A massively ambitious album of derivative, quasi-plagiaristic tunes. Ah, if only young Cope didn't take himself so bloody seriously! Produced by Clive Langer.

## TENPOLE TUDOR
**Let the Four Winds Blow** (Stiff)
Yobbo rock in the purest British tradition of verve and healthy vulgarity. And a zest of primeval rockabilly to make the mixture prosper. Has an amateurish charm, I suppose, which helped the group to two and a half hits in the UK. But I don't think worldwide fame will automatically follow. Worth a chuckle.

## THEATRE OF HATE
**Westworld** (Burning Rome)
Theatre of Hate are one of the last rabid outposts of unadulterated British punk, full of rage, bitterness and rancour. Unpolished, often unmusical thrashings where energy is the only redeeming feature. Produced by Mick Jones.

## THIRD WORLD
**You've Got the Power** (CBS/Columbia)
Impressive reggae album by one of the foremost bands in the field boasts highly-polished and slick production by big name US musician in a bid to reach crossover market. Stevie Wonder also guests on two tracks. Produced by Stevie Wonder.

## BARBARA THOMPSON AND ROD ARGENT
**Ghosts** (MCA)
Pleasant middling jazz ballads by veteran jazz blower and soft-voiced crooner with bona fide pop roots. Easy-listening in a tasteful style. Produced by Jon Hiseman.

## LINVAL THOMPSON
**Look How Me Sexy** (Greensleeves)
Reggae singer with soft crooning voice and a lesser preoccupation with rasta creeds. Backing by Roots Radics. Produced by Linval Thompson.

## RICHARD AND LINDA THOMPSON
**Shoot Out the Lights** (Hannibal)

| | |
|---|---|
| Don't Renege on Our Love | Shoot Out the Lights |
| Walking On A Wire | Back Street Slide |
| Man In Need | Did She Jump Or Was She Pushed |
| Just The Motion | Wall of Death |

A change of label and a return to the producer of Thompson's epochal band Fairport Convention seem to have worked wonders and this new album sees the Thompsons at the awesome height of their musical power. Always a superlative guitarist whose technical ability never overshadowed his simmering emotions, Richard Thompson has carved a unique niche for himself and his wife: a corner of gothic/electric folk rock. Painting bleak aural vistas of brooding intensity, Richard and Linda Thompson have come up with

an album in a thousand. Produced by Joe Boyd.

## THOMPSON TWINS
**Set** (T) (US title: In the Name of Love (Arista))
Strong percussion effects on this set of quirky dance tunes by a new British band who have since fragmented. Intelligent but faceless modern rock still in search of the elusive sparkle that will make all the difference. Produced by Steve Lillywhite.

## THE TIME
**The Time** (Warners)
Minnesota band discovered by glam funkster Prince. Strong rock-tinged soul often reminiscent of Funkadelic. Produced by Morris Day and Jamie Starr.

## THE TIMES
**Pop Goes Art** (Whaam)
Whimsical art-school satirical ditties in an English eccentric tradition. Gentle, naïve fun while it lasts. Okay first time round, but doesn't improve with repeated listenings.

## TOOTS AND THE MAYTALS
**Knock Out** (Island/Mango)
Routine reggae outing by a reliable purveyor. Melancholy mood dominates throughout. Produced by F. Toots Hibbert.

## TANYA TUCKER
**Live** (MCA)
Junior country jailbait gone to fat, seed and a veneer of sophistication. Gutsy versions of all the old hits. Produced by Snuff Garrett.

## TV PERSONALITIES
**Mummy You're Not Watching Me** (Whaam)
Modern British rock much too clever for it's own sake. Pretentious, I'd call it. Lurches back to the 1960s with gay abandon.

## TV 21
**A Thin Red Line** (Deram)
Anonymous new Scottish band. Derivative. Mildly pleasant. Any other convenient adjectives going cheap?

## 23 SKIDOO
**Seven Songs** (Fetish)
The combined spectral souls of Captain Beefheart, Ornette Coleman and Roland Kirk live on in this strongly experimental jazz-influenced set by a British band. Adventurous rhythms and dissonances but not easy to dance to. An ambitious record which, at least, doesn't settle for the bland canyons of easy acceptance facility. Priced cheaply also. Produced by Tony, Terry and David.

## DWIGHT TWILLEY
**Scuba Divers** (EMI)

Twilley's fourth album (this time without his usual cohort Phil Seymour who has also gone down the solo rag and riches path) after a three year break. His voice is still as pure and youthful, vibrating its way through delicately crafted melodic pop. Jangling guitars à la Buddy Holly and hooks of Beatles similitude situate where Twilley lives on the map of rock, and there are much worse places to be at. Produced by Dwight Twilley, Geoff Workman, Chuck Plotkin, Noah Shark and Max.

# U

## UFO
**Mechanix** (Chrysalis)
One of the more professional heavy metal outfits on yet another studio recording. Just what the denim crowd want: powerhouse riffs, shrieking vocals and a perfect lack of subtlety. A few ballads to rest the ears, though. Produced by Gary Lyons.

## URIAH HEEP
**Abominog** (Bronze/Mercury)
A prehistoric precursor of the heavy metal brigade rises from the grave where most of us had long banished them. A new line-up but the mixture as before. Produced by Ashley Howe.

# V

## VARDIS
**Quo Vardis** (Logo)
How do you say 'The Curse of Heavy Metal Strikes Again' in Latin?

## VARIOUS
**Amarcord Nino Rota** (Hannibal)

An engaging jazz homage to Nino Rota who wrote the music for most of Federico Fellini's films. A wonderfully varied group of US musicians offer their own versions of his principal themes and tunes. Features Debbie Harry and Chris Stein, Carla Bley, Jaki Byard, Steve Lacy, Dave Samuels, Bill Frisell, Sharon Freeman, Richard Abrams, David Amran and many others. A labour of love. Produced by Hal Willner.

## VARIOUS
**A Country Fit for Heroes** (No Future)
A punk manifesto featuring 12 tracks from 11 generally unknown British skin bands in full flight of fury and resentment against society.

## VARIOUS
**Echoes of an Era** (Elektra)
An interesting American collection featuring modern soul performers with updated versions of fifties numbers (recorded under elementary fifties conditions, which does spoil the pleasure somehow). Includes contributions by Chaka Khan, Freddie Hubbard, Chick Corea, Stanley Clarke. Produced by Lenny White.

## VARIOUS
**A Fresh Selection** (Fresh)
Sampler for one of the more enterprising British independent labels (which has since gone under). Features Family Fodder, Wilko Johnson, Bernie Torme, UK Decay, The Wall, Cuddly Toys. Varied and diverse roster.

## VARIOUS
**Genius of Rap** (Island)
First-class compilation of US rap masters for British consumption. Includes dizzy verbal improvisations by the likes of Twennynine, T/Ski Valley, Dr. Jeckyll and Mr. Hyde, Afrika Bambaataa, Grandmaster Flash, Bon Rock. A good introduction to a new musical genre.

## VARIOUS
**Hell Comes to Your House** (Riot State/Bemisbrain)
A selection of crude but lively Los Angeles punk groups: 45 Grave, Christian Grave, 11 Flowers, Rhino 39, Super Heroines, Social Distortion, Legal Weapon, Red Cross, Modern Warfare, Secret Hate and The Conservatives.

## VARIOUS
**Punk and Disorderly** (Abstract/Posh Boy)
Another punk compilation of up and coming and struggling bands from the UK, plus a US 'name' contribution from the already-infamous Dead Kennedys. In the line-up on parade: UK Decay, Peter and the Test Tube Babies, Blitz, Vice Squad, The Addicts, Disorder, Disrupters, Red Alert, The Partisans, Demob, The Insane, Abrasive Wheels, Chaos UK, Outcasts and G.B.I.

## VARIOUS
**Raiders of the Lost Dub** (Island/Mango)
Introduction to the spare features of reggae dub for the white market. Features a bevy of leading Jamaican bands: The Paragons, Ijahman, Black Uhuru, Burning Spear, Wailing Souls, the ViceRoys and Junior Delgado.

## VARIOUS
**Rap Tracks** (Virgin)
A further varied introduction to rap for the British audience. Original formula with two 12-inch albums playing at 45 rpm, presumably for better penetration into the disco market. The tracks include The Treacherous 3, Frankie Smith, Disco Four, Midnight Blue, Doctor Ice, Funk Fusion Band, Captain Sky and Count Coolout.

## VARIOUS
**Rodney at the ROQ Vol. 2** (Posh Boy)
Selected by the eponymous Rodney Bingenheimer for his West Coast radio show, a sampler of lesser-known US bands with strong punkoid leanings: Target 13, Social Distortion, Shattered Faith, Black Flag, Minutemen, Red Cross, CH3, Agent Orange, Red Rockers, Unit 3, The Stepmothers, Gleaming Spires, Levi and the Rockats, Little Girls, Twisted Roots and Geza.

## VARIOUS
**The Secret Policeman's Other Ball – The Music** (Springtime/Island)
Following the success of the charity show's comedy sketches, now comes the album of the music. A powerful 'Message in the Bottle' by an acoustic Sting stands out amongst more varied material by a selection of name stars like Donovan, Bob Geldof, Jeff Beck, Eric Clapton, Phil Collins, etc. . . . . In favour of Amnesty International. Produced by Martin Lewis.

## VARIOUS
**A Splash of Colour** (Warners)
Under a suitable garish, multicoloured cover comes a British compilation of new pyschedelic bands. Patchy, to say the least. Features The Barracudas, Miles Over Matter, The Earwigs, Marble Staircase, Mood Six, The Times, The Silence and The High Tide.

## VARIOUS
**Stars of the Street Encore** (Cachalot)
An enterprising compilation (as the title reveals, in fact a second such one) of New York busker and street artists. All styles of music are here: rock, jazz, bluegrass, folk, calypso, country. . . . Refreshing. Produced by Eric Dufaure and Allan Steckler.

## VARIOUS
**Tokyo Mobile Music 1** (Phonogram)
Compilation of Japanese electro-pop chosen by club man David Claridge. Includes the usual Yellow Magic Orchestra offshoots, soloist and cronies.

## VARIOUS
**To The Shores of Lake Placid** (Zoo)
A retrospective sampler album and history of the independent Liverpool born label Zoo. Tracks by Teardrop Explodes, Echo and the Bunnymen, Big in Japan, Dalek (I Love You), Lori and the Chameleons, Those Naughty Lumps and Julian Cope under a pseudonymous funny hat.

## VARIOUS
**Your Secret's Safe With Us** (Statik)
Another compilation of British regional bands, this time from the north of England. Compiler Nigel Burnham's previous 'Hicks from the Sticks' has a good track record so it's a fair bet that one or two names from the legion of 18 unknown bands featured here will emerge again to individual acclaim.

37

## ALAN VEGA
**Collision Drive** (Celluloid)
Hypnotic, driving electronic rockabilly with unusual strength and intensity by Alan Vega, half of the minimalist US group Suicide, who applies a similar treatment to more traditional forms of rock. Has proved surprisingly successful in Europe. Certainly worth investigating with an open mind even if rockabilly has never been your brew. Produced by Alan Vega.

## THE VICEROYS
**We Must Unite** (Trojan)
Supposedly cult reggae vocal trio in a powerful demonstration of fluent, mellow tunes, with backing from the omnipresent Roots Radics. Produced by Linval Thompson.

## VISAGE
**The Anvil** (Polydor)

Visage are a group who exist only in the darkness of recording studios, consisting of a variety of electro-rockers from other horizons (Midge Ure, Gary Barnacle, Rusty Egan, Billy Currie, Dave Formula) fronted by man-about-fashionable-London-town Steve Strange. Their first album was catchy and produced a few hits, but this new effort is bland and unmemorable and lacking in both passion and inventiveness. A sad waste of money, considering the extent of the promotion and the luxury sleeve courtesy of Helmut Newton (photo), Peter Saville (sleeve texture and old/modern typographics), Antony Price (clothes), etc. . . . . Produced by Midge Ure and the group.

## VOGGUE
**Voggue** (Atlantic)
French Canadian female disco duet. Formula stuff. Produced by Michel Daigle and François L'Herbier.

JOHN WATTS

# W

## THE WAITRESSES
**Wasn't Tomorrow Wonderful?**
(Polydor/Ze)
The newest darlings of New York clubland, The Waitresses on their initial album outing. Perky, intelligent new wave pop with almost chanted vocals by the distinctive Patty Donahue and generally conceived by guitarist Chris Butler as day-to-day parables of life's foibles and follies. A bit samey. Judgment will have to await the next album to ascertain whether this promising new group has the staying power and capacity to innovate further. This'll do for now. Produced by Kurt Munkacsi and Chris Butler.

## BOBBI WALKER
**Bobbi Walker** (Alfa)
Jazz-accented soul from mellifluous vocalist with prized backing by the likes of Joe Sample, Wilton Felder and The Crusaders. Produced by Steve Tyrell.

## WAR
**Outlaw** (RCA)
Black rock band with minor successes in the '70s now turns more ethnic and makes long forays into soul, jazz and funk territories in search of necessary new audience. Slick but automatic. Produced by Jerry Goldstein and Lonnie Jordan.

## JACKY WARD
**Night After Night** (Elektra)
Subdued country album from a performer best at ease with melancholy ballads of woe and lost love. Produced by Mike Post.

## JOHN WATTS
**One More Twist** (EMI)
Minor but pleasant album from a former member of little-sung band Fischer-Z. Modern rock with a modicum of intelligence but a lack of originality. Produced by Richard Mainwaring and John Watts.

## WEATHER REPORT
**Weather Report** (CBS/Columbia)
Another fine album by the pioneers of fusion/electronic jazz with the magical bass of Jaco Pastorius and orchestrations of Joe Zawinul. Much the same as before with few concessions to modern electronic or dance trends. Jazz limbering up on the furthest borderlines of progressive rock. Produced by Joe Zawinul.

## PATTY WEAVER
**Patty Weaver** (Warners)
Shapely, blonde American sitcom actress with an album of fluent, middle-of-the-road songs with a zest of rock. She has a surprisingly fine voice and the overall sound is clear cut and vivacious thanks to fine production work, but was there any point? Goes in one ear, comes out the other. Produced by Steve Barri.

## BRANDI WELLS
**Watch Out** (WMOT)
Nicely varied soul set by new US singer. A few very strong, danceable songs but the rest does suspiciously sound like filler material. Various producers.

## HELEN WHEELS BAND
**Post Modern Living** (Real American)
Strictly speaking an EP, this, from a veteran of the New York new wave club scene who's never truly made it to the spotlight like her similar colleague in po-

etry and rock soul Patti Smith. Six powerful songs that deserve a larger audience. Produced by Joe Bouchard.

### THE WHISPERS
**Love Is You Where You Find It**
(Solar)
Ever so slick album from veterans of the soul circuit. One side of the album is designated 'For Romancin'' and the other 'For Dancin'' and the music skilfully fulfils all expectations.

### WHITE HEAT
**In the Zero Hour** (Valium)
Murky, non-descript debut album by British band with too many Springsteen mannerisms.

### KIM WILDE
**Kim Wilde** (Rak/EMI)
American 1982 release for Kim Wilde's blockbusting first European album. Being carefully groomed as a younger Blondie under the careful auspices of her father, brother and Micky Most, Wilde proves highly adaptable and this is almost a collection of hits, actual and potential. Contains 'Kids in America', 'Water on Glass', 'Chequered Love'. An infectious, joyfully commercial album. Produced by Ricky Wilde.

### KATE WOLF
**Close To You** (Kaleidoscope)
Heartfelt folk rock by American vocalist. Laid back and unassuming. Produced by Bill Griffin and Tom Diamont.

### WRABIT
**Wrabit** (MCA)
Mainstream rock from new Canadian band with four singers taking lead vocals which dispels some of the monotony and evenness of the tone and tempo of the material. Produced by Paul Gross.

### ROBERT WYATT
**Nothing Can Stop Us** (Rough Trade)
Robert Wyatt's first full-fledged album in an eternity is in fact a hotch-potch of past, experimental singles and tracks by guest poets. Lacks any real unity as a result. Wyatt's voice and textures are still as unique as ever and it's nice to have his beautiful version of Billie Holliday's 'Strange Fruit' and Mexican revolutionary classic 'Caimanera'. Also included is a sardonic, ambiguous version of 'The Red Flag' and a stunning rendition of Chic's 'At Last I Am Free'. Certainly a heteroclit album but when it's good, it's just sublime. Produced by Robert Wyatt.

# X

### XTC
**English Settlement** (Virgin/Epic)
A double album in England which was slimmed down to a single platter for US consumption. The general feeling is more diffuse than on 'Black Sea', their previous album, where their eccentricity had been carefully kept to an acceptable minimum.

Otherwise, it's a sprawling catalogue of all of XTC's idiosyncratic revisions of the currents of British pop sensibility. Andy Partridge remains as quirkily witty as ever, while Colin Moulding's more direct melodic numbers betray a heavy dose of pastoral romanticism. One of the more intelligent pop bands going the rounds in these early 1980s and worthy of their growing following. Produced by Hugh Padgham and the group.

# Y

### YELLOW MAGIC ORCHESTRA
**Solid State Survivor** (Alfa)
An early record by the ubiquitous Japanese electro-synth formation. Made in 1979 this has been superseded since by more thorough experimentation and tunes. Instrumentals are a strong feature. But, for YMO collectors only. Produced by Haruomi Hosono.

### STEVE YOUNG
**To Satisfy You** (Rounder)
Strong, vigorous country rock by a singer whose sparse past recorded output was more in a folk vein (he is the writer of the oft-recorded 'Seven Bridges Song'). One of the best records of the year in this particular genre, and well worth hunting down as its distribution through independent channels is patchy. Produced by Jerry Shook, Mac Gayden and Steve Young.

# Z

### ANDY Z AND LESLIE
**Opportunity Rocks (and Rolls)**
(Snow Beach)
The Z stands for Zwerling. And Leslie is his sister, taking lead vocals on this set of innocent mid-seventies tunes that has the rough feel of a demo tape recorded in a garage for love and the sheer fun of it. 13 songs in a minor but highly enticing vein. More than just a curiosity in the style of eternal adolescent Jonathan Richman, this is also a finely crafted pop album. Investigate.

### ZOUNDS
**The Curse of Zounds** (Rough Trade)
The political naïvety and the accomplished lack of musicianship of, say, the Sex Pistols mix on this debut independent album by a run-of-the-mill British punk group who seem to have jumped on the wagon a many few years too late.

KIM WILDE

## A

### ABC
**Lexicon of Love** (Neutron/Mercury)

Show Me
Poison Arrow
Many Happy
  Returns
Tears Are Not
  Enough
Valentine's Day
The Look Of Love
  (part one)
Date Stamp
All Of My Heart
4ever 2gether
The Look Of Love
  (part four)

Hate the suave image; love the music. White boys might not be able to sing the blues, but these Sheffield newcomers have white funk pouring out of their fingernails. Although there is little doubt that the package is eminently fabricated and tailor-made to today's pop sensibility, and the numerous hit singles lifted off the album bear witness to its popularity, these tunes keep your feet moving. Smooth, witty. What else should a popster want? Music to change the world by? We'll leave that to Springsteen. Until then, this will do. Produced by Trevor Horn.

### ROY ACUFF
**Back in the Country** (Elektra)
A rare vinyl excursion for an old country hand. Decent assortment of backing musicians and a balance between nostalgic melodies and more modern ballads make this just a touch more than a superfluous trip down memory lane. For fans only, though. Produced by Wesley Rose.

### BRYAN ADAMS
**You Want It, You've Got It** (A&M)
There was once a time when the record industry offered us our yearly 'new Dylan'. Times have changed and these are the halcyon days of Springsteen clones. Bryan Adams is one; he has the image and idiosyncrasies down pat: street-wise lyrics and thundering piano runs. But it's still glorified rubbish.

### GAYLE ADAMS
**Love Fever** (Epic)
Pedestrian glossy funk. Scored minor hit with title track but then sped towards oblivion, where it always belonged. Produced by Willie Lester and Rodney Brown.

### AIR SUPPLY
**Now and Forever** (Arista)
Off the group's platinum mould, but somehow lacking in genuine pizzazz this time around. Romantic ballads with a strong touch of the melodramatic, but, at the end of the day, quite unmemorable and hollow. Will sell a million and adorn the cocktail hour blues in dimly-lit bars from Poughkeepsie to Portland (Oregon). But I still don't like it. Produced by Harry Maslin.

### ALESSI
**Long Time Friends** (QWest)
Mid-tempo polished, safe, aseptic rock by an American duo doomed to linger forever in the Sargasso of US late-night radio. Ah, to see the light of day. Plastic pap but well-done. Produced by Michael Ostin and Christopher Cross.

### ALKATRAZZ
**Radio Five** (RCA)
Identikit heavy metal mayhem.

### ALLIANCE
**Alliance** (Handshake)
Pleasant but vapid debut by new American poppish balladeers. Very safe, very mainstream. Here today, gone today. Produced by Ron and Howard Albert.

### LUTHER ALLISON
**South Side Safari** (Red Lightnin')
Seven live Chicago blues tracks by a master guitarist. Adequate mix of classic tunes and new, self-penned, numbers. Produced by Craig Moore.

### HERB ALPERT
**Fandango** (A&M)
As the title indicates, Alpert is back in a Spanish vein. Innocuous elevator music, all instrumentals bar one, with big-name Latin arrangers and others. Produced by Jose Quintana and Herb Alpert.

### ALTERED IMAGES
**Pinky Blue** (Epic)

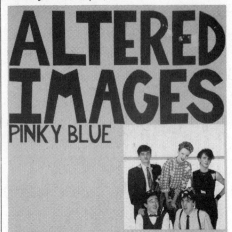

Altered Images' first album (see elsewhere in this volume) was genuinely invigorating and snappy. This hurried second effort (no doubt accelerated by the mega-success of 'Happy Birthday') puts on a bubbly front but soon succumbs to terminal cutesy-poo and lemonade poisoning. The group's virtues have been obliterated and Miss Grogan's little-girl giggles smother the whole record in a most unendearing way. Schooldays were never like this. A cover of Neil Diamond's 'Song Sung Blue' vies for worst track of the year. Produced by Martin Rushent (boo . . .).

### AMBROSIA
**Road Island** (Warner)
Faceless group with more faceless music. This time around, it's not Foreigner, but Ambrosia, but who can really spot the difference? Nothing offensive about it; on the other hand, there's also nothing remarkable by any stretch of the imagination. Produced by James Guthrie.

### JON ANDERSON
**Animation** (Polydor/Atlantic)
Anderson's bleating, castrati tones never really bothered me in the early days of Yes, drowned as they often were in a torrent of virtuosity and potent energy. Later dabblings in 'fantasy' lyrics that gave fantasy a bad name and concept albums that sounded the death knell of concept albums further aggravated his case as Yes began losing members. The canny if dubious musicianship of Vangelis once more muddied the waters of assessment after Anderson went solo, but here the man is naked and properly insufferable. Self-

appointed guru of the whey-faced effeminate set and the scrapings of bedsit land, he stands accused: this music rots teeth!

## LAURIE ANDERSON
**Big Science** (Warners)

| | |
|---|---|
| From The Air | O Superman (For |
| Big Science | Massenet) |
| Sweaters | Example 22 |
| Walking & Falling | Let X=X/It Tango |
| Born, Never Asked | |

A new York performance artist previously noticed for collaborations with seminal poetry and beat figures like John Giorno or William Burroughs, Laurie Anderson revives my faith in the future of music. At last, listening to record after record, ranging from excretory substances to merely pleasant, comes something truly original. Furthermore, it even sold well! The songs/pieces on the album come from her multi-media stagework 'United States I–IV' and, although in a minimalist mode, benefit from multi-layered studio techniques which subtly emphasize their unassuming quirkiness. The eerie title track with its whale-like yodelling and visions of technology in an urban landscape is a personal favourite, but the whole album makes for fascinating listening. Buy. Produced by Laurie Anderson and Roma Baran.

## ANGELIC UPSTARTS
**Still From The Heart** (Zonophone)
Working-class punk survivors adapting to the times and testing new waters with a sprinkling of reggae, a zest of electronic dirge music and naive Clash-like politics. E for Effort and F for Failure nonetheless. Produced by Steve Levene.

## DAROL ANGER/BARBARA HIGBIE
**Tideline** (Windham Hall)
Interesting attempt at a form of rock chamber music, as violinist Anger duets on delicately carved tunes with Higbie's piano. A touch of the jazz-according-to-ECM, but worth looking out for. Produced by Darol Anger.

## ANTI-NOWHERE LEAGUE
**We Are . . . The League** (WXYZ)
First album by neo-punk revivalists. Really not the sort of stuff you could expect me to be impartial about, is it? You can feel the rage, the vengeful spirit et al; the drums and shrieking guitars keep it all going at a fair pace, heavy-metal style; the lyrics are inane but genuinely sincere. The way music was. Produced by Aurable.

## ANVIL
**Metal on Metal** (Attic)
High energy heavy metal from seasoned Canadian group. All the screams and riffs of the fair are dutifully present. Produced by Chris Tsangarides.

## ASHFORD & SIMPSON
**Street Opera** (Capitol)
A schizophrenic album, Ashford & Simpson's first for a new label. The first side features a series of polished, ultra-romantic songs familiar to the duo's followers while the second one consists of a realistic song cycle about the life of a poor black family in contemporary America. This is where the meat is and it's most effective, melodramatic and poignant. An unusual departure which should gain A & S a larger public, beyond the limited social awareness of the dance floor. Produced by Ashford and Simpson.

## THE ASSOCIATES
**Sulk** (Associates/Sire)

A frustrating album from one of Britain's most promising bands. While their first album often recalled the Bowie of 'Young Americans', this third one (the second was a collection of singles) lacks unity beyond the magnificent warblings of Billy MacKenzie. The Associates are in turn histrionic, epic, whimsical and cryptic, sometimes all under the aegis of the same song. Still, even when functioning on only one piston, as often appears here, they are so much superior to three quarters of the other records released with fanfare elsewhere. The American release of the album features a different selection of tracks from the British version. Both avatars are worth a purchase. Produced by Mike Hedges and the Associates.

## AXE
**Offering** (Atco)
Hard melodic rock/heavy metal/power pop. Choose your cliché. Produced by Al Nalli.

# B

## BALLISTIC KISSES
**Total Access** (Don't Fall Off The Mountain)
New York punk agit-prop rock. The curse of Talking Heads strikes again, but this US quartet ignore the fact that Byrne's band have a strong melodic feel and, admit it, talent. Ballistic Kisses are no doubt young, sincere and angry, but it sure ain't enough to make an LP that stands on its own two feet. Tentative glimpses of class shine through the murky atmosphere of this record but they are few and far between. Some people just take themselves too seriously!

## THE BAND AKA
**The Band Aka** (Epic)
Smooth funk. Set the controls for the heart of Saturday night . . .

## MOE BANDY
**She's Not Really Cheatin' (She's Just Gettin' Even)** (Columbia)
Traditional beer-drinking music from a reliable country stalwart. Produced by Ray Baker.

## BOBBY BARE
**Ain't Got Nothin' to Lose** (Columbia)
Strong set from an established country stylist. A satisfactory blend of ballads, reminiscences and humour. Produced by Allen Reynolds.

BOBBY BARE

## BATTLEFIELD BAND
**The Story So Far** (Temple)
The Battlefield Band are one of the last remaining, staunchly traditional, British folk bands. This album, commemorating their tenth anniversary (despite a number of changes in the line-up), charts their progress and celebrates their contribution to British folk. Features one unreleased track. Not only for folk purists and sandal-wearing freaks.

## PETER BAUMANN
**Repeat Repeat** (Virgin/Portrait)
A past member of German synthesiser doodlers Tangerine Dream switches to mainstream dance pop. Rather anonymous but not unpleasant, this caught me with at least each toe twitching and ready to trip a mild disco beat over my kitchen floor. Produced by Robert Palmer and Peter Baumann.

## BEACH BOYS
**Sunshine Dream** (Capitol)
Another compilation for the sand, sun and water season. The formula is safe and a minimum amount of sales are always guaranteed. Breezy surfing and blue sky minor classics, and those harmonies, god those harmonies! A double set, of course. Produced by the Beach Boys. By the way, what are they doing now?

THE BEATLES (1964)

## THE BEATLES
**Reel Music** (EMI/Capitol)
Not a bad idea, this. A well-devised compilation of songs from Beatles movies from 'A Hard Day's Night' to 'Let It Be'. All your favourites and mine are here. Strange how so many Beatles songs strike a resonant chord in the memory of us over-30s. I'll always remember that summer on a Spanish beach and the girl who was beside me when I heard 'Eleanor Rigby' for the first time on a tinny transistor radio. But that's another book, folks (see: Jakubowski, fiction) and anyway that particular song isn't even on this album . . . Produced by George Martin and The Beatles.

## THE BEATLES
**Talk Downunder** (Goughsound/PVC Raven)
A rip-off, of course. But fun. A record of interviews with the fab mop-tops on the occasion of their 1964 Australian tour. No Ringo (he was ill) but some forgotten hero called Jimmy Nicol (who? – sign him up for a book, fast!) deputized, it appears. Did you know that?

## ADRIAN BELEW
**Lone Rhino** (Island)

Sideman guitarist to the modern stars (Bowie, Zappa, Talking Heads, etc . . .) Adrian Belew is, at time of writing, firmly ensconced in the more recent and lasting incarnation of King Crimson. His solo album never ceases to impress by its virtuosity, wit and imagination. A distinctive guitar player, Belew shows a chameleon-like stance and we see here touches of Bowie, Byrne and Fripp plus a few personal idiosyncrasies. Most solo outings usually prove unnecessary; while this one won't convert Jews to the Palestinian cause, it won't bore you either. Produced by Adrian Belew.

## BELLAMY BROTHERS
**When We Were Boys** (Elektra)
All self-penned material, heavily into rom-
ance and starry-eyed nostalgia. Professional blandness. Produced by David & Howard Bellamy and Jimmy Bowen.

## MIKE BERRY
**Memories** (Polydor)
Old Merseybeat rockers never die, they just turn into sitcom actors and record albums of old MOR stalwarts by Irving Berlin. Strictly for the working men's club and pink cocktail set. Produced by Mike Berry and Chas Hodges.

## BIG TWIST AND THE MELLOW FELLOWS
**One Track Mind** (Flying Fish/Red Lightnin')
Big Twist is none other than Larry Nolan, a strong blues singer backed by a group of white musicians deeply steeped into grassroot club blues traditions. Old-fashioned but reliable. For Dr. Feelgood early-day nostalgics. Beats the overrated Blues Brothers and Blues Band any day. Produced by Jim Tullio.

## BLACK UHURU
**Chill Out** (Island)
Why are reggae artists so prolific? It's not that this latest Black Uhuru effort is bad, far from it, but a sense of repetitiveness soon dulls the senses and due appreciation is muted. A strong militant flavour permeates this album, with strong rhythm backing from diamond-sharp producers extraordinaire: Sly Dunbar and Robbie Shakespeare.

## CARLA BLEY
**Live!** (Watt)
Carla Bley's big band jazz flirts outrageously with rock, vaudeville and surrealistic military marches. A true original whose recorded career is now most substantial, Bley has long since left the avant-garde regions with which too many critics still associate her music. On the contrary, she couldn't be more accessible. This is fun music. Leave your prejudices at the door. Produced by Carla Bley.

## BLONDIE
**The Hunter** (Chrysalis)

| | |
|---|---|
| Orchid Club | War Child |
| Island of Lost Souls | Little Caesar |
| Dragonfly | Danceway |
| For Your Eyes Only | (Can I) Find the |
| The Beast | Right Words (To Say) |
| | English Boys |
| | The Hunter Gets Captured By The Game |

Blondie's first major flop. After the unpopular experiments of their last album, an attempt to recapture the liveliness of pop exuberance of the early days fails to co-

DEBBIE HARRY, BLONDIE

alesce. Snatches of reggae, rap and rock with few distinguishable features. Production and musicianship are first class, but a lack of enthusiasm permeates 'The Hunter' as if the group were now just going through the motions. Another of my favourite bands grows old; sad. Unnoticed by other critics, though, is 'English Boys', a delicate, almost innocent paean by Stein and Debbie Harry to days gone by. Otherwise, it's all much the same. Produced by Mike Chapman.

### BLUE ORCHIDS
**The Greatest Hit** (Rough Trade)
A nicely ironical title for this first album from a young British group whose Martin Bramah was once in the Fall. A gentle, unassuming debut with strong emphasis on organ, this suffers a bit from the obvious comparison with other, maybe more adept British new music exponents of angst and doom (Joy Division, Associates, U2, Comsat Angels), but is worth looking out for in bargain bins until their next album creates further ripples. Produced by Tony Roberts and Blue Orchids.

### BLUE OYSTER CULT
**Extraterrestrial Live** (CBS/Columbia)
Pompous and bombastic, this new double live set from Blue Oyster Cult comes much too soon after their last double live set. For fans of the group only. Refer to their single album studio sets for much more polished versions of all the material. Produced by Sandy Pearlman and George Geranios.

### GARY US BONDS
**On the Line** (EMI)
Springsteen continues his healthy patronage of Bonds with more sure-fire material

off his seemingly unending mental panoramas of night, cars, dance and rock 'n' roll. This second album in the Bonds resurrection isn't as invigorating as 'Dedication' and the general mood is more subdued and reflective, the extra-special Springsteen touch only truly coming into its own in up-tempo songs like 'Club Soul City'. Will certainly do until you-know-who's next LP. Produced by Bruce Springsteen and Miami Steve.

### BOW WOW WOW
**Last of the Mohicans** (RCA)
McLaren's tribal beat teeny-bop answer to Adam and the Ants. Mixed EP of new material released in the US market.

### BOXCAR WILLIE
**Good Ol' Country Songs** (K-Tel)
A staunchly traditionalist US country singer who sells remarkably well in the UK. 16 tracks covering a lot of ground from cowboy ballads to songs of the bayou and the wild west. Reliable. Star backing musicians offer a guarantee of quality.

### THE BOYS BAND
**The Boys Band** (Asylum)
Anonymous soft rock. Produced by Peter Granet.

### BOYS TOWN GANG
**Disc Charge** (ERC/Raws Horn)
Lush disco revivalists from San Francisco cover six dance floor anthems. Who would ever have thought that disco would emerge from the tomb so fast; we'd just about buried it . . .

### BRASS CONSTRUCTION
**Attitudes** (Liberty)
Strong funk to fuel the patent leather dance shoes into higher gear. Great brass. Produced by Randy Muller.

### BRITISH ELECTRIC FOUNDATION
**Music of Quality and Distinction**
(Virgin)
Ball Of Confusion (Tina Turner)
The Secret Life Of Arabia (Billy McKenzie)
There's A Ghost In My House (Paul Jones)
These Boots Are Made For Walking (Paula Yates)
Suspicious Minds (Gary Glitter)

You Keep Me Hanging On (Bernie Nolan)
Wichita Lineman (Glenn Gregory)
Anyone Who Had A Heart (Sandie Shaw)
Perfect Day (Glenn Gregory)
It's Over (Billy McKenzie)

A great idea (though not a new one, Bowie and others have beaten the B.E.F. boys to it long ago) from the Human League splinter group going for critical kudos rather than world domination. The only problem is that none of these modern covers of major (and very minor) hits either adds to the original or presents a radically new interpretation. So, curiosity value mostly. Sandie Shaw and Gary Glitter both on the come-back trail don't convince and only the lesser known Glenn Gregory (of Heaven 17) and Billy MacKenzie (of the Associates) impress. Produced by Martyn Ware and Ian Craig Marsh.

### DENNIS BROWN
**Love Has Found Its Way** (A&M)
Crossover between reggae and gentle funk. Recorded in Jamaica, the rhythm section carries the tunes and imposes a strong dance feel, even to the more devotional material. Produced by Joe Gibbs and Willie Lindo.

DENNIS BROWN

### SHEREE BROWN
**Straight Ahead** (Capitol)
Second division soul, sometimes reminiscent of (but nowhere as poignant as) Minnie Ripperton. Produced by Richard Rudolph.

### BRYGADA KRYSIS
**Brygada Krysis** (Fresh)
Polish punk rock recorded live before the military clampdown on Solidarity and their supporters. The music sounds like early Clash with the occasional reggae toon. Difficult to assess the lyrics but they sound sufficiently impassioned. Give it the (liberal) benefit of the doubt.

### BUCKS FIZZ
**Are You Ready?** (RCA)
A second album of clever, ultra-polished, well-crafted pop for children, mums and dads by one of the few groups to survive the Eurovision Song Contest and not die a death. Much of this is due to Andy Hill's songwriting which carefully avoids aiming

at the lowest common denominator and instead goes for a touch of class and cheerful glamour. Contains all the hit singles, of course. Produced by Andy Hill.

### KENI BURKE
**Changes** (RCA)
One-man band funk machine. Self-produced and written. Body-shaking music. Effective but unmemorable.

### BURNING SPEAR
**Farover** (Radic/Heartbeat)
Stalwart reggae performer singing here with larger than usual group of musicians. Easy listening within its own genre. Produced by Burning Spear.

# C

### CABARET VOLTAIRE
**2 x 45** (Rough Trade)
Ambient music for the electronic age from the Sheffield band that appears to have lost out in the fame stakes to Human League and ABC. Obscure stuff barely distinguishable from their previous, numerous, vinyl excursions. Comes as two 12-inch 45s.

### CALAMITY JANE
**Calamity Jane** (Columbia)
Female quartet from the USA in an easy access version of country music, obviously devised for cross-over into the larger rock audience. Produced by Billy Sherrill.

### RANDY CALIFORNIA
**Euro-American** (Beggars Banquet)
He could have been a contender! Now he just plugs his electric axe in and goes through the Hendrix-imitation motions on automatic pilot. Although some of his ex-Spirit cohorts join him here, Randy California never recaptures the joy and wit of his earlier group at its heyday. Produced by Randy California and Steve Sollars.

### CAMEL
**The Single Factor** (Decca)
Bland pomposities by a now forgotten group who should have remained that way. Not worth the effort.

### CAMEO
**Alligator Woman** (Casablanca/Chocolate City)
Energetic soul abounds on this second album for the new band fronted by Larry Blackmon. The second side pales after the strong opening, and points to unnecessary hurry in putting the record together. Should reach beyond the black market. Produced by Larry Blackmon.

### CAPTAIN SINBAD
**The 7 Voyages of Captain Sinbad** (Greensleeves)
Reggae as she is spoken. Standard dub fare from the Roots Radic team. Produced by Henry 'Junjo' Lawes.

### CAPTAIN SKY
**Return of the Captain** (AVI)
A funk classic of 1979 messed about, with new, so-called improved mixes and a few new tracks. Refer back to the original 'Pop Goes the Captain' for ze real thing.

### JEAN CARN
**Trust Me** (Motown)
A new recruit to the ageing Motown stable. Promising debut with secure contributions by the Temptations and High Energy, with a slight jazzy feel beefing up the soul banalities. Produced by Norman Connors.

### JOE 'KING' CARRASCO & THE CROWNS
**Synapse Gap** (Mundo Total/MCA)

Zany Carrasco tones down the Texas rockabilly mood of his first album with an injection of more thoughtful material and even a touch of lilting reggae. A garage band growing up and going places, even if the direction is still unclear. Allow not all this critical bumph to distract you, it's still great fun and damn the words!

### JIM CARROLL BAND
**Day Dreams** (CBS/Atlantic)
This American poet's first album of songs with neo-heavy metal backing had its attractions for many, due in large part to the strong, obsessive subject matters permeating his lyrics. 'Day Dreams' seriously fails to consolidate on the earlier success and what were once annoying idiosyncrasies become insistent mannerisms. Although the song lyrics/poems are as heartfelt as ever, repetitive high power riffs now spoil the broth. A sparser musical setting would have been so much more appropriate. Maybe next time? Produced by Earl McGrath.

JIM CARROLL

Ain't No Money
Down On Love
I Wonder
Oh Yes I Can
Looking For A
  Corner

It Hasn't Happened
  Yet
That's How I Got To
  Memphis
Third Rate Romance
I Look For Love
Somewhere In The
  Stars

Rosanne Cash's third album (if you ex-clude an unofficial German bootleg of sorts) is everything one could reasonably have expected. She just keeps on getting better and now vies with Emmylou Harris for the title of crossover country queen. One of the purest and most expressive voices around with heart-breaking material by Rodney Crowell, Susanna Clarke, Tom T. Hall, Russell Smith and John Hiatt; add to this the crème de la crème of today's country musicians: Emory Gordy, Albert Lee, Ricky Skaggs, Hank DeVito and many others and the platter is a sheer gossamer delight. Surprise appearance by 'Pa' Johnny Cash on 'That's How I Got To Memphis'. Indispensable. Produced by Rodney Crowell.

### JOHNNY CASH/JERRY LEE LEWIS/ CARL PERKINS
**The Survivors** (CBS/Columbia)
Recorded live off a West German tele-vision show when Jerry Lee and Perkins came on as guests, this is an impromptu, necessarily ragged but endearing session of revamped rock and country chestnuts. Produced by Lou Robin and Rodney Crowell.

### ROSANNE CASH
**Somewhere in the Stars** (Columbia/ Ariola)

### CHANGE
**Sharing Your Love** (London/Atlantic)
By all accounts one of the best disco and dance albums of the year. Change are a group of studio musicians who have since taken to playing live. Verve, funk and ex-citement. Produced by Jacques Fred Petrus and Mauro Malavasi.

### CHAS 'N' DAVE
**Mustn't Grumble** (Rockney)
A new, wider release for the Cockney duo's earlier album of boozy London boo-gie. Very popular in some circles. Person-ally, it makes me cringe. Beer-drinking music. I'm a Coca Cola (TM) man myself! Produced by Chas and Dave.

### CHEAP TRICK
**One On One** (Epic)
Nondescript album by a tired power pop outfit who never quite made it to the top and now appear to be sliding their way down the slippery slope. Produced by Roy Thomas Baker.

CHAS 'N' DAVE

## CHEETAH
**Rock and Roll Women** (Epic/Albert)
Led Zeppelin-type music by a duo of lissome Australian sisters. You can't really say it has balls but the Hammond sisters certainly do their best to create an illusion of freak biological engineering by putting their hearts and throats into the material with vengeful élan. Worth seeing on stage for an impressive example of rock role reversal in the sexist stakes, but a lacklustre record. Produced by Vanda and Young.

## CHELSEA
**Evacuate** (Step Forward/IRS)
Primal punk protest in its most elemental form; strictly for the ripped tee-shirt and bondage gear mob. Produced by Harry Murlowski.

## CHER
**I Paralyze** (CBS/Columbia)
Run-of-the-mill Las Vegas cabaret ballads from an old trooper. Produced by David Wolfert.

CHER

## CHICAGO
**Chicago 16** (Full Moon)
A change of label for Chicago offers a pleasant return to the early virtues of brass rock and swing. An unexpected hit from the album has also given the group a new lease of life. Bill Champlin, once with the much underrated Sons of Champlin is now in the group and the injection of new blood has worked well. Predictable but Chicago buyers know what they want. Produced by David Foster.

## CHIPMUNKS
**Chipmunk Rock** (RCA)
After 'Chipmunk Punk' and 'Urban Chipmunk' a third album of distinctive cover versions by your favourites and mine. Look out for their 'Bette Davis Eyes'! Produced by Janice Karman and Ross Bagdasarian.

## CHRIS & COSEY
**Trance** (Rough Trade)
Quirky electronic British pop from an offshoot of the notorious Throbbing Gristle outfit. Not as danceable as, say, Depeche Mode or Human League, but more sincere and stimulating.

## CHRISTIAN DEATH
**Only Theatre of Pain** (Frontier)
American occult punk rock, in the tradition of the Cramps. Fronted by female singer Rozz Williams, this debut album offers bleak, destructive anti-religious anthems in a cryptic mood. Takes some getting used to. Produced by Thom Wilson.

## CHROME
**3rd From The Sun** (Don't Fall Off The Mountain/Siren)
Droning music for industrial sleep-walkers. Hails from San Francisco where psychedlia once held sway. Produced by Chrome.

## CIRCLE JERKS
**Wild In The Streets** (Faulty/Step Forward)
Los Angeles punk rock at its most primeval captures with unerring accuracy the rage and feeling of social resentment of the early days of pre-Jubilee punk in Britain. 15 short but vengeful tracks most unlikely to adorn American (or British) airwaves.

## ERIC CLAPTON
**Timepieces** (RSO)
A safe compilation of the best of Clapton post-'Guitar Wizard' period. All the easy-listening hits are here: 'I Shot the Sheriff', 'Layla', 'Cocaine', 'After Midnight,' etc. . . . Various producers.

## ROY CLARK
**Live From Austin City Limits** (Churchill)
Quality country guitar instrumentals culled

from a radio appearance by Clark. C & W classic tunes and newer material. Produced by Roy Clark.

## JOHN COOPER CLARKE
**Zip Style Method** (Epic)
Poetry to music from the self-styled Salford (near Manchester, England) bard. Delightfully idiosyncratic once you get accustomed to Clarke's nasal tones. The staccato delivery of the poems blends effortlessly with sympathetic backing by Martin Rushent and acolytes. Produced by the Invisible Girls.

## THE CLASH
**Combat Rock** (CBS/Epic)

| | |
|---|---|
| Know Your Rights | Overpowered By |
| Car Jamming | Funk |
| Should I Stay Or | Atom Tan |
| Should I Go | Sean Flynn |
| Rock The Casbah | Ghetto Defendant |
| Red Angel Dragnet | Innoculated City |
| Straight To Hell | Death Is A Star |

A single album this year after the double and triple excesses of previous years, which sees a leaner, hungrier and generally less-indulgent Clash. As militant as ever, though the strong messages and exhortations to change the state of things blend more easily with a metallic-edged music with the usual blend of reggae, rapping and funk influences. Produced by the Clash.

## ANGELA CLEMMONS
**Angela Clemmons** (Portrait)
Soul with a strong injection of gospel fervour dominates Angela Clemmons' first album. A noticeable debut from this Connecticut singer. Produced by Paul Leka.

## PATSY CLINE & JIM REEVES
**Remembering** (MCA)
More plundering of the vaults by opportunist executives. Reeves and Cline both died in (separate) air crashes and were foremost in the realm of country warbling. This album is, however, cheating as it only

includes one duet ('I Fall to Pieces') and the rest consists of solo cuts, all used to death on previous albums, compilations and whatnots. Produced by Owen Bradley, Chet Atkins and Bob Ferguson.

## CLOCKS
**Clocks** (Boulevard)
A new group from Wichita with crisp, quality modern rock often reminiscent of groups like Cars or Shoes. All the material is self-penned. Produced by Mike Flicker.

## JERRY CLOWER
**Dogs I Have Known** (MCA)
Novelty country album with 15 songs involving dogs! 'Puppy Love' is the opening track which should give you the flavour . . . Produced by Snuffy (sic) Miller.

## BILLY COBHAM'S GLASS MENAGERIE
**Observations &** (Elektra Musician)
Cobham is a survivor of the pioneering days of fusion jazz and this new departure with a younger quartet sees him flirting with soul and rock, albeit with a strong percussive emphasis. Produced by Bill Cobham.

## JOE COCKER
**Sheffield Steel** (Island)

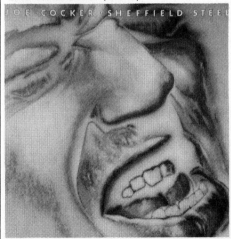

A change of label for the old trooper, and the reliable team of Sly and Robbie in charge of the rhythm section in the hallowed halls of Compass Point Studios in Nassau. Much the same as before, soulful cover versions of songs by Jimmy Cliff, Steve Winwood, Randy Newman, Dylan and others; the emotion is there in Cocker's distinctive, growling voice, but it just doesn't carry any more. Produced by Chris Blackwell and Alex Sadkin.

## COCKNEY REJECTS
**The Wild Ones** (Arena)
According to the critics in the know, the nec plus ultra of punk heavy metal, or as they say in informed circles, Herbert Metal. You've been warned. Produced by Pete Way.

## COLD CHISEL
**Circus Animals** (Polydor/Elektra)
High-speed rock from an Australian band in the AC/DC and Rose Tattoo mould. Produced by Mark Optiz and Cold Chisel.

## ORNETTE COLEMAN
**Of Human Feelings** (Antilles)
A new label with rock connotations for the jazz veteran. This album was recorded with the group Prime Time, back in 1979, but only sees the light of day three years later through the usual accidents that the record industry is familiar with. This is free-form jazz at its best and deserves a crossover audience, even if Coleman makes no concessions whatsoever to commercialism. Thank God. Produced by Ornette Coleman.

## COLLAGE
**Do You Like Our Music?** (Solar)
Indifferent soul/funk/disco outing by the Whispers under another name. Produced by the Whispers.

## WILLIAM BOOTSY COLLINS
**The One Giveth, The Count Taketh Away** (Warners)
Parliament/Funkadelic solo offshoot. Multi-instrumentalist never strays from the path of fire funk and this will delight all addicts. Produced by William 'Bootsy' Collins.

## JOHN CONLEE
**Busted** (MCA)
Noteworthy country album devoid, for once, of the smothering strings that mar so many of them. Produced by Bud Logan.

## RY COODER
**The Slide Area** (Warners)
The customary, slick mix of styles and sensitivities from the US singer and guitarist, now making a niche for himself as a contemporary cult figure. Contrary to most, I found this 10th solo album (not counting the numerous film soundtracks) predictable and lacklustre. The right ingredients are here, from electronic im-

RY COODER

provisations and Tex-Mex ballads to Dylan and Curtis Mayfield covers but one gets a strong feel of Cooder sleepily going through the motions. Pleasant but too laid back for comfort. Produced by Ry Cooder.

### GREG COPELAND
**Revenge Will Come** (Geffen)
A strangely compelling debut by a new American singer-songwriter. Strong vindictive lyrics with a moralistic streak surprise by their sheer intensity and, despite a few easy targets, score several bull's eyes. Lean, sympathetic backing by the customary battery of LA session supremos. Investigate at your own cost; Copeland is a disturbing new talent. Produced by Jackson Browne (who also discovered that other atypical LA sombre rocker, Warren Zevon).

### JOHNNY COPELAND
**Copeland Special** (Demon Fiend/Rounder)
Voted Blues Album of the Year in 1981 in the USA, but released much later in the UK. Copeland is a young Texas guitarist specialising in generally up-tempo blues with little or no antiquarian feel. Certainly worth looking out for. Produced by Dan Doyle.

### ELVIS COSTELLO
**Imperial Bedroom** (F-Beat/Columbia)

| Beyond Belief | The Loved Ones |
| Tears Before | Human Hands |
|    Bedtime | Kid About It |
| Shabby Doll | Little Savage |
| The Long | Boy With A Problem |
|    Honeymoon | Pidgin English |
| Man Out Of Time | You Little Fool |
| Almost Blue | Town Cryer |
| . . . And In Every | |
|    Home | |

A quick return to vengeful form by Costello after last year's misconceived and erratic country and western flirtation on 'Almost Blue' (a song of the same title appears on this platter, no relation though

RANDY CRAWFORD

. . .). Lush, string-infested production, for 15 new songs tackling Costello's eternal obsessions with the war of the sexes. 'Beyond Belief' with its almost spoken narration impresses as a strong departure from his customary spiteful delivery, but the bitter, analytical tone soon re-emerges thereafter and sustains a strong pitch throughout the album. Produced by Geoff Emerick.

### JOHN COUGAR
**American Fool** (Riva)
Seger/Springsteen imitator proving yet again that mediocrity is all too often the name of the game. Boring and predictable (and basically dishonest). Sold a bomb (and more). Produced by John 'Cougar' Mellencamp and Don Gehman.

### KEVIN COYNE
**Politicz** (Cherry Red)
Coyne is one of the last great British musical eccentrics (school of Syd Barrett and Robert Wyatt). Equal to himself, he seldom strays from the heartfelt path of angst and social deprivation. Compassion oozes from his songs and his umpteenth album can't truly be reviewed: it's the same as before and it's as good as before. If you've ever liked Kevin Coyne, you'll want this album. Despite the synthesised backing which is the only novelty and doesn't always work too well.

### RANDY CRAWFORD
**Windsong** (Warners)
No expense spared for the superlative American soul singer on her fifth album. Lilting ballads from Don Covay, Stevie Wonder, Leon Russell, Marvin Hamlisch and Carole Bayer Sager, Bill LaBounty and other established values. Exaggeratedly commercial and unerringly tailored for a quality market. Produced by Tommy LiPuma.

### CRAWLING CHAOS
**The Gas Chair** (Factory Benelux)
Strong punk image in fact hides a potpourri of basically folk influences with a strong, quirky, touch of humour. Uneven.

### MARSHALL CRENSHAW
**Marshall Crenshaw** (Warners)
First album by American rock's big new white hope. Crenshaw, straight from a Beatles impersonators theatre show, is a strange regressive artist working in the narrow pop tradition of Buddy Holly and the Byrds. Short, snappy songs with deliberately trivial subjects like girls, love and cars, but the overall effect sure does work even if I kept on hoping for the occasional spark of passion or madness that might ignite the album. It never comes, and the feeling it leaves is strangely unemotional. Certainly investigate this; no way is it the future of rock, but it agreeably wastes 40

minutes. It will be most intriguing to see in what direction Crenshaw develops on his next album. Produced by Richard Gohterrer.

### THE CRUSADERS
**Royal Jam** (MCA)
Double album of a 1981 show at the London Royal Festival Hall highlighting The Crusaders with the help of B. B. King and the Royal Philharmonic Orchestra. Turgid mush. Produced by Joe Sample, Wilton Felder and Stix Hooper.

### THE CURE
**Pornography** (Fiction/A&M)

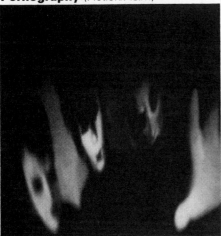

Gloomy atmospherics, ghostly melodies lacking in substance. The title is the most exciting (and misleading) thing about the whole sorry package. The Cure are a good group, but self-indulgence wins the day on this latest album heavily reliant on fatalistic clichés and dullness. Produced by Phil Thornally and the Cure.

# D

### THE DARK
**Chemical Warfare** (Fresh)
Grey and lifeless debut by new British band in the punk/heavy despair category. Already forgotten. Produced by Sean Purcell and the Dark.

### DATA
**Opera Electronica** (Illuminated)
Electronic pop featuring Georg Kajanus, who used to front Sailor, and female backing vocals against a background of synthesiser improvisations. A bit pretentious but listenable. Produced by Georg Kajanus.

### MILES DAVIS
**We Want Miles** (CBS/Columbia)
Another two-record set from the legendary jazzman. Long, lazy mood improvisa-

MILES DAVIS

tions pierced from time to time by the eerie, angry sound of Davis' trumpet before it fades again and leaves his musicians grooving in a dull funk mood. Patchy. For Miles Davis completists (and there are many around). Produced by Teo Macero.

### PAUL DAVIS
**Cool Night** (Arista)
Cool American pop; British release long after a couple of hits Stateside. Davis is a veteran and his métier shows. Safe but danceable.

### DEADLY ERNEST AND THE HONKY-TONKY HEROES
**The Modern Sound of . . .** (Wheeler 82)
Workmanlike country set with a nod in the direction of the early Sun days by a new US band. Produced by Bo Deadly (!)

### THE DEEP FREEZE MICE
**The Gates of Lunch** (Mole Embalming)
Great name! Great title! Great label! Pretentious neo-psychedelic music of uncertain British origins.

### DEEP PURPLE
**Deep Purple In Concert** (Portrait)
Oh no, not again! And it's a double set! For the sake of information freaks, this is 1970–1972 material with the Blackmore, Lord, Gillan, Paice and Glover line-up.

### DEFUNKT
**Thermonuclear Sweat** (Hannibal)
Furiously disjointed jazz funk led by trombonist Joseph Bowie. A bit more complex and intelligent than the usual US dancefloor groups and squarely aimed at the white new wave audience. Produced by Joe Boyd and Joseph Bowie.

### DEL-BYZANTEENS
**Lies To Live By** (Don't Fall Off The Mountain)
Sophisticated New York new wave pop in the most modern style. A satisfying blend of standard toe-tapping rock and subtle experimentation. A band to look out for in the future. Produced by Charlie Walden and the Del-Byzanteens.

### NEIL DIAMOND
**Live Diamond** (MCA)
More gold from the vaults. MCA seem to have elevated the Neil Diamond compilation album to a fine art since he departed, long ago, for another label.

### DISCHARGE
**Hear Nothing See Nothing Say Nothing** (Clay)
Barrage of punk noises. No more, no less.

### JEDRZEJ DMOCHOWSKI
**Stallions of my Heart** (Whaam)
A name to remember (excuse the obvious

STALLIONS OF MY HEART

*Jedrzej Dmochowski*

. . .). Dmochowski is a delightful original, blending touches of the late Marc Bolan and the quirkiness of Kevin Ayers. Cheerful Dada music in a deliberately happy mood. Produced by Jedrzej Dmochowski.

## DOKKEN
**Breakin' The Chains** (Carrere)
Heavy metal, man. Pass me the beer and try not to spill it all over my favourite jeans. All the clichés of the fair.

## THOMAS DOLBY
**The Golden Age of Wireless** (Venice In Peril/Harvest)
More British electronic pop. Dolby is another of the hordes of wizards of the synthesiser creeping out of the woodwork with easy listening melodies punctuated by the de rigueur rhythm box. The tunes are, however, unmemorable despite stalwart support from other British new wave luminaries like Andy Partridge of XTC, Lene Lovich and Bruce Woolley. Produced by Thomas Morgan Dolby Robertson.

## THE DRAGONS
**Parfums de la Révolution** (Blitzkrieg)
Alleged Chinese punk with a suspicious French connection.

## THE DRAMATICS
**New Dimension** (Capitol)
Bland Detroit-based sophistico-funk. All the right notes are played to cater for a safe, mainstream audience but not much imagination is otherwise on display. Produced by Ron Banks.

## MIKEY DREAD
**Swalk** (Dread at the Controls)
Street-wise British reggae from a Clash associate. Produced by Michael Campbell.

## DRINKING ELECTRICITY
**Overload** (Survival)
Thinly-stretched British electronic pop with female vocals from yet another hopeful group on yet another independent label. Tasty sleeve though.

## D TRAIN
**D Train** (Epic)
New York funk according to the dance floor gospel. Palatable on Saturday nights only . . . in small doses.

## DURAN DURAN
**Rio** (EMI/Capitol)

Lacking the awesome pretensions of Spandau Ballet, Duran Duran seem set to be the band that best survives the dreadful new romantic image. With this, their second album, they comfortably slot into a tasteful territory of lush, expansive melodies, infectious hooks and first division pop. Give them a listen and overcome your inititial prejudices: Duran Duran might well be more than just pretty faces. Produced by Colin Thurston.

## RONNIE DYSON
**Phase 2** (Cotilion)
US concept dance LP. Classy production and ballads. Produced by Bobby Eli.

# E

## DAVE EDMUNDS
**Dave Edmunds 7** (Arista/Columbia)
Veteran rock; which doesn't mean to say that anything about this record is tired, far from it. As usual Edmunds offers us a clean-cut, uncomplicated set of songs in a diversity of styles raging from cajun, Chuck Berry, bar-room boogie, and country to blues. And a new tune donated by Bruce Springsteen provides the good rock seal of approval. Produced by Dave Edmunds.

## ENO
**Ambient 4. On Land** (EG)
Music to fill spaces with. Both surreal and bland, Eno's ambient music mixes atmospherics and electronics to suit the listening environment. Could be any vaguely evocative, futuristic muzak. But it just happens to be Eno, so will sell to his devoted fans. Produced by Brian Eno.

## DAVID ESSEX
**Stage Struck** (Mercury)
British warbler now firmly ensconced in the collective mind of the great silent majority television viewer as an impersonation of the acceptable (cute) face of rock. Most of the material on this umpteenth comeback record is self-penned and with a light disco touch. 'Me and My Girl (Nightclubbin')' stands out, the rest is so-so. Produced by David Essex.

## THE EXPLOITED
**Troops of Tomorrow** (Secret)
Punk batallions on the rampage. Noisy.

# F

## FANTASY
**Sex and Material Possessions** (Pavilion)
Decent disco. Energetic vocal trio going through the classic motions. Produced by Tony Valor.

## LEE FARDON
**The God Given Right** (Aura)
Listen carefully to Lee Fardon and don't let initial impressions of a poor man's British Springsteen deceive you. A passionate lyricist whose music is not always up to the fiery emotion of his words and stories, Fardon is a true original. Few contemporary writers can wrestle as he does with the heartbreak and anguish of memory and broken love affairs. This is an angry and committed album which deserves a place in anyone's collection alongside Cohen's 'Songs From a Room', Springsteen's 'Darkness at the End of the Street' and Van Morrison's 'Astral Weeks'. Yes, it's almost that good. Produced by Lee Fardon and Jim Hall.

## FASHION
**Fabrique** (Arista)
Good, solid British modern dance music, very much in the (very recent) tradition of ABC. But the hooks aren't so catchy, the production not so glossy and the melodies just drift away without truly connecting with the memory cells. But, all in all, a very promising electro-funk debut. Produced by Zeus B. Held.

## FAT LARRY'S BAND
**Breakin' Out** (WMOT/Virgin)
Philadelphia funk by the effervescent Larry James. Dance music diet extraordinaire. Produced by Larry James and Nick Martinelli.

THE FIXX

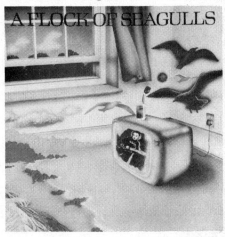

Yes, another electro-pop band from old blighty (and doing remarkably well in America, by the way) but one of the better examples. Catchy and haunting melodies where emotion is never subjugated to industrial effect. 'I Ran' is one of my favourite singles of the year. Lousy cover might put some people off. Look inside the jacket and savour. Produced by Mike Howlett.

## FLYING SAUCERS
**Flying Tonight** (EMI)

Rockabilly revamps from British revivalists. Produced by Sandy Ford.

## JANE FONDA
**Jane Fonda's Workout Record**
(CBS/Columbia)
Following on the mega-success of her book on aerobic exercises, now comes the record . . . La Fonda intones gravely the instructions to stretch and pull all those recalcitrant muscles as the CBS roster of hits dutifully fills the background: Jacksons, Boz Scaggs, Brothers Johnson, etc . . . For fitness fanatics. Produced by Mary Kushner.

## FEAR
**The Record** (Slash)
Faceless Los Angeles punk. Comes ten years too late and the energy expenditure goes wasted.

## RICHARD 'DIMPLES' FIELDS
**Mr Look So Good** (Epic)
Suave soul for sweet sisters of Saturday set.

## FIREWORKS
**Sightseeing At Night** (MCA)
Polished rock with soaring harmonies and flashy instrumentals from a group of evangelizing Christians. Ignore the lyrics and it's surprisingly effective. Jesus might have another hit yet! Produced by Marty McCall and Jerry Gaston.

## FIST
**Back With A Vengeance** (Neat)
Heavy metal from Newcastle. Gutless.

## FIVE OR SIX
**A Thriving And Happy Land**
(Frizbee)
Doom rock. Britain. School of 1982. Substandard. Back to square one.

## THE FIXX
**Shuttered Room** (MCA)
Moderately successful first album by a new British band in the electro-pop tradition but with a lesser emphasis on electronic instrumentation. Moody. Produced by Rupert Hine.

## ROBERTA FLACK
**I'm The One** (Atlantic)
Easy listening fodder from someone who was once great. The abundance of producers is a guide to the indecision surrounding this muddled record. Produced by Ralph McDonald, William Eaton, Roberta Flack, William Salter, Burt Bacharach and Carole Bayer Sager.

## FLIPPER
**Album Generic Flipper**
(Subterranean)
Velvet Underground lives! Powerful primal music from a hitherto unknown California band that owes little to punk or new wave but sure teaches illiterate musical upstarts some lessons. Irreverent, loud and witty. A discovery of the first order. Produced by Flipper, Gary Kriman and Chris.

51

## 4-SKINS
**The Good, The Bad and the 4-Skins**
(Secret)
Oi punk thrashings, with a nod of the shaven barnet to heavy metal. The lyrics aren't quite in the same league as Rod McKuen . . . Produced by the 4-Skins and Tim Thompson.

## FOSTER AND ALLEN
**A Bunch of Thyme** (Ritz)
Irish ballads. Scored a surprise, and lone single hit in the UK, where a tradition of freak novelty records has always existed.

## GLENN FREY
**No Fun Aloud** (Asylum)
Now that the Eagles have officially disbanded into the mellow Californian sunshine, the time for solo albums has come. Glenn Frey progresses no further than Eagles-filler tunes and exhibits all the boring characteristics of LA laid-back-itis. Wallpaper music done with taste and relish. Music for pickled brains. Pass that toke, man. Will sell a million. Produced by Glenn Frey, Allan Blazek and Jim Ed Norman.

## DEAN FRIEDMAN
**Rumpled Romeo** (Epic)
Sincere love songs, plaintive voice, compassionate wimpishness; Friedman is a balladeer who bears all the wrong stigmata. Score another one for romantic bedsit land. Produced by Dean Friedman.

## EDGAR FROESE
**1974–1979** (Virgin)
A retrospective look at Tangerine Dream's main keyboards fuhrer's years of solo recording. Ranges from quirky electronic doodles to truly evocative atmospherics but lacks overall unity. Produced by Edgar Froese.

## FUNKAPOLITAN
**Funkapolitan** (London/Pavilion)
White boys sing the funk. Bona fide producer and stylish cocktail-set Peter Saville cover, all the ingredients are right but it all sounds so strained and unnatural. The dance feel is missing as if some mysterious filter castrated all the group's undoubted immediacy in the studio. Too polished by half. Produced by August Darnell.

## THE FUREYS
**When You Were Sweet Sixteen**
(Ritz)
Folk group with a rare crossover pop hit with 'When I was Sweet Sixteen'. The material is undiluted traditional fare, a bit insipid but all very sincere. Produced by Phil Coulter and Finbar Furey.

## DIAMANDA GALAS
**The Litanies of Satan** (Y)
Punk opera, experimental screams, make of this what you want. Still, there's nothing new, remember Yma Sumac or Cathy Berberian and other arch female warblers. . . . A record which cannot be judged by normal standards of criticism. All you can do is experience it. Nuff said.

## RORY GALLAGHER
**Jinx** (Chrysalis/Mercury)
Safe, predictable, competent and jolly. The umpteenth album of vivid rock in a strong blues vein by the diminutive Irish guitarist. He has now reached the stage where he knows what his faithful audience wants and provides them with it. Could do with a lot more imagination. Produced by Rory Gallagher.

## GANG OF FOUR
**Songs of the Free** (EMI/Warners)

A surprisingly pleasant fourth album from the Gang of Four whose harsh, literate version of punk fades into yesteryear as bassist Sara Lee mellows their sound after replacing Dave Allen and the whole band veer towards a strong dance stance. Accessible, dare I say commercial? 'I Love A Man In A Uniform' has hit written all over it. Who could have believed such a rapid metamorphosis would take place in such an uncompromising group without any concessions being made. Produced by Mike Howlett, Jon King and Andrew Gill.

## THE GAP BAND
**Gap Band IV** (Mercury/Total Experience)
Fourth album for one of the most popular soul outfits around. More of the same despite an American change of label and the blend still works to dancing perfection. Produced by Lonnie Simmons.

## TERRY GARTHWAITE, BOBBIE LOUISE HAWKINS & ROSALIE SORRELS
**Live At The Great American Music All** (Flying Fish)
Badly recorded album taken from a live performance by three different American performers. Terry Garthwaite, from the lamented Joy of Cooking, emerges as the only real winner with smooth and joyful acoustic blues improvisations; Hawkins is a poet and, as such, can't be reviewed here from any musical point of view (I like her, though); Sorrels is an old folkie whose singalongs make one cringe and suffers from a bad echo. An engaging oddity.

## GASKIN
**No Way Out** (Rondelet)
Heavy metal mess of indeterminate origins.

## CRYSTAL GAYLE
**Love Songs** (Liberty)
A compilation of ballads from country's gentle lady of commercial sorrows.

## GENESIS
**Three Sides Live** (Charisma/Atlantic)
It's record company live cash-in time again, folks! Yes, another record duplicating well-known tracks you all know and love and already have is foisted upon the weary public. With the new Genesis double, however, some executive ingenuity has been working overtime so as to extract the maximum possible cash from Genesis die-hard fans: the British and American releases have one side which is completely different. While the three live sides concentrate on the biggest hits (or thereabout) of the post-Gabriel Genesis, the fourth is the one that changes: in Britain, it contains 3 songs with the 1976 line-up including 'If/Watcher of the Skies' while the US release contains 5 brand new studio tracks from 1979 and 1982 (including latest hit singles). Produced by Genesis.

## RENEE GEYER
**Renee Geyer** (Portrait)
Debut American album for a female vocalist already popular in her native Australia. Gruff but pleasant voice which suits more uptempo material is seen tackling a varied assortment of genres: blues, rock, reggae, r&b . . . Classy back-up musicians but still to be filed under easy listening. Produced by Rob Fraboni.

## TERRI GIBBS
**Some Days It Rains All Night Long** (MCA)
Female country but with guts and determination and none of the usual masochistic clichés of the genre. The fact that Terri Gibbs has been blind from birth may have

nothing to do with it, but there is an underlying strength in her songs of loneliness and despair which no Dolly Parton or Crystal Gayle can even approach. Even if country music bores you, give this one a listen. Produced by Ed Penney.

### GIRLSCHOOL
**Hit And Run** (Stiff America)
Strongly macho all-female heavy metal quartet's debut American LP. Riff-mad and hard-hitting sturm und drang. Effective. Produced by Vic Maile.

### GIRLSCHOOL
**Screaming Blue Murder** (Bronze/Mercury)
Third British album from the girls who have balls, after a line-up change, sees them unfailingly rocking and blowing away most of the similar male competition. Under the heavy metal din, there are evident signs that a lot of musicianship has in fact gone into their sound. Produced by Nigel Gray.

### THE GO-BETWEENS
**Send Me A Lullaby** (Rough Trade)

First album from an endearingly simple new band from Australia. Jingle jangle instrumentation and plaintive male and female vocals ride a tightrope between whimsy and Velvet Underground-like slice of life experimentation in a minor mode. Takes a few plays but quickly grows on you. Produced by the Go-Betweens and Tony Cohen.

### VIC GODDARD AND THE SUBWAY SECT
**Songs For Sale** (London)
A would be Sinatra-swinger for the 1980s, Vic Goddard certainly stands out and scores points for originality. A few standards and a majority of new material in the style of 1940. Amusing but ultimately pointless.

### GOOMBAY DANCE BAND
**Seven Tears** (Epic)
German novelty act who even stoop to fire-eating in addition to lousy harmony singing. Scored a surprise massive British hit but then mercifully faded away. The album sold doodly shit, as Mr. Vonnegut says. Thanks for small mercies. Produced by Jochen Petersen.

### LARRY GRAHAM
**Sooner Or Later** (Warners)
Mellow dance funk by Sly and the Family Stone's erstwhile bassist. Produced by Larry Graham and George Duke.

### GRAND PRIX
**There For None To See** (RCA)
Second album of safe, featureless American mainstream rock. A bit like manuscript editors (like a certain MJ) often receive from would-be authors who've majored Stateside in so-called creative writing: the technique is right, but there's just no emotion.

### AMY GRANT
**Age To Age** (Myrrh)
Gospel goes funk rock. Smooth but solid slice of syrupy devotions. Produced by Brown Bannister.

### FREDI GRACE & RHINESTONE
**Get On Your Mark** (MCA)
Male-female soul duo with synthesiser-driven backing. Produced by Peabo Bryson and Ed Howard.

### GRAUZONE
**Grauzone** (EMI)

Swiss electronic band specializing in the customary grey synthesiser doodles posing as clever atmospherics. Elevator muzak at its most dynamic. Produced by Grauzone and Urs Steiger.

### AL GREEN
**Higher Place** (Hi-Cream)
Once upon a time, in a long ago faraway land called the 1960s, there was this soul singer with a voice mellow enough to make honey run and a passionate love of life. Religion captured him, I fear, and now he churns out slick devotional offerings you can still tap your toes to, as well as embarrassing revamps of 'Battle Hymn of the Republic' and 'Amazing Grace'.

### LEE GREENWOOD
**Inside And Out** (MCA)
Country crossover material for new US singer. Good voice, duff material. Produced by Jerry Crutchfield.

### GROW UP
**(Without Wings)** (Up)
Self-financed debut for a young Manchester band. Arty and earnest, but nothing to be ashamed of. Very British and loaded with idiosyncratic would-be-clever touches. Keeps you attentive, which not every record does, as the sadly sarcastic tone of many of the reviews in this book bears witness to. Investigate, it could be your cup of tea.

### ADRIAN GURVITZ
**Classic** (Rak/Geffen)
Calculated stab at the US chart with a polished dosage of easy listening and highly pretentious and bombastic ballads by a British rocker who was never that good in the first place. The USA is welcome to him, should they want him. Produced by Adrian and Paul Gurvitz.

### GWEN GUTHRIE
**Gwen Guthrie** (Island)
Former soul session songstress, Gwen Guthrie is here given the full Compass Studios treatment and the results are obviously heavily tinged with reggae rhythms. Gentle but bland. Good Bob Marley cover with 'Is This Love?' Produced by Sly Dunbar, Robbie Shakespeare and Steven Stanley.

# H

### NINA HAGEN
**Nunsexmonkrock** (CBS/Columbia)

Fraulein Hagen has always been an acquired taste and her new album will sell to the converted, unlikely as it is to make new recruits on the altar of her dual-language screaming. You have been warned, as some anonymous Nazi once said. Produced by Mike Thorne.

## HAMBI AND THE DANCE
### Heartache (Virgin)
New Liverpool group whose singer has a most strong and distinctive voice. The production gives the band room to move and a deep, orchestral sound and the effect is quite dramatic. The songs are what let the band down, though: predictable and reminiscent of all too many efforts of yesteryear from others. Produced by Mick Glossop.

## HERBIE HANCOCK
### Lite Me Up (CBS/Columbia)
Hancock now seems to have once and for all deserted the barren shores of jazz and his new album even features him over one side as vocalist in addition to his multikeyboards. Quality soul throughout, particularly as the second half of the record features guest vocalists. Produced by Herbie Hancock, Jay Graydon and Narada Michael Walden.

## HANOI ROCKS
### Oriental Beat (Johanna)
Glam heavy metal on this second album from the curious Scandinavian band that sounds like a cross between the New York Dolls and early Rolling Stones, with an added touch of obligatory orientalism.

## TIM HARDIN
### The Homecoming Concert (Kamera)
A poignant reminder of the sad career of Tim Hardin, this live recording made shortly before his death shows how the magic was fading fast. But through the rambling, drunken in-between songs dialogue with his audience, Hardin still wore his heart on his sleeve as he performed some of his classic songs. A valuable document.

## HAWKWIND
### Friends And Relations (Flicknife)
Eight highly miscellaneous tracks divided between a studio and live side. Many tracks don't in fact feature Hawkwind but 'friends' like Michael Moorcock, Nik Turner and other acolytes. A shambles in the old Hawkwind tradition this; really a jigsaw album.

## HEART
### Private Audition (Epic)
A slightly more varied collection of songs than is usually the case from the Wilson sisters, trying to escape the female Led Zeppelin image they had cultivated for some years. A touch of Motown and an old-fashioned music-hall turn prove the versatility is still there, but the ethereal feeling of their early album 'Dreamboat Annie' is the sound I'd like to see them tackle again. Worthy. Produced by Connie and Howie.

## HEATWAVE
### Current (Epic)
Exciting soul set tailored for the dance market. Strong British connection this time around with Rod Temperton material and guest vocals by Imagination. Herbie Hancock and Paulinho da Costa also make impromptu appearances. Produced by Barry Blue and Johnnie Wilder Jr.

## HERMINE
### The World On My Plates (Crammed)

A mini album of six tracks by a French singer in the old cabaret tradition, this set exerts a strange fascination (if only because Hermine's accent conforms to all ze French accent stereotypes). Every song is a cover version, in many cases utterly transformed and unrecognizable from the original, of Nick Lowe, Roy Orbison, etc. . . . It's a fun little album but I suspect there's a strong tongue-in-cheek element involved, or is there? Nice textured sleeve.

## JOHN HIATT
### All Of A Sudden (Geffen)
Hiatt's first album since his highly-praised association with Ry Cooder. He has rid himself of some of the more obvious Costello-like mannerisms but this has also disposed of some of the bitter aggression he displayed on earlier records and this album veers towards the bland. A rough mixture of rocking styles sees Hiatt going through razor-sharp motions but the spark seldom really ignites. Better luck next time. Produced by Tony Visconti.

HERBIE HANCOCK

RUPERT HINE

# I

### THE INDIVIDUALS
**Fields** (Plexus)
Highly promising first album by a new, tight New York band who don't rely on electronics. A quartet including ex *New York Rocker* managing editor, The Individuals function in the modern pop tradition with lean, staccato instrumentals and catchy hooks, crisp vocals. A band for tomorrow. Produced by Gene Holder.

### INKENBRANDT
**Passenger** (Friendship)
Glossy mainstream rock of American origins. Big sound, small ambitions. Produced by Peter Schekeryk.

### INFA-RIOT
**Still Out of Order** (Secret)
Oi aural assault in the now all-too-familiar storm-trooper of British inner cities style. Produced by Tim Thompson and Infa-Riot.

# J

### DAVID JACKSON
**The Long Hello** (Butt)
Or the late, lamented by some, Van Der Graaf Generator under another name, that of their erstwhile saxophone player. This album also features vocalist Peter Hammill and Guy Evans in re-treads (shelved tracks) of VDG blueprint songs.

### JOE JACKSON
**Night and Day** (A&M)

| | |
|---|---|
| Another World | Breaking Us In Two |
| Chinatown | Cancer |
| T.V. Age | Real Men |
| Target | A Slow Song |
| Steppin' Out | |

### BERTIE HIGGINS
**Key Largo** (Epic)
Debut album by a new American singer-songwriter steeped in the adventurer myths of Bogart years and smugglers shores in the sunny Caribbean. Sounds a bit like Gordon Lightfoot at times, but deserves a listen for his almost cinematic cameos. Produced by Sonny Limbo and Scott MacLellan.

### RUPERT HINE
**Waving Not Drowning** (A&M)
Rupert Hine is a true individualist and fascinating singer who has appropriated all the tricks of the British electronic new wave and married its cold efficiency with slightly operatic tunes and pungent lyrics of alienation by Jeanette Obstoj. You don't listen to Hine, you experience him. He is one those rare examples of singers who lives by his emotions and the mental panoramas he paints are quite haunting.

Some might find him an acquired taste. I know what *I* like: more. Produced by Rupert Hine.

### THE HONEYMOON KILLERS
**Les Tueurs de la Lune de Miel**
(Crammed)
Avant-garde Belgian group with jazz influences and double-headed male-female vocals with an often manic delivery.

### JOHN LEE HOOKER
**Tantalizing With The Blues** (MCA)
Compilation of tracks recorded by the blues master between 1965 and 1971.

### HOUND DOG TAYLOR AND THE HOUSEROCKERS
**Genuine Houserocking Music**
(Alligator)
An anthology of the now dead blues performer's better tracks from the 1970s. Electric. Produced by Bruce Iglauer and Wesley Race.

JOE JACKSON

### DAVID JOHANSEN
**Live It Up** (Blue Sky)

One of the superior stylists of contemporary rock, Johansen has never received the praise that should be his, despite two excellent albums and one more dubious one. This live album for once justifies the whole hackneyed idea of recording public performances for it displays an infectious joy that seems to be the essence of David Johansen in front of an audience. This is an uncluttered, unpretentious, triumphant act of faith in the future of rock 'n roll as we know it and should be a must for any disillusioned listener. The marvellous Animals medley even had some commercial success, so there's still hope. Produced by Ron Nevison.

### ELTON JOHN
**Jump Up** (Rocket/Geffen)
Elton's best album in a long time will do a lot for his flagging reputation. Since it's already his 23rd LP, about time too. A return to a leaner, less cluttered sound and a renewal of his early writing partnership with Bernie Taupin (and a collaboration with Tim Rice: 'Legal Boys'). Produced by Chris Thomas.

### JOHNNY AND THE ROCCOS
**Scots On The Rocks** (Magnum Force)
Scottish outfit who have frequently functioned as backing band for visiting US artists to Britain. Solid, workmanlike rock and roll, with rockabilly cover versions.

### QUINCY JONES
**The Best** (A&M)
The track record speaks for itself, although all the excellent material collected here is from before Quincy Jones' 'Dude' success and offers latter-day fans a chance to check up on his earlier days. Various producers.

### LONNIE JORDAN
**The Affair** (Boardwalk)
Solo effort by member of War. Romantic soul ballads. Produced by Lonnie Jordan.

---

A return to vocal form for Joe Jackson after his 'Jumpin' Jive' album of Cab Calloway-like music. A night side and a day side of songs heavily influenced by the feel and emotions of a long sojourn in New York city. Jackson's untrained, gritty voice lends conviction to the aimlessness and resigned despair of his subject matters while a strong percussive undertow is imprinted on the proceedings by the dynamic use of versatile Sue Hadjopoulos. Produced by David Kershenbaum and Joe Jackson.

### BOB JAMES
**Hands Down** (CBS/Tappan Zee)
Big city fusion jazz with a big, big beat. Produced by Bob James.

### RICK JAMES
**Throwin' Down** (Motown/Gordy)
Major album by the so-called prince of punk-funk. Boasting the impressive help of names like Grace Slick, Narada Michael Walden, Roy Ayers, Teena Marie and the Temptations, James literally sets fire to the grooves of disco-soul land with a collection of strong, hook-laden, immediate melodies. Produced by Rick James.

### BERT JANSCH
**Heartbreak** (Logo)
Bert Jansch has always held a place in my heart as one of the first prime exponents of British folk-rock, before his days with Pentangle. This umpteenth album was recorded in America and is much the same as before – Jansch will never change – gentle, melodic tunes. It won't stop the world from turning, but nice to have all the same.

### JEAN-MICHEL JARRE
**The Concerts in China** (Polydor)
Seductive, but in the long run awesomely superficial, the music of Jean-Michel Jarre is perfect 1980s muzak, blending the right mixture of spacey electronics, lush and romantic melodies and kitsch (let us not forget that his father, Maurice Jarre, is the prominent film score specialist for all seasons). Having broken new ground by performing a few concerts in China, it was natural that a live recording (double album, bien sûr) of the occasion should percolate out of the event. Familiar tunes from his albums plus a few Oriental concessions and use here and there of a classical Chinese ensemble. Easy listening. Suspicions of much studio doctoring back in Paris to bring the recording quality up to par with overdubs and whatnots, though.

### JETHRO TULL
**Broadsword and the Beast** (Chrysalis)
Injection of synthesiser earnestness into the customary ponderous pastoral mood of Jethro Tull makes this a touch different, but still for fans only (and they're legion). Produced by Paul Samwell-Smith.

## JUNIOR
**Ji** (Mercury)
First album by a young British soul performer with an endearing and joyful innocence in his tunes. At times reminiscent of middle-period Stevie Wonder, this is an exciting discovery. Produced by Bob Carter.

# K

## KANSAS
**Vinyl Confessions** (Kirshner)
Clean-cut example of semi-pomp mainstream US faceless rock. Formula stuff, guaranteed to please or bore, depending on your attitude to the genre. Produced by Ken Scott and Kansas.

## JANET KAY
**Capricorn Woman** (Solid Groove)
One-hit ('Silly Games') breeds a whole album of similar reggae concoctions which Janet Kay's thin voice can barely carry adequately. Good material but a rush job spoils the broth. Produced by Dennis Bovell.

## THE KENDALLS
**Stickin' Together** (Mercury)
American country duo. Sanitized twang for the trucker diner juke-box market. Produced by Roy Dea and the Kendalls.

## RICHARD KERR
**No Looking Back** (A&M)
Songwriter turns singer. Possibly less depressing than Barry Manilow (for whom he wrote 'Mandy') but still nothing to write home about on the saccharin ballad front. Produced by Richard Kerr.

## KID CREOLE AND THE COCONUTS
**Tropical Gangsters** (Ze)
**Wise Guy** (Sire)
Don't fret: it's the same record – title and label vary according to the country you're in. Ironical that Kid Creole and his motley

bunch of calypso/soul cocktail lounge serenades should garner hits from this, his weakest album. Mind you, it's not bad, it's just that he's capable of so much better. A toe-tapping collection, always entertaining in a genre that the Kid and Andy Hernandez have almost appropriated as their own patch. Produced by August Darnell.

## GREG KIHN BAND
**Kihntinued** (Beserkly)

Fresh-eyed pop rock with a touch of both class and feigned innocence. Kihn is an exemplary writer and performer, a rock journeyman who here exhibits a surprising variety of styles and slots like a chameleon into all sort of grooves. Recommended if you like unpretentious music. Produced by Matthew King Kaufman.

## KILLING JOKE
**Revelations** (EG)
Third album (and final one with the initial line-up) from the prime (and almost lone) exponents of existential punk thrash. Noteworthy energy but doesn't really lead anywhere. Produced by Conny Plank and Killing Joke.

## B. B. KING
**Love Me Tender** (MCA)
A sad record despite B.B. King's assertion on the sleeve that it's the best he's ever done. The veteran blues guitarist here wastes his time covering highly inappropriate material by the likes of Willie Nelson, Doc Pomus, Mickey Newbury, etc . . . in a country or Muscles Shoals style, plus insipid strings smothering the whole mess. Better to ignore this one, for the sake of memories. Produced by Stewart Levine.

## KING CRIMSON
**Beat** (EG)
Today's King Crimson has few similarities with the group's earlier incarnations (in fact, back when guitarist and inspiration Bob Fripp had long, frizzy hair!). The Talking Heads influence, introduced by Adrian

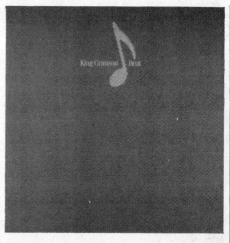

Belew, having been duly absorbed in the preceding 'Discipline', the group now turn their attentions to a concept album of sorts, evoking the days of Kerouac, the beats and the existential road. Personally, I don't see the connection between subject matter and music, but I am greatly impressed by the record. You know the saying 'I know what I like'. If you need any convincing, just lend an ear to the hypnotic beat of 'Heartbeat'. Even for people who've never liked King Crimson. Produced by Rhett Davies.

## KISS
**Killers** (Casablanca)
Not even released in the USA, this collection of banal new songs by Kiss has, at the time of writing, only seen the light of day in the UK and Europe. How the mighty have fallen!

## KLIQUE
**Let's Wear It Out** (MCA)
Dance machine fodder. All the right notes and beats are there. Roger and out. Produced by Michael Cooper, T. Fuller, Felton Pilate, David Crawford and Isaac Suthers.

## DIE KRUPPS
**Volle Kraft Voraus** (WEA)
Electronic/punk new modern German music. A bit faceless but grows on you once the language barrier fades into aural muzak. Very minimalist, very chic m'dear. Produced by Engler and Schnekenburger.

# L

## LA CONNECTION
**LA Connection** (MCA)
Soul/funk from the Blackmon/Cameo factory of beaty, meaty, big and bouncy dance floor hits. Produced by Larry Blackmon.

**BIRELLI LAGRENE**
**Routes to Django** (Antilles)
1979 recording of young prodigy 13-year-old gypsy guitar player. As the title and homage imply, very much in the footsteps of the legendary Django Reinhart. Technically impressive. Produced by Jan Jankeje.

**THE LAST RESORT**
**A Way of Life- Skinhead Anthems**
(Last Resort)
Badly recorded Oi punk. You've heard one, you've heard them all.

**THE LATE BRONZE AGE**
**Isles of Langerhan** (Landslide)
New group led by ex-Hampton Grease Band frontman, Hampton Coles. Versatile rock, very American and satisfyingly blending all angles in contemporary music from blues to country and an understanding of new wave dynamics. Produced by The Late Bronze Age and Eddie Offord.

**BETTY LAVETTE**
**Tell Me A Lie** (Motown)
Debut album for a 36-year old black singer working in the mainstream of the Motown soul tradition. Promising if formula stuff.

**THE LEAGUE UNLIMITED ORCHESTRA**
**Love & Dancing** (Virgin/A&M)

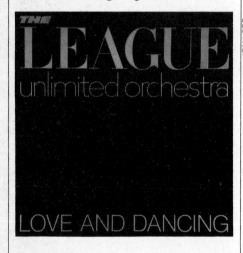

THE LEAGUE unlimited orchestra
LOVE AND DANCING

An intriguing semi-follow up to the Human League's (for it is them) bestselling 'Dare'. Producer Martin Rushent has manipulated the backing tracks and erased 90% of the vocals to obtain a dance mix that sounds surprisingly familiar but also new. One new song.

**LARRY LEE**
**Marooned** (Columbia)
Solo outing by a member of country band the Ozark Mountain Daredevils. On his own, he veers more towards the blues and medium-speed easy rock. Palatable, no more. Produced by John Ryan.

JON LORD

**IJAHMAN LEVI**
**Tell It To The Children** (True Roots)
Reggae artist from the burgeoning independent sector. Walks a straight line between Rasta sermonizing and expansive celebrations of love and life.

**LIQUID LIQUID**
**Successive Reflexes** (99)
Punk salsa, if you can believe the recipe, from a young New York outfit on this EP of quirky rhythms and undoubted talent. Deserves a larger audience.

**LITTLE GINNY**
**My Dixie Darling** (Pastafont)
British female country singer recorded in the holy land of Nashville. Could pass for the real product, which coming from me is not a compliment. Cringe, cringe . . . Produced by Paul Kirkby.

**JON LORD**
**Before I Forget** (EMI)
Classical rock from Deep Purple and Whitesnake's keyboards virtuoso. You've heard it all before and you'll hear it all too often again, but it's safe, a trifle bombastic and superficially impressive.

**JIM & JESSE & CHARLIE LOUVIN**
**Jim & Jesse & Charlie Louvin**
(Soundwaves)
Invigorating set of country and bluegrass by noted songwriters pairing up again after a long interruption for solo efforts. Splendid mandolin playing by Jesse McReynolds to the fore. Produced by Jimmy Capps, Charlie Louvin and Jim and Jesse McReynolds.

**LOVE TRACTOR**
**Love Tractor** (dB)
New band from Athens, Georgia (what is it about the place? Shades of musical Midwich Cuckoos!) with a strong, compelling set of not quite instrumentals but rather songs without vocals. It works. Pity it's on local label which will preclude too large a circulation. Produced by Bruce Baxter and Love Tractor.

**CARRIE LUCAS**
**Still In Love** (Solar)
Dull love threnodies in a soul vein, with a fashionable synthesiser beat aiming the whole package upmarket. Instantly forgettable. Various producers.

### LYDIA LUNCH
**13.13** (Situation Two/Ruby)
New York punk madonna Lydia Lunch recorded with 13–13, a band she has since disbanded. Angry, apocalyptic, disturbing slabs of often primeval noise. After a while, it makes sense. Persevere. Produced by Lydia Lunch and 13–13.

### CHERYL LYNN
**Instant Love** (CBS/Columbia)
Mellifluous soul ballads and duets that display the genre at its easy-listening best. Produced by Luther Vandross.

# M

### M
**Famous Last Words** (Sire)
Ever since the phenomenal 'Pop Muzik' success, M (alias Robin Scott) has found it hard going and his quirky observations on the modern dance angst appear to have mostly missed their targets. This new album is much the same as before, but again lacks immediacy. Clever. Produced by Robin Scott.

### MADNESS
**Complete Madness** (Stiff)
Exemplary compilation of past hits by the nutty British boys. 16 memorable, snappy tunes that communicate the sheer enjoyment Madness get from their music. Odd that their success has not been equalled outside the UK. Produced by Clive Langer and Alan Winstanley.

### MELISSA MANCHESTER
**Hey Ricky** (Arista)
A new, short haircut does wonders for warbler Manchester who moves a few notches up with this surprisingly varied set of torch songs, rockers and ballads (the 'Chariots of Fire' theme) distancing herself from a past cabaret image. Duet with David Gates of Bread and a better than usual choice of material sees Melissa Manchester as more than just a pretty voice. Produced by Arif Mardin.

### BARBARA MANDRELL
**In Black and White** (MCA)
Well-established and lissome (male chauvinist pig speaking . . .) country performer veers towards the rock market with a slickly produced set of pop with r & b nuances. Produced by Tom Collins.

### CHUCK MANGIONE
**Love Notes** (CBS/Columbia)
New label for the flugelhorn funkster. Innocuous summery improvisations which now owe little to his jazz roots. Produced by Chuck Mangione.

### BARRY MANILOW
**Live in Britain** (Arista)
All the schmaltz is here in thin, anaemic settings. Blame the producer. Recorded at the Royal Albert Hall in London early in 1982. Produced by Barry Manilow.

### JOHN MARTYN
**Glorious Fool** (Warners/Duke)
Belated US release for Martyn's last album on the new label set up by Genesis. A posse of big name guests like Eric Clapton and Phil Collins and a heavily orchestral sound dim the usual immediacy and sensuality of Martyn's slurred vocals and highly idiosyncratic songs. Certainly a more commercial sound. but I still pine for the unadulterated Martyn. Produced by Phil Collins.

### MASSACRE
**Killing Time** (Celluloid)
Loud experimentation by an ad hoc trio of ex-Henry Cow guitarist Fred Frith and the funk Material rhythm section of Bill Laswell and Fred Maher. Abstract and metallic, Recorded live in the studio; could have done with more attention and overdubs & cleaning up. Interesting, as a US girl I knew always said.

### JOHNNY MATHIS
**Friends In Love** (CBS/Columbia)
Consummate ballad singing from the old master of the form with a nod to more contemporary material (Stevie Wonder, Andrew Lloyd Webber's future perennial 'Memory') and a couple of sentiment-oozing duets with Dionne Warwick. Produced by Jack Gold and Jay Graydon.

### PAUL McCARTNEY
**Tug of War** (EMI/Columbia)

| | |
|---|---|
| Tug of War | Ballroom Dancing |
| Take It Away | The Pound Is |
| Somebody Who | Sinking |
| Cares | Wanderlust |
| What's That You're | Get It |
| Doing? | Be What You See |
| Here Today | (Link) |
| | Dress Me Up As A |
| | Robber |
| | Ebony And Ivory |

Although I would agree with the majority of critics that this is McCartney's best album in an age, there are still deep flaws present that preclude any Beatles comparison which the hype machine has seen fit to spray in the public's direction. 'Ebony and Ivory' with Stevie Wonder strikes me as a particularly maudlin hit with ingratiating lyrics and senseless singalong chorus for liberal softies. The production is grandiloquent but perfectly tailored to McCartney's style of composition with fleeting appearances from all the man's friends: Wonder, Ringo Starr, Carl Perkins, Stanley Clarke, Steve Gadd, Eric Stewart, Andy McKay, Dave Mattacks and Denny Laine.

MADNESS

Young Paul is such a prolific and easy writer that it's sad to see him go down the easiest path and opt for gentility when he shows (on some tracks) that he still has the original fire somewhere within him. Try harder next time, Paul, it'll still sell a million or two, but my review might be a better one. Consider this a bribe! Produced by George Martin.

## CHARLY McCLAIN
**Too Good To Hurry** (Epic)
Another long-legged Nashville lady makes tentative overtures towards the pop market, with disco strings and electric piano tickling the listener's dance mood. Produced by Chucko Productions.

## GWEN McCRAE
**Gwen McCrae** (Atlantic)
Strong black funk in the Tina Turner mould.

## McCRARYS
**All Night Music** (Capitol)
Male-female harmonies from a large orchestral and vocal group playing middle-of-the-road easy-listening funk. Wall-paper music. Produced by Wayne Henderson.

## RONNIE McDOWELL
**Love To Burn** (Epic)
Country singer who's paid his dues, now making a grab for the Presley-ballad territory. Lousy backing vocals give the game away. Produced by Buddy Killen.

## REBA McENTIRE
**Unlimited** (Mercury)
Run-of-the-mill female country singer. Slick pop hooks. Produced by Jerry Kennedy.

## BOBBY McFERRIN
**Bobby McFerrin** (Elektra Musician)
Jazz keyboards man goes for larger audience with soulful vocals on other people's songs. Material by Van Morrison, Smokey Robinson and the Miracles, Orleans. Duet with Phoebe Snow. McFerrin has a peculiar and intriguing vocal style and this should make him some fans despite the purple patches. Produced by Linda Goldstein.

## KATE & ANNA McGARRIGLE
**Love Over And Over** (Polydor)
The endearing Canadian sisters in usual form. This is modern folk of unmistakeable quality with little or no traditional stereotypes. Material is a bit samey, but they have me hooked for life so who am I to criticize. Mark Knopfler from Dire Straits makes a fleeting guest appearance, which

serves to demonstrate the esteem in which the McGarrigle sisters are held in the rock world for their infectious, joyful melodies. Produced by Kate, Anna and Jane McGarrigle.

## FREDDIE McGREGOR
**Big Ship** (Greensleeves)
Reggae session drummer now graduating to vocal outing. Very much easy listening rasta fare aimed at the white market. Passable within the compromised parameters. Produced by Linval Thompson.

## MELANIE
**Arabesque** (RCA/Blanche)

The hippie madonna grows up and returns after many a year out in the cold. And she sounds just the same; maybe some hint of gravity in her songs but her voice and lush ballads remain as individual as ever. It had become fashionable to be dismissive of Melanie; this album demonstrates that fashion is not always the place to be. Produced by Peter Schekeryk.

## MEN AT WORK
**Business As Usual** (Epic/Columbia)
A bestselling album back in native Australia, this is Men At Work's first Anglo-US outing. Quality new wave rock with strong melodies and saxophone playing. A band

we should hear more about. Produced by Peter Mclan.

## PAT METHENY GROUP
**Offramp** (ECM)
Atmospheric jazz in an electronic mood veers more and more towards rock as Pat Metheny gains a greater audience with the more progressive segments of the pop public. Guitarist Metheny and keyboard cohort Lyle Mays slowly explore the romantic side of technology. Produced by Manfred Eicher.

## METHOD ACTORS
**Dancing Underneath** (Armageddon)
A prolific bunch, these Method Actors, what with their second album (and the first was a double . . .) this year. The individualistic duo from Athens, Georgia, are featured here on material which in fact pre-dates 'Little Figures' and serves as a blueprint for that important offering's pieces. Energetic.

## CHARLIE MIDNIGHT
**Innocent Bystander** (Decent)
Debut LP by Bob Seger/Paul Rodgers clone minus the talent. Yet more wasted vinyl. Produced by Kash Monet.

## MIGHTY FIRE
**Mighty Fire** (E1)
Saturday night-confectioned funk. Produced (self-written and on lead guitar) by Mel Bolton.

## MILK FROM CHELTENHAM
**Tryptich of Poisoners** (It's War Boys)
Experimental art-school pap. An independent recording, naturelement.

## FRANKIE MILLER
**Standing On The Edge** (Capitol)
From soul revivalist to Bob Seger/Free imitations (Free's Andy Fraser collaborated with Miller on most of the songs), the gravel-voiced Scotsman walks down those mean American highways with not an inch of true emotion in his soul. Going through the motions. Banal, antiseptic Muscles Shoals muzak for the airwaves. Produced by Barry Beckett.

## STEVE MILLER BAND
**Abracadabra** (Mercury/Capitol)

| | |
|---|---|
| Keeps Me Wondering Why | Things I Told You Young Girl's Heart |
| Abracadabra | Goodbye Love |
| Something Special | Cool Magic |
| Give It Up | While I'm Waiting |
| Never Say No | |

An old and true professional at work and play. After his disappointing 'Circle of Love' last year, Miller reverts to laid back, mellifluous form with a deceptively easy set of new songs (allegedly recorded at

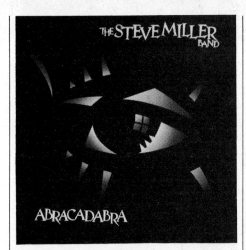

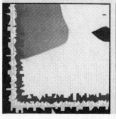

the same sessions as the preceding album – Miller dislikes too frequent studio work!) many of which have quickly become hits. No longer a guitar wizard or space-age impressionist as in the heyday of his psychedelic San Francisco days, Miller has now perfected to a tee the craft of short, snappy songwriting. Few can better him, even if many of the tunes on the album were in fact penned by members of his band . . . their master's touch and all that. Enjoy an unpretentious pop record. Produced by Steve Miller and Gary Mallaber.

### STEPHANIE MILLS
**Tantalizingly Hot** (Casablanca/20th Century Fox)
Medium warm, no more, soul in the gentle Motown tradition. A slick album with Mills at her best on two Ashford-Simpson songs. Produced by Stephanie Mills.

### RONNIE MILSAP
**Inside** (RCA)
R&B and country specialist demeaning himself in easy-listening country. What the world doesn't want is another Gilbert O'Sullivan or, Gods of Mammon help us, a second Barry Manilow. Produced by Ronnie Milsap and Tom Collins.

### THE MISFITS
**Walk Among Us** (Ruby)
New York city rotting metropolis punk. Rough and ragged along the edges and an empty void center. Been this way before, I fear.

### THE MISUNDERSTOOD
**Before the Dream Faded** (Cherry Red)
The Misunderstood are a US group from the psychedelic days, sufficiently obscure to have become legendary in the UK thanks to earnest, plugging via various DJs. Guitarist Glen Campbell (no, not *the* GC!) displays similarities to Hendrix but these tracks salvaged from the past barely have any curiosity value today. Sometimes, it's better to remain obscure and misunderstood.

### MODERN ENGLISH
**After the Snow** (4AD)
School of Joy Division angst & shadows, but the melodies are strong and the instrumentation lush without too many electronic ostentatious touches. Will depress you just enough to appreciate a ray of sun. Produced by Modern English and Hugh Jones.

### EDDIE MONEY
**No Control** (Columbia/CBS)
Identikit power pop. Eddie Money has an archetypal rock voice but the material is trite and self-pitying. One more victim of the Springsteen syndrome. Produced by Tom Dowd.

### MORE
**Blood and Thunder** (Atlantic)
Riff-mad heavy metal. Produced by More, Kenny Cox and Vic Rush.

### PABLO MOSES
**Pave The Way** (Island)
Tepid reggae made easy.

### THE MOTELS
**All Four One** (Capitol)
How ironical that the Motels should score big, at any rate in the USA, with what I feel is their weakest album! A sultry, melodramatic singer at best, Martha Davis has always been at the heart of this oddly melodic, rare, West Coast new wave band and her searing delivery and savagely repressed emotions have characterized the immediacy of the Motels. Following the departure of guitarist Tim McGovern, the group scrapped a first version of this third album and this new effort is strangely subdued, with a lush production muting all Martha Davis' best qualities. Still beats most Los Angeles groups around today, but could have been so much better. Produced by Val Garay.

### THE MOTHMEN
**One Black Dot** (Do It)
Experimental reggae with jazz overtones from British sources. Puzzling, beat-infested music. Produced by Hugh Jones.

### MOTOR BOYS MOTOR
**Motor Boys Motor** (Albion)
A British band whose debut offers a curious but compelling hybrid of savage R & B with old Captain Beefheart overtones. Displays all the raw energy of punk. It's different. I hope they stay that way. Produced by John Brand.

### HUGH MUNDELL
**Mundell** (Greensleeves)
Smooth, fluent reggae with a nice

EDDIE MONEY

additional touch of brass. Usual rasta ballads by an interesting performer. Produced by Henry 'Junjo' Lawes.

# N

## THE NAMES
**Swimming** (Crepuscule)
Introspective electronic improvisations by a new group. Produced by Martin Hannett.

## NATIONAL HEALTH
**D.S. Al Coda** (Europa)
National Health reform for one album to pay homage to Alan Gowen, their keyboards player, who died in 1981. The playing is as fluent as ever, as you would expect from such British jazz rock luminaries, but the principle of only performing Gowen compositions holds back the strong improvisatory streak that was the group's forte. Interesting moments. Produced by National Health and Nick Bradford.

## BILL NELSON
**The Love That Whirls** (Mercury/PVC)

Bill Nelson is one of the precursors of the British electronic new wave, but has never truly earned the credit for his pioneering efforts. This new solo album displays his customary, impeccable musicianship and odd, crafty melodies with a strong Eastern influence. A lack of warmth mars what is otherwise an imaginative album. A second, home-recorded, platter comes free with 'The Love That Whirls': instrumental background music to a stage production of 'The Beauty and the Beast'. Produced by Bill Nelson.

## WILLIE NELSON
**Diamonds in the Rough** (Delta)
1961 demo tracks from the days before fame had struck. Rough, ready and of interest beyond Nelson's fan club. Produced by Willie Nelson.

## NERVOUS GENDER
**Music From Hell** (Subterranean)
Experimental electronic drones from L.A. Produced by Nervous Gender.

## NEW ASIA
**Gates** (Situation 2)
Puzzling studio album of electronic mood pieces and chanting oddities. Phil Manzanera does a guest stint on guitar. Apart from that, a bit of a 'see me twiddling all those knobs, mum' effort by engineer and producer Ian Little.

## THE NEW HIGH LEVEL RANTERS
**The New High Level Ranters** (Topic)
Very traditional British folk music from a group of old hands (though suffering the loss of some original members). Varied instrumentation keeps tedium away but all very predictable. Produced by Tony Engle.

## NEW MATH
**They Walk Among You** (415)
More voodoo punk rock from the US West Coast. Potent, evil, posturing music but surprisingly compelling. Investigate at your own peril this heady brew.

## NEW MUSIK
**Warp** (Epic)
Vapid electronic pop with a soft centre. Produced by Tony Mansfield.

## JUICE NEWTON
**Quiet Lies** (Capitol)
Seasoned country pop by a youthful veteran now benefiting from the crossover of more established stars like Rondstad or Parton to richer fields. Studious, demure, tasteful but utterly lacking in fire or personality. Produced by Richard Landis.

## NICOLE
**A Little Peace** (CBS)
Eurovision schoolgirl winner with a smile all innocence and naivety with a re-run of sentimental euroballads. Schmaltzy is too restrained an epithet for this pap. Love the cynical change of image in the latter part of 1982, though, as the moneymen pulling the strings try for an increased share of the market beyond the fabled lands of Eurovision. . .

## TOM NIELSEN AND THE PARKER BROTHERS
**Pretty Boy Floyd** (ABI)
Soap operas stars woo the rock market. Banal. Produced by Al Basi.

## NIGHTWING
**Black Summer** (Gull)
Heavy metal for lumberjacks. Has all the subtlety of a falling tree. Produced by Gordon Rowley.

## THE NOLANS
**Portrait** (Epic)
The hackneyed album title betrays the dearth of originality in this soapy compilation of ballads by Pa Nolan's quartet of daughters. Not only are they hugely popular in British seaside towns but also in Japan. Strange folk, these Japanese. Produced by Ben Findon, Nicky Graham and Robin Smith.

## PETER NOONE
**One Of The Glory Boys** (Johnston)
Alias Herman of Herman's Hermits (those were the days . . .) now mature enough to tackle the melodic rock market. A bit anonymous, with an injection of urgency by the Tower of Power horn section. Not a noticeable comeback, but no failure either. Produced by Spencer Proffer.

## TED NUGENT
**Nugent** (Atlantic)
The well-worn gonzo rock and roll thrash from Nugent on this first album for a new label. The sound is instantly recognizable and the formula perfected over so many years on the road and in the studio is followed with not an iota of divergence. Will satisfy the fans. Produced by Ted Nugent.

## JUDY NYLON
**Pal Judy** (On-U Sound)

New York new wave rocker and friend of the stars (Eno, John Cale) belated first album blends all the right amount of innovation and solid backbeat. A remarkable voice contorts its way through a compelling mixture of rap, diluted reggae and film noir narratives. A record that succeeds in trying to be all things to all people and guaranteed to keep you alert and keen throughout. Produced by Adrian Sherwood.

## O

### O'BRYAN
**Doin' Alright** (Capitol)
Rhythm and blues ballads with a tenuous degree of funk. Tepid. Produced by Don Cornelius, O'Bryan Burnette II, Melvin Davis and Ron Kersey.

### ODYSSEY
**Happy Together** (RCA)
Slick harmony-based funk from one of the 'in' trios of the genre. Every song sounds like a hit. Great version of the Turtles 'Happy Together' and assistance by the Chic Organisation round off an excellent album. Produced by Jimmy Douglas.

### THE O'JAYS
**My Favourite Person** (Philadelphia Int.)
Mushy soul ballads by a group in search of new inspiration. Really gives a feeling of the O'Jays just going through the (money-making) motions. With eight producers involved, no wonder.

### JANE OLIVOR
**In Concert** (Columbia)
Big-tonsiled US cabaret singer going through a familiar repertoire of soothing material (yes, 'Chariots of Fire' with words emerges again . . .) Produced by Jason Darrow.

### JEFFREY OSBORNE
**Jeffrey Osborne** (A&M)
Former lead singer for funk outfit, Ltd, goes solo with a remarkably stylish set of romantic, warm ballads. Much help from his friends the Brothers Johnson, the Average White Band and Larry Graham. A confident debut. Produced by George Duke.

### THE OSBORNE BROTHERS
**Bluegrass Spectacular** (RCA)
Live country recording with mighty picking and harmonies. Produced by Sonny Osborne.

### MICHAEL O'SHEA
**Michael O'Shea** (Dome)
Unique and endearing Irish busker who plays zither through electronic enhancers and distortion treatment; unclassifiable but well worth a half hour or so of your time. Produced by Gilbert and Lewis.

### OUTLAWS
**Los Hombres Malos** (Arista)
Southern rock boogie by veterans. Sounds tired, aged and facile. Heard all the clichés and riffs before. Faceless American music. Produced by Gary Lyons.

### PAUL OVERSTREET
**Paul Overstreet** (RCA)
Mainstream easy-listening country rock by a new solo performer who uses a cohort of guests, all of them rather minor names, to polish up this inoffensive debut. Produced by Ron Haffkine.

### OZARK MOUNTAIN DAREDEVILS
**It'll Shine When It Shines** (A&M)
Another year, another album of laid back country boogie from the Ozark boys who must have recorded this in their sleep.

## P

### RAY PARKER Jr.
**The Other Woman** (Arista)
Raydio's main personality on first solo effort. Silky soul ballads from an accomplished performer. Smooth-talking romance for the ladies and other softhearted folk. Produced by Ray Parker Jr.

### THE ALAN PARSONS PROJECT
**Eye In The Sky** (Arista)
Although generally unnoticed in the UK, Alan Parsons and his pretentious orchestral rock concept platters sell like hot cakes in most other territories (and not only Italy where they have a healthy instinct for pomp and bombast). More of the same again here: neo-cosmic bilge with a big sound. Pseud rock. Produced by Alan Parsons.

### GRAM PARSONS AND THE FALLEN ANGELS
**Live 1973** (Sierra)

Recorded by a radio station six months before Gram Parsons' tragic and premature death this live album is another 'best of' package (could Parsons be coming into fashion?) with familiar songs in rougher, looser settings. Produced by John Delgatto and Marley Brant.

### GRAM PARSONS
**Gram Parsons** (Warners)
14 classic Gram Parsons tracks compiled

THE O'JAYS

THE PASSAGE

by Elvis Costello remind us how good and ahead of his time the American country pioneer was. Material is taken from Parsons, two solo albums and includes duets with Emmylou Harris. Contractual problems presumably nixed the idea of a more complete retrospective by inclusion of some Byrds and Flying Burrito Brothers tracks with Parsons. If you haven't got the originals, this is a must.

### DOLLY PARTON
**Heartbreak Express** (RCA)
Slight return to form for Dolly Parton after a few easy listening sorties. This new album is in a soft country mood which suits her voice and temperament better. Produced by Dolly Parton and Gregg Perry.

### THE PASSAGE
**Degenerates** (Cherry Red)
Quality minimalist rock from one of Britian's more intriguing new wave bands. Tenuous melodies stretched out to reveal the very structure of the music as Dick Witts and his cohorts intone their puzzling lyrics of social anger and delicate introspection. Takes some getting into, but rewards you at the end with the feeling you've been through a genuinely new experience. Produced by The Passage.

### JOHNNY PAYCHECK
**Winners and Losers** (Epic)
Run-of-the-mill, country outlaw deep-voiced ballads. Produced by Billy Sherrill.

### ANNETTE PEACOCK
**Sky Skating** (Ironic)
A still youthful-looking veteran of the jazz/experimental scene now more at ease on her own independent label. Once an inspiration for many rock personalities (Bowie being not the least of them), An-

nette Peacock indulges in freeform improvisatory pieces, putting her most extraordinarily flexible voice through its paces. Often pretentious but never less than fascinating. A unique talent at work. Produced by Annette Peacock.

### KEVIN PEEK
**Life and Other Games** (Ariola)
Sky's lead guitarist with second solo album. Safe, cushy instrumentals with nary a nod to the rock audience. For insomniacs only. Produced by Trevor Spencer.

### PEYR
**As Above** (Shout)
It means 'thaw' in Icelandic and that's where this uncommonly strong dose of punk thrashings comes from. Rather melodic and sung in English. A notch above the average British doom rocker on the edge of the world.

### Ph. D.
**Ph. D.** (WEA/Atlantic)
Wimpish but immaculately presented

light-weight rock by a British studio duo. Scored major British hit with the catchy 'I Won't Let You Down'. Rest is much in the same mould. Produced by Ph.D and Cy Langston.

### ANTHONY PHILLIPS & ENRIQUE BERRO GARCIA
**Private Parts & Pieces III: Antiques** (PVC)
Semi-classical duets involving every type of guitar in the manufacturers' catalogues. Arty and clever, but it ain't rock 'n roll, man. Produced by Anthony Phillips.

### RICHARD PINHAS
**L'Ethique** (Pulse)
Pinhas is one of the most accessible synthesiser Eurorockers and his new album is probably his best. Searing guitar runs, reminiscent of the Fripp 'Red' period, played against synthesiser programmes, overlap with one of the most potent rhythm sections this side of hell (ex-Magma musicians) resulting in an impressive wall of sound that is the nearest electronic rock has come to heavy metal without the customary redundant clichés. A reverent homage to science fiction also colours Pinhas' subject matter. Raw energy of the best kind. Produced by Olivier Lamit.

### THE PIN-UPS
**The Pin-Ups** (Columbia)
German female quartet built on the Abba easy-listening assembly line. Produced by Ingeborg Hauke.

### PLACEBO
**England's Trance** (Aura)
Guitar/synthesiser duo from the North of England in the form of a wife and husband team. Sensitive, minimalist but melodic improvisations rather than tunes, much in the vein of the lamented Young Marble Giants. Takes some getting used to, but in the end will be remembered as an endearing and courageous experiment that positively goes against all the prevailing fashions of 1982. Produced by Placebo.

### PLAYGROUP
**Epic Sound Battles. Chapter One** (Cherry Red)
More Adrian Sherwood-produced dub studio experiments from an assortment of white and coloured musicians.

### THE PLUGZ
**Better Luck** (Fatima)
Somewhat colourless L.A. vinyl. Not as fierce and anti-social as many of their would-be punk contemporaries. The Plugz seem to have an eye on radioland's Springsteen territory. Wishful thinking.

POINT BLANK

## POINT BLANK
### On A Roll (MCA)
Predictable American energy rock with a flourish of keyboards pyrotechnics. Produced by Bill Hamm.

## NOEL POINTER
### Direct Hit (Liberty)
Decent soul/funk warblings with a touch of the jazz influences. Mellow and commercial. Produced by Richard Evans and Noel Pointer.

## POSITIVE NOISE
### Change of Heart (Statik)

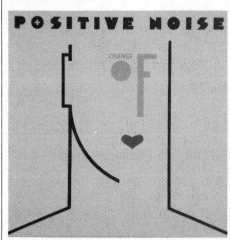

Second album from this promising British group, recorded shortly after the departure of founder member Ross Middleton. The primal African sound and rhythms of 'Heart of Darkness' have faded to be replaced by a gentle, funky dance beat with electronic trimmings. Unspectacular but reliable. Produced by Nik Launay and John Walker.

## PURRKUR PILLNIK
### Googooplex (Gramm Gramm)
Incomprehensible and muddled Icelandic rock. Very experimental and going nowhere.

## ARTIMUS PYLE BAND
### Artimus Pyle Band (MCA)
Familiar, and tepid, Southern rock boogying by the ex-Lynyrd Skynyrd drummer and his new band. Produced by Jerry Eubanks, Doug Gray and George McCorkle.

# Q

## QUEEN
### Hot Space (EMI/Elektra)

| | |
|---|---|
| Staying Power | Put Out The Fire |
| Dancer | Life Is Real |
| Back Chat | Calling All Girls |
| Body Language | Las Palabras De Amor |
| Action This Day | Cool Cat |
| | Under Pressure |

A contemptible record by a contemptible group with millions of devoted fans worldwide. Queen's irresistible rise in the days of pomp/classical rock was the result of a clever manipulation of image and professional marketing. Their subsequent malleability and willingness to espouse and imitate changes in musical fashion and ride on every successive new wave was blatant calculation. But this newest album with songs in Spanish, neo-rockabilly, tributes to Lennon and (why did he do it?) a collaboration with Bowie ('Under Pressure') is opportunistic and gratuitous. You get it, I hate it. Produced by Queen-Mack.

## THE QUICK
### One Light in a Blackout (Epic)
Titled 'Fascinating Rhythm' in the UK, this is the first album by the British duet of George McFarlane and Colin Campsie who work in the USA. It's blue-eyed dance music with a sting in the tail, a bit like Hall & Oates with a stronger beat and electronic heart-beeps. Infectious fun. Produced by The Quick and John Luongo.

# R

## RADIO STARS
### 2 Minutes Mr Smith (Moonlight)
Compilation of a now-deceased pub rock British band who never quite made the grade when punk came and washed all impurities of the British scene away. Disposable.

## RAGE
### Nice 'n' Dirty (Carrere)
Hard-edged blitzkrieg heavy metal on this second album from the British band once known as Nutz. Loud but effective.

## RAINBOW
### Straight Between the Eyes
(Mercury/Polydor)
Decibel rock from Ritchie Blackmore's group of seasoned veterans. Massed synthesisers to the rescue on most tracks. If it's heavy metal you want, you might as well get the real thing. Produced by Roger Glover.

## ERIC RANDOM AND THE BEDLAMITES
### Earthbound Ghost Need (New Hormones)
Silly name for an average British electronic band associated with Cabaret Voltaire. Remodelled version of Ravel's 'Bolero' stands out amongst the moods and doodles.

## RAVEN
### Wiped Out (Neat)
Heavy metal rock in constant fourth gear

if not overdrive; after a while it all sounds much the same.

## OTIS REDDING
**Recorded Live** (Atlantic)
Dubious skeleton dug up from the Atlantic vaults. Although Redding's voice is in fine fettle, the supporting musicians backing him on the occasion at the Whisky are sadly out of tune and sympathy. Produced by Nesuhi Ertegun and Ed Michel.

## THE REDDINGS
**Steamin' Hot** (Believe In A Dream)
Safe soul fare. The late Otis Redding's son, Dexter, vocalises on a new, flat version of 'Dock of the Bay'. Room for improvement. Produced by Russell Timmons Jr with the Reddings.

## JERRY REED
**The Man With The Golden Thumb** (RCA)
Despite the title, this is an album where Jerry Reed generally eschews his virtuoso guitar-picking in overdrive for more sedate and thoughtful ballads. Rather anonymous. Produced by Rick Hall.

## DAVID REILLY
**Life On Earth** (MCA)
No, not the TV series but a US record of unassuming lightweight pop. Produced by Nick Tauber.

## THE RESIDENTS
**The Tunes of Two Cities** (Ralph)

Another puzzling outing by San Francisco's leading mystery band. The second instalment in their projected 'Mark of the Mole' trilogy, this dishes out the customary weird mix of wit, unsalubrious noises and out-of-this-world tape-jumble and experimentation. The growing army of Residents fans won't take much convincing; others will scratch their heads despairingly. Write to me c/o the publisher if you know the question to the answer. Produced by The Residents.

## REVELATION
**Revelation** (Handshake)
Yet more polished soul funk from the US of A. The hits keep on coming. Shades of middle-period Earth, Wind and Fire. Produced by Tom Tom 84 (!), Bruce Gray and Dunn Pearson Jr.

## RICO
**Jama Rico** (Two-Tone)
Nine reggae instrumentals by the veteran and popular saxophonist with a little help from his friends, including Jerry Dammers from the Specials and Dick Cuthell on cornet and flugelhorn. Produced by Dick Cuthell.

## JIMMY RILEY
**Put The People First** (Shanachie)
Competent reggae outing with the ubiquitous Sly and Robbie on the rhythm machine. Nice, dreamy voice but usual clichés in the subject matter. Produced by Jimmy Riley.

## RIOT
**Restless Breed** (Elektra)
Brutal heavy metal mayhem (and one forlorn big sound ballad) for Riot's latest, their first with new singer Rhett Forrester. Produced by Steve Loeb and Billy Arnell.

## RIP RIG AND PANIC
**I Am Cold** (Virgin)

Coming in fast succession to the group's previous, ambitiously-named 'God', this second double 45 rpm set of albums from Rip Rig and Panic confirms them as one of the most promising and original British groups of the day. A strong and adventurous blend of free-form jazz (Don Cherry, whose daughter plays with the group, lends a helping hand), African ethnic music, latin rhythms and an infectious joy of playing dominate this unique set. Produced by Rip Rig and Panic.

## THE RITCHIE FAMILY
**I'll Do My Best** (RCA)
Competent soul dance tunes, good voices

and accurate (but anonymous) backing. Produced by Fred Petrus.

## MARTY ROBBINS
**Come Back To Me** (Columbia)
Old country gravel-voiced balladeers never fade away, they just keep on recording more sad songs of womanly deception and woe. Par for the course and for Robbins' fans. Produced by Bob Montgomery.

## TOM ROBINSON
**North by Northwest** (Panic/IRS)
Once one of the great white British hopes of new wave music, Tom Robinson has gently faded away from the scene, to the extent of now living in Germany. This new album has a wistful and warm quality to it as Robinson gently ponders on his past and future without recourse to sloganeering or shock effect. Not a spent force yet. Produced by Richard Mazda.

## ROMEO VOID
**Never Say Die** (415)
A four song extended EP to whet one's appetite until next quarter's presumably major album. One of the USA's most individual new wave bands capable of combining thrash bombast and more delicate phrasing against a strong melodic background. A tasty appetiser. Produced by Rick Ocasek and Ian Taylor.

## THE ROLLING STONES
**Still Life** (EMI)

| | |
|---|---|
| Under My Thumb | Let Me Go |
| Let's Spend The Night Together | Time Is On My Side |
| | Imagination |
| Shattered | Start Me Up |
| Twenty Flight Rock | Satisfaction |
| Going To A Go-Go | |

Recorded on their 1981 American concert tour, a brief glimpse of the Stones live on stage. The new versions of the old standards are the most interesting, although revealing few changes in the playing or interpretation. A general emphasis on the R&B side of the Stones generally pays off as this energetic set doesn't betray any sign of tiredness. Produced by the Glimmer Twins.

## ROSE ROYCE
**Stronger Than Ever** (Epic)
Quality funk by a known quantity. Love Ricci Benson's mellifluous vocalising. A treat of professionalism. Produced by Norman Whitfield.

## DAVE ROWLAND
**Sugar Free** (Elektra)
Middle-of-the-road country singer with a ton of strings and more than a handful of female vocalists breaking wind and other delicacies in the cluttered background. Produced by James Stroud.

## ROXY MUSIC
**Avalon** (EG/Warners)

| | |
|---|---|
| More Than This | The Main Thing |
| The Space Between | Take A Chance |
| Avalon | With Me |
| India | To Turn You On |
| While My Heart Is | True To Life |
| Still Beating | Tara |

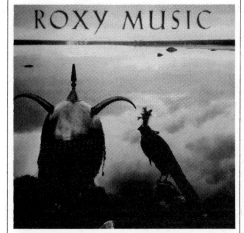

Eight songs, two instrumentals on this most polished and elegant latest offering from Bryan Ferry's group. All the glossy excesses of earlier Roxy Music incarnations have now been ruthlessly pared down to a clean, romantic sound that can but charm the pants off you. Ferry has finally managed to transfer his sartorial elegance wholesale to his music and this is the result. Clever use of synthesiser atmospherics blends in well with the general melancholy mood of the title track and other hits like 'More Than This' and 'Take A Chance With Me'. Produced by Rhett Davis and Roxy Music.

## RPM
**RPM** (EMI)
Boringly competent but truthfully unimaginative debut album by new American group. Power pop variety. Produced by Brent Maher.

## PATRICE RUSHEN
**Straight From The Heart** (Elektra)
Smooth transition from soul to a more generally accepted combination of soul and rock sees Patrice Rushen delivering an almost perfect album. Addictive tunes and stunning musicianship (Patrice herself plays piano, synthesisers and percussion) make this a must for lovers of quality music. Produced by Charles Mims Jr. and Patrice Rushen.

# S

## RIUICHI SAKAMOTO & DANCERIES
**The End of Asia** (Nippon Columbia)
Collaboration between the Yellow Magic Orchestra man and a classical ensemble specializing in the loving recreation of medieval music. Pleasant but highly academic exercise.

## DAVID SANBORN
**As We Speak** (Warners)
Crossover jazz outing by the talented alto sax stylist. Synthesised orchestral backing dominates throughout. Produced by Robert Margouleff.

## CHAS SANDFORD
**Parallax View** (Elektra)
First album by new LA singer/songwriter with a strong pop vein, akin to Tom Petty but without the urgency. Produced by Chas Sandford.

## SARACEN
**Heroes, Saints and Fools** (Nucleus)
Run-of-the-mill heavy metal for new British group in the Judas Priest lineage. Produced by Robert Bendelow (who plays guitar for the group) and Roy Neave.

## SAXON
**The Eagle Has Landed** (Carrere)
Brimstone live heavy metal performances by one of Britain's leading groups. Captures the fire and manic energy of the band perfectly as they go through their repertoire of flash, thrash and smash. Also features their new drummer Nigel Glockler. Quality incendiary stuff.

## LEO SAYER
**World Radio** (Chrysalis)
A highly successful record commercially but a sad artistic downfall, showing without the shadow of a doubt how Leo Sayer, once an individualistic, quirky and affectionate singer, has now joined the massed snoozing ranks of cabaret entertainers. Safe, boring material and not an ounce of expression. Move over, Barry Manilow. Produced by Arif Mardin.

## JOHN SCHNEIDER
**Quiet Man** (Scotti)
Soap opera star performs middle-of-the-road country chestnuts. Pleasantly innocuous and antiseptic. produced by Tony Scotti and John D'Andrea.

## SCHNEIDER WITH THE KICK
**Exposed** (Mirage)
European singer goes rock with a vengeance. A mite strident but certainly lacks no energy, although still safely mainstream. Produced by Helen Schneider.

## SCIENTIST
**Wins The World Cup** (Greensleeves)
Topical reggae that offers no surprises. Produced by Henry 'Junjo' Lawes.

## EARL SCRUGGS & TOM T. HALL
**The Storyteller and the Banjo Man** (CBS/Columbia)
Strained collaboration between two country artists with highly different styles. While Hall's drawling ballads dirge on, Scruggs often appears to be picking his bluegrass melodies in a world apart. A curiosity at most. Produced by Randy Scruggs and John Thompson.

LEO SAYER

## SECTION 25
**The Key of Dreams** (Factory Benelux)
Second division Joy Division (school of drab and dreary) meet the ghost of funk (school of Earth, Wind and Fire minus the panache and joy).

## THE SEQUENCE
**The Sequence** (Sugarhill)
Glossy, glitter rap outfit with sequin outfits and all! Well-dressed funk clichés. Produced by Sylvia Robinson.

## 707
**Megaforce** (Boardwalk)
Forceful power rock from the USA. More where they come from, and better. Produced by George Tutko and Kevin Russell.

## SHAKATAK
**Night Birds** (Polydor)
Smooth and finely polished blue-eyed soul background music from a (mostly) white British group. The gloss is pleasant but superficial. Elegant but vacuous dance music performed in the very best of taste. Produced by Nigel Wright.

## SHAKIN' PYRAMIDS
**Celts and Cobras** (Virgin)
If it shakes, it's British rockabilly! Scottish trio on their second album with strong beefing up of the sparse, acoustic sound in the studio with the help of guests. Produced by Roger Bechirian and Bob Andrews.

## SHAKIN' STEVENS
**You Drive Me Crazy** (Epic)
Heart-throb British neo-rockabilly singer's US album regrouping all his European hits in a bid for Stateside success. If God had wanted Stevens to be another Elvis, he would have had him born in Mississippi. Various producers.

## SIDE EFFECT
**All Aboard** (Elektra)
Sparkling soul harmonies in a mellow vein. Produced by Augie Johnson.

## RICHARD SIMMONS
**Reach** (Elektra)
Bestseller US exercise mini-guru narrates the usual legs up, legs down, tummy in instructions for a healthy body and sane mind although, this time around, the music is not a pot-pourri of anonymous, tested hits but new material (by Bruce Roberts and Allee Willis). It's still glorified muzak, though. Produced by Hank Medress and Dave Appell.

## SKA DOWS
**Ska'd for Life** (Skate)
Dance floor reggae. Score half a point for the puns.

## SKY
**Sky 4 Forthcoming** (Ariola)
Safe, classical bastardization of rock by the foremost exponents of the genre. In fact, little rock even emerges on this fourth album which includes Wagner's 'Valkyries', Berlioz, Khatchaturian, Bach and . . Hoagy Carmichael. Laid back, coffee-table music. Produced by Sky, Tony Clark and Haydn Bendall.

## LESLIE SMITH
**Heartache** (Elektra)
Agreeable pop soul, featuring clear-voiced singer. Includes duet with Merry Clayton on 'Before the Night Is Over' and fluent backing by non-soul specialists like Ned Doheny and Norton Buffalo. Leslie Smith has taste and he should be a name to look out for in the future. Produced by Peter Bunetta and Rick Chudacoff.

## PAUL SMITH
**Mysterious Barricades** (Flying Fish)
Clever banjo instrumentals in a country vein, with a zest of jazz thrown in for good measure. Produced by Paul Smith.

## SNOWY RED
**The Right To Die** (Dirty Dance)
Do-it-yourself home electronics by young Englishman still full of all the obligatory Bowie and Kraftwerk influences. E for Effort. Produced by Micky Mike.

## SOFT CELL
**Non Stop Ecstatic Dancing** (Some Bizarre)
6-track mini LP of dance/disco electronic mixes of winning songs from their recent first album and one new track 'What'. An interesting formula as long as groups don't indulge in it too often (see Human League/League Unlimited Orchestra). Produced by Mike Thorne.

## SONIC YOUTH
**Sonic Youth** (Neutral)
Experimental funk broken down and reconstituted in odd atonal sequences by a NY group on minimalist Glenn Branca's independent label. Monotonous and self-indulgent, but rewarding if you're in the right frame of mind.

## SOUNDTRACK
**The Animal Film** (Rough Trade)
Droning electronic atmospherics by Robert Wyatt for the controversial animal liberation film narrated by Julie Christie and directed by the committed Victor Schonstein. Unworthy of Wyatt's talent.

## SOUNDTRACK
**The Boat** (Atlantic)
Klaus Doldinger's score for the latest submarine epic. Bitty stuff, with martial tunes, French songs and generally uninspiring mood stuff in unhappy cohabitation.

## SOUNDTRACK
**Cat People** (MCA/Backstreet)

A surprisingly effective soundtrack outside of the context of the (controversial) movie. Although Bowie's contribution is limited to the eerie, compelling 'Putting Out Fire', probably his best song since 'Ashes to Ashes', the general mood conveyed by Moroder's synthesiser music and subtle orchestrations is strongly atmospheric in the right sense of the term and makes you want to see the film. A rare success in a usually barren field. Produced by Giorgio Moroder.

## SOUNDTRACK
**Countryman** (Island/Mango)
Double-album for Island's first major film production. A modern sort of Western shot in Jamaica, this obviously features the cream of the crop of Island's roster of superior reggae artists. No new major material though, all chestnuts from the bulging vaults: Bob Marley, Aswad, Steel Pulse. Rico, Lee Perry, Toots and the Maytals, etc . . . Produced by Chris Blackwell.

## SOUNDTRACK
**Diner** (Elektra)
'American Graffiti'-style of '50s and '60s familiar minor classics, features Dion and the Belmonts, Tommy Edwards, Elvis Presley, the Del Vikings, etc . . . Captures the feel of the times. Produced by Carol Thompson and Roger Mayer.

## SOUNDTRACK
**Grease II** (RSO)
The same mixture as first time around, but like the film the magic is no longer there. Familiar blend of youth ballads and gently up-tempo teenage rave-ups. Four Tops with 'Back To School Again' come out with the only honours. Produced by Louis St. Louis.

## SOUNDTRACK
**Soup For One** (Mirage)
Film soundtrack crafted by Rodgers and Edwards of Chic. Mixes both old material

and newer stuff by the likes of Carly Simon, Fonzi Martin and Teddy Pendergrass. All benefit from the Chic connection, while existing songs by Sister Sledge, Debbie Harry and Chic themselves polish off an attractive collection.

## SPARKS
### Angst In My Pants (Atlantic)

Amusing diversions by the ever unchanging Mael Brothers now on their umpteenth label. Clever European feel tinged with Californian surf-like teenage anxiety subject matters, Russell's distinctive high notes and Ron's impassive keyboards and orchestration work: a breezy cocktail. Produced by Giorgio Moroder.

## SPLIT ENZ
### Time and Tide (A&M)

Once exponents of quirky glam rock in the truest art-school tradition, New Zealand group Split Enz changed directions and

SQUEEZE

their last album was a sheer delight of melodies and harmonies in lush romantic moods. This new album, while carefully assembled and polished, lacks the hooks and emotions of its predecessor. Listening to it on various occasions I kept on expecting the spark that would set it alive, but it never comes. Sadly bland; can do better. Produced by Hugh Padgham and Split Enz.

## SQUEEZE
### Sweets From A Stranger (A&M)

Twelve more songs from the prolific Difford-Tilbrook team on their usual obsessions of romance and unsatisfaction. Uneven, but benefiting greatly from the contribution of new keyboards man Don Snow who injects a subtle R&B feel to the urban ballad mood of the group. When music and lyrics marry up well, Squeeze can be almost perfection but the combination is not achieved too regularly. Nevertheless, this is a better album than 9 out of 10 of the competition's and will endear itself to all and make new fans as Squeeze craft their way to the top. Produced by Squeeze and Phil McDonald.

SPLIT ENZ

**69**

## JOE STAMPLEY
**I'm Goin' Hurtin'** (Epic)
Stampley here eschews the honky-tonky sound he usually indulges in with partner Moe Bandy for more thoughtful country ballads. Smooth, self-indulgent, middle-of-the-road fodder. Produced by Ray Baker.

## THE STATLER BROTHERS
**The Legend Goes On** (Mercury)
Country veterans sing country harmonies for country fans. Strictly specialized. Produced by Jerry Kennedy.

## STATUS QUO
**1982** (Vertigo)
Three chord boogie formula stuff by the inventors of the genre. After twenty years in the business of repeating hit after hit, Status Quo are unassailable. This is more of the same; just what the people want. Produced by Status Quo.

## STEELY DAN
**Gold** (MCA)
Compilation of past Steely Dan gems. Only 'FM', previously included on a soundtrack album, is partly new. If you've missed out on their previous albums, you could do worse than this taster. Produced by Gary Katz.

## RAY STEVENS
**Don't Laugh Now** (RCA)
Mild country pop and no humour for Stevens on this latest album. Pleasant, just about. Produced by Bob Montgomery and Ray Stevens.

## BARON STEWART
**In Temperature Rising** (MCA)
'Beach boogie woogie' according to the artist. Upbeat, bubbly rock. All self-penned material except for one Dylan cover. From the US of A, home of power pop. Produced by Baron Stewart and Stu Cook.

## GARY STEWART & DEAN DILLON
**Brotherly Love** (RCA)
Attractive album with a diversity of country moods ranging from straight honky-tonk tunes to romantic ballads; also a light humourous touch on some songs. Produced by Eddie Kilroy.

## STRAIGHT EIGHT
**Straight To The Heart** (Logo)
Workmanlike British rock with no particular signs of individuality. Produced by Martin Rushent.

## GEORGE STRAIT
**Strait From The Heart** (MCA)
Texas country set of heartbreak and honky-tonk boogie. Produced by Blake Mevis.

## TERESA STRALEY
**Never Enough** (Alfa)
Previously known as a songwriter for Suzi Quatro, Jefferson Starship, Kiki Dee and others, Teresa Straley now makes a solo outing. Polished, quality pop. A bit featureless. Produced by David DeVore and Jim Ed Norman.

## STRANGE FRUIT
**Debut** (President)
Medium-pace jazz funk. Reliable but dull. Produced by Mike Jarratt.

## STRANGER
**Stranger** (Epic)
Power pop/heavy metal from new Florida group. Decent thrash, very anonymous, could be one of a dozen faceless bands playing. Produced by Tom Werman.

## STRAY CATS
**Built For Speed** (EMI)
First US album release for the New York rockabilly revivalists who had to move to England to find success. This album collects a representative sampling from their British albums. I personally find them a bit of a holier-than-thou bore but there's no denying an innocent sort of infectious energy. Make your own mind up. Produced by the Stray Cats, Dave Edmunds and Hein Hoven.

## STUTZ BEAR CATS
**Stutz Bear Cats** (Multimedia Tapes)
A new British group who devote their time to recreating a mellow, cabaret, palm-tree lounge 1930s sound. It worked for Manhattan Transfer, so who says talentless imitators can't make it?

## STYLISTICS
**1982** (Philadelphia Int.)
Eight new tracks (only?) of close male harmonies and strident falsettos by the master quartet of soul. Smooth, effortless and gentle funk. No innovations, but just what the punters want again and again. Produced by Jefferson, Wansel, Gamble, Bryant, Thompkins, Johnson & Biggs (phew! Just don't expect first names even if this reviewer is being paid by the word . . .).

## NIKKI SUDDEN
**Waiting On Egypt** (Abstract)
First solo album by member of Swell Maps. Straight rock and roll with a nod to the energy of punk and the drive of the Stones. Raw and eclectic but worth a listen.

## SUGAR BLUE
**Cross Roads** (Europa)
American bluesman and harmonica player carving a reputation for himself under European climes. Predictable wailing but pleasant all the same. Produced by Dominique Buscail.

## SUN
**Let There Be Sun** (Capitol)
Mediocre funk with pretentious cosmic overtones. Pass. Produced by Beau Ray Fleming and Byron Byrd.

## SURVIVOR
**Eye Of The Tiger** (Scotti)
The title track from this mainstream rock group's third album has soared to dizzy heights in the wake of its choice for the 'Rocky III' soundtrack. The rest is mucho bland and superbly anonymous. Produced by Frankie Sullivan and Jim Peterik.

STEELY DAN

## SWELL MAPS
**Collision Time** (Rough Trade)
Following the demise of the group, a 15 track compilation capturing their endearing experiments in style and moods. New wave rock at its most amateurish as well as adventurous. Deserved a better fate.

## SYLVIA
**Just Sylvia** (RCA)
Sophisticated country ballads with a beady eye on mainstream acceptance. Produced by Tom Collins.

# T

## TANGERINE DREAM
**White Eagle** (Virgin)

Prolific atmospheric machine from Germany delivers new platter. Stop. Sounds much the same as before. Stop. American Indian feel dominates major track 'Mohave Plan'. Stop. For fans only. Over and out. Produced by Edgar Froese, Chris Franke and Johannes Schmoelling.

## A TASTE OF HONEY
**Ladies of the Eighties** (Capitol)
Supremes clones in the best of sophisticated American soul tradition. Upbeat dancefloor pop with a novelty Japanese angle following their 'Sukiyaki' success. Produced by Al McKay, Ronald LaPread, Janice Marie Johnson and Hazel Payne.

## LINDA TAYLOR
**Taylor Made** (Groove)
Blue-eyed soul in a funky groove by erstwhile British veteran session singer on the solo trail. Powerful. Produced by Chris Palmer.

## T.C. MATIC
**T.C. Matic** (Statik)
Belgian group who haven't yet quite transmuted all their influences into a distinctive, personal style. Snatches of PIL, punk

bleakness and American funk blend uneasily.

## T-CONNECTION
**Pure and Natural** (Capitol)
Copybook disco tracks from US group. Produced by T. Coakley.

## TEEZER
**Teezer** (Sepico)
Independent album debut for new US midwestern band playing gentle mainstream pop. A bit of a concept based on 'Prince Lucifer' (the rock opera of dreaded memory returns?) runs through the record. Produced by Dick Young.

## TELEX
**Sex** (PVC)
Quirky Belgian electronic trio here with music set to the usual offbeat lyrics of Ron and Russell Mael's Sparks. Produced by Telex.

## THE TEMPTATIONS
**Reunion** (Motown/Gordy)
Features the return to the fold of David Ruffin and Eddie Kendricks. Clever use of more modern synthesiser funk featuring Rick James on keyboards on the first side, while the second is in a more classic mellow soul harmonies mood for which the Temptations are renowned. Various producers including the Gordys, Rick James and Smokey Robinson.

## THEATRE OF HATE
**He Who Dares Wins** (Burning Rome)
Live album recorded in Berlin in September 1981 of violent, earnest British postpunk anthems of despair. Searing, angry music. Produced by Terry Razor.

## 38 SPECIAL
**Special Forces** (A&M)
Southern rock boogie with a metallic edge. Produced by Rodney Mills.

## B. J. THOMAS
**As We Know Him** (MCA)
Disappointingly dull and lifeless material for a usually interesting US singer. Furthermore, Thomas is drowned under an orgy of strings more appropriate to the cabaret easy-listening market. Produced by Nick DeCaro.

## THOSE FRENCH GIRLS
**Those French Girls** (Safari)
All-male outfit from Glasgow with a sharp touch in clever group names. Pretentious and highly derivative glam rock which went out of fashion a rock-aeon ago.

## MEL TILLIS
**It's A Long Way To Daytona** (Elektra)
Decent country singer with the usual preoccupations: broken love and shady women. Produced by Billy Strange.

## THE TINS
**Buying in Bulk** (Tintrax)
Young US garage band with a neat parodic touch.

## TOILING MIDGETS
**Sea of Unrest** (Instant)
Melodramatic copies of Lou Reed and David Bowie. Not all independent records are good. This is a fine mess.

## BERNIE TORME
**Turn Out The Lights** (Kamaflage)
Solo album for Gillan's erstwhile lead guitarist. Not so much heavy metal as one might have expected from his past associations, but solid, competent hard rock. Voice lets the package down, though. Produced by Nick Tauber and Bernie Torme.

## TOTO
**Toto IV** (Columbia)
The epitome of US faceless rock. Pompous concoctions with a zest of rock, bal-

38 SPECIAL

lads, R&B, but no direction or guts. Immaculate musicianship, of course, from such experienced session players but such a lack of fire. Smash hit with 'Roseanna' so critics be damned. Produced by Toto.

## PETE TOWNSHEND
### All The Best Cowboys Have Chinese Eyes (Atco)

| | |
|---|---|
| The Sea Refuses No River | Uniforms |
| Communication | Prelude |
| Exquisitely Bored | Somebody Saved Me |
| North Country Girl | Face Dances Part Two |
| Slit Skirts | Stardom In Action |
| | Stop Hurting People |

As the Who's albums go from bad to worse, Townshend's solo efforts keep on getting better and better. This is a major album by any name or standards. Obviously wracked by doubt and remorse, Townshend also makes it his most personal ever. Loss of love, the perils of stardom, religion and growing older are the main themes tackled on 'Cowboys' and, despite a few lapses and self-indulgent forays, a strong sense of commitment allied to great melodies and musicianship dominates the whole album. A serene set about self-doubt. Particular favourites for me are the lush and expansive 'The Sea Refuses No River' and the stunning 'Slit Skirts'. Until now, I'd been a lukewarm admirer but no great fan of the Who; now, I no longer wonder about the Who, I know Pete Townshend has become the major talent so many others said he was long before my own conversion to the cause. Produced by Chris Thomas.

## TOYAH
### The Changeling (Safari)
Fifth album from the hyped-up actress with spunk but no talent. A mixture of cosmic or social preoccupations to an electronic beat shuffle. I still remain unconvinced. Produced by Steve Lillywhite.

TOYAH

## JEANIE TRACY
### Me And You (Fantasy)
Black gospel music from a session singer familiar in jazz fusion circles. Strong, powerful voice and somewhat religious overtones in the lyrics.

## TRAMPOLIN
### Gonna Make It Alright (CBS)
European sludge rock par excellence. Ciao and au-revoir.

## TRIUMPH
### Triumph (Attic)
Hendrix-inspired heavy metal from a Canadian trio. Fiery but run-of-the-mill decibel thrash. Produced by Mike Levine and Doug Hill.

## TROUBLE FUNK
### Drop The Bomb (Sugarhill)
Superior rapping funk dance jams by a Washington septet of immeasurable energies and rhythm. Ideal party record demonstrating the versatility of Trouble Funk outside of the restraining confines of rap.

## TRUE SOUND OF LIBERTY
### Dance With Me (Frontier)
Vindictive vintage '77 punk by latecomer US group. Noisy.

## TRUST
### Savage (Epic)
Strongly political heavy metal by a leading French group unfortunately trying to sing in English. Not quite Maurice Chevalier in leather gear intoning Clash-like left-wing credos, but not far off.

## TRUC OF AMERICA
### Outa Control (UFR)
Good-natured pop tunes from a Florida-based band, with a nod of recognition towards Dr. Hook. Produced by Marc Fett and Truc of America.

## MARSHALL TUCKER BAND
### Tuckerized (Warners)
Extra-sophisticated country rock from a known quantity. Carefully tailored for maximum radio impact. A ballad here, a Randy Newman song there and no-nonsense

boogie throughout. A proven recipe. Produced by Garry Klein.

### TUXEDO MOON
**Divine** (Operation Twilight)
The alluringly experimental San Francisco band now resident in Europe with an exquisite album of background music for a Maurice Béjart ballet dedicated to Greta Garbo. Snatches of dialogue from Garbo

movies punctuate seven operatic rhapsodies where violin and synthesizers blend most lyrically. An undeniable and fascinating challenge.

### McCOY TYNER
**Looking Out** (Columbia)
Jazz pianist's debut on new album bears witness to an increasing interest in pop, what with Carlos Santana providing guitar licks and Phyllis Hyman a number of vocals. At times, you can almost dance to funk rhythms. Sounds all a bit too calculated to me. Produced by McCoy Tyner.

### JUDIE TZUKE
**Shoot The Moon** (Chrysalis)
No, not a soundtrack to the Alan Parker film but a touch of serendipity for the young, ever-promising British singer. Strong touch of the heavy rocks dominate her new songs and while the sensitivity is well on display in the lyrics, the music does sometimes swamp her. Still, it's one way to escape the 'wimp' image she was well on the way to getting. Needs a few plays before you really appreciate what she's trying to do. Points for courage. Produced by Paul Muggleton.

JUDIE TZUKE

# U

### UK SUBS
**Endangered Species** (NEMS)
Courageous attempt by one of the eponymous punk bands to move out of the genre rut. Added melody and variety to the strident anthems and guitar thrash make this a not always successful but definitely worthy effort.

### UNIT 5
**Scared of the Dark** (Clone)
The first big miss from Akron, small town with strong musical spawns. Would-be new wave meanderings leading nowhere fast.

### UNIVERS ZERO
**Ceux Du Dehors** (Recommended)
Dour European dirges.

### UTOPIA
**Swing To The Right** (Bearsville)
Todd Rundgren takes a back chair and blends in with his group for this album. Strong political stance but chirpy anonymous songs. Produced by Todd Rundgren.

# V

### VAN HALEN
**Diver Down** (Warners)
Reliable heavy rock by one of the most popular US bands around. Stylish and incendiary. Interesting cover versions of material by the Kinks, Roy Orbison and the classic 'Dancing in the Streets' in addition to the self-penned material. No surprises, but then Van Halen fans just want more of the same. Produced by Ted Templeman.

### VARIOUS
**Bowling Balls II** (Clone)
Second instalment in the Akron, Ohio compilation series 'Bowling Balls from Hell'. Features new wave rock from the likes of the Waitresses, Tin Huey, Unit 5, Bizarros, Hammer Damage, Totsuzen Danball, Susan Schmidt and Debbie Smith. Produced by Nick Nicholis.

### VARIOUS
**Dr Rhino and Mr Hyde** (Beggars Banquet/Rhino)
One of the more astute US independent record labels shows off its wares with a selection from past and present roster of artists including a wealth of eccentric California comedy performers as well as the Temple City Kazoo Orchestra, Wild Man Fisher, Randy California and Arthur Lee.

## VARIOUS
**Hot Shower** (RCA)
Rag-bag selection of heavy metal: Hawkwind, Budgie, Slade, Triumph, Alkatrazz, Grand Prix and Heaven.

## VARIOUS
**Metal Massacre** (Metal Blade)
Heavy-you-know-what compilation of unsigned Los Angeles bands. All sadly going through stereotyped motions: Bitch, Steeler, Avatar, Pandemonium, Cirith Ungol, etc. . . .

## VARIOUS
**No Future** (No Future)
Anthology of primal British punk bands on a Finnish label (!). A taster of Blitz, the Partisans, Red Alert, Peter and the Test Tube Babies, Crux, Hostile Youth, Blitzkrieg, Distortion, the Samples and the Violators. Oi, oi reigns even up beyond the polar circle, it would appear . . .

## VARIOUS
**Reggae Crossing** (Burning Sounds)
Quality showcase for reggae artists often in slower, mellower, more accessible moods; as a result this compilation never bores or sounds too similar. Included are Janet Kay, Alton Ellis, John Holt, Augustus Pablo, Delroy Wilson, Hortense Ellis, etc

## VARIOUS
**Reggae Sunsplash 81 (Warners)**
Although subtitled 'A Tribute to Bob Marley' this double album is really a soundtrack for the film of the 1981 Jamaican festival featuring the crème de la crème of reggae artists: Mighty Diamonds, Black Uhuru, Third World, Dennis Brown, Steel Pulse, Eek-a-Mouse, I-Threes, Gregory Isaacs, Sheila Hylton, Carlene Davis and the Melody Makers. Produced by Jay Steinberg.

## VARIOUS
**Riotous Assembly** (Riot City)
Fourteen identikit British neo-punk amateurs on a quick outing straight from the woodwork: a few riffs and screams and back they go to deserved obscurity. Namechecks: Vice Squad, Resistance '77, Havoc, Chaos UK, Undead, Lunatic Fringe, Abrasive Wheels, the Expelled, Organised Chaos, Court Martial, etc . . .

## VARIOUS
**Rockers Variation** (Dread at the Controls)
Reggae vocalists anthology: Hopeton Lindo, Rod Taylor, Sugar Minott, all produced by the ubiquitous Mikey Dread.

## VARIOUS
**Sex, Sweat and Blood. The New Danceability** (Beggars Banquet)
Funk and techno-pop compilation. Basically what the UK has been most active in fieldwise this year. Fashion, Medium Medium, Lora Logic, 23 Skidoo, Perry Haines, the Dance, David Gamson, Ministry, Maximum Joy are the chosen protagonists. Not a valid selection, methinks.

## VARIOUS
**Wargasm** (Pax)
Punk against the bomb anthology. Features the Angelic Upstarts, the Dead Kennedys, Infa Riot, Rat Scabies, Canker Opera, Quite Unnerving, the Mau Maus, the System, Captain Sensible, Flux of Pink Indians and Poison Girls all contributing new material in aid of the cause. Worthy, but sadly predictable music.

## VARIOUS
**A Young Person's Guide to Compact** (Compact)
Lavish boxed set wherein Compact seeks to resurrect the lamented 1960s with its curious roster blending unabashed nostalgia and techno-pop. Mari Wilson and the Wilsations, Shake Shake, Virna Lindt and Cynthia Scott uneasily share company. Love the box and all the generous giveaways but a bit perplexed at the label's policy and commercial acumen.

## BILLY VERA
**Billy Vera** (Alfa)
Having ditched his sidekicks the Beaters, Vera has moved to Muscle Shoals for a clean set of R&B songs with the right touch of romance and sophistication. Produced by Jerry Wexler.

## TOM VERLAINE
**Words From The Front** (Virgin/Warners)
Third solo album for the frontman of Television, one of the most important (and sadly short-lived) groups of the late '70s. A vibrant guitar player capable of searing emotion, Verlaine is often let down by his somewhat whining vocals. Moody, rambling songs set in an indeterminate territory beyond dreams or reality come to life on every guitar lick and there will be enough here to confirm to his admirers that Verlaine is still a contender. But I think his best is still to come (if the record industry allows). Produced by Tom Verlaine.

## VICE SQUAD
**Stand Strong Stand Proud** (Zonophone)
Socially angry British punk with female vocalist Beki Bondage to the fore. Somewhat more articulate and thoughtful lyrics than most of the bands lumped in the same category, but the wall of rancour sound begins to grate after a while. Produced by Park Byrne.

## VOICE FARM
**The World We Live In** (Optional)
Experimental San Francisco trio with a neat electronic touch. Weird and wacky and very self-indulgent. A curio.

## ANDREAS VOLLENWEIDER
**Behind the Gardens, Behind the Wall – Under the Tree** (CBS)
European harp player with sickly romantic compositions that veer towards pomp rock. What the world doesn't need is another Mike Oldfield. Produced by Eric Merz.

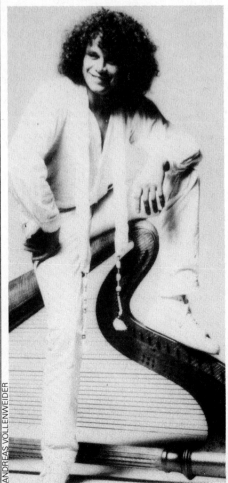

ANDREAS VOLLENWEIDER

# W

## JOHN WAITE
**Ignition** (Chrysalis)

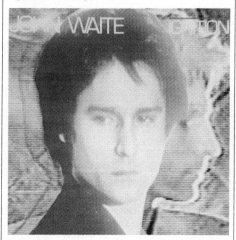

Solo effort by a member of the Babys. Using a bevy of experienced US new wave musicians to back him in the studio, he comes across with undeniable vitality but the results are still too calculated and glossy to satisfy entirely. Maybe with a different producer? Produced by Neil Geraldo.

## NARADA MICHAEL WALDEN
**Confidence** (Atlantic)
Despite the inanities of the inner sleeve blurb, full of cringe-worthy cosmic self-help tips, this is an accomplished soul set by a distinctive singer with a sure commercial touch and feelings galore. Transcends disco by a mile. Produced by Narada Michael Walden.

## WENDY WALDMAN
**Which Way To Main Street** (Epic)
Yet another folk/rock performer infected by the Springsteen big heart big sound virus. Wendy Waldman, though, seems capable of mastering the genre and this is a rewarding album coming as it does after a few silent years. A fine writer of songs and pointed, personal lyrics, Waldman seems at ease with the larger than life production. Investigate. Produced by Eddie Kramer.

## WALDO
**Love Don't Grow On Trees**
(Columbia)
Washington, DC based soul group with strong horns and a characteristic jazz influence. Great dance material. Produced by Willie Lester and Rodney Brown.

## THE WALL
**Dirges and Anthems** (Polydor)
Drab blend of punk preoccupations and

JOHN WAITE

Joy Division-like minimalism. In fact, the title of this album by an anonymous new British group gives the whole game away.

## WALL STREET CRASH
**In Central** (Magnet)
Cabaret harmonies and posturing in another attempt to revive, in vain, the spirit of the '30s and '40s. Made in Britain, not a million miles from Broadway, in fact. Produced by David Mackay.

## HANK WANGFORD BAND
**Live** (Cow Pie)
A reverent homage to the sounds and subjects of American country music by a talented group of British musicians (all hiding under careful pseudonyms – Wangford is in civilian life a gynaecologist!). Recorded in 'Sincere-O-Round' in a London pub, this is not only funny but also very good country music. Produced by B. J. Cole.

## DIONNE WARWICK
**Friends in Love** (Arista)
A carefully chosen repertoire of songs culled from the pens of soul's finest stylists; a duet with Johnny Mathis; spare-no-dollar backing and orchestration; Warwick's dulcet tones; we have lift-off. Produced by Jay Graydon.

## JIMMY WEBB
**Angel Heart** (CBS/Columbia)

A long-awaited album by one of pop's most celebrated songwriters, still deserving recognition for his own output, rather than cover versions consecrating other people. Although half of California's laid back set guests on the record, it's Webb's sweet, vulnerable voice which dominates on lyrical, romantic songs full of hurt and deadly metaphors. Produced by Matthew McCauley and Fred Mollin.

### BOB WELCH
**Bob Welch** (RCA)
Easy, melodic pop rock from an erstwhile Fleetwood Mac alumni. Still has a touch of the Fleetwoods. Fun, unassuming album.

### WEST STREET MOB
**West Street Mob** (PRT)
Highly imaginative rap performances. Produced by Sylvia Robinson.

### KIM WILDE
**Select** (RAK)

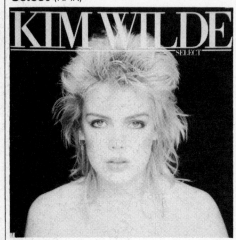

Stage (and album) two in the irresistible rise of Miss Wild to the top. Carefully crafted songs by father and brother capably devised for her sometimes limited vocals, the right amount of hooks, riffs and staged melodrama. This is manufactured pop of the better kind and suffers from a certain monotony and sameness. Kim Wilde, however, is here to stay and we could fare worse. Includes the adventurous 'Cambodia'. Produced by Ricky Wilde.

### BEAU WILLIAMS
**Beau Williams** (Capitol)
Easy grooving soul made simple by US singer with a nod of the beat towards the shores of rock 'n roll. Produced by Johnny Pate.

### DENIECE WILLIAMS
**Niecy** (CBS/ARC)
Classy soul from one of the better UK black artists. Seductive ballads dominate her second album and her voice reaches

DON WILLIAMS

amazing heights while remaining utterly tuneful. A minor gem. Produced by Thom Bell.

### DON WILLIAMS
**Listen to the Radio** (MCA)
Easygoing country ballads of woe and mighty sorrow by the veteran gravel-voiced singer oozing emotion from every chord. Reliable. For fans, principally. Produced by Don Williams and Garth Fundis.

### HANK WILLIAMS JR
**High Notes** (Elektra)
Country singer with a famous name switches direction from honky tonk rave-ups to more thoughtful ballads and slower tempo. Material is not quite up to standard, though, and the results are somewhat somniferous. Produced by Jimmy Bowen.

### JOSEPH WILLIAMS
**Joseph Williams** (MCA)
Album debut for the son of film-score composer John Williams. Middle-of-the-road pop with a fleeting jazz feel. Might have required some of his father's touch with instantly familiar hooks to make this more memorable. Produced by Jay Gruska.

### BOBBIE WOMACK
**The Poet** (Motown/Beverly)
A breakthrough album for a gritty-voiced soul veteran. After a career of supplying hits for others (Rolling Stones, Eric Clapton), Womack has come up with a superb LP blending infectious up-tempo dance numbers with a series of moody, reflective and moving ballads. A cool, often subdued record which sees Womack perfectly in control of his material.

### STEVIE WONDER
**Original Musiquarium 1** (Motown)
A double set with only three new tracks might seem something of a cheat, but it's always a pleasure to hear many of Stevie's past material in a new light or context. The older songs are all compiled from his '70s output and include a brace of smash hits ('Superstition', 'You Are The Sunshine Of My Life', 'Isn't She Lovely' and others). The new pieces (there were four but delays in the record's release allowed one to become a single hit – 'That Girl' – thus reducing the count to three) blend in quite effortlessly. Produced by Stevie Wonder.

### WOO
**Whichever Way You Are Going, You Are Going Wrong** (Sunshine Series)
Quiet, moody tunes from a British independent. Heavy on the atmospherics without heavy reliance on synthesiser magic. Adventurous and clearly unfashionable. Deserves a detour.

### REN WOODS
**Azz/izz** (Elektra)
Black American actress with a medium paced soul-pop outing aimed squarely at the easy-listening market. Produced by Chuck Jackson.

### WORLDBACKWARDS
**Flesh** (Illuminated)
Young British experimental trio with seventeen tracks ranging from the heavy dirge to the slow monotony of meticulously crafted despair. Vocalist Dinah Mulholland's voice is electronically treated and rather effective. Interesting if you have the time.

BILL WYMAN

# Y

## YELLOWMAN
**Mister Yellowman** (Greensleeves)
Master Jamaican DJ (his name stems from his being an albino) with a collection of dynamic, rapping hits. Produced by Henry 'Junjo' Lawes.

## YELLOWMAN AND FATHEAD
**One Yellowman** (Hitbound)
Pulsating DJ raps from Yellowman and sidekick Fathead. If you like the style, you'll like the vinyl.

# Z

## PIA ZADORA
**Pia** (Elektra)
Elektra was once an ace label who had no need to sign Lolita-like starlets sponsored by millionaire husbands. Scantily-clad Zadora sings and pouts her way through middle-of-the-road and disco standards in a clean, antiseptic fashion. The cover is heavily retouched: even nudity isn't what it used to be! Produced by Jimmy Tract.

## FRANK ZAPPA
**Ship Arriving Too Late To Save A Drowning Witch** (Barking Pumpkin)
The usual reliable and idiosyncratic concoction from old father Zappa: time shifts, loony lyrics, non-sequiturs and, miracle of miracles, a major hit with his daughter Moon intoning 'Valley Girl'. Now they'll say he's sold out! Though, if truth be told, this is much the same quirky, uncommercial mixture as before. Produced by Frank Zappa.

## ZZ HILL
**Downhome** (Malaco)
Identikit Southern boogie rock. Move down that mean, dusty road, man.

## BILL WYMAN
**Bill Wyman** (A&M)
The amiable Rolling Stones bass player with a summery set of sheer pop tunes in distinct contrast to the heavier Stones material he has lived with so long. Amiable divertimento where Wyman has enrolled a whole bevy of helping hands: the Stray Cats, Chris Rea, Mel Collins, Dave Mattacks, etc. . . . Exhibits all the usual indulgences of solo albums by members of megagroups but always remains unassumingly pleasant nevertheless. Produced by Bill Wyman and Chris Kimsey.

## TAMMY WYNETTE
**Soft Touch** (Epic)
Undiluted schmaltz churned out by the groove in good ole country tradition. Yecchh. Produced by George Richey.

# X

## XAVIER
**Point of Pleasure** (Liberty)
Manic funk in the George Clinton-tradition by a new eight-piece group also fluent on a few ballads. Ideal dance floor fodder.

FRANK AND MOON ZAPPA

## A

**ABWARTS**
**Der Westen Ist Einsam** (Mercury)
Dense and furious German proto-punk. Grinding rhythms and dissonances punctuate joyless cries of despair. As the title puts it, 'the West is lonely. . .' Hard on the soul and hard on the ears. Produced by Nick Launay.

**KING SUNNY ADE AND HIS AFRICAN BEATS**
**Juju Music** (Island/Mango)

Surprising modern African music from Nigeria, blending infectious, traditional rhythms with unusual electric instrumentation and synthesisers. Dub, talking drums and even steel guitar incongruously mix in a fascinating brew that evokes the twang of the Ventures, the chanting of Fela Kuti and much more besides. A minor enchantment. Produced by Martin Meissonier.

**AEROSMITH**
**Rock In A Hard Place** (CBS/Columbia)
New guitar front line for the hard-rocking US group but vocalist Steve Tyler's characteristic warbling keeps the package instantly recognisable. Raw and nasty, the way the fans want it. Produced by Jack Douglas, Steven Tyler and Tony Bongiovi.

**WILLIE ALEXANDER**
**Solo Loco** (Bomp)
A mixture of rock stalwarts ('Be Bop A Lula', 'Tennessee Waltz') and newer bluesy compositions by the Boston ever-hopeful. Not bad, but lacking in fire. Produced by Willie Alexander.

**WILLIE 'LOCO' ALEXANDER AND THE CONFESSIONS**
**Autre Chose** (New Rose)
Double live set recorded in France. Bland, bluesy honky-tonk music in a drunken bar-room tradition. Superfluous.

**THE ALLEY CATS**
**Escape From Earth** (MCA)
Basic rock 'n' roll with a touch of punk minimalism by a new Los Angeles trio featuring Randy Stodola on guitar and Dianne Chai on bass and vocals. Not as polished as X, but going in the right direction. Produced by Randy Stodola.

**ALLEZ ALLEZ**
**African Queen** (Kamera)
Six-piece Belgian band with strong per-

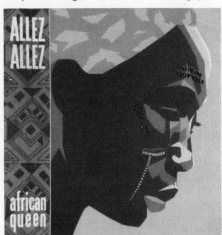

cussion. Pronounced African feel highlighted by vocalist Sarah's vulnerable tones make this more than the usual ethnic rip-off. Thoughtful, intelligent and you can dance to it. Worth looking out for.

**AMERICAN EXPRESS**
**Jazz-Funk Fusion** (Supermusic)
Faceless fusion jazz by British session musicians on the Shakatak/Spyrogyra trail. Sadly predictable and bland.

**ALISTAIR ANDERSON**
**Steel Skies** (Topic)
Quality traditional British folk, although all the tunes are self-penned. Sober and clean-cut.

**CARL ANDERSON**
**Absence Without Love** (Epic)
Interesting soul debut by Carl Anderson, previously an actor. Cool, calculated and composed. Produced by Richard Rudolph.

**JAMES ANDERSON**
**Strangest Feeling** (Kat Family)
Run-of-the-mill American radio muzak, featuring ballads and raunchy anonymous rock. Eminently forgettable. Produced by Paul Davis and Phil Benton.

**ANTIPASTI**
**Caution To The Wind** (Rondelet)
Archetypal punk formation seeks diversification in the minor heavy metal league. E for Effort.

AEROSMITH

### APRIL WINE
**Power Play** (Capitol)
Quality, melodic heavy metal from Canadian band on their fourth album. Slowly but surely going places. Produced by Myles Goodwyn and Mike Stone.

### ARTERY
**Oceans** (Red Flame)
Tortured art-school rock from a new British group hailing from Sheffield (the Athens, Georgia of the UK? viz Human League, BEF, ABC, Cabaret Voltaire, etc. . .). Often pretentious and impenetrable but gets better if you persevere.

### ASWAD
**Not Satisfied** (CBS)
Superlative reggae set by veteran exponents of the genre. Produced by Aswad and Michael Campbell.

### SWEET PEA ATKINSON
**Don't Walk Away** (Ze)
Singer from the Was Not Was troup now on solo outing. Soul-like tones carry well on this dance rock set of great vitality. Produced by Don Was, David Was and Jack Tann.

### ATLANTA POPS ORCHESTRA
**Just Hooked On Country** (Epic)
Segue of instrumental country tracks. All the fun and all the dreary clichés (and handclaps) of the fair. Avoid. Produced by Albert Coleman.

### THE AU PAIRS
**Sense And Sensuality** (Kamera)
Uncompromising British group on their second album. Husky feminist mouthpiece Lesley Woods on lead vocals often mistakes the intensity of the message with the emotion but overall the lush, almost orchestral sound captivates. Produced by Martin Culverwell and the Au Pairs.

### AUSTRALIAN CRAWL
**Sons Of Beaches** (EMI)
Scintillating power pop with hummable melodies and a bevy of catchy hooks. Australian sextet's third album. Strong classical guitar is featured throughout. Straightforward but reliable. Produced by Mike Chapman.

### THE AVERAGE WHITE BAND
**Cupid's In Fashion** (Arista)
Easy listening groove by experts in the field. No great hits here but a consistent level of middle-aged funk with a minor sting in the tail. Good for summer evenings and over-40s but not much use elsewhere. Sadly out of fashion. Produced by Dan Hartman.

### BAD COMPANY
**Rough Diamonds** (Swansong)

First album by a once major group after a three-year lay-off. Paul Rodger's voice is still an archetypal rock and roll instrument and the sheer ease and professionalism of Bad Company remain seductive. However, a lack of innovation and a surfeit of lyrical clichés soon bury this album in a quagmire of sluggishness. Could do better. Produced by Bad Company.

### LISA BADE
**Suspicion** (A&M)
Appealing female rocker from Australia in the school-of-Joplin hard and tough manner. Well-chosen material and pared-down instrumentation make this a most promising debut. Produced by David Kershenbaum.

### SCOTT BAIO
**Scott Baio** (RCA)
Once a teenage lead in Alan Parker's movie 'Bugsie Malone', Baio has now emigrated to sitcom land and this debut album is all too smooth, middle of the road and predictably sterile. Produced by Bob Reno and Stephen Metz.

### BALANCE
**In For The Count** (Portrait)
Second hard rocking album for an East Coast group with fire and brimstone percolating out from all bodily orifices. A bit monotonous but classy nonetheless. Produced by Doug Katsaros, Bob Kulick, Peppy Castro and Tony Bongiovi.

### BARCLAY JAMES HARVEST
**A Concert For The People** (Berlin) (Polydor)
Two-year-old live recording of a British band who are absolutely huge in Europe and long forgotten elsewhere. Tasteful in the extreme, bombastic and redundant.

For the fans only. Produced by Barclay James Harvest/Martin Lawrence and Ian Southerington.

### CHRIS BARRETT
**Introducing** (Wandon)
Suave cocktail lounge, happy hour muzak ballads of indeterminate Yankee origin. Produced by Peter Dean, John Lepine and Frank Wehr.

### BARTOCK AND LANSKY
**On The Air** (MCA)
Anonymous new US duo from San Diego. Run-of-the-mill pop rock with a zest of modernity through use of synthesisers. Might grow on you, though I didn't allow it time to do so on me. Produced by Craig Bartock and Harlan Lansky.

### THE B B & Q BAND
**All Night Long** (Capitol)
Multi-racial soul group from Brooklyn, the Bronx and Queens (B B & Q, gettit?). Clever and dynamic disco material with a surefire touch of quality. Produced by Jacques Fred Petrus.

### THE BEATLES
**The Complete Silver Beatles** (Audiofidelity)
The historic demo tape which the Beatles made for Decca (who turned them down) now generally available outside of the bootleg circuit. Of dubious historical interest. Amateurish and reedy, though one or two hints of future qualities are detectable.

### BOB BELAND
**Bob Beland** (What)
Whimsical American art-school rock with more than a nod to Jules and the Polar Bears whose members are much in evidence throughout; quirky but danceable. Produced by Stephen Hague.

### THE BELLAMY BROTHERS
**Greatest Hits** (Warners)
I find it difficult to spot more than a couple of very medium-sized hits on this souvenir album of gentle country rock with ten cuts. Wimpish. Produced by Phil Gernhard, Tony Scott, Michael Lloyd and Jimmy Bowen.

### BARRIE BIGGS
**Wide Awake** (Afrik)
Smooth velvety reggae. Pleasant throughout; includes a curious cover of Gerry and the Pacemakers' 'Don't Let The Sun Catch You Crying'. Ideal dance-floor, soft-light time music. Produced by Barry Biggs.

### THE BIRTHDAY PARTY
**Junkyard** (4AD)
Primal screams and grating guitars on this uncompromising and disturbing album by

the neo-punk Australian group. Takes some getting used to but ultimately makes harrowing sense. Audience participation and willingness badly needed. Awful cartoon sleeve art.

### BITCHES SIN
**Predator** (Heavy Metal)
Duelling heavy metal set. Heard it all before, he mutters, listening to his grey hairs grow.

### BLACKFOOT
**Highway Song** (Atco)
Live heavy rock set by popular American band. Solid, reliable thunder and lightning thrash with all the right trappings and posturings. Produced by Al Nalli.

### BLACK SLATE
**Six Plus One** (Top Ranking)
Gentle reggae nodding towards the crossover, easy listening market. All sounds very familiar and soothingly predictable.

### BLACK UHURU
**Black Sounds Of Freedom** (Greensleeves)
1977 set by one of today's better-established reggae groups. Reliable, smooth material. Produced by Prince Jammy.

### BLANKET OF SECRECY
**Blanket Of Secrecy** (Warners)
Anonymous, identikit techno-pop of uncertain provenance. Assured and romantic, accessible music with guitars, heavenly choir and massed banks of synthesisers to the rescue. Produced by Blanket of Secrecy; 'directed' by Roger Bechirian.

### BLOODSTONE
**We Go A Long Way Back** (T-Neck)
Return of a black group with a mediocre set of syrupy ballads and medium fast dance numbers. Indifferent funk at best. Produced by the Isley Brothers and McKinley Jackson.

### THE BLUES BAND
**Brand Loyalty** (Arista)
Unnecessary revivalist rhythm and blues by a white band steeped in reverence and clichés. This new album features a majority of new tunes instead of the warmed-up cover versions of yore but the overall sound is so derivative. Produced by the group and Richard Dodd.

### BLURT
**Blurt** (Red Flame)
Jarring experimental doodles by Ted Milton and his saxophone-led trio. Much too gratuitous and lacking in melodies or feeling. Pass.

### HAMILTON BOHANNON
**Bohannon Fever** (Phase II)
Mixed funky set by the famous drummer. A blend of smooth disco, with African rhythms in a bow to British fashion, rock riffs and Funkadelic neo-psychedelic soul. A hotchpotch, and not a very effective one at that. Produced by Hamilton Bohannon.

### BOW WOW WOW
**I Want Candy** (EMI/RCA)
British and US releases have different track listings but in both instances we have a 'Greatest Hits' package of sundry tracks by the semi-fashionable British daughter-of-punk group with a decidedly peppy pop personality. Bow Wow Wow have never been my cup of tea, but their effervescent enjoyment and liveliness has gained them many fans. At any rate, they have now successfully transcended their dubious manufactured-punk origins and stand proudly at the crossroads of rock and insouciant pop. Produced by Malcolm McLaren, Kenny Laguna, Ritchie Cordell, Brian Tench, Colin Thurston and Alan Tarney.

### BOW WOW WOW
**12 Original Recordings** (Harvest)
US release of another combination of Bow Wow Wow's greatest hits, combining recent chart material with earlier, more quirky and subversive songs initially released only in cassette form. The earlier pieces are still very effective and less basic than later songs with which they have gained some form of popular success. Produced by Malcolm McLaren, Colin Thurston and Alan Tarney.

### PAUL BRADY
**Hard Station** (WEA)
Re-mix of last year's critically acclaimed folk rock album by the ex-member of Planxty and the Johnstons. Quiet urban ballads in a subdued but effective mood. Electric rock intrusions provide the occasional grittiness. A sleeper. Produced by Hugh Murphy and Paul Brady.

### BRAND X
**Is There Anything About?** (CBS/Passport)
Laidback jazz-rock tunes with a strong improvisatory feel by British veterans featuring Phil Collins of Genesis and solo fame. A pleasant way to spend three-quarters of an hour with your feet up, but none of the melodies survive the test of time to make this anything more than competent muzak. Produced by Robin Lumley and Steven Short.

### KAREN BROOKS
**Walk On** (Warners)
Another impressive country-rock female performer in the hallowed footsteps of

Emmylou Harris and Rosanne Cash. Although the choice of producer and a starry cast of musicians and back-up collaborators is near perfect, Karen Brooks' voice and writing shine strongly throughout the album, both melodic and tough in the customary brittle manner, and make her a name to look out for. Produced by Brian Ahern.

### THE BROUGHTONS
**Superchip** (Sheet)
Somewhat humorous heavy rock by survivors of one of the all-time eponymous hippie bands. Worth a minor detour.

### CLARENCE 'GATEMOUTH' BROWN
**Alright Again!** (Demon)
Big band Texas swing set by the 48-year-old legend in his own time. Live and infectious. Ideal good time party music with a lot of fizzle, pop and exhilaration.

### RUTH BROWN
**The Soul Survives** (Flair)
Live recording of an old soul stalwart at the Blues Alley in Washington, D.C. Competent. Produced by Norman Schwartz.

### U BROWN
**Ravers Party** (Trojan)
Familiar toastin' artist improvising on reggae pieces. Ordinary.

### ED BRUCE
**I Write It Down** (MCA)
Songwriter on solo outing, featuring material made famous by a score of others. Laidback and easy. Produced by Tommy West.

### BUCKS FIZZ
**Bucks Fizz** (RCA)
Familiar collection of middle of the road material with strong panache by Britain's answer to Abba in the easy listening, boys and girls together stakes. Lots of class and clever hooks. Produced by Andy Hill.

### BUGATTI AND MUSKER
**The Dukes** (Atlantic/WEA)
Singer/songwriters for the AOR multi

tudes go disco on a big scale. Polished soul excursion lacking the fire and sparkle of, say, Hall and Oates. Safe and commercial. Produced by Arif Mardin.

### T-BONE BURNETT
**Trap Door** (Warners)
Six song mini-album by a veteran of Dylan bands and the late-lamented Alpha Band. A bitter collection of tunes which includes an almost cynical revamp of 'Diamonds Are A Girl's Best Friend', this is an impressive set which puts Burnett up in the first division of US folk-rock performers. Powerful affirmation of rock (and Christian) values. Produced by Reggie Fisher and T-Bone Burnett.

### BURNING ROME
**Burning Rome** (A&M)
Promising American new wave band, still halfway between emotion-swept proto-punk and a more melodic variation of power pop. Lead singer Vicki Thomas has a strong distinctive voice and comes across as a promising personality. One for tomorrow. Produced by Liam Sternberg and Ed Stasium.

### GEORGE BURNS
**Young At Heart** (Mercury)
Very old actor on vocal country outing. Deplorable set of standards. Produced by Jerry Kennedy and Charles Fach.

### THE BUS BOYS
**American Worker** (Arista)
Second album by a black US band who move with consummate ease between a varied assortment of musical genres, from reggae to soul boogie. But a heavy dose of rock dominates which is the one area in which they are ill at ease. Blame the management or the producer. Their first album was so much wittier, even if it did have annoying novelty aspects. Produced by Pete Solley.

### KATE BUSH
**The Dreaming** (EMI)

Sat In Your Lap
There Goes A
 Tenner
Pull Out The Pin
Suspended In
 Gaffa
Leave It Open

The Dreaming
Night Of The
 Swallow
Houdini
Get Out Of My
 House

A year in the making, Kate Bush's new album is a highly ambitious stab at self-conscious artistry. Blending weird elements of ethnic rhythms and sounds with almost parodic vocals ranging from shrieks to whispers, this is definitely not an easy set of songs to absorb, with no single concession to market exigencies. Impressionistic at the best of times, the album has few familiar hooks or potential hit singles and, as such, one should admire Kate's unnerving courage. However, the mixture doesn't really come off and, at the end of the day, one is left with patchy memories of what could have been, while the evident mistakes dominate the listener's picture of the record. Admirable individualism, though. Produced by Kate Bush.

KATE BUSH

# C

### TANE CAIN
**Tane Cain** (RCA)
Striking new American songstress on an easy-listening outing with mild rock touches to keep the pulse going after encountering her likeness on the album cover. Produced by Jonathan Cain and Keith Olsen.

### JOHN CALE
**Music For A New Society** (Ze/Island)
A striking return to form by John Cale with an ascetic, almost despairing collection of laments and existential ballads. The sparse instrumentation recalls the bleak production job he was responsible for on Nico's 'Desertshore'. Solemn modern dirges; music doesn't come any harder but I beg you to listen. This is an important album by a sadly neglected musician who deserves more than just cult status. Produced by John Cale.

## THE CANNIBALS
**Bone To Pick** (Hit)
Garage punk R&B. Badly recorded injection of voodooish rockabilly. Energetic but not very innovative.

## CAPTAIN BEEFHEART
**Ice Cream For The Crows** (Virgin/Epic)
Familiar broken rhythms and quirky tunes from the good Captain. Much the same as before: you either like it or hate it. Eccentric poet on free jazz/rock improvisatory meanderings. Nobody does it like Beefheart! Produced by Don Van Vliet.

## CAPTAIN SENSIBLE
**Women And Captain First** (A&M)
A whole album of Captain Sensible? After the cloying strains of the surprisingly successful 'Happy Days', the mind rebels at the thought of more, but on attentive listening this proves to be a nicely varied set of novelty items and genuinely touching childhood memories set to innocuous melodies and music. Innocent fun (or is it? What about those collaborations with Crass and Robyn Hitchcock . . .). Produced by Tony Mansfield.

## CARAVAN
**Back To Front** (Kingdom)
The Canterbury art-rockers reform (have they ever been away?) with their initial line-up. Studious and predictable. Produced by Caravan.

## KIM CARNES
**Voyeur** (EMI)

A follow-up to the mega 'Bette Davis Eyes' hit, 'Voyeur', both the album and title track, cleverly exploits Carnes' distinctive raspy voice and aggressive melancholy sultriness. There is a hard rock edge of much of the material which is to be admired. Quality stuff throughout. Produced by Val Garay.

## LARRY CARLTON
**Sleepwalking** (WEA)
Somnolent jazz funk from a veteran jazz guitarist now slumming down these mean crossover streets. Forgettable.

## CARMEL
**Carmel** (Red Flame)
Debut mini-album by new British singer with an appealing style of torch song in the grand cabaret of old tradition. Pared down accompaniment suits her to a tee and the old-fashioned result spells class in large letters. Produced by Ablette.

## PAUL CARRACK
**Suburban Voodoo** (Epic)

Overwhelmingly pleasant debut album by the British musician known for his past affiliations with Ace and (briefly) Squeeze. Good time rock and roll with a bow to the blues and a nod to smokey pub backrooms. Unambitious but perfectly done. Produced by Nick Lowe.

## MARTIN CARTHY
**Out Of The Cut** (Topic)
Acoustic folk from one of Britain's great stylists. Produced by Jerry Boys and Martin Carthy.

## JOHNNY CASH
**The Adventures Of Johnny Cash** (Columbia)
Reunion between Cash and his former Sun producer yields what is possibly his best album in a long time. The usual assured delivery and tight orchestration on the customary blend of sad love songs and train dirges. Produced by Jack Clement.

## CASIOPEA
**Mint Jams** (Alfa)
Japanese jazz-funk group recorded live. Mellow to soporific. Pointless album in an already crowded field of mediocrities. Produced by Shunsuke Miyazumi.

## LACKSLEY CASTELL
**Morning Glory** (Negus Roots)
Gentle reggae vocalising by a new Jamaican singer, not unlike Hugh Mundell in tone and voice.

## CATHOLIC GIRLS
**Catholic Girls** (MCA)
Strong debut for new US East Coast all-girl group. Tougher than the Go-Go's, more in the Robin Lane, Chrissie Hynde tough-girl mould and very effective at that. Vocalist Gail Petersen stands out. Produced by Evan Pace.

## MARSHALL CHAPMAN
**Take It On Home** (Rounder)
First album on an independent label for one of my favourite maverick country rock singers of the female persuasion, after a couple of overlooked outings with major companies. Lean, well-paced hard rockers with swing and humour. Not to be overlooked too long.

## CHARGE
**Caged And Staged** (Trikont)
Recorded live in Germany, eighteen blustering tracks by a stalwart British band still caught in that old timewarp of punk. High-level energy and a minimum of sensitivity. Formula stuff but good within those parameters.

## CHARGED GBH
**City Baby Attacked By Rats** (Clay)
Hopelessly confused outing full of sturm and drang from punk revivalists. Loud, nasty and vibrant.

## AVA CHERRY
**A Streetcar Named Desire** (Capitol)
Surprisingly varied first album by a black US singer better known for backing Bowie some years back. Useful synthesiser backdrop to a collection of sultry love songs with just a hint of disco. Never completely convinces but always interesting. Produced by Bob Esty.

## THE CHURCH
**Blurred Crusade** (Carrere)
Second dollop of neo-psychedelia by Australian band. Romantic and fresh if you can overcome the naivety. Pop as it was. Produced by Bob Clearmountain.

## STANLEY CLARKE
**Let Me Know You** (Epic)
Jazz veteran now pandering to the pop audience with a tasteful but oh-so-sterile mixture of dance-floor soul, mainstream rock and vacuous lyrics in the old Motown tradition. Carlos Santana guests on guitar and injects some momentary fire into the dullish proceedings. Produced by Stanley Clarke.

## JIMMY CLIFF
**Special** (CBS/Columbia)
First album for a major label by the veteran reggae performer. No rough edges and the customary pleasant mix of sweet, lilting melodies and understated political

commentary. Sly Dunbar, Ansell Collins and Roy Wood help out. Produced by Chris Kimsey.

## COCKNEY REJECTS
**The Wild Ones** (Akai)
Assembly-line punk/heavy metal. A familiar din. Produced by Pete Way.

## COCTEAU TWINS
**Garlands** (4AD)
British experimental trio strong on dirge and trance meanderings. Too many Siouxsie and Joy Division influences as yet undigested for the Cocteau Twins to make a genuine impact.

## DAVID ALLAN COE
**David Allan Coe** (Columbia)
Fine interpretative album by a neglected country artist who can pack a mean punch. Songs by Kristofferson, Jimmy Buffett, B. J. Thomas, etc. . . Produced by Billy Sherrill.

## THE COMSAT ANGELS
**Fiction** (Polydor)
Third album by one of the more promising young British bands. The preoccupation with SF subject matter continues unabated and 'After the Rain', the post-nuclear opening track, sets a bleak mood for the rest of the platter. Much the same as before as the Comsat Angels fail to achieve lift-off from the doomed disaster area of entropy rock. Intense as ever, but seemingly unable to shift into any higher (joyful?) gear. Impressive but despairing. Produced by Peter Wilson and the Comsat Angels.

## CONEY HATCH
**Coney Hatch** (Anthem/Mercury)
Strong rocking pop fare from a new Canadian quartet. Unpleasant misogynist lyrics mar an otherwise competent album. Produced by Kim Mitchell.

## EARL THOMAS CONLEY
**Somewhere Between Right And Wrong** (RCA)
Uniformly polished album of self-penned country material by a particularly stylish US performer. Sensual mood dominates. Produced by Nelson Larkin and Earl Thomas Conley.

## CHICK COREA
**Touchstone** (Warners)
Assured return to the fusion fold by the jazz pianist. Smooth use of electronics and famous friends: Stanley Clarke, Lenny White, Lee Konitz, Paco DeLucia, Al Di-Meola and Gayle Moran. Small scale and controlled. Produced by Chick Corea.

## JOSIE COTTON
**Convertible Music** (Elektra)
Good-time rock from a peppish new US

singer. High school love ditties and infectious hooks abound on this old-fashioned album of simple but effective values. Uncluttered production and soaring harmonies. An unassuming success. Produced by Bobby and Larson Paine.

## CRASS
**Christ The Album** (Crass)

Apocalyptic boxed set of two albums by the most fervent British exponents of the uncompromising punk ethos. Full of fire, venom and anarchistic hate against systems of authority, the package comes (at a very low, accessible price) with a poster and a detailed booklet. The first album features 15 new pieces, while the second is a mix of live tracks, radio tapings and general miscellania. Indignant thrash of sustained intensity from the other side of the road. Unique.

## CRAZY HOUSE
**They Dance Like This From As Far Off As The Crazy House** (TW)
Independent British UK electro-pop duo on virgin outing. Confused, naive but appealing in its simplicity.

## CREATION REBEL
**Lows And Highs** (Cherry Red)
Patchy album of experimental studio reggae. Produced by Adrian Sherwood.

## CREEDENCE CLEARWATER REVIVAL
**Chooglin'** (Fantasy)
Yet another 'Greatest Hits' compilation of the many hits of the late and lamented CCR. Perennial classics that stand up to the test of time. Come back, John Fogerty, all is forgiven. Produced by John Fogerty.

## STEVE CROPPER
**Night After Night** (MCA)
Laidback Memphis soul-rock by a crew of seasoned veterans. Guitarist Steve Cropper reveals new talents on vocals on this pleasant collection of rhythm and blues in a finger lickin' mood. Produced by Steve Cropper and Bruce Robb.

## CROSBY, STILLS AND NASH
**Daylight Again** (Atlantic)
Return of the golden-voiced California trio after a period of five years in the solo doldrums. The sweetness is still there, mellow and infuriating; the musicianship is impeccable and the songs are just plain boring. Some comebacks aren't what they used to be! Ghastly sci-fi cover with no bearing whatsoever on any of the songs on the album. Produced by C, S & N, Stanley Johnson, Steve Gursky and Craig Doerge.

## CROWN HEIGHTS AFFAIR
**Think Positive!** (De-Lite)
Muscular disco dance-floor workouts by large black formation. Smooth and fluent, ideal for Saturday night outings in search of both energy and sentiments. Produced by Raymond Reid and William Anderson.

## ANDRE CYMONE
**Livin' In The New Wave** (FC)
Prince's bass player on solo outing. An interesting blend of soul and electronics. Robotic funk at its best. Produced by Andre Cymone.

# D

## LACY J. DALTON
**16th Avenue** (Columbia)
Quiet, almost philosophical record from one of the most popular US country singers around. Bluesy, laidback sound and attractive selection. Produced by Billy Sherrill.

## THE DAMNED
**Strawberries** (Bronze)
Pleasantly varied album from old punk veterans now basking in the limelight of Captain Sensible's chart success. His whimsical tone permeates this surprising album of gentle pop material in a highly traditional mould. Produced by the Damned and Hugh Jones.

DANCE CLASS

### THE DANCE
**Soul Force** (Statik)
Quirky New York new wave funk group. Already their second album of jerky dance tracks. Deserves better than the bargain bins. Produced by the Dance.

### DANCE CLASS
**Dance Class** (A&M)
Mediocre new wavish fillers from a Newcastle band badly in need of inspiration. Average pop.

### THE DANSE SOCIETY
**Seduction** (Society)
Theatrical debut outing by a new band from Yorkshire. Treading a thin line between bombast and fashion, this is a highly ambitious album that doesn't always come off but is worth the detour. We might hear about Danse Society again, methinks.

### THE DARK
**The Living End** (Fall Out)
Mini-album by a now-defunct British band. Dark, doom-laden punk anthems recorded live. Achingly sincere and dishevelled. For the future historians of the after-punk era only.

### THE DAWGS
**My Town** (Star Rhythm)
Boston bar band playing in the style of twenty years ago and no worse for wear. Fun stuff, no questions asked. Produced by Cub Coda.

### DAYTON
**Hot Fun** (Liberty)
Clean-cut US funk in the Shalamar-style. Bootsy guests on a couple of tracks. Their third album already. Fun but no real progress down these well-trodden soul avenues.

### DeBARGE
**All This Love** (Gordy)
Jackson Family clones. Same style, same tunes (almost), same town. Thanks but no thanks. Produced by Iris Gordy and Eldra DeBarge.

### THE DECORATORS
**Tablets** (Red Flame)

Tablets

Modernist new British band with strong saxophone player in a dense, doomy set of mostly self-penned material. Stark arrangements and moody atmosphere. A promising debut.

### DEEP PURPLE
**Live In London** (Harvest)
Live recording by the eponymous precursors of classy heavy metal, going back to 1974 and the band's second line-up. All the hits, but haven't we heard them all before in god knows how many live or studio combinations? Produced by Pete Dauncey and Jeff Griffin.

### DEMON
**The Unexpected Guest** (Carrere)
Satanic dose of heavy metal. Play loud and stay out of the room. . . Produced by Pete Hinton.

### DEODATO
**Happy Hour** (Warners)
Sleek, familiar instrumental disco workouts (with background vocals; a first for the Brazilian virtuoso). Crisp and funky. Produced by Eumir Deodato.

### DEPECHE MODE
**A Broken Frame** (Mutesirc)
Second album for the fresh-faced Basildon electro-poppers, although this time without the composing talents of Vince Clarke now prospering with Yazoo. 'Tinky-bonk whimsy' said *Smash Hits* and I can find no better definition for these gently crafted, innocent songs in a teenage pop tradition that goes a long way back. Pleasant but cloying. Produced by Daniel Miller.

### THE DESTRUCTORS
**Exercise The Demons Of Youth** (Illuminated)
18 intense tracks by a new band from Peterborough. Rough and somewhat slipshod but trying hard and sincere.

### KEVIN ROWLAND AND DEXY'S MIDNIGHT RUNNERS
**Too-Rye-Ay** (Mercury)

| | |
|---|---|
| The Celtic Soul Brothers | Plan B |
| Let's Make This Precious | I'll Show You |
| | Liars A To E |
| All In All | Until I Believe In My Soul |
| Jackie Wilson Said Old | Come On Eileen |

The con of the year. The distasteful little Mr Rowland has now abandoned his soul-boy working-class image for a newfangled (and unshaven) persona paying dubious homage to his Irish roots in the guise of a fiddle player with dollops of insincere anguish. He isn't the Van Morrison he wants to be, and this sad album goes down in my books (and I'm in a minority if one is to believe the charts) as a vast compendium of posturings . . . and bad, derivative music. Directed (and that's a pointer to the pretentiousness of the enterprise, if ever there was one) by Clive Langer, Alan Winstanley and Kevin Rowland.

### TOM DICKIE AND THE DESIRES
**The Eleventh Hour** (Mercury)

Clean-cut pop from a new American group. Anonymous but quietly effective; a nice way of wasting three-quarters of an hour pinned to the radio. Rock and roll as she is spoken.

### STEVE DOUGLAS
**Hot Sax** (Fantasy)

Veteran saxophone player on a solo instrumental outing. Impeccably put together and brimming with classy musicianship. Still very boring I found (and no, please not another version of 'Peter Gunn'!). Produced by Steve Douglas and Phil Kaffel.

SHEENA EASTON

KEVIN ROWLAND: DEXY'S MIDNIGHT RUNNERS

### DOWNCHILD
**Blood Run Hot** (Attic)

Thirteen-to-the-dozen bar boogie band reworking those 12 bar tunes until hell freezes over.

### MIKEY DREAD AND CO.
**Rockers Vibration** (Dread At The Controls)

Dub reggae outing featuring the usual crowd. Most of these dub records seem interchangeable. Not only does the music all sound the same to old-fashioned Western ears, but the musicians always appear to be identical. . .

### THE DUB SYNDICATE
**Pounding System** (On U Sound)

Experimental dub, with a generous helping of sound effects. Produced by Adrian Sherwood.

### SLY DUNBAR
**Sly-Go-Ville** (Taxi)

Standard reggae outing by a session veteran who has appeared on probably half this year's Jamaican records. Despite heavyweight friends in the studio, all rather lacklustre. Produced by Sly Dunbar and Robbie Shakespeare.

### ERROL DUNKLEY
**Special Request** (Carousel)

More anonymous reggae. Solid, reliable and bland. Produced by Errol Dunkley.

# E

### SHEENA EASTON
**Money, Madness And Music** (EMI)

Thanks to shrewd career management, the young Scottish waif has now con-

quered America and this third album follows in strong Grammy-AOR mood. Up-tempo rockers of a very safe and sterile nature. Sheena still seems to be more at ease on the slower, ballad material but this calculated album of high superficial gloss will find its market with ease. Produced by Christopher Neil.

### JACKIE EDWARDS
**King Of The Ghetto** (Black Music)

Veteran Jamaican crooner now into a strong reggae mood with an assured album. Both classic and innovative. Usual complement of star backing musicians.

### EEK-A-MOUSE
**Skidip!** (Greensleeves)

Toasting reggae tracks with Roots Radics in strong control. Rambling, salty, druggy references. Produced by Linval Thompson.

### 805
**Stand In Line** (RCA)

Cautious, uninspired new American power pop ensemble. A set of easy options; not for export (I hope). Produced by Dennis MacKay.

### ELOY
**Planets** (Heavy Metal)

German sword and sorcery heavy metal. Not quite on the Wagnerian scale but a loud and dirty barrage of guitar and synthesiser outbursts. There's a concept hiding in there somewhere, but I'll be damned if I can pinpoint it. Produced by Frank Bornemann and Eloy.

### THE EX
**History Is What's Happening** (More)

Barricade-manifesto punk rock from Holland. Sincere and boringly pointless.

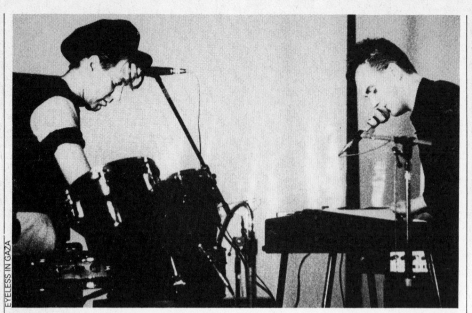

EYELESS IN GAZA

## EYELESS IN GAZA
**Drumming The Beating Heart**
(Cherry Red)
Third Cherry Red (one of the most enterprising and interesting British independent labels) album for a young British group who, although deeply entrenched in the electro-rock niche, easily transcend its limitations with a healthy knack for melodies and feeling. Brief, dramatic songs and sounds that will stay with you for a long time. Produced by the group and John Rivers.

# F

## FAIRPORT CONVENTION
**Moat On The Ledge** (Woodworm)
A live recording of a Fairport Convention reunion with many (but alas not all, what with Sandy Denny now dead and Ian Matthews in the US) of the past line-ups present. Exuberant and full of memories, if a trifle rough at the edges. Produced by Dave Pegg and Simon Nicol.

## THE FALL
**Room To Live** (Kamera)
Budget-priced offering from the prolific, uncompromising, British experimentalists. Quirky, idiosyncratic and earnest. Much the same as before, this slipshod effort won't gain Mark Smith's band new fans, but the regulars will like it. Produced by Kay O'Sullivan.

## GEORGIE FAME/ANNIE ROSS/ HOAGY CARMICHAEL
**In Hoagland** (DRG)
A homage to the late Hoagy Carmichael featuring a selection of his songs in a jazzy mood by Georgie Fame and Annie Ross. Also includes Carmichael's last record-

ings. An affectionate album. Produced by Georgie Fame, Rod Slade and John Lambe.

## FAMILY PLAYERS
**I Love Funk 'n' Roll** (MCA)
Unpretentious funk workouts (and a Joan Jett 'I Love Rock 'n' Roll' parody) recorded in New Orleans. Produced by Isaac Bolden.

## THE FIBONACCIS
**The Fibonaccis** (Index)
A seven-song EP with a quirky tribute to spaghetti westerns ('Sergio Leone') and odd, melodic little songs in a deliberately minor but clever vein. Fun. Produced by the group and Philip Randal.

## THE FITS
**You're Nothing You're Nowhere**
(Rondelet)
Competent, hostile British punk with rough edges and metallic, doomy outlook on life. Par for the course.

## FLEETWOOD MAC
**Mirage** (Warners)

| | |
|---|---|
| Love In Store | Empire State |
| Can't Go Back | Straight Back |
| That's Alright | Hold Me |
| Book Of Love | Oh Diane |
| Gypsy | Eyes Of The World |
| Only Over You | Wish You Were Here |

First studio album for Fleetwood Mac since the ambitious double-set 'Tusk' (which I enjoyed very much, despite many reviewers' reservations). Generally bland but impeccably performed set of songs and sweet melodies, rising harmonies and jingle-jangle guitar work. Quiet, unassuming but in the long run disappointing album. Fleetwood Mac might be the epitome of California cool music but this

new offering lacks the fire and life to make it as memorable as earlier platinum (or pre-platinum) efforts. Produced by Lindsey Buckingham, Richard Dashut, Ken Caillat and Fleetwood Mac.

## THE FLESH EATERS
**Forever Come Today** (Ruby)
Earth-moving primeval rock 'n' roll from a new California outfit led by Chris D. Literate, romantic and full of fire. A good one. Produced by Chris Desjardins.

## STEVE FORBERT
**Steve Forbert** (Nemperor)
Gutless new album for Forbert, once one of my great white US hopes. Indifferent material (bar an interesting cover of Jackie de Shannon's 'When You Walk In The Room'), glossy, vacuous production and a general lack of commitment. Ever since his brilliant debut album, Forbert has been going downhill fast in my books, and this collection confirms the slippery trend. Produced by Steve Burgh.

## TENNESSEE ERNIE FORD
**Back Where I Belong** (Applause)
Country old-timer with a subtle mix of old and newer songs. Comfortable, middle-of-the-road Nashville fodder. Produced by Jerry Gillespie and Buck Ford.

## 48 CHAIRS
**70% Paranoid** (Relentless)
Manchester band on initial effort. Synthesisers, brass and the whole kitchen sink. Pleasantly poppish. Produced by John Scott and Tony Roberts.

## THE FOUR TOPS
**One More Mountain** (Casablanca)
Formula soul from a group who've seen better days. Just going through the sentimental motions, I fear. A bit of a mess.

## PETER FRAMPTON
**The Art Of Control** (A&M)
In a vain attempt to recapture past glories and audiences, Peter Frampton has taken

PETER FRAMPTON

a snarling leaf from the new wave book of flash and suffer. Nervous contribution from Mark Goldenberg, from the under-rated Cretones. The result is an unsatisfying hybrid with Frampton never quite sounding right for the part. Straight towards the cut-out bins is a mighty mean road to go. Produced by Eddie Kramer and Peter Frampton.

### ARETHA FRANKLIN
**Jump To It** (Arista)
Sophisticated excursion by the first lady of soul into the murkier borderline areas of disco/funk. Duet with Levi Stubbs of the Four Tops is prominently featured on this short, 8-song collection of dance material with a gentle vengeance. A commercial and artistic success. Produced by Luther Vandross.

### FRIDA
**Something's Going On** (Epic/Atlantic)

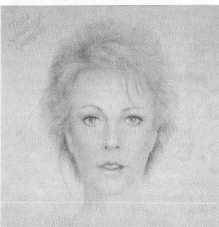

Abba's redhead warbler in her first English-language solo album. Clever choice of songs from British and Swedish sources and the Phil Collins connection

ropes in the classy Earth Wind and Fire brass section (although he also spoils the broth with a cringe-cringe duet). Diffident, calculated and professional. Produced by Phil Collins.

### DAVID FRIZELL
**The Family's Fine, But This One's All Mine** (Warners)
Standard country and western fare by a performer who, in fact, seldom appears solo these days (viz the album's title). Innocuously pleasant. Produced by Snuff Garrett and Steve Dorff.

---

# G

---

### PETER GABRIEL
**Peter Gabriel** (Charisma) – **Security** (Geffen)

| | |
|---|---|
| Rhythm Of The Heat | Shock The Monkey |
| San Jacinto | Lay Your Hands On Me |
| I Have The Touch | Wallflower |
| The Family And The Fishing Net | Kiss Of Life |

Truly a thing of beauty. No mincing of words. Gabriel's fourth solo outing since departing from the Genesis fold offers a beautiful blend of haunting melodies with a strong African rhythm mood and a shimmering but discreet touch of electronic wizardry. The result is both adventurous and reliable and the often incongruous subject matter ('Shock The Monkey') takes on almost menacing, brooding dimensions. Experience; I envy you the pleasure. Produced by David Lord and Peter Gabriel.

### GANG'S BACK
**Gang's Back** (Handshake)
California sextet playing in the hallowed fields of funk and R&B. Polished to shining, aseptic production with every piece of brass in the right place. Strong pop leanings should make this a popular item with white audiences. Produced by Barney Perkins and Tony Coleman.

### GEZA X
**You Goddam Kids** (Final Gear)
Eclectic power pop with a strong individualistic touch from the California boondocks. Produced by Geza X.

### THE GHOULIES
**Dogged By Dogma** (Lounging)
New Welsh band with sundry guests (Dave Stewart, Green from Scritti Politti). Led by Charlie Summers, they work their way through idiosyncratic melodies and intricate songs with gentle abandon. Produced by Ben and Charlie.

### GILBERT, LEWIS AND MILLS
**Mzui** (Cherry Red)
Aural doodling by Wire survivors and illustrator Russell Mills (Hi, Russ!) on the occasion of the setting-up of an exhibition. Rather boring out of context.

### GILLAN
**Magic** (Virgin)
Intelligently watered-down heavy metal by a set of old troopers. What it loses in occasional bombast, the music gains in subtlety. Pleasant in a most predictable way. But why can't Gillan ever get a better deal for their cover illustrations. Bloody awful sleeve again. . . Produced by Mick Glossop.

### MICKEY GILLEY
**Put Your Dreams Away** (Epic)
Crooning country cowboy who still knows how to rip up the honky-tonk from time to time. Ballads predominate this time around however, a genre in which he isn't quite so adept. Produced by Jim Ed Norman.

### TOMPALL AND THE GLASER BROTHERS
**After All These Years** (Elektra)
Polished country outlaw music. Soaring harmonies and stronger than usual melodies make this a fan's delight. Produced by Jimmy Bowen.

### THE GO-GO'S
**Vacation** (IRS)

| | |
|---|---|
| Vacation | Get Up And Go |
| He's So Strange | This Old Feeling |
| Girl Of 100 Lists | Cool Jerk |
| We Don't Get Along | The Way You |
| I Think It's Me | Dance |
| It's Everything But | Beatnik Dance |
| Partytime | Worlds Away |

Summer sun tunes from the girls who created last year's big surprise with their debut album of unassuming pop ditties. This is very much a follow-up offering the punter much more of the same formula. It's full of fizz, jangling guitar work and soppy, girl-meets-boy lyrics but the initial freshness is beginning to wear thin giving

GO-GO'S

the nice gals in the Go-Go's a bit of a fabricated image. A record to hum along to with a smile on your lips, but the centre isn't soft, just very empty. Watch out for terminal cuteness. Produced by Richard Gohterer.

### ROBERT GORDON
**Too Fast To Live, Too Young To Die** (RCA)
A mixture of old and newer songs for the rockabilly veteran now breaking through into a tentative new pop market with de-

ceptive ease. Assured and easy-going, but conceals a touch of fire. Various producers.

### THE GRASSROOTS
**Powers Of The Night** (MCA)
Rob Grill returns as lead singer of the quartet whose hour of glory came back in the venerable sixties. Bland mainstream pop. Produced by Evan Pace and Leon Tsilis.

### GRIFFIN AND SYLVESTER
**Griffin and Sylvester** (Polydor)
A collaboration between Bread and Hollies past vocalists. No surprises in the amiable nature of the resulting album: laid-back harmonies and super-bland songs with a strong touch in unmemorable melodies. A turkey. Produced by Griffin and Sylvester.

### THE GUN CLUB
**Miami** (Animal)
The Gun Club have toned down their manic energy for this second album under the auspices of Chris Stein's enterprising new label. But there's still enough steel and muscle on display (and the inspiration of John Fogerty feels stronger than ever) and one can recommend this set of blues-based rockers to the most jaded ears. One of the best new American

bands. California doesn't deserve them: their brimstone aura belongs more to the New York Lower East Side! Produced by Chris Stein.

### BUDDY GUY/JUNIOR WELLS
**Drinkin' TNT 'n' Smokin' Dynamite** (Blind Pig)
Live blues date recorded in Montreux, Switzerland in 1974. Unremarkable if reliable performances from masters of the form. Vintage picking for the fans. Produced by Bill Wyman.

# H

### MERLE HAGGARD AND GEORGE JONES
**A Taste Of Yesterday's Wine** (Epic)
Interesting set of duets by old country performers usually reminiscing in bittersweet tones about the past and the perils of ageing. Strong on the melancholy but an intriguing combination all the same. Produced by Billy Sherrill.

### KIT HAIN
**Looking For You** (Mercury)
Past member of the short-lived duo Marshall-Hain, Kit is a British singer with a characteristic style halfway between smooth ballads and gentle rockers that fits into today's commercial criterions with surprising ease. Nice. She'll have another hit one day; she deserves it. Produced by Mike Thorne.

### HARLEQUIN
**One False Move** (Columbia)
Faceless power pop by a Canadian group already on their third album. Produced by Jack Douglas.

### GARY HARRISON
**To The Night** (Unicorn)
New American singer/songwriter still trying to shake off his influences (Springsteen is one). Good sense of rhythm and catchy melodies. We might hear from him again. Produced by Paul Leim, Joe Chemay and Ed Barton.

### LISA HARTMAN
**Letterock** (RCA)
Once known as a singer, Lisa Hartman emigrated to TV soap opera land and now relies on media exposure for this return to the grooves. Where she once belonged to country ranks, she now rocks along with the best with aggression and confidence. Effective. Produced by Denis Pregnolato.

### HAWKWIND
**Church Of Hawkwind** (RCA)
Mostly a compendium of past glories from the hippie band that can never die. Fans only.

### HAWKS
**30 Seconds Over Otho** (Columbia)
Second album of competent but faceless rock (REO Speedwagon, Journey, school of) by a midwestern band. Produced by John Ryan.

### BONNIE HAYES WITH THE WILD COMBO
**Good Clean Fun** (Slash)
Beach party, West Coast music from a new San Francisco band who've emerged smiling from the underground circuit without a trace of punk contamination. Full of fizz and enthusiasm. Better than the Go-Go's who occupy a similar territory of the pop weltanschaung. Produced by Steve Savage.

### HEADPINS
**Turn It Loud** (Atco)
Fierce power pop barrage. Clean-cut and ambitious, this new band are fronted by the defiant Darby Mills and know exactly where they are going. Produced by Brian MacLeod and Bill Henderson.

### MARK HEARD
**Victims Of The Age** (Home Sweet Home)
Socially-conscious rockers with a background of shrieking and wailing guitarwork by an American singer on a usually inspirational label. Lots of guts. Produced by Mark Heard.

### RICHARD HELL AND THE VOIDOIDS
**Destiny Street** (Red Star)
Five years after 'Black Generation', Richard Hell's second album. The New York punk venom and dissonances are still overwhelmingly present, but time has passed by and rendered the whole exercise particularly redundant. This is a courageous attempt at recapturing the past and Hell's voice has never been more weary and disillusioned, while Quine and Naux on guitars also share in the ephemeral glory. Worth looking out for despite my reservations. S for (absolute) Sincerity. Produced by Alan Betrock.

### JIMI HENDRIX
**The Jimi Hendrix Concerts** (CBS/Warners)
Double set of vintage performances (authorised by the Hendrix estate) from old concerts in San Francisco, London, San Diego, Berkeley and New York. 11 classic cuts for both Hendrix completists and those who never did experience him alive; all the well-known hits are present. Produced by Alan Douglas.

### DON HENLEY
**I Can't Stand Still** (Asylum)

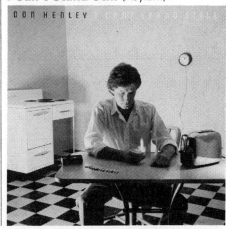

As the Eagles go the solo route, Don Henley's first foray easily outclasses Glenn Frey's similar effort. Where Frey only conserved the terminal mellowness of the group, Henley tries harder and injects a necessary sense of immediacy into his songs. The general sound is as lush and smoothly polished as the group, but Henley has things to say (about America, politics, himself) and says them well. Produced by Don Henley, Danny Kortchmar and Greg Ladanyi.

### HI-FI
**Moods for Mallards** (First American)
Out of nowhere, one of the surprise arrivals of the year. This is the album no one noticed. On an unknown independent US label a new group featuring Ian Matthews and David Surkamp, the high-pitched voice singer of the late, late Pavlov's Dog. An unusual combination at best, this works incredibly well even if one pines after the dulcet tones of Matthews' earlier efforts. Based in Seattle, the band coalesce various styles with jangling guitar and organ to the fore, while the two lead singers surprisingly cannot be distinguished from each other. Strong melodies and songs make this the major sleeper of 1982 in my humble books. Produced by Ian Matthews.

### HIGH FASHION
**Feelin' Lucky** (Capitol)
Studio-manufactured disco and highly sophisticated at that. Fronted by singers Erick McClinton, Alyson Williams and Melissa Morgan, this is exuberant dance-floor material with a couple of stings in the tail. Produced by Jacques Fred Petrus and Mauro Malavasi.

### LIGHTNIN' HOPKINS
**Strums The Blues** (Score)
Representative compilation of class blues performances by the late black pioneer.

### HUGHES-THRALL
**Hughes-Thrall** (Boulevard)
Made-to-measure chart rock by transfers from Deep Purple and the Pat Travers Band. Safe, mainstream thrash with all the right notes and shrieks. Doesn't amount to much. Produced by Andy Johns, Hughes-Thrall and Rob Fraboni.

### CON HUNLEY
**Oh Girl** (Warners)
Country artist moves to sunny LA and crosses over the rock borderline. Strong rhythm and blues feel with Chi-Lites and Four Tops cover versions. Not bad, but a trifle calculated. Produced by Steve Dorff.

### THE HUNT
**Thrill Of The Kill** (Passport)
Fifth-gear Canadian heavy metal.

THE GUN CLUB

**89**

## ROBERT HUNTER
**Promontory Rider** (Relix)

Best of compilation for the quirky but decidedly underrated lyricist for the Grateful Dead. Collects material from his first four albums (one of which never seems to have surfaced anywhere near my shores – ah, woe is me). From sturdy drinking songs to accapella dirges and poignant ballads. Will sell to all Dead-heads but deserves a much larger audience: in his own right, Hunter is a remarkable writer and very original singer.

## CINDY HURT
**Talk To Me** (Churchill)
Lachrymose country warbling by a lady with a lot of problems (at any rate in her lyrics . . .). Produced by Bob Milsap and Joe Bob Barnhill.

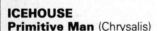

## ICEHOUSE
**Primitive Man** (Chrysalis)

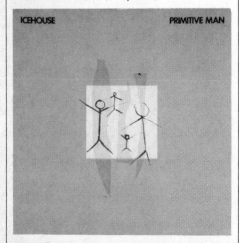

Although strongly reminiscent at times of David Bowie and Roxy Music, this second album for Iva Davies' Australian group (with a drastic line-up change since the debut LP) remains a strong and evocative

IVA DAVIES: ICEHOUSE

collection of atmospheric vignettes. Seductive. Produced by Iva Davies and Keith Forsey.

## BILLY IDOL
**Billy Idol** (Chrysalis)
The would-be angelic-looking blonde singer from punk loser band Generation X deserts British shores to seek fame and fortune in the American colonies where he devises this, his first solo album. Formula easy-listening pop replete with riffs and sundry commercial hooks. Well-done but calculatingly familiar to the ears. Could be anybody. Produced by Keith Forsey.

## IMAGINATION
**In The Heat Of The Night** (R&B/MCA)
Infectiously danceable funk from a British trio who have been reaping a fine measure of success. Lousy leopard-skin and Roman armour-plate image but the funk is on course like a rutting express train. 'Just An Illusion' leads the toe-tapping honours. Clever guys, Imagination! Produced by Tony Swain and Steve Jolley.

## INNER CITY UNIT
**Punkadelic** (Flicknife)
Led by ex-Hawkwind stalwart Nik Turner. Punkadelic are a powerful and eclectic British band combining psychedelics, power pop and disco riffs with effectiveness. The result never amounts to much but it's fun music nonetheless. These tracks were recorded over a long period of time and bear witness to the band's progress. The humour (often political), you'll either like or dislike. Don't expect any middle-ground.

## WELTON IRIE
**New Style** (Pioneer International)
Second album of DJ rap on the thriving reggae beat. Considered to be one of the best around.

## GREGORY ISAACS
**Mr. Isaacs** (Shanachie)
Older Isaacs reggae with a dash of politics and social commentary. Harmonies by the Heptones and rhythm by Evolutional Revolutionaries. Produced by Gregory Isaacs.

GREGORY ISAACS

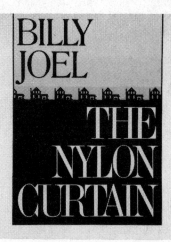

### GREGORY ISAACS
**Night Nurse** (Island)
Lyrical and lovingly-crafted set of new songs by one of the leading reggae singers left since the death of Bob Marley. Less of a preoccupation with ganja and Jamaican politics allow Isaacs to devote most of the songs to the pleasures and fears of love and this is an ideal field for his soft, crooning vocals dripping with expressiveness on every chord. Produced by 'Flabba' Holt and 'Style' Scott.

### THE ISLEY BROTHERS
**The Isley Brothers** (Epic/T-Neck)
A return to form for the Isley Brothers with a sure-fire combustible set of up-tempo funk and dance numbers which they tackle with their characteristic smoothness. Age doesn't appear to affect them one iota. Produced by the Isley Brothers.

# J

### JACK OF DIAMONDS
**Dodge City** (Ransom)
A three years in the making independent release album by a group of polished American rockers. Unspectacular but effective. A touch of heavy metal here, a pinch of funk rhythms there, stir in some jazz inflections and presto! we have an album. Produced by Jack of Diamonds.

### JERMAINE JACKSON
**Let Me Tickle Your Fancy** (Motown)
Michael Jackson's brother gets into higher gear for an entry into the major league. Carefully crafted material, contributions by Devo, Syreeta and clever choice of material make this his best album. Smooth soul and funk with grace and elegance, this is often reminiscent of Stevie Wonder. Produced by Jermaine Jackson and Berry Gordy.

### STONEWALL JACKSON
**Solid Stonewall** (Phonorama)
Traditional country for the genre die-hards. Assured and predictable. Produced by Pete Drake.

### JEWEL
**Cut 'n' Polished** (Erect)
Polished rhythm and blues halfway between the brassy fire of Earth, Wind. . . and the suave elegance of Philadalephia International black acts. Mellow but pleasant. Produced by Jim Porter.

### BILLY JOEL
**The Nylon Curtain** (CBS/Columbia)

| | |
|---|---|
| Allentown | She's Right On Time |
| Laura | A Room Of Our Own |
| Pressure | Surprises |
| Goodbye Saigon | Scandinavian Skies |
| | Where's The Orchestra |

Mature, reflective album from Billy Joel, his first studio work in 2½ years. Moving from small-town heartaches and personal relationships to a grander scale of political commentary (the Vietnam war as seen by its lowly US participants in the ambitious but effective 'Goodbye Saigon'), Joel appears in a more sombre mood and without the annoying bombast and aggressiveness that marred many of his past successes. The album gives out a sad general feeling which shares an uneasy seat with the often Broadway-like orchestrations. Could well be a very important collection of songs. Time will judge. Produced by Phil Ramone.

### KARIN JONES
**Under The Influence of Love** (Handshake)
Anonymous black soul outing by a new artist. Danceable; big ballads; cluttered backing. Produced by (hold your breath) Howard King, Ed Moore, Jim Tyrrell, Eddie Levert, Dennis Williams and Bruce Hawes.

### TOM JONES
**Country** (Mercury)
Old crooner seeks new horizons. Competent if laughable in intent. Produced by Gordon Mills and Steve Popovich.

### JUDAS PRIEST
**Screaming For Vengeance** (CBS/Columbia)
Blitzkrieg heavy metal from one of the more established names in the cluttered (and noisy) field. Rob Halford and cohorts come up with a concept album of sorts based on the exploits of some imaginary winged warrior in the Conan blood-and-guts mould. A fast succession of pagan lung-bursting anthems that should satisfy most fans. Produced by Tom Allom.

# K

### SI KAHN
**Doing My Job** (Flying Fish)
Political folk songs as you haven't heard them since the 1960s. Kahn is a cottonmill organizer and his songs reflect the harsh life of the American working class in Kentucky mines and factories. Nice country touches. Worth the detour.

### HENRY KAISER
**Aloha** (Metalanguage)
Double album of experimental guitar pieces by an acolyte of Fred Frith. At times

tedious, at other times entrancing. Should have been edited down for stronger listener-effect.

### KAS PRODUCT
**Try Out** (RCA)
Enigmatic debut album from a duo out of France (although vocalist Mona Sonyoc is from the USA). Rambling melodies with strong electronic and keyboards wall of white noise backgrounds. A decidedly adventurous pair. Could catch on; worse could happen.

### FELICITY KENDAL
**Shape-Up And Dance** (Lifestyle)

How to keep fit in 1,001 easy movements. . . Narrated by the popular British actress against a soothing background of recent and older pop hits. Satisfies a demand, as it sold over ¼ million copies in the UK alone.

### DAVID KENT
**David Kent** (Epic)
Solo album by the keyboards player for Hall and Oates. Workmanlike mellow pop guaranteed not to leave any after-effect, or any memories of the music. Produced by John Anthony.

### THE KIDS FROM FAME
**The Kids From Fame** (BBC)

One of the surprise mega-hits of the year in Britain because of the canny positioning of the TV series in close proximity to the perennial 'Top Of The Pops'. Catchy set of numbers by the various performers of the sitcom, but does not include the title song. Lightweight, gentle pap. Produced by Barry Fasman.

### EVELYN KING
**Get Loose** (RCA)
Soft soul and disco album by a polished, assured performer. No sparks but a gentle feel throughout. Produced by Morris Brown.

### KOOL AND THE GANG
**As One** (De-Lite)
Quality, bopping black dance music by the experts of the genre. Infectious enthusiasm and non-stop rhythm. The material is pretty uneven but if you let yourself go with the non-stop flow, you won't notice it too much. Produced by Eumir Deodato and Kool and the Gang.

### AL KOOPER
**Championship Wrestling** (Columbia)
Six years since Kooper's last solo album, but he only appears as vocalist on two tracks on this new album! The other vocals are shared between Valerie Carter, Mickey Thomas and Ricky Washington. Brassy compositions in collaboration with the ubiquitous Jeff Baxter span many moods and styles. An interesting record. Produced by Bill Szymczyk.

# L

### BIRELI LAGRENE
**15** (Island/Antilles)
Third album from the infant prodigy guitarist. Gypsy jazz guitar in a most fluent mood. Produced by Carlos Albrecht.

### NICOLETTE LARSON
**All Dressed Up And No Place To Go** (Warners)

Mellifluous and gentle West Coast songster on a standard set of carefully crafted and somewhat somnolent laidback material. Drowns in good taste. Produced by Andrew Gold.

### THE LAST MAN IN EUROPE CORPORATION
**Songs From The Ark** (Situation 2)
Directionless synthesiser doodles and experimentation from a new British quartet in an arty mood; the only problem is that they don't know what 'Art' is truly about. A misguided muddle. Produced by David Motion and the group.

### STACY LATTISAW
**Sneakin' Out** (Cotilion)
Once a nymphet of soul, Lattisaw is now being groomed to tread in the footsteps of Aretha Franklin. Smooth production, safe uptempo dance numbers falling just that degree short of aggression and passion, polished vocals. Class product. Produced by Narada Michael Walden.

### THE LAUGHING CLOWNS
**Mr Uddich-Schmuddich Goes To Town** (Prince Melon)
Quirky Australian group on the extreme limits of the jazz map. Strident guitar and saxophone work-outs recall the Velvet Underground's wall-of-noise. Never works to my entire satisfaction but superior to, say, Pigbag when they get into a strong swing and dance mood. Another band for tomorrow, maybe.

### ADRIAN LEE
**The Magician** (DJM)
Wide-screen pomp rock from Toyah's ex-keyboards player. Swirling washes of synthesised sound and the right degree of bombast and circumstance make this most predictable. Will find its own fans without my saying too much about it, though. Someone else's cup of tea. Produced by Adrian Lee, Phil Garding and Nick Tauber.

### LEGAL WEAPON
**Death Of Innocence** (Arsenal)
High-energy independent US rock band with strong female singer. Patchy but has its fiery moments.

### LEGEND
**Death In The Nursery** (Workshop)
Heavy metal from Jersey. . . Horrid production and virtually inaudible music. To be buried and forgotten mighty fast.

### LEVEL 42
**The Pursuit Of Accidents** (Polydor)
British fusion funk in a strong but predictable groove. Brass and electronics cocktail for the small hours of the dance floor night. Pleasant but won't make the earth move. Produced by Mike Vernon.

LIGHT OF THE WORLD

### MARCY LEVY
**Marcella** (Epic)

### LIGHT OF THE WORLD
**Check Us Out** (EMI)

Quality solo outing by a practiced session and back-up singer with impressive stints to her credit with Leon Russell and, principally, Eric Clapton's band. More big-voiced ballads than rockers and a strong obsession with all American forms of romance make this a bit of a disappointment, though. Could do better, and no doubt will (if given another chance). Produced by John Boylan and Frank Rand.

### JERRY LEE LEWIS
**The Best Of Jerry Lee Lewis Featuring '39 & Holding'** (Elektra)
'Best of' package in a country mood compiled after Jerry Lee's departure from the Elektra fold. Ballads and the rare barrelhouse rocker. A fair selection of past glories. Produced by Eddie Kilroy and Bones Howe.

British disco group with a strong American sound. This is a new line-up since a split in the band last year and sees a return to form. Rich and fruity funk. Produced by Nigel Martinez.

### LILIPUT
**Liliput** (Rough Trade)
Swiss all-female line-up once known as Kleenex. Now down to a duo responsible for formless chanting and rough anthems of woe. A futile series of unending drones, I fear.

### FRED LOCKS AND HIS CREATION STEPPERS
**Love And Only Love** (Regal)
Listless reggae. Truly bland fourth division material.

### KENNY LOGGINS
**High Adventure** (Columbia)
Wimp rock supreme. Already Loggins' fifth album since the saccharin strains of Loggins and Messina. A maudlin selection of self-conscious material is not improved by a tenuous touch of rock and the help of Journey's Steve Perry on one cut. Produced by Bruce Botnick and Kenny Loggins.

### THE LONE RANGER
**Hi-Yo, Silver, Away!** (Greensleeves)
Sweet reggae tones by another of the cohorts of Jamaican singers rhapsodising on about the merits and visions of ganja. Sly and Robbie backing. Produced by the Lone Ranger and Clive Jarrett.

### THE LOOK
**Look Again** (RFC/Quality/Plastic)
Second album from the Detroit group with a strong emphasis on good time, simple rocking music. Bluesy touches and energy to spare. Produced by Mark Sax.

### LORDS OF THE NEW CHURCH
**Lords Of The New Church** (Illegal/IRS)
Punk heavy metal by one of the first new music supergroups (ie formed by musicians with more failed groups to their credit than hot meals). Pretentious thrashing about at speeds approaching that of sound. Stiv Bators (ex-Dead Boys) and Brian James (ex-Damned) are the main culprits. Produced by the Group.

### THE LOST JOCKEY
**The Lost Jockey** (Crepuscule)
Experimental minimalist music from a British ensemble. Strongly influenced by Philip Glass (one side is devoted to 'Hoovering the Beach' – shades of 'Einstein On The Beach'). Full of silences and deliberate repetitions.

### LUDUS
**Danger Came Smiling** (New Hormone)
Indifferent album by British duo of Linder and Ian. Lightweight, at times funny, but generally weak material.

### LUDUS
**Riding The Rag** (Expanded)
Cleverly-conceived compilation of Ludus' best recorded tracks of the past three years. Sharp and uncompromising, Linder's voice soars over the cluttered, experimental din. Dense and sometimes rewarding.

### LORETTA LYNN
**Making Love From Memory** (MCA)
Reliable country tear-jerkers by one of the best emoters in the business. Will have them crying tears of gold in the cornfields. Produced by Owen Bradley.

PHIL LYNOTT

## PHIL LYNOTT
**The Philip Lynott Album** (Vertigo)
All-star cast of friends: Mark Knopfler, Midge Ure, Mel Collins and a bevy of other veterans to assist Lynott on this new solo outing away from Thin Lizzy. Conveniently romantic and soft-edged but still betraying too many derivative influences. Easy-listening for night moods. Produced by Philip Lynott and Kit Woolven.

## MAD PROFESSOR
**Dub Me Crazy!** (Ariwa)
Peckham, London-based dub expert. Jolly reggae dance tracks with pungent aural running commentary. Produced by the Mad Professor.

## MAGAZINE
**After the Fact** (Virgin/IRS)
Best of virtually no hits for the now-defunct Magazine; a group which bathed in critical acclaim for its adventurous approach and new wavish music with a strong touch of intellect, but never really shifted any decent quantity of product. Moody, cryptic material which deserved a better fate than relative obscurity. All your old, underrated faves are present. Various producers.

## THE MAINES BROTHERS
**Hub City Moan** (Country Roads)
Good-time country music in a contemporary vein. Cajun, barrelhouse boogie and Texican rockers fight for space with rich Rodney Crowell material. One for the real fans. Produced by the Maines Brothers.

## MALARIA!
**Emotion** (Crepuscule)
Earnest doom-rock sung with chilling conviction by an all-girl group from Berlin. Oozing emotion from the grooves, Malaria! bulldoze their rhythms through electronic, mechanistic filters. Strong stuff. Approach with caution.

## BARBARA MANDRELL
**He Set My Life To Music** (MCA)
From country to gospel is not a major step for Mandrell whose devotional strains always remain most melodious. Duets with B. J. Thomas and Andrae Crouch and a nice lachrymose mood with choral backing and child choir. Distasteful but tastily done. Produced by Tom Collins.

## MANOWAR
**Battle Hymns** (Liberty)
Powerful heavy metal blitz by a new but impressive band. All cylinders firing on tales of rape and destruction, featuring the sonorous tones of Orson Welles as narrator on Viking saga 'Dark Avenger'. But 'Citizen Kane' this ain't; lacks subtlety. Produced by Bob Currie.

## FRANK MARINO
**Juggernaut** (CBS/Columbia)
Identikit American power pop, i.e. heavy metal with a thin veneer of melody. The Jimi Hendrix influence still pervades Marino's guitar work on this fifth album (the group was previously known as Mahogany Rush). Tepid. Produced by Frank Marino.

## JOHN MARTYN
**Well Kept Secret** (WEA)
A disappointment this, as John Martyn indulges in a rock vein and allows his delicate melodies and muted vocals to be overshadowed by a gamut of sound, the nearest he could in fact get to heavy metal. Some of the tunes have an infectious beat but the general tone is cluttered and unsuitable to Martyn's moody, jazzy style. Still better than a majority of the albums churned out by others, though. Produced by Sandy Roberton.

## MAYDAY
**Revenge** (A&M)
Second album by a US heavy metal group. This new effort sees a laudable effort towards varying the brew somewhat: jazz-fusion work-outs and some shades of techno-rock punctuate the loud proceedings. Produced by Don Silver and Ben Wisch.

## KEVIN McCORMICK & DAVID HORRIDGE
**Light Patterns** (Sheet)
Minimalist guitar atmospherics from a British duo of virtuosi. Tedious.

## MICHAEL McDONALD
**If That's What It Takes** (Warners)

The first solo album from the mainstay of the Doobie Brothers. Smoothly unobjectionable, laidback material on which McDonald's melodious voice and elegant keyboard work dominate, despite the heavyweight presence of a galaxy of

94

helpers. Typical aseptic rock which goes down a bomb on American airwaves but impresses on this side of the great divide by the lack of meat or life. Pedestrian was the word I was searching for. Won't harm you, though. Produced by Lenny Waronker and Ted Templeman.

### MISSISSIPI FRED McDOWELL
**Shake Em On Down** (Labor)
Live 1971 recording of the venerable bluesman and his incomparable slide guitar playing. A classic.

### RALPH McTELL
**Water Of Dreams** (Mays)
Once a highly-regarded folk performer, McTell is now somewhat forgotten. An expressive singer with a knack for sweet melodic material, this new album on a minor British independent label sees him true to past form. It's not so much that McTell hasn't progressed but that musical trends have moved fast beyond him. Worth looking out for as an example of intelligent, tuneful writing. Produced by Ralph McTell and Martin Levan.

### MEAT PUPPETS
**Meat Puppets** (SST/Thermidor)
Innovative American group based in Phoenix, Arizona. 14 high octane rock and roll songs to be played at 45 rpm, map the history of rock, reinterpreted à la Frank Zappa, but with an infectious enjoyment and a rough edge that bears witness to the strong immediacy of the music. A major album . . . if you can find it.

### MECO
**Swingtime's Greatest Hits** (Arista)
Mechanistic dance treatment to classic oldies from the golden age of swing. 19 tracks make this value for money for the Saturday night disco hordes. Produced by Meco Monardo, Dan Levine, Lance Quinn and Tony Bongiovi.

### RANDY MEISNER
**Randy Meisner** (Epic)
Gentle, forgettable laidback snooze-rock from another past Eagle on the loose in the vinyl jungle. Produced by Mike Flicker.

### MIDNIGHT STAR
**Victory** (Solar)
Consummate, tuneful quality funk. Heard it before, will hear it all again but it passes the time of night in the meantime. Produced by Reginald Calloway and Midnight Star.

### MINNY POPS
**Sparks In A Dark Room** (Factory Benelux)
Moan and croon doom rock from a Belgian group. Drab and monotonous and going nowhere in a hurry. Produced by the Group.

### MISSING PERSONS
**What's Wrong With A Tune You Can Whistle** (Less)
Naive, goodtime music with a strong feel of the deliquescent hippies.

### THE MONOCHROME SET
**Eligible Bachelors** (Cherry Red)

Flippant rock from a decidedly humorous band who veer between preciosity and hilarity without ever really blending the ingredients satisfactorily. The ultimate in art-school rock, I suppose; in which case, welcome to the working-class blues. Produced by Tim Hart.

### MOTHER'S RUIN
**Road To Ruin** (Spectra)
Average pop strains from a new British band out on the independent circuit.

### ALPHONSE MOUZON
**Distant Lover** (Highrise)
Predictable disco-funk dance floor music from a musician with a strong jazz heritage. Never objectionable but also rarely infectious enough to make it a must. Produced by Alphonse Mouzon.

### ALPHONSE MOUZON
**Step Into The Funk** (Metronome)
Workmanlike disco pop with criss-cross rhythms galore.

### JUDY MOWATT
**Only A Woman** (Shanachie)
Solo debut by a member of Bob Marley's female backing group the I Threes. Assured and polished set of reggae with strong soul ballads to disperse the occasional monotony of the Jamaican rhythms. A confident debut. Produced by Judy Mowatt.

### ANNE MURRAY
**The Hottest Night Of The Year** (Capitol)
Reliable country performer for the middle-aged comfortable slipper set. All the saccharin ballads but a slight and pleasing emphasis on more up-tempo material which suits Anne Murray's temperament well, including a sprightly revival of Bruce Channel's 'Hey, Baby!' Produced by Jim Ed Norman.

THE MONOCHROME SET

### MUSIC FOR PLEASURE
**Into The Rain** (Polydor)
At times quite compelling set of doomy rock with strong evocative atmospherics from a British band treading in familiar furrows. Not as monotonous as many of their rivals. Worth investigating. Produced by Mike Hedges and the Group.

### NAFFI
**Yum Yum Yum Ya** (Ark)
Heteroclit rock from a new Liverpool duo displaying a welter of sundry influences ranging from rockabilly rhythms to Caribbean strains. Innovative and fresh.

### NATASHA
**Captured** (Towerbell)
Contrived pop from the wife of the record label's owner. Scored a few minor hits in the UK. Sounds fresh but when you peer at the would-be sexy sleeve artwork and young Natasha's features (and hints of body) you soon realize that this is rip-off stuff performed by old farts.

### NAZARETH
**2 X S** (Nems/A&M)
15th album from veteran rockers who've suffered many line-up changes. The material is lacklustre power rock and undistinguishable from too many similar US bands playing around in the same division. Might earn more shekels in the US than in their own British homeland but ultimately disappointing. Produced by John Punter.

### WILLIE NELSON
**The Best Of Willie** (RCA)
The Best of the RCA years (60s and 70s), to be pedantic. Well-known material whether sung by Nelson or penned for others. Produced by Bill Haynes.

### WILLIE NELSON AND WEBB PIERCE
**In the Jailhouse Now** (Columbia)
Two old masters at work and play. Mostly modern country versions of Pierce's hits of the 50s. Pleasing chestnuts. Produced by Willie Nelson and Chips Moman.

### NERVOUS GERMANS
**Desolation Zone** (Rondelet)
Anonymous metallic thrash. Next. . .

### JIMMY C. NEWMAN
**Cajun Country** (Delta)
Lively set of infectious cajun romps with the statutory strains of rampaging accordion supplied by Bessyl Duhon. Produced by 'Gary Lynn' Petty.

WILLIE NELSON

### NIGHTHAWKS
**Times Four** (Adelphi)
Barrelhouse boogie rock from a reliable source. These are unreleased tracks going back to 1977 and 1979; one record is a live performance while the other is a studio set. Basic but great fun. Produced by the Nighthawks, Bill McCullough, OB Obrien, Jon Curlin.

### NIGHT PLANE
**Night Plane** (Handshake)
Lightweight jazz-flavoured rock by a new US duo. High-gloss stuff with session musicians filling in every little gap. Reggae strains and nice saxophone work make the package sufficiently distinctive. Produced by Jeffrey Weber.

### THE NITWITZ
**The Scorched Earth Policy** (Vogelspin)
Minimal experimentalism and silliness from Holland on this extended EP.

### KENNY NOLAN
**Head To Toe** (MCA)
Sickly set of romantic ballads sounding dangerously like some family favourite male performers I would rather not give a mention to again. Pass and pass again. Produced by Kenny Nolan, Jay Senter and Freddie Perren.

### NOVO COMBO
**The Animation Generation** (Polydor)
Second album of reggae-rock by a set of Police-clones. Assured and fluent but highly derivative. Produced by Novo Combo and Elliot Scheiner.

### NON-FICTION
**Don't Let Your Love** (Mega)
Modern rock from a new American West Coast group who've learned their musical lessons well: a touch of synthesiser electronics, jumpy time signatures, quirky but not too worrying lyrics and girl vocalist in the person of Karen Selden. Packaged rock. Produced by Jerry Marcellino.

## GARY NUMAN
**I Assassin** (Beggars Banquet/Atco)
Gazza the automaton strikes again. Some reviewers have detected traces of progress in this new album by the whey-faced one. As far as this humble scribe is concerned, Numan is still the master rip-off artist and if David Bowie is no longer the main burgled influence then OMD, Simple Minds and Bryan Ferry are new additions to the case history. To avoid like the plague if I were you. Produced by Gary Numan.

## BOBBY NUNN
**Second to Nunn** (Motown)
Light-handed touch of the dance-floor ethos on this debut album by a talented keyboards player and mellifluous singer. Produced by Bobby Nunn and Winston Monseque.

## THE NYLONS
**The Nylons** (Attic)
Four voices, handclaps and simple percussive effects in this Canadian acapella revival. Old stalwart hits are the subject of the treatment. Might have been more persuasive with original material but all the same unusual and fun. Produced by Sean Delaney and the Nylons.

## BILLY OCEAN
**Inner Feelings** (Epic)
Fourth album of mellow, unspectacular funk. Never less than pleasant, never truly memorable either. Produced by Billy Ocean and Nigel Martinez.

## OINGO BOINGO
**Nothing To Fear** (A&M)

Second album from a frantic US new wave band with the right touch of quirkiness and individuality to make a name for themselves. Cluttered but danceable stuff with a strongly featured three-man brass sec-

tion adding fire to the proceedings. Produced by Oingo Boingo and Joe Ciccarelli.

## ORCHESTRA MAKASSY
**Agwaya** (Virgin)
Pleasing African dance band strong on rhythms and political anthems you can dance to. Part of the 1982 rush by record companies to sign up most of the Black continent in search of another money-making tribal beat. Produced by Norman Mighell.

## ORLEANS
**One Of A Kind** (Radio)
Dull and uninspired collection of laidback material by a band who have been through better (and more creative) days. Produced by Don Silver and Ben Wisch.

## JOHNNY OSBORNE
**Never Stop Fighting** (Greensleeves)
Backed by the ever-present team of Roots Radics, another smooth as silk reggae singer. A trifle anonymous. Produced by Henry 'Junjo' Lawes.

## OSMOND BROTHERS
**The Osmond Brothers** (Elektra)
The standard harmony treatment is this time around given to a set of proven country standards. Produced by Rick Hall.

## JOHN OTWAY
**All Balls And No Willie** (Empire)
Eccentric British singer verging on the manic with a solo album of tender elegies and ridiculous loony tunes. For fans only; beware: the Otway fun-formula can sometimes be contagious. Produced by John Otway and Tim Summerhayes.

## OZONE
**Li'l Suzy** (Motown)
Workmanlike Motown eight-person funk outfit (with help from stablemate Syreeta on one track). A predictable, competent groove to wear in your dancing shoes. Produced by Ozone and Art Stewart.

## PALAIS SCHAUMBURG
**Palais Schaumburg** (Kamera)
Quirky pop funk by a German group strong on experimental touches and tongue-in-cheek humour. Jerky cut-up rhythms and sardonic lyrics (sung in German) make this an intriguing debut in a style all of their own. Produced by David Cunningham.

PALAIS SCHAUMBURG

## BILLY PARKER AND FRIENDS
**(Who's Gonna Sing) The Last Country Song** (Soundwaves)
Sincere country songs of woe and wanton women from an ex-Texas Troubadour. Par for the course. Produced by Joe Gibson.

## DOLLY PARTON
**Greatest Hits** (RCA)
Spans most of Ms Parton's career and bears witness to a smoothly engineered transition from traditional country fare ('Applejack') to cross-over pop ('9 to 5') and almost back again. If you haven't the original recordings, this is the one to have. Produced by Dolly Parton, Gregg Perry and Gary Klein.

## THE PASSIONS
**Sanctuary** (Polydor)

Patchy new album by a British band that remains ever promising but still fails to deliver. Barbara Gogan's ethereal voice is as effective and distinctive as ever but the material doesn't live up to expectations. And why a song sung in French with atrocious accent to the fore? Surely the heights of pretentiousness. Some good tracks, though.

## ROBBIE PATTON
**Orders From Headquarters** (Atlantic)
Blandola West Coast rock despite Patton's British connections. All lilting guitars and soporific musicianship of the highest calibre. Produced by Peter Coleman with Robbie Patton.

## PAYOLAS
**No Stranger To Danger** (IRS)
Average power pop in a typical 80s modern rock outing. Competent but uninspired. Produced by Mick Ronson.

## LESLIE PEARL
**Words and Music** (RCA)
Adult contemporary ballads as the US biz-speak puts it. Melodic but cluttered orchestral backing. Produced by Leslie Pearl.

## TEDDY PENDERGRASS
**This One's For You** (Philadelphia International)
Immaculately classy ballads full of funk and feeling. The record is all the more poignant because of Pendergrass' accident and physical incapacity. Old-fashioned funk with a sweetness of touch that has always been Pendergrass' hallmark. Produced by Gamble, Huff and various producers.

## PERE UBU
**The Songs Of The Bailing Man** (Rough Trade)
Heteroclit assemblage of experimental musical patchwork by a band with a strong tradition of innovation but now sadly lacking any further imagination. For the fans only. An acquired taste, if not as opaque as, say, the Residents.

## THE PERSUASIONS
**Good News** (Rounder)
Effective ensemble acapella singing on old soul classics by Sam Cooke, David Ruffin and others. Seductively strong stuff, in its deliberately old-fashioned way. Produced by Jerry Lawson.

## WILLIE PHOENIX
**Willie Phoenix** (A&M)
Black US singer in a strong hard rock outing. Also at ease on softer ballad material. Produced by David Anderle and Joe Ciccarelli.

## CHARLIE PICKETT AND THE EGGS
**Live At The Button** (Open)
Live bar-room rock with an easy, relaxed feel of unbridled abandon. Good-time music badly recorded but still much to enjoy here. Memories of a sweat and beer night in Florida.

## PIECES OF A DREAM
**We Are One** (Elektra)
Second jazz funk outing for a promising US soul outfit. Expert help from luminaries such as Grover Washington, Herb Smith and Ralph McDonald add swing to the occasional female vocals, although the majority of the album is in an instrumental mode. Reliable. Produced by Grover Washington Jr.

## PINK FAIRIES
**Live At The Roundhouse** (Chiswick)
The final outing recorded for posterity of the British psychedelic precursors of heavy metal. A bit of a shambles but a good time was had by all over the many years the band rambled on from free concert to free concert. A touch of affection and nostalgia and forgettable music.

## PINSKI ZOO
**The Dizzy Dance Record** (Dug-Out)
Extended EP (or mini-album?) by British jazz experimentalists. Shades of Albert Ayler, Coltrane or Roland Kirk with a rock backbeat. Has its rough charms.

## ROBERT PLANT
**Pictures At Eleven** (Swansong)
Plant's first solo album sees him following closely in the musical footsteps of Led Zeppelin. Owner of the definitive hard rock voice, Plant carefully avoids treading unfamiliar ground and has surrounded himself with seasoned musicians like Robbie Blunt, Cozy Powell, Phil Collins, Paul Martinez, keeping the echoes of Jimmy Page guitar wizardry at bay. Safe, reliable mix of impressive heavy metal and soft bluesy ballads. The acceptable face of heavy rock. Produced by Robert Plant.

PAYOLAS

## THE PLATTERS
**Platterama** (Mercury)
Compilation of well-worn standards and a medley of past hits. For the over-40's.

## PLUNKY AND THE ONENESS OF JUJU
**Everyway But Loose** (Buddah/Sutra)
Strong dancefloor material with a smattering of reggae and African rhythms injecting some originality into the relentless funk. Roots and pop for all boppers. Clever. Produced by Plunky and Muzi Nkabinde.

## PLUTO
**Again** (KR)
Comedy reggae songs in Jamaican patois most of the time. For specialists only. Produced by Leighton Shervington.

## POINTER SISTERS
**So Excited** (Planet)
Sweet, swaggering classy funk by expert purveyors of harmony and fiery vocals. Gets better with every play. Produced by Richard Perry.

## IGGY POP
**Zombie Birdhouse** (Animal)

Striking return to form by the Igg under the auspices of Blondie's Chris Stein's new label. Strong material in a surprisingly commercial vein. Avoid past prejudices and give this a close listen, Iggy's versatility and sheer quirky melodiousness will surprise. Loved it. Produced by Chris Stein.

## BILLY PRESTON
**Pressin' On** (Motown)
Veteran funkster going through the motions; full of pep, soul and pop but all somewhat mechanical. Produced by Billy Preston, Ralph Benatar and Glen Senogles.

## PRINCE LINCOLN THOMPSON AND THE ROYAL RASSES
**Ride With The Rasses** (God Sent)
Strong roots-oriented reggae. Seven

GERRY RAFFERTY

drawn-out tracks with powerful vocals. Produced by Prince Lincoln Thompson.

## PRODIGAL
**Prodigal** (Heartland)
New American band still steeped in too many midstream rock influences (Chicago, Who, Eagles). Strong guitar and keyboards but unmemorable. Produced by John Phelps.

## THE PRODUCERS
**You Make The Heat** (Portrait)
Quaint mainstream rock from Atlanta, Georgia band on second album. Full of hooks and aggression. Produced by Tom Werman.

## PSYCHEDELIC FURS
**Forever Now** (CBS/Columbia)

Superlative album of undeniable power and atmospherics by an underrated British band. However, singer Richard Butler sounds more and more like middle-period Bowie and this derivative influence spoils a lot of the pleasure. The vocal mannerisms are exaggerated and constantly refer the listener to memories of the real thing. Pity. A lot of talent on evidence here though I fear the Furs (get rid of that misleading 'Psychedelic' tag) are one of those perennial loser bands who can't stop themselves falling at the first hurdle. Produced by Todd Rundgren.

# Q

## Q-TIPS
**Live At Last** (Rewind)
Ultimate souvenir of a British band who have since disbanded. Polished funk with a strong brass contribution. Hommage to Stax and smoky rooms permeated with the spirit of the true rhythm and blues. Another example of white boys playing the blues to no avail. A gentle curiosity.

## QUEEN CITY KIDS
**Black Box** (Epic)
Power pop in the standard vein of anonymity and predictability from a Canadian quartet. Good riffs, naff material. Produced by Rob Freeman.

# R

## GERRY RAFFERTY
**Sleepwalking** (EMI/Liberty)
Subdued ballads by the gentle Rafferty after a year away from the active music scene. Much the same appealing mixture as before and, despite the injection of syn-

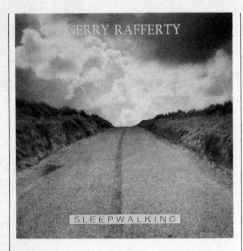

GERRY RAFFERTY
SLEEPWALKING

thesised electro-pop elements, old-fashioned and boring. Not a success. Produced by Christopher Neil and Gerry Rafferty.

## PETER RANKING AND GENERAL LUCKY
**Jah Standing Over Me** (Silver Camel)
Workmanlike DJ rapping reggae album.

## LOU RAWLS
**Now Is The Time** (Epic)
Tasty collection of uptempo funk dance tracks from an expert crooner. Mellow weaving of time-hardened magic. Produced by Mtume, Lucas and Bell.

## SHARON REDD
**Redd Hot** (Prelude)
Soulful, efficient disco songs by a gutsy black vocalist. Funky handclaps and unceasing rhythms win the day. Produced by Eric Matthew.

## BLAINE L. REININGER
**Broken Fingers** (Crepuscule)
Mixed results on this eclectic solo album by the violin player from Tuxedo Moon. A strong Bowie touch mars the vocals but ethnic musical moods come off successfully and provide a varied feel to the album.

## REO SPEEDWAGON
**Good Trouble** (Epic)
12th album of reliable hard-riff rock from expert purveyors to the cluttered but conservative American airwaves. Fat guitar sound and inane lyrics according to the winning past formula. Predictably successful. Produced by Kevin Cronin, Gary Richrath, Kevin Beamish and Alan Gratzer.

## BARRY REYNOLDS
**I Scare Myself** (Island)
Contributor to Marianne Faithfull's album accompanied by the crème de la crème of Island backing musicians on a pleasant solo debut with smooth melodies and Irish ballads in a more modern vein. Soothing. Produced by Alex Sadkin.

CLIFF RICHARD

## L. J. REYNOLDS
**Travelin'** (Capitol)
Reliable soul from an ex-member of the Dramatics. Adequate blend of funky ballads and up-tempo dance numbers. Produced by L. J. Reynolds and Don Davis (one side each).

## RHEINGOLD
**Fan Fan Fanatic** (Harvest)
Four-track mini LP by a new German synthesiser group in a dance mood. Catchy hooks. Produced by Rheingold and Conny Plank.

## BOBBY RICE
**Bobby's Back** (Audiograph)
Varied country set switching genres and mood with confidence: ballads, honky-tonk, swing and hard rocking numbers co-exist cleverly. Produced by Charlie Fields.

## CLIFF RICHARD
**Now You See Me, Now You Don't** (EMI)
Although 'The Only Way Out' is consummate pop done to a tee, the rest of Cliff Richard's album drowns ·in a morass of religious messages. While the craft is near perfect, the subject matter tends to dominate the proceedings and a whole record of Christian proselytising becomes a bit much. Produced by Craig Preuss and Cliff Richard.

## ANGELA RIPPON
**Shape Up And Dance Volume 2** (Lifestyle)

SHAPE UP & DANCE with ANGELA RIPPON
Look Good! Have Fun! Feel Fit!
Exercise With these Hits PHYSICAL SLOW HAND HANDS UP LAND OF MAKE BELIEVE TURN YOUR LOVE AROUND IT'S A LOVE THING And more...!!
FREE 8-PAGE BOOKLET

More exercise routines narrated, this time around, by the stern British television newsreader and journalist. Jaunty music in the background.

## DAVID ROBERTS
**All Dressed Up** (Elektra)
Sleek debut by a Canadian singer aiming straight at the jugular of American easy-listening radio programmes. Heard it all too often from other sources already (Boz Scaggs, Christopher Cross, Doobie Bros) but well-done. Produced by Greg Mathieson.

### STEVE ROBERTS
**Do You Know Who I Am?** (Exploited)
Drummer from punk pioneers the UK Subs on a sloppy solo outing of slap-dash rock with a decided lack of polish and discipline. A mixture of cover songs and derivative new compositions. An indulgent record.

### B. A. ROBERTSON
**R & BA** (Asylum)
Relaxed pop from the Scottish singer (and occasional TV personality these days). Very self-conscious tunes wallowing in cleverness. With help from his friends Cliff Richard, Paul Jones, Maggie Bell, Alan Gorrie, Billy Bremner. Produced by B. A. Robertson.

### THE RODS
**Wild Dogs** (Arista)
Very, very loud heavy metal indeed on this second album by the US rockers of the Rods. For a trio, they certainly can develop a great deal of power and project energy. Cluttered and deafening. Unrecognizable version of Diana Ross' 'You Keep Me Hangin' On'. Produced by Carl Canedy, David Feinstein and Martin Pearson.

### KENNY ROGERS
**Love Will Turn You Around** (Liberty)
Rogers' last album for Liberty before moving over to RCA sees him in the customary easy-going country style which sells so well in the USA but just won't connect in England. Velvet-voiced ballads with a strong melancholy touch emerging through the welter of pedal steel guitar playing. Has its undeniable charms. Produced by Kenny Rogers, Val Garay, David Mallow, Brent Maher and Randy Goodrum.

### RON ROGERS
**Don't Play With My Emotions** (Ze)
New York dance music from a Kid Creole associate. Slick and danceable but generally unremarkable. Produced by Ron Rogers and Vince Traina.

### ROMEO VOID
**Benefactor** (CBS/415)

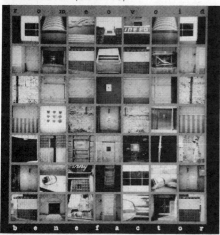

Art rockers Romeo Void come under the umbrella of a major label and their second album is an assured and polished set of quirky songs about the seamier side of life. Highly ambiguous lyrics (conveniently printed on the inner bag) over a storm of aural aggression characterise this innovative American group. Deborah Iyall is tough and gutsy on vocals with no little-girl or pseudo-macho mannerisms, defiant through and through. One for new wave nostalgics. Produced by Ian Taylor.

### THE ROOM
**Indoor Fireworks** (Red Flame)
Debut for a new Liverpool group. Moody atmospheres in the grand old Joy Division tradition, but singer David Jackson conveys every inch of expressiveness with distinct fervor. A promising platter. Produced by Dave Kitson and the Group.

### CHARLIE ROSS
**The High Cost Of Living** (Town House)
Diverse country album with some soul and pop mixed in to vary the menu. Digestible, just about. Produced by Walt Aldridge, Tom Brasfield and Ernie Phillips.

### MICHAEL ROTHER
**Fernwarme** (Polydor)
Rambling evocative synthesiser and guitar ballads with strong cosmic feeling. Much the same as before from Rother who somehow succeeds in avoiding the mawkishness of Oldfield's similar compositions. Music to make love to or indulge in euphoric illegal substances.

### THE RUNAWAYS
**Best Of The Runaways** (Mercury)
Following the American success of Joan Jett, it's rip-off time and Mercury are quick to plunder the archives. Girl-group rock with a rough, clumsy edge. Never worked back then even with the scantily-clad theatrics of Cherie Currie; works even less today. Various producers.

### RUSH
**Signals** (Mercury)

Limp new album from the bestselling Canadian trio until now ensconced in the heavy metal niche. The pomp rock formula of old is now tinged by fashionable synthesiser swirls which do not, however, conceal a dire lack of melodies and good tunes. Pretentious and already selling like a bomb. What can a poor critic do? Produced by Rush and Terry Brown.

### MIKE RUTHERFORD
**Acting Very Strange** (WEA/Atlantic)
Solo album by the Genesis bass player. Straightforward pop with Rutherford's gravel voice to the fore and help from a crew of studio veterans: Daryl Stuermer, Stewart Copeland, Gary Barnacle. Unspectacular but honest and appealing. Produced by Mike Rutherford.

### RUTS DC
**Rhythm Collision** (Bohemian)
Now on their own independent record label, the Ruts move further away from their punk beginnings towards a more intelligent and experimental reggae-tinged base. Instrumentally strong with an emphasis on dub techniques. Produced by Paul Fox, David Ruffy and John Segs.

### MITCH RYDER
**Smart Ass** (Safari)
Mild come-back by a Detroit veteran of funk and roll. Nothing special about this new set: competent but no real innovations. Feels dated.

# S

### MARC SADANE
**Exciting** (Warners)
Strong soul outing with outstanding production values and a fiery sting in the tail. Powerful vocals and class material. Produced by James Mtume and Reggie Lucas.

### SAD LOVERS AND GIANTS
**Epic Garden Music** (Midnight Music)
A mini-album from a new, young British band. Modernistic and very derivative art-school rock with Banshees and Bunnymen undigested influences. Produced by Nick Ralph and Steve Burgess.

### SAGA
**In Transit** (Polydor)
Bombastic heavy metal assault from the Canadian band recorded live in Germany and Denmark.

### FREDDIE SALEM AND THE WILDCATS
**Cat Dance** (Epic)
Solo effort by a member of Outlaw with strong guitar orientation. Mostly own,

fluent compositions with Todd Rundgren and Buffalo Springfield covers. Innocuously pleasant. Produced by Freddie Salem.

## SANTANA
**Shango** (CBS/Columbia)

How time passes! This is already Carlos Santana's fourteenth album and the seams are beginning to show. As much as I enjoy his quick-silver guitar playing, the generous blend of rhythmic influences from various ethnic cultures and the Coltrane-like serenity for some passages, I must confess there are few nuggets on this new platter. The band calmly go through the motions on automatic pilot and the vocals are excruciatingly mannered and irritating. Formula stuff, alas. Produced by Bill Szymczyk, John Ryan, Carlos Santana and Gregg Rolie.

## SAX MANIAX
**Oversaxed** (Penthouse)
Bouncy day-to-day pop with strong brass thrust. Indifferent. Produced by Step Morley.

## TOM SCOTT
**Desire** (Elektra Musician)
Live laid-back fusion jazz from the best West Coast session musicians around. Mostly instrumental soul and pop workouts with a cocktail lounge feel. Easy, easy. Produced by Jeffrey Weber.

## GIL SCOTT-HERON
**Moving Target** (Arista)
Barbed-wire political lyrics couched in a deluge of jazzy tunes by a noted US black poet whose anger comes through strongly. Exquisite musicianship makes the blend all the more effective.

## SCRITTI POLITTI
**Songs To Remember** (Rough Trade)
Reggaefied, jazzy melodies in a surprisingly commercial (and sometimes) bland mood from a British independent band of long-standing only now making an album

debut. Flows most gracefully with rippling saxophone to the fore; lyrics are self-conscious but the general package leaves you with that old 'so what?' feeling when all is said and done.

## SEARCH
**Search** (Phillyworld)
Anonymous funk clichés played with indifferent gusto.

## PHIL SEYMOUR
**Phil Seymour 2** (Boardwalk)
Pleasant dose of rhythmic power pop. No great shakes in the originality stakes on this second outing by Dwight Twilley's

ex-cohort but passes the time of day and has a fresh, youthful feeling to it.

## SHADOWS
**Life In The Jungle** (Polydor)
Studio set with live album included free in the package. Varied material stronger on cover versions like Vangelis' 'Chariots of Fire' theme, 'Lili Marlene', 'High Noon'. Sounds rather familiar and old-hat. Produced by the Group.

## JAH SHAKA
**Ten Commandments of Dub** (Shaka)
Heavyweight reggae dub. Very much for the fans of the genre.

THE SHADOWS

SHANGHAI

## SHALAMAR
**Greatest Hits** (Solar)
Round-up of past material by the soul group's previous label. The songs aren't as immediate as their recent hits. Average disco, no more.

## SHANGHAI
**Shanghai** (Chrysalis)

A new-fangled line-up for a group previously known (or should it be unknown) as Spider. Quality American power pop in the Benatar-Blondie mould (and Chrysalis should know. . .) with Amanda Blue on vocals. Has its moments but overall monotony of tone keeps the whole album bogged down in no-man's-land. Produced by Bruce Fairbairn.

## ROCKIE SHARPE AND THE REPLAYS
**Shout! Shout!** (Chiswick)
Tedious British revivalist rock and roll. Compilation of past dubious glories for retarded greasers. Produced by Mike Vernon.

## BILLY JOE SHAVER
**Billy Joe Shaver** (Columbia)
Lyrical country singer with slight outlaw overtones. Pleasing brew of remorse, twang and rock. Produced by Richie Albright.

## BIM SHERMAN
**Across the Red Sea** (On U Sound)
Reggae crooning with less experimentation than usual from the producer's console. Sly and Robbie on duty. Sensitive, effective tunes by an overlooked Jamaican artist. Produced by Adrian Sherwood.

## SHOES
**Boomerang** (Elektra)
The wistful lyricism of the Shoes' earlier albums I found very reminiscent of the younger Beatles: memorable hooks and fluent melodic harmonies tinged with a touch of deliberate naivety characterised the music of both groups. On this fourth album, the Shoes have adopted a harder approach with voices mixed back and heavy guitar work in stronger evidence. The result lacks the immediacy of their previous approach but they still remain complete masters of the 2½ minute pop song. Not many can achieve that. Produced by the Shoes.

## SHOOTING STAR
**III Wishes** (Virgin)
Third album of floundering heavy metal bop pop with few redeemable qualities by a second division US band. Produced by Kevin Elson.

## SHRIEKBACK
**Tench** (Y)

Mini-album with six tracks of adventurous, innovative music by a motley trio of British musicians including Barry Andrews, late of XTC and Fripp's League of Gentlemen and Dave Allen from the Gang of Four. Synthesised percussion and experiments in sound and rhythm to satisfy the most jaded ears. Try it, you'll be surprised.

## JANIS SIEGEL
**Experiment in White** (Atlantic)
Assured solo debut from one of the Manhattan Transfer vocalists. Blend of straight pop, jazzy ballads and New Orleans blues. A satisfying journey. Produced by Joel Dorn.

## SIMPLE MINDS
**New Gold Dream '81, '82, '83, '84** (Virgin)

Someone
  Somewhere In
  Summertime
Colours Fly And
  Catherine Wheel
Promised You A
  Miracle
Big Sleep
Somebody Up
  There Likes You

New Gold Dream
  (81–82–83–84)
Glittering Prize
Hunter And The
  Hunted
King Is White And
  In The Crowd

Jim Kerr's band of Scotsmen are fast forging one of the most distinctive sounds around. Already on their sixth album, they offer a most innovative blend of synthesiser rock with emotive vocals to the fore while halting but compelling rhythms shudder through in the background. This is the stuff that wide-screen romance is made of. Original and heartening. Produced by Peter Walsh.

## SIR COXSONE SOUND
**King Of Dub Rock Part 2** (Regal)
Superior dub reggae. Pungent, social and humorous. One of the best dub records around in an overcrowded field.

## RICKY SKAGGS
**Family And Friends** (Rounder)
Acoustic selection from Skaggs and friends (including Peter Rowan, Jerry Douglas and the White Family) in a bluegrass mood, recorded some years back before Skaggs signed to a major following his involvement with Emmylou Harris. Simple, unadorned country close to its roots. Produced by Ricky Skaggs.

## RICKY SKAGGS
**Highways And Heartaches** (Epic)

More contemporary material on Skaggs' second album for Epic. Still a strong traditional tinge to the music, though, with guitars and dobro in full flight behind Ricky Skaggs' expressive tones. Produced by Ricky Skaggs.

## SKIDS
**Fanfare** (Virgin)
The obligatory compilation and celebration

now that the group is no longer. Traces the meandering path from neo-punk to quirky country soil anthems followed by Richard Jobson and Stuart Adamson and their constantly changing acolytes. Of undoubted historical merit. Includes hits and near-misses like 'Working For The Yankee Dollar', 'Masquerade', 'Charade', 'Circus Games', etc. . . Various producers.

## SLOW CHILDREN
**Mad About Town** (Ensign/RCA)
Second idiosyncratic album from the duo of Pal Shazar and Andrew Chinich. Quirky pop in an accelerated mood, often reminiscent of Sparks in their heyday. Endearing nonsense. Produced by Jules Shear and Stephen Hague.

## JIMMY SMITH
**Off The Top** (Elektra Musician)
Veteran jazzman in an accessible, fusion mood; Smith is helped along by Ron Carter and George Benson on a patchy set of contemporary pieces and more traditional material on which they vent their improvisatory skills with the usual talent.

## SNIFF 'N' THE TEARS
**Ride The Blue Divide** (Chiswick)

Sniff 'n' the Tears are always seen as a second-rate Dire Straits and share with Knopfler's outfit the same sense of romance and adventure in subject matter. This fourth album (with the customary stunning cover illustration by singer Paul Roberts) combines the impossible by being both laidback and electrifying. B-movie narratives redolent of nights in seedy hotel-rooms, flight from responsibility and moral anguish: mighty subjects for music that flows quite effortlessly. A soft spot of mine. Produced by the Group.

## SNUFF
**Snuff** (Elektra-Curb)
Adequate new US band on unrestrained pop debut with cajun and country feel in places. Produced by Phil Gernhard.

## GINO SOCCIO
**Face To Face** (RFC)
Funky disco loony tunes from Canada and an independent label.

## SONS OF JAH
**Universal Message** (Natty Congo)
Positive rhythmic reggae on this fourth album by a now well-established band.

## SOUNDTRACK
**The Best Little Whorehouse In Texas** (MCA)
Songs and music from the uninspiring film by Colin Higgins about goings on in a Texas brothel, a star vehicle for Dolly Parton and Burt Reynolds. Predictable Parton tunes; dull otherwise. Produced by Gregg Perry.

## SOUNDTRACK
**Brimstone and Treacle** (A&M)
Music for the Richard Loncraine movie of the controversial Dennis Potter play. Sting stars as a charming but malevolent figure with demonic overtones and contributes the quaint 'Spread A Little Happiness'. The rest of the soundtrack is very much a collection of Copeland-stable copyrights what with reprises of established hits by the Police, the Go-Gos, Squeeze, etc. . . An unnecessary piece of vinyl.

## SOUNDTRACK
**Fast Times At Ridgemont Hill** (Full Moon)
Double-album extravaganza tied-in to a dubious film about high-school pranks. Irving Azoff tries to repeat the 'Urban Cowboy' success and presents 18 acts spanning the whole spectrum of US musical tastes: includes Led Zeppelin, Go-Gos, Jackson Browne, Quarterflash, Rainbow, Joe Walsh, Billy Squier, Donna Summer, Stevie Nicks, Don Henley and many others. Hasn't got that much to do with the film, really. Various producers.

## SOUNDTRACK
**Laura** (Barclay)
Patrick Juvet bland romanticism by numbers and tepid disco for the David Hamilton soft-porn movie. Produced by Patrick Juvet.

## SOUNDTRACK
**Night Shift** (Warners)
Although Burt Bacharach wrote this film's score, the vinyl counterpart is more a fashionable compilation: Talk, Talk, Marshall Crenshaw, Quarterflash, Rod Stewart, Pointer Sisters, Al Jarreau, etc. . . The film is an amiable, if vulgar, comedy. Various producers.

## SOUNDTRACK
**Rocky III** (Liberty)
'Eye of the Tiger' dominates the record,

otherwise adorned with three hesitant vocals by Sylvester's own brother, Frank Stallone. Rubbish. Produced by Bill Conti.

## SOUNDTRACK
### Summer Lovers (Warners)
Adolescent skin-flick under pretence of romance in the Greek islands. Yet another mixture of rag-bag tracks from name performers: Elton John, Stephen Bishop, Chicago and others. Various producers.

## SPACE PEOPLE
### Space People (Capitol)
Mini-album put together by A Taste of Honey's Hazel Payne. Drum-driven disco covers of famous Motown hits. Works well. Produced by Paul Ring and Hazel Payne.

## SPITTIN IMAGE
### Spittin Image (MCA)
First album by a new US band. Competent pop with reggae leanings, front vocals by Mimi Rousseau. Produced by Robin Jenney.

## SPLIFF
### Spliff (CBS)
Nina Hagen's former back-up band. German rock: ponderous, heavy and clichéd. Lyrics in English lighten the load.

## SPLIT BEAVER
### When Hell Won't Have You (Heavy Metal)
Room temperature metal with mighty ambitions but no real guts.

## BRUCE SPRINGSTEEN
### Nebraska (CBS/Columbia)

| | |
|---|---|
| Nebraska | Used Cars |
| Atlantic City | Open All Night |
| Mansion On The Hill | My Father's House |
| Johnny 99 | Reason To Believe |
| Highway Patrolman | |
| State Trooper | |

Like Bowie, Springsteen does just what you don't expect next. As most will now know, this is an album of pared down, acoustic songs recorded in his own front-room with the E-Street Band out in the cold. Echoes of Hank Williams, Woody Guthrie and early Dylan come to mind but this is nevertheless pure, unadulterated Springsteen Americana. The bleak panoramas of broken homes, cars and highway desolation are rendered even more acute by the naked treatment and quiet acquiescence Springsteen wraps around the songs. And it works! Chillingly so. This is the sort of record you can write fifty-page

essays about. A masterpiece. But then we should have known long before that Bruce would never fail. Recorded by Mike Gatlin.

## SPROUT HEAD UPRISING
### Early Spring (Rocksteady)
Weirdish blend of pop, country, reggae and many genres by a group of Manchester experimentalists. Endearingly funny. Produced by Michael Mafia.

## SPYS
### Spys (EMI)
Melodramatic rock from a new outfit formed by two departing members of Foreigner. Same pomp and loud tunes. Soaring solos on the old electric guitar and raunchy vocals. Won't change lead into gold. Produced by Neil Kernon.

## BILLY SQUIER
### Emotion in Motion (Capitol)
Tough-boy rock with Warhol cover to boot. Polished high-tech power pop with all the studio gloss that money can buy. Doesn't, however, hide the fact that Squier is a mediocre songwriter and a one in a thousand heavy metal vocalist with more scream than actual voice. Produced by Mack.

## JOHN STARLING
### Waitin' On A Southern Train (Sugar Hill)
Smooth, well-crafted country music by a mellow-voiced singer of great appeal and future. Produced by John Starling and Paul Craft.

## CANDI STATON
### Suspicious Minds (Sugarhill)
Danceable soul ballads and up-tempo ravers from a lady who's been away some time since her 'Young Hearts Run Free' hit of years ago. Nothing as catchy here, but a pleasant groove to relax by. Produced by Dave Crawford.

BRUCE SPRINGSTEEN

STIFF LITTLE FINGERS

### JON STEVENS
**Jon Stevens** (MCA)
Workmanlike new Australian vocalist in a laidback, almost West Coast style of singing. Abetted by John Helliwell of Supertramp and members of Rufus. No great shakes. Produced by Trevor Lawrence.

### STIFF LITTLE FINGERS
**Now Then** (Chrysalis)
Neo-punk, anti-establishment pieces. The same as before and lacklustre as Stiff Little Fingers fail to recapture their initial energy and anger and sound as if they are just going through the vengeful motions. Can do better. Produced by Nick Tauber.

### THE STRANGLERS
**The Collection 1977–1982** (Liberty)
Interesting retrospective for the band once steeped heavily in a punk-with-Doors-organ runs groove and who later espoused a smoother, highly effective and evocative pop mood which has served them well. Includes 'Peaches', 'No More Heroes', 'Golden Brown', 'Strange Little Girl'. Protean. Various producers.

### MARTY STUART
**Busy Bee Cafe** (Sugar Hill)
Although an album debut, this is not Marty Stuart's first record appearance: he is a veteran of the Lester Flatt band and an assured country performer and multi-instrumentalist. Witness to his reputation are the many guest musicians on show here: Johnny Cash, Doc and Merle Watson, Earl Scruggs, Jerry Douglas and others. Rewarding. Produced by Marty Stuart.

### DONNA SUMMER
**Donna Summer** (Geffen)

| | |
|---|---|
| Love Is In Control | Livin' In America |
| Mystery Of Love | Protection |
| The Woman In Me | (If It) Hurts Just A Little |
| State Of Independence | Love Is Just A Breath Away |
| | Lush Life |

Long-awaited collaboration with Quincy Jones by the arch-mistress of soul disco. Patchy but when it's good, it's superlative. Driving rock, stirring anthems and melodrama galore (particularly on Springsteen's 'Protection' with the man himself on guitar). 'State of Independence', with a choir that money can't buy, manages to transcend the maudlin lyrics (by chief wimp Jon Anderson) and reaches an incantation level that few others can match. And 'Love Is In Control' is all hooks and riffs that stick in your brain like a fish bone.

Forget the torch singing parts and the naive life-embracing paeans and sleeve notes: this is quality stuff. Produced by Quincy Jones.

### JOE SUN
**The Best Of Joe Sun** (Elektra)
Collects some earlier Ovation material. Identikit country fare. Produced by Brian Fisher.

### SUPER HEROINES
**Cry For Help** (Bemisbrain)
Independent Californian atmospherics à la Manchester/Liverpool gloom and doom school of despair. Produced by Steve Sinclair.

### SWINGERS
**Counting The Beat** (Backstreet)
Australian arty rock with quirks and high spirits galore. Catchy pop (includes an ex-member of Split Enz) with a lot of relaxed humour. Produced by David Tickle.

# T

### YUKIHIRO TAKAHASHI
**What. . . Me Worry?** (Alfa)

Yet another album from the YMO stable. To put matters into the right perspective, this is in fact a recently-recorded opus (most of Takahashi's previous output had been released in the West in random order at almost fortnightly intervals). Indifferent electro-pop with a cast of thousands including Zaine Griff, Ronny, Bill Nelson. Produced by Yukihiro Takahashi.

### TALK TALK
**The Party's Over** (EMI)
Assured debut album by a new British pop band functioning inside a safe, danceable pop groove. Gentle melodies with muted synthesiser background patterns and positive harmonies make this eminently pleasant if a little light-hearted. Produced by Colin Thurston.

**TAVARES**
**New Directions** (RCA)
Despite the title, nothing very new. Standard soul funk watered down for the white radio audience. Produced by Kenny Nolan, Jay Senter, Ric Wyatt Jr. and Benjamin F. Wright.

**TAXXI**
**States Of Emergency** (Fantasy)
Workmanlike rock from a San Francisco trio with no particular indications of genuine talent. Produced by Phil Kaffel.

**B. E. TAYLOR GROUP**
**Innermission** (MCA)
Middle of the road American rock with brass in full flight. All original material bar the Ronettes 'Be My Baby'. Ordinary. Produced by Mark Avsec and Donnie Iris.

**TECHNO TWINS**
**Technostalgia** (PRT)
Electro-pop made easy. Floundering originals are calculatedly mixed in with synthesiser versions of old chestnuts like 'In The Mood' or 'Falling In Love Again'. Dubious. Very.

**TELEVISION PERSONALITIES**
**They Could Have Been Bigger Than The Beatles** (Whaam)
Ironic title for a collection of unreleased tracks recorded between 1976 and 1980 for the now-defunct band led by Dan Treacy. Neo-psychedelia, humour and electric guitar showcases blend satisfactorily and call for a reassessment of an overlooked band.

**TELEX**
**Birds And Bees** (Interdisc)
Belgian fizzy electro-pop duet. An improvement on past efforts as melodies get the better of idiosyncratic touches and some tracks are even quite catchy in a frivolous sort of way.

**10 CC**
**Ten Out Of Ten** (Warners)
American release for recent Gouldman/Stewart material. As usual, witty, melodic vignettes leading nowhere but always great on the ears and mind. Quirky but always strongly commercial. Produced by Eric Stewart and Graham Gouldman.

**BARBARA THOMPSON'S JUBIABA**
**Barbara Thompson's Jubiaba** (MCA)
1978-reissue for a big band jazz sound with strong ethics strains. Emphasis on Latin rhythms and percussion. Rather ordinary. Produced by Chris Tsangarides.

**TRACEY THORN**
**A Distant Shore** (Cherry Red)
Plaintive little-girl vocals by an errant member of Everything But The Girl.

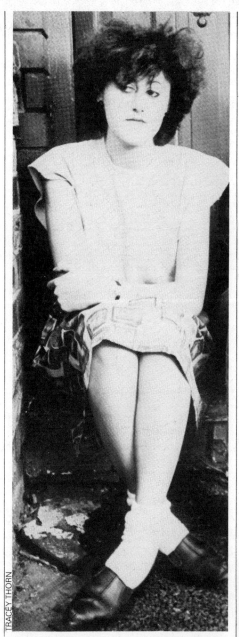

TRACEY THORN

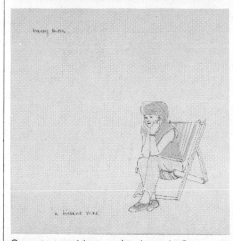

Sweet, touching and ethereal. Cover of the Velvet Underground's 'Femme Fatale' is totally misunderstood, however. Fey.

**GEORGE THOROGOOD AND THE DESTROYERS**
**Bad To The Bone** (EMI)
Unadulterated boogie in constant overdrive from the paramount US blues revivalist. Abetted by Stones cohort Ian Stewart on keyboards, Thorogood and his blistering band go through Isley Brothers, Chuck Berry, John Lee Hooker, Jimmy Reed and other numbers with gusto and energy. No surprises but then no disappointments either. Produced by the Delaware Destroyers.

**THRASHER BROTHERS**
**Country In My Soul** (MCA)
Country vocal quartet in traditional mood. Palatable in small doses. Produced by Jim Foglesong.

**THROBBING GRISTLE**
**Journey Through A Body**
(W. U. Schallfolien)
Final studio outing by T.G. in Rome, March 1981. Sound patchwork and strident excess as usual. This is a limited edition of 1,000. Some masochists do collect this now-defunct band's output. They should have this in their collection already.

**THE TIGERS**
**Savage Music** (Strike)
Not heavy metal as one might reasonably expect, but reasonably intelligent British modern pop with a touch of the Elvis Costellos. Literate and keyboards-oriented. Worth looking out for. Produced by TJ and Alvin Clark.

**TIGHT FIT**
**Tight Fit** (Jive)

Although a studio-constructed band cleverly handled by management (and record company), Tight Fit's sound, if you discount the unrepresentative but bestselling 'The Lion Sleeps Tonight', veers towards Abba-land and the majority of their album displays strong harmonies, melodies ('Fantasy Island', 'I'm Undecided') that stick in your mind and luscious orchestra-

**107**

TIGHT FIT

tions. Conquer your prejudices and overlook the group's visual image. Produced by Tim Friese-Green.

### MEL TILLIS
**Mel Tillis' Greatest Hits** (Elektra)
As Tillis moves to another label, the predictable compilation. Includes 'Southern Rains' and 'Your Body is an Outlaw'. Produced by Jimmy Bowen and Billy Strange.

### THE TIME
**What Time Is It?** (Warners)
Second album for the black Minneapolis funk outfit. Rocking strongly towards doomsday and full of sexual bravado, this comes as a minor disappointment and is nowhere near as distinctive as their first effort. Produced by Morris Day and the Starr Company.

### TOMORROW'S EDITION
**A Song For Everyone** (Atlantic)
East-Coast black soul quartet album debut. Mixed material borrowed from Lou

Reed and The Staples amongst others. Lots of vitality and powerful vocal harmonies. Produced by Amir Bayyan.

### THE TOONS
**Looking At Girls** (Rhino)
Six man band from San Francisco treading Beach Boys sun, summer, girls and fast cars territory. Strong harmonies but derivative material. Produced by Cal Bell and John Milne.

### TORONTO
**Get It On Credit** (Network)
Third album of nondescript rock by an American group. Produced by Steve Smith.

### TREES
**Sleep Convention** (MCA)
Trees conceals the persona of multi-instrumentalist Dane Conover. Strong, upfront soul for the dance-clubs; reminiscent of Prince without the provocative sexuality. Produced by Dane Conover.

### TRIO
**Trio** (Mercury)
Minimal novelty pop from Germany. Takes the fun in electro-pop and simplifies it to absurd proportions. Like a Chinese meal, doesn't provide too much nourishment but if it's humour you're after, this will keep you happy. Produced by Klaus Voorman.

### PAT TROIANI
**Somewhere In Paradise** (Wounded Knee)
Workmanlike country rock with fiddle and pedal steel and Spanish/Mexican influences from an independent label. Pleasing but slight. Produced by Pat Troiani.

### TROUBLEFUNK
**Drop The Bomb** (Sugarhill)
Hot disco soul from a new Washington DC outfit. Virtually non-stop frantic rapping in fourth gear and above, this has energy to spare and will prove to be contagious once your toes start tapping along to the criss-cross rhythms. Produced by Leo Edwards.

### MAUREEN TUCKER
**Playin' Possum** (Trash)
The drummer for the late-lamented Velvet Underground makes a comeback of sorts after a career and a half as a Mid-West housewife. Recorded in her garage (and it sounds that way) this is an affectionate but desperately naive set of interpretations of hits (Dylan's 'I'll Be Your Baby Tonight' and Reed's own 'Heroin' are the worst to suffer). A dire atrocity which should not have been allowed to see the light of day.

### TANYA TUCKER
**The Best of Tanya Tucker** (MCA)
Anthology of early Tucker tracks in a strong country mode: 'Pecos Promenade', 'Rodeo Girls', 'Texas (When I Die)', etc. . . Various producers.

### TANYA TUCKER
**Changes** (Arista)
Teenage country singer now grows older and follows the high road to cross-over, middle-of-the-road acceptance with a change of label and a watering down of her traditional influences. Slick. Produced by Dave Malloy.

### TONY TUFF
**Tuff Selection** (Grove Music)
Pleasant British reggae with Aswad on the rhythm section. Produced by King Sounds.

### TWISTED SISTER
**Under The Blade** (Secret)
Whining orgy of glam heavy metal from a new mutant American outfit leading the current ugliness stakes. Unsubtle satura-

TRIO

## UK PLAYERS
**No Way Out** (A&M)
Superfluous and mundane British jazz funk.

## UTOPIA
**Utopia** (Network)
First album for a new label by Todd Rundgren and his clever synthesiser cohorts. Predictably hard-driving hooks and memorable melodies. The only problem with Rundgren is that he makes it all sound so easy that one soon has doubts about his musical sincerity. A minor genius or a conniving technician? Produced by Todd Rundgren and Utopia.

# V

## THE VALENTINE BROTHERS
**First Take** (Bridge)
Big sound emotional soul panorama with rhythmic tunes and soaring vocals. An impressive album with vitality to spare and first-class musicianship. Produced by the Valentine Brothers.

## VANGELIS
**To The Unknown Man** (RCA)
Compilation of past Vangelis ethereal synthesiser paeans released in the USA following the success of his 'Chariots of Fire' soundtrack. Strong melodies, profound meaning, perfect for the apprentice philosopher. Produced by Vangelis.

## VANILLA FUDGE
**The Best Of Vanilla Fudge** (Atco)
One from the musty vaults. Pompous mush we've all heard too often. From 'You

---

tion assault on the senses. Some will enjoy it, good luck to them. Produced by Pete Way.

## CONWAY TWITTY
**Conway's No. 1 Classics Vol. I** (Elektra)
New recordings of Twitty's numerous past hits. Fans will spend much time comparing and weighing merits. Includes 'Hello Darlin' ', 'You've Never Been This Far Before' and 'I Can't See Me Without You' and other country notables. Produced by Jimmy Bowen and Conway Twitty.

## CONWAY TWITTY
**Dream Maker** (Elektra)
Gentle ballads and half-assed rockers from the country stylist now showing signs of age. Produced by Jimmy Bowen and Conway Twitty.

## TYGERS OF PAN TANG
**The Cage** (MCA)
Slick British heavy metal nodding in the direction of American radio acceptance and the patch of Journey/Foreigner/REO Speedwagon and other mega-platinum bores. Well-done but pointless waste of energy. Produced by Peter Collins.

# U

## UB 40
**The Singles Album** (Graduate)
A compilation of the band's past singles, including 'The Earth Dies Screaming',

'Food For Thought', 'Dream A Lie' and others. Produced by UB 40, Bob Lamb and Ray Pablo Falconer.

## UB 40
**UB 44** (DEP International)
Second album for the successful racially-mixed Birmingham band sees them accentuate the reggae groove with the customary topical, angry lyrics. Earnest and grim preoccupations blend uneasily with the laidback sleepy rhythms and make this a highly frustrating album.

TYGERS OF PAN TANG

Keep Me Hanging On' to 'Season of the Witch' and not forgetting their massacre of 'Ticket to Ride'. Will make some feel younger and highly embarrassed. Produced by Vanilla Fudge and Shadow Morton.

## VANITY 6
### Vanity 6 (Warners)

Female trio talk dirty to soul music backing (courtesy of Prince). Invigorating tunes crafted with much skill and the girl's lingerie image only serves to emphasize the X-certificate lyrics. Interesting, interesting. Produced by Vanity 6 and the Starr Company.

## JOHNNY VAN ZANT BAND
### The Last Of The Wild Ones (Polydor)
Boogie good-time Southern rock sweating it out with the best of them. Hot and raunchy and derivative. Produced by the group, Gregory M. Quesnel and Al Kooper.

## VARIOUS
### Another Saturday Night (Oval)
A re-release for this quality sampler of good-time cajun tunes featuring Johnny Allan's 'Promised Land' and other Louisiana melodies.

## VARIOUS
### The Barclay Towers Compilation Album (Supermusic)
Interesting compilation tracks recorded by seminal Scottish bands and lesser luminaries from north of the border at Barclays Towers studios. Includes the Rezillos, Another Pretty Face, Boots for Dancing, etc. . .

## VARIOUS
### Bay State Rock Vol. 1 (Star Rhythm)
An anthology of Massachusetts rock 'n' roll. Obscure Boston area bands recorded in the mid-60s. A majority of Beatles clones that never made the grade. Of historical interest for unearthing names like Teddy and the Pandas, the Chessmen, Improper Bostonians, Reveliers and Rockin' Ramrods. Produced by David Pierce.

## VARIOUS
### The Best of British Jazz Funk Vol. 2 (Beggars Banquet)
Double album of dance music by Beggar & Co, Freez, Light of the World, Linda Taylor, Linx, Ray Carless, Morrissey Mullen and Incognito. 14 tracks of extended 12-inch efforts. Various producers.

## VARIOUS
### Bumper to Bumper (Calibre)
Double album of extended disco singles featuring Jesse Green, Imagination, Savanna, Illusion, Oneness of Juju, K.I.D. and Fonda Rae. Throbbing and full of hooks.

## VARIOUS
### Bustin' Surfboards (GNP Crescendo)
Surf sagas of the early 60s. Timeless summer tracks by the Beach Boys, Dick Dale, Ritchie Valens, Jim Messina, Bobby Fuller and others. Produced by Neil Norman and Jim Pewter.

## VARIOUS
### A Chance Encounter – The First Essex Rock Album (Rambert)
Very local compilation of uncertain virtues. One band dominates the proceedings with little difficulty: Nightshade. But it's still no great shakes.

## VARIOUS
### Deutschland Compilation (Buro/Cachalot)
US-released anthology of German new wave acts: Xao Seffcheque und Gute Freunde, Palais Schaumburg, Der Plan, Wirtschaftswunder, Pyrolator, Einsturzende Neubauten, SYPH, Die Krupps, Die Doraus und Dien Marinas, Fehlfarben, Abwarts, Der Moderne Man, Malaria, Ja Ja Ja and Der KFC. Many already have debut albums released so this serves as a good appetiser.

## VARIOUS
### Fear And Fantasy (Armageddon)
Compilation of mostly new wave bands that have appeared at London's Moonlight Club: the Room, the Chefs, Flying Club, Out On Blue Six, Patrik Fitzgerald Group, the Pinkies, Dr Mix and the Remix and Artery.

## VARIOUS
### First Edition (EG)
Showcase sampler album for the innovative and experimental Editions EG rock and minimalist roster. Features Jon Hassell, Robert Fripp, Penguin Café Orchestra, Edikanfo, the Lounge Lizards, Brian Eno, Phil Manzanera, Snatch, David Byrne (collaborating with EG mastermind Eno). A challenging choice of cuts.

## VARIOUS
### For Dancers Only (Kent/Modern)
Northern soul compilation. Smooth and soothing dance music in the good old traditions of the genre, mostly dating back to the 60s. Includes a young Ike and Tina Turner, the Ikettes, ZZ Hill, Lowell Fulsom, Mary Love, Felice Taylor, etc. . .

## VARIOUS
### Heavy Metal Thunder (Carrere)
Loud noises from the reliable home of the riffs chez Carrere: a roster which includes Saxon, Rose Tattoo, Biff, Rosy Tatts, Demon, Dokken, Rage. . . All sound the same to me, but we all know what a philistine I can be.

## VARIOUS
### The Indipop Compilasian Album (Virgin)
British new wave with an Oriental touch. Contrived and awkward but has its moments: Monsoon, Thika, Sons of Arga, Dishari, John Keliekor, Sulaeman (in fact from Indonesia and plays flute but no rock. . .) are part of the package put together by David Claridge.

## VARIOUS
### Jive Rhythm Trax (Jive)

Not a record to listen to, but one to play along or rap with. Indeed this is a basic set of no-frills rhythm tracks (with various bpm's – beats per minute) for the Saturday night stay at home fantasist or the deejay with the gift of the gab. Produced by the Willesden Dodgers.

## VARIOUS
### Life In The European Theatre (Elektra)
Anthology with a political slant, proceeds of which are going to the anti-nuclear movement. Mostly new wave contributors from both sides of the water: Clash, Peter Gabriel, the Undertones, Madness, Bad Manners, the Jam, the Beat, the Specials, XTC, the Stranglers, Echo and the Bunnymen, the Au Pairs but also the

Doors from earlier times with a similar peace-loving vocation.

**VARIOUS**
**Mastermixes** (Epic/Prelude)
Extended disco mixes of major dance floor hits from the USA. Infectious stuff with re-modeled contributions from Sharon Redd, Jeanette, D Train, Empress, Gayle Adams, Secret Weapon, the Strikers and others.

**VARIOUS**
**Music And Rhythm** (WEA/PVC)

Double album of celebration of African and other ethnic musics, delineating their healthy influence on various strands of contemporary rock and jazz. Possibly the best sampler of the year, this blends in an invigorating manner contributions by Peter Gabriel (who organised the parallel WOMAD festival), the Beat, Holger Czukay, XTC, Byrne and Eno, Morris Pert with the real stuff from the Burundi Drummers, Shankar, Mighty Sparrow, and many others. Also a Pete Townshend track. A must.

**VARIOUS**
**Oi Oi That's Yer Lot** (Secret)
One more yobbo rock compilation with undistinguished, roisterous, superficially angry pieces from the no-less undistinguished Business, Five-O, the Oppressed, Subculture, Crux, the Warriors, Attak, Arthur Afters, Frankie and the Flames, the Gonads, Attila the Stockbroker, Judge Dread. Reggae influences pervade side two. A minor blessing to break up the loud monotony.

**VARIOUS**
**The Only Alternative** (Rondelet)
More punk rejects from the gristmill of fame. Features such unforgettable but forgotten names as Special Duties, Catwax Axe Co, Dead Man's Shadow, Antipasti, Riot Squad, the Fits . . . Snore. . . .

**VARIOUS**
**Plurex Hours** (Plurex)
Mostly Dutch new wave compilation with A Blaze Of Colour, X-Mal Deutschland, Nasmak, Minny Pops and the Project supplying jaunty poppish experimentation. British outfit Eric Random and the Bedlamites also make a surprise appearance.

**VARIOUS**
**Punk And Disorderly: Further Charges** (Anagram)
More anti-establishment anthems most of which seem to be flirting with heavy metal in the volume stakes. On display are the wares of GBH, the Expelled, the Insane, One Way System, Court Martial, Action Pact, Erazerhead, the Enemy, Abrasive Wheels, Riot/Clone, Channel 3, the Dark, the Violators and the Wall. Take your sad pick.

**VARIOUS**
**Recommended Records Sampler** (Recommended)
Sampler for a small but imaginative British independent label. Double album with lots of innovative stuff from This Heat, Faust, Robert Wyatt, the Residents, Art Zoyd, Univers Zero, Vogel, Picchio Dal Pozzo, and other cheerful European experimentalists.

**VARIOUS**
**Soul Daze: Soul Nights** (Ronco)
TV advertised British soul compilation with tracks by Aretha Franklin, Lee Dorsey, Fontella Bass, Rufus Thomas, Candi Staton and scores more.

**VARIOUS**
**Sounds d'Afrique II – Soukous** (Island)

Second Island sampler presentation of authentic African music concentrates on the area of the Congo. Fascinating material showing the cross-breeding of cultures as electric guitars and horns blend in all so effectively with more ethnic instruments and rhythms. More than just a curio.

**VARIOUS**
**Soweto** (Rough Trade)
Invigorating sounds from South African bands recorded under primitive conditions in the Soweto township. New Ducky Boys, Kid Bera-Bera and Mister King Jerroo, S. Tshabalaka, John Motha, Elfas Zondi and A. M'Kosane are names which appear on the WOMAD double album but these longer pieces show them in full stride.

**VARIOUS**
**Steel Crazy** (Abstract)
Yet another heavy metal anthology. Includes the disreputable likes of the Rods, Twisted Sister, Stampede, Starfighters, Anvil, Geordie, Praying Mantis, Krokus, Lautrec and Girlschool.

**VARIOUS**
**Summer Means Fun** (CBS/Columbia)
Double dose of suntanned plastic compilation. Not always the original groups on some of these beach and hot rod chestnuts; beware. Performing for real, though, are Bruce and Terry, the Rip Chords, Johnny Rivers, Jan & Dean, the Hot Doggers and Flash Cadillac and the Continental Kids. Produced by Terry Melcher and Bruce Johnston.

**VARIOUS**
**This Is Boston, Not LA** (Modern Methods)
Irreverent compilation of aggressive modern rock in a punk tradition from mightily unknown US bands.

**VARIOUS**
**US Metal Vol. 2** (Shrapnel)
Guitar-orientated compilation of US heavy metal heroics. On display are Mike Batio, the Rods, Wild Dogs, Cinema, Le Mans, Vixen, Virgin Steele and Failsafe. Formula thrash.

**VENDETTA**
**Vendetta** (Epic)
US heavy metal trio out of a familiar mould which they should throw away some day soon before the rot sets in once and for all. Mediocre bombast.

**HOLLY BETH VINCENT**
**Holly And The Italians** (Virgin/Epic)
Holly now takes the solo route (although the album's title is misleading). Tough girl stance and wide-screen production job hardly conceal the lack of inspiration and common touch of Miss Vincent. Has the loser stamp all over it; squandered talent. Produced by Mike Thorne.

**VOYAGE**
**One Step Higher** (Atlantic)
French session musicians go disco with a rancid vengeance. Formula stuff and a

waste of time. Produced by Marc Chantereau, Pierre-Alain Dahan, Slim Pezin and Roger Tokarz.

## C. W. VRTACEK
**Victory Through Grace** (Leisuretime)
Minimal minimalist experiments in experimentalism. Uh?

## BUNNY WAILER
**Hook, Line And Sinker** (Solomonic)
Reggae master indulging in demonstrative soul warblings. Somewhat unexpected but grows on you.

## WALL OF VOODOO
**Call Of The West** (IRS)
Idiosyncratic modern American pop in the best traditions of the genre. Imaginative, disjointed and fun. Already their second album and getting better all the time. Superior to the twee Devo by a length and a synthesiser. Produced by Richard Mazda.

## LEON WARE
**Leon Ware** (Elektra)
Polished black medium-paced funk with half the jazz cross-over world seemingly helping out in the studio: Gato Barbieri, Jeff Porcaro, David Paich, David Ganson, David T. Walker. . . Soothing rhythmic excursions. Produced by Marty Paich and Leon Ware.

## JENNIFER WARNES
**The Best Of Jennifer Warnes** (Arista)
An oddly premature compilation from this sadly underrated US singer after only two albums and a few soundtrack songs (her

later duet with Joe Cocker in 'An Officer and a Gentleman' was released long after this album). However, the material is nigh perfect rocking ballads and most expressive they are at that: 'I Know A Heartache When I See One', 'Right Time Of The Night' and many other melancholy pieces. A third album is very much overdue. Various producers.

## GENE WATSON
**This Dream's On Me** (MCA)
Predictable, sentimental country schmaltz. Produced by Russ Reeder.

## DOTTIE WEST
**Full Circle** (Liberty)
Bland, anonymous middle of the road ballads from a deserter from the country field. Doesn't suit her either; she should have stuck to what she knew (and could sing) best. Produced by Larry Gatlin.

## JAMES WHITE AND THE BLACKS
**Sax Maniac** (Animal)
Ragged, rough at the edges fusion jazz

from a veteran of the New York jazz and art scene. Uncompromising and difficult music, not to everyone's taste; sample with due care. Produced by James White.

## ROBERT 'GOODIE' WHITFIELD
**Call Me Goodie** (Total Experience)
Upbeat soul disco with help from the Gap Band and Yarbrough & Peoples. Slick and highly danceable. Produced by Lonnie Simmons.

## THE WHO
**It's Hard** (Polydor/Warners)

| | |
|---|---|
| Athena | I've Known No War |
| It's Your Turn | One Life's Enough |
| Cooks County | One At A Time |
| It's Hard | Why Did I Fall For |
| Dangerous | That |
| Eminence Front | A Man Is A Man |
| | Cry If You Want |

And seldom has an album title proved so appropriate! Never have The Who and Pete Townshend's inspiration sounded so tired and resigned to the fact. The lyrics and subject matter are more convoluted than ever and the music lacks thrills of the mildest kind. Synthesiser runs fail to trigger any vibrant response from Daltrey's vocal clichés and no track really stands out as memorable. Produced by Glyn Johns.

WALL OF VOODOO

## HANK WILLIAMS JR.
**Hank Williams Jr.'s Greatest Hits** (Elektra)
Glossy anthology of strong, past country successes. Sturdy mini-classics like 'Texas Women', 'Dixie On My Mind' and 'Whiskey Bent and Hell Bound'. Produced by Jimmy Bowen.

## WIND CHYMES
**Arrival** (RCA)
Smooth and toe-tapping Southern soul from a new nine-piece band of funk experts. Produced by Anthony A. Lockett.

## PAUL WINTER
**Missa Gaia Earth Mass** (Living Music)
Liturgical mish-mash spread over two albums. Ambitious but highly fallible modern mass mixing elements of rock, African rhythms, whale noises and jazz. Worthy but oh so long. Produced by Paul Winter and Oscar Castro-Neve.

## STEVE WINWOOD
**Talking Back To The Night** (Island)

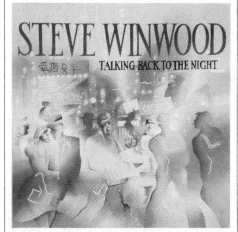

After the heartening success of 'Arc Of A Diver', Winwood's new solo album comes as a bit of a let down. Deliberately low-key and strongly introspective, the songs never take off from a gentle funky beat and drown in a veritable morass of naive sentiments. Immaculate musicianship and Winwood's sweet, rasping tones are as fresh as ever but the excitement is gone. 'Valerie' is the only track to stick in the mind (mostly by virtue of constant radio play). Good taste taken to too much of an extreme. Produced by Steve Winwood.

## ROY WOOD
**The Singles** (Speed)
Almost classic British pop of yesteryear from a now almost forgotten craftsman of the genre. Features familiar tunes like Move stalwarts 'Flowers in the Rain' and 'Fire Brigade' to Wizzard and solo recording by the endearing Roy Wood. 15 cuts. Various producers.

## THE WORK
**Slow Crimes** (Recommended)
Old-fashioned experimentalism from British musicians, one of whom, Tim Hodgkinson, was in Henry Cow. Wails and meanders in all directions.

## X
**Under The Big Black Sun** (Elektra)

Third album from the ever-improving Los Angeles punk band now transcending their origins with assured, powerful music. Raw energy and angry despair rail against the American way of life in furious way. Combines the virtues of primal punk with a fluent form of musicianship, full of fervor. An important album which explodes the loser-myth of West Coast punk and laidback clichés. Produced by Ray Manzarek.

## YAZOO (YAZ in the USA)
**Upstairs At Eric's** (Mute/Sire)

The first album from Vince Clarke and his acolyte blues singer Alf Moyet (a she. . .). The combination of synthesiser work by the ex-Depeche Mode mastermind and the strong, deep blues tones of the singer strike a fruitful combination and make this a major release. Memorable melodies and songs marred only here and there by Clarke's dabblings in the studio with voice cut-ups and overlays. Produced by E. C. Radcliffe and Yazoo.

## YELLOWMAN AND FATHEAD
**Live At Aces** (Jah Guidance)
Reggae dance hall session with clever, polished and witty deejay dub. Ideal party record.

## Y & T
**Black Tiger** (A&M)
Run-of-the-mill American second division heavy metal. Limp, and that's no compliment when it comes to this kind of music.

## ZAPP
**Zapp II** (Warners)
Disco-soul syncopation in an overdrive, robotic groove throughout. Lots of intricate studio work but the results are infectious and easy-going. Accomplished funk. Produced by Roger and Zapp Troutman.

## WARREN ZEVON
**The Envoy** (Asylum)
An out-of-focus album where the talented Zevon flounders in search of unity. Moving from fluent, plaintive, love ballads and raucous idiosyncratic rockers, Warren Zevon never settles for a mood as he keeps on exorcising his private ghosts. Still miles ahead of most US West-Coast singer-songwriters nevertheless. Stand-outs are the beautifully ironic 'The Hula-Hula Boy' and the vicious 'Charlie's Medicine'. Produced by Greg Ladanyi, Waddy Wachtel and Warren Zevon.

## ZINC
**Street Level** (Jive)

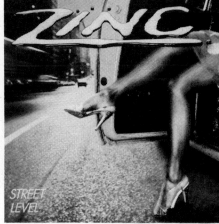

First rate urban soul funk-out. Very much a recording studio creation but immaculately crafted and with not a beat missing to get your feet, body and mind into the right dancing groove. Produced by Jacques Fred Petrus and Mauro Malavasi.

# A

## ABBA
### The Singles-The First Ten Years
(Epic/Atlantic)
Recapitulating an era: all the clean-cut, infectiously clever hit songs from the Swedish money-making machine. Early smasheroos still hold up well and the whole set is a practical demonstration of sheer glossy professionalism. On the menu: 'S.O.S.', 'Waterloo', 'Dancing Queen', all the way to more recent (and gently subdued efforts) like 'The Day Before You Came' and 'Under Attack'. Indispensable as a testimony to what pop music is all about (that is, if you haven't already got all the preceding albums). Produced by Benny Anderson and Bjorn Ulvaeus, all 23 hits of them over two albums. . .

## ABRASIVE WHEELS
### When The Punks Go Marching In
(Riot City)
Million miles an hour punk anthems with energy to spare, firing in all directions with joyous indiscrimination. Banal lyrics and lots a' noise.

## THE ABYSSINIANS
### Forward (Alligator)
Sensuous, lilting reggae tones from one of Jamaica's more popular bands. Ubiquitous Robbie Shakespeare helps out together with Zoot Sims and Earl 'Chinna' Smith. Pleasing. Produced by the Abyssinians.

## ACCEPT
### Restless And Wild (CNR)
Third release by thunderous German heavy metal outfit. Speed freak music in constant fifth gear, if not overdrive. One for the connoisseurs of loud music.

## THE ADICTS
### Sound of Music (Razor)
Surprisingly effective punk album with, could one have believed it, a trenchant sense of humour! Strong and joyful pop strains combined with the manic energy of minimal punk blend with ease and make this an album to look out for. It's better, much better than you might think. Investigate. Produced by Harry T. Murlowski and Steve Tannet.

## AFTER THE FIRE
### Der Kommissar (CBS)
ATF Christian-rock compilation culled from past albums. The only problem is that ATF have never had any hits to speak of. Dreary.

## RIKK AGNEW
### All By Myself (Frontier)
US punk solo effort (Agnew led Southern California outfit The Adolescents). Hardcore energy encapsulated with gusto. Produced by Thom Wilson and Rikk Agnew.

## WYVON ALEXANDER
### Wyvon (Gervasi)
Blurred-voiced country newcomer. Smokey and melancholic, but also retains some touches of humour. Produced by Jerry Shook and Bob Saporiti.

## ALFONZO
### Alfonzo (Larc)
New black singer/songwriter with a strong touch of the early Motown ballads. Energetic and ideal dance-floor material. Should go further down the road to the big time. Produced by Clay McMurray.

## PETER ALLEN
### The Best (A&M)
A past label retrospective of assured, middle-of-the-road songs which never quite achieved immortality. Cocktail lounge schmaltz with a modicum of pep and wit. Produced by David Foster, Joel Dorn, Mike Post, Marvin Hamlisch, Peter Allen and Ed Thacker.

## ALLEZ ALLEZ
### Promises (Virgin)
Pleasant if moody debut album by the Belgian group with British vocalist Sarah Os-

ALLEZ ALLEZ PROMISES

bourne. Swirls of ethnic rhythms surround her sultry, chanteuse tones while an over-elaborate production job adds a touch too much gloss to the proceeds. You can dance to it, just about. Will do better, but sufficiently entrancing for now. Not many bands can say that for themselves so early. Produced by Martyn Ware.

## AMERICA
### View From The Ground (Capitol)
Saccharine-streaked wimp rock from foremost warblers of the genre.

## AMUZEMENT PARK
### Amuzement Park (Our Gang)
New Chicago-based soul outfit on debut outing. Strong horn workout in a dance groove that swings with gentle abandon. Produced by Dunn Pearson Jr.

## JOHN ANDERSON
### Wild and Blue (Warners)
Stark, unadulterated country with few concessions to rock or crossover audiences. Anderson's fourth album is packed with felicities, and first-rate musicianship (banjos, fiddles, steel guitars and dobros dominate the proceedings) stands out. Contributions from Emmylou Harris and Merle Haggard. Recommended for purists and everyone. Produced by Frank Jones.

## CATHERINE ANDREWS
### Fruits (Cat Tracks)
Wafer-thin melodies with a touch of terminal whimsy from a young British painter. Patchy but often too coy for words. Might prove to be an acquired taste; time will tell.

## HORACE ANDY
### Exclusively (Solid Groove)
Sweetish US-produced reggae which goes down well but offers few distinctive features. Produced by Lloyd Barnes.

## ADAM ANT
### Friend or Foe (CBS/Epic)
Young Adam now wanders the pop roads quite antless and the results are much the same as before, even if the hits are not so easy to achieve. A strong autobiographical series of comments on the vagaries of fame provides a self-pitying mood, but the enthusiasm is still quite infectious. Some progress is slowly being made; the problem is – in which direction? Produced by Adam Ant and Marco Pirroni.

ADAM ANT

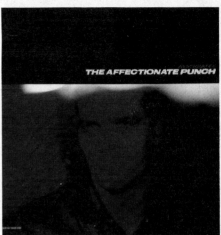

### AUGUST REDMOON
**Fools Are Never Alone** (Metalworks)
5-track mini-album of strong mainstream rock from a new American band. The riffs are impeccable and the vocalist screams just right. Good formula stuff.

### AVALON
**Everyman A King** (Capitol)
Short mini-LP with only four US heavy metal tracks in a decidedly mellow mood which might not satisfy the ravenous hordes of the pagan god Riff.

### HOYT AXTON
**Road Music** (A&M)
Easy-rider ballads with a twang in the country tail. Gravel-voiced and appealing.

### AZYMUTH
**Cascades** (Milestone)
Brazilian fusion jazz trio in a poppish, entertaining mood. Veers from ethereal to sleek percussion with equal pleasure. Easy listening of the better kind. Produced by Jose Roberto Bertrami.

# B

### BAD MANNERS
**Forging Ahead** (Magnet)
Accessible, danceable pop with zest and fun to the fore. Less of a reggae influence than on previous outings and the pop leanings of Bad Manners emerge triumphant. Fun time music with all the hits of the fair: 'My Boy Lollipop', 'Samson and Delilah', etc. . . Produced by Roger Lomas.

### BAD RELIGION
**How Could Hell Be Any Worse?** (Epitaph)
Prototype L.A. punk with hate and resentment of all things bright and beautiful at its core. Heard it all before (and better). Produced by Bad Religion.

### APES OF WRATH
**Apes Of Wrath** (Media Master)
Late period psychedelia excursion; rambling, spineless songs with few signs of distinction. Produced by Ted Dodson.

### ARKANSAW MAN
**Arkansaw Man** (Subterranean)
New American trio moving effortlessly from rock to post-psychedelia with a remarkable lack of originality and punch. Produced by the group and Richard Kelly.

### THE ASSOCIATES
**The Affectionate Punch** (Fiction)
Both one from the vaults and a new one: the Associates' first (1980) album with a radical re-mix which revitalises the material but also subtracts some of its urgent immediacy. 'A memorable one . . . often reminiscent in its romantic, operatic bleakness of the David Bowie of "Station to Station". . .', I said back in 'The Rock Yearbook 1981'. I see no reason to change my views.

## RAZZY BAILEY
**A Little More Razz** (RCA)
Slick and gritty country singer with rock velleities. Appealing crossover attempt with enough integrity to please both country and rock camps. Produced by Bob Montgomery.

## BAR-KAYS
**Propositions** (Mercury)
The epitome of the Memphis funk sound brought up to date for the dance mood of the 1980s. Fiery and gripping stuff with Larry Dodson taking on the vocal mantle with a talent worthy of his predecessors in the group. Produced by Allen A. Jones.

## BARON ROJO
**Larga Vida Al Rock And Roll/ Volumen Brutal** (Kamaflage)
A double helping of raucous heavy metal from, of all places, Spain. The first album boasts lyrics in Spanish but 'Volumen Brutal' recorded later sees the mandatory switch to English and confirms the fact that Baron Rojo (The Red Baron) stick to all the clichés of HM in their decided lack of subtlety and hackneyed riffs.

## TONI BASIL
**Word Of Mouth** (Radialchoice/Chrysalis)

Lightweight pop propelled to the heights by the freak success of the Chapman and Chinn 'Mickey'. Infuriatingly coy and knowing covers of Bacharach, Essex, Devo and other familiar songs. Just an old lady playing at being young again; the gloss and vivacity are artificial in the extreme. Easy to listen to, though. Produced by Greg Mathieson and Trevor Veitch.

## MARTYN BATES
**Letters Written** (Cherry Red)
Ten-inch package of ethereal, delicate mood pieces by the singer from Eyeless in Gaza. Monotonous and poetic, seldom ignites into something bigger. A curio, no more.

## BATTLEFIELD BAND
**There's A Buzz** (Temple)
One of Britain's best folk outfits, using a satisfying blend of old instruments and more modern synthesisers to reinterpret traditional music in an innovative manner. Reliable.

## THE BATS
**How Pop Can You Get?** (Gustav)
Youthful American power pop despite the garish cover. Crisp and bouncy material with power and gusto. Produced by The Bats.

## BAUHAUS
**The Sky's Gone Out** (Beggars Banquet/A&M)
Pretentious serving of gothic, obscure neo-psychedelia. Fleeting flirtations with other genres (disco, pop, doom rock) show the whole dishonesty of the affair. Scored a minor UK hit with a David Bowie cover. File under 'No Future'. Produced by Bauhaus.

## THE BEAT (known as **THE ENGLISH BEAT** in the USA)
**Special Beat Service** (Go-Feet/IRS)
Third album by the popular British group whose carefree mixture of disparate styles here works to a tee, enhanced by digital recording. A multi-racial team, they move with visible enjoyment from reggae to pop, with deft touches of calypso, toasting and large screen ballads. Can't be faulted. Produced by Bob Sargeant.

## THE BEATLES
**20 Greatest Hits** (Parlophone/Capitol)
A twentieth anniversary commemoration of the Beatles, regrouping all their hits in (almost) chronological order. Every tune is familiar but the sequencing throws up interesting insights and this is, without any doubt, a value-for-money collection for younger generations who missed out on the thrill of it all. Produced by George Martin.

## THE BEATNIKS
**The Beatniks** (Statik)
Collaboration between Japanese stars Yukihiro Takahashi and Keiichi Suzuki. Bland and much too faceless electro-pop. Ambles along and does no great harm. Somewhat useless. Produced by the artists.

## TOMMY BELL
**Tommy Bell** (Gold Sound)
Samey-voiced new country performer equally at ease on ballads, rockers and traditional weepers. Also a welcome touch of r&b. Produced by Tommy DeVito.

## BELLAMY BROTHERS
**Strong Weakness** (Elektra-Curb)
Diluted country by the duo, with reggae and pop touches. Frothily lightweight and inconsequential. Passes a half hour effortlessly but is forgotten as quickly. Produced by Jimmy Bowen and the Bellamy Brothers.

## PAT BENATAR
**Get Nervous** (Chrysalis)

US prima donna of easy acceptability heavy metal for the masses (and the young boys) with another selection of unmemorable, hard-driven rock done with gloss, money and everything lack of talent can buy. Dull, dull, dull. Produced by Neil Geraldo and Peter Coleman.

## MICHEL BERGER
**Dreams In Stone** (Atlantic)
Unashamedly romantic concept album about life in New York, created by a Frenchman with the help of a bevy of US lyricists, recorded on the West Coast and featuring solo outings by Jennifer Warnes, Rosanne Cash, Max Gronenthal and Bill Withers. Highly cinematic; the parts are better than the whole. Produced by Michel Berger and Philippe Rault.

## BERLIN
**Paradise Victim** (Enigma)
Infectious electro-pop from Los Angeles with a slight sting in the tail. Solid hooks and melodies fronted by female singer Teri Nunn bring back short-lived memories of many other groups but the formula works well. Produced by Daniel Van Patten and the Maomen.

## BLANCMANGE
**Happy Families** (London)
Silly names and titles and even sillier cover for what is, in fact, one of the more vital electro-pop releases of the year. Dramatic delivery coupled with strong, soaring melodies make this new British duo a power to contend with in the field, now that precursors like OMD appear to be on the creative wane. Produced by Mike Howlett.

## THE BLASTERS
**Over There – Live At The Venue London** (Warners/Slash)
A six-song EP recorded on the occasion of a recent British visit by the Los Angeles punk/neo-rockabilly outfit. Second-rate material (minor early rock pieces and derivative originals) disappoint and the band's true power is missing. Nice piano touches à la Jerry Lee Lewis hint at the Blasters' real strength. A wrong career move soon to be forgotten.

## BLITZ
**Voice Of A Generation** (No Future)
Sub-Ramones speed punk from British group in dire need of a few extra grey cells. Obscure rantings against a wall of sound that allows no respite.

## BLOTTO
**Combo Akimbo** (Blotto)
Satirical rock from previous winners in this sparse category. Sex comes in for a beating but the music is lightweight and generally fun. Buck Dharma of Blue Oyster Cult joins on 'Metal Head'. Produced by Blotto and Chris Cassone.

## KURTIS BLOW
**Tough** (Mercury)
Unimaginative album of five rap tracks by one of the genre's pioneers. Too many (bad) puns for comfort. Try Grandmaster Flash instead.

## BLUE ORCHIDS
**Agents Of Change** (Rough Trade)
Another EP to add to this year's flood of albums. More shimmering musical lacework from Martin Braham's guitar and Una Baines' keyboards. A work of transition still veering between dirge and monotony but often achieving great emotional heights. Look forward to the next artefact from Blue Orchids.

## BLUE RONDO A LA TURK
**Chewing The Fat** (Virgin)

Or the triumph of style over content! One of Britain's hypes of the year which didn't come off despite columns of print and media attention. The vinyl results come as a bit of an anticlimax, but this is in fact not that bad: mild, lilting sambas and carioca rhythms from a bunch of poseurs but honest musicians. Good for dancing, even. They should have allowed the music to speak for itself. Soulful. Produced by Pete Wingfield, Mike Chapman, Godley and Creme, Clanger and Winstanley.

## ARTHUR BLYTHE
**Elaboration** (Columbia)
Good-time swing jazz with mucho funk and soul. A delightful blend of melody and dance rhythms courtesy of New Orleans at its best.

## BONEY M
**Mary's Boy Child (The Christmas Album)** (Hansa/Atlantic)
Compilation of seasonal massacres from the epitome of purveyors of kitsch (or bad taste – depends on where you are sitting). Even includes 'Jingle Bells' à la disco sauce; nuff said. Produced by Frank Farian.

## BOXCAR WILLIE
**The Best Of Boxcar Vol. 1** (Main Street)
Retrospective of Boxcar Willie's 1975–1979 years. Rugged, folky country paeans. Safe and familiar. Produced by Jim Martin.

## THE BOXTOPS
**Greatest Hits** (Rhino)
Compilation of Alex Chilton's now almost legendary band. Obvious inclusions are 'The Letter' and 'Cry Like A Baby' but the other songs bear rediscovery. Produced by Dann Penn, Tommy Cogbill and Chips Moman.

## BRICK
**After 5** (Bang)
Unpretentious but danceable brand of

ARTHUR BLYTHE

ROCKY BURNETTE

### BUZZ
**Buzz** (Asylum)
And another funk album hits the dance floor. Anonymous toe-tappers.

### DONALD BYRD AND 125TH STREET N.Y.C.
**Words, Sounds, Colors and Shapes** (Elektra)
Jazz trumpet virtuoso Byrd on a slumming excursion into dance floor soul territory with the help of Hot Buttered Soul, Hayes and a whole cohort of assorted instrumentalists. Bland and lacking in momentum. Produced by Isaac Hayes.

# C

### CABARET VOLTAIRE
**Hai!** (Rough Trade)
Britain's (or Sheffield's) most adept synthesised doom distillation unit recorded live in Japan. As *NME* puts it: 'monotony and sub-aquatic vocals' dominate the joyless, but intense proceedings. Music for paranoiac moods only.

### GLEN CAMPBELL
**Old Home Town** (Atlantic)
A change of label for the country man sees him veering between two chairs and indulging in some whimsy. Side two, brooding and melancholy, comes off best. Still one of the best male voices in the business. Produced by Jerry Fuller.

### CAN
**Delay 1968** (Spoon)
One from the past, recorded back in 1968 before the momentous Monster Movie and never released before. Not just of historical interest, this shows Can were then already a major, innovative force, even if much was still in gestation. Malevolent exorcisms that were to mark the next decade are seen here in shorthand form: Malcolm Mooney's satanic tone, the trance elements, the unleashed wall-of-sound fury. In advance of its time then and still vitally important now.

### FREDDY CANNON
**14 Booming Hits** (Rhino)
Exemplary anthology of familiar songs by a much-underrated early rock and blues pioneer. Includes 'Tallahassee Lassie', 'Way Down Yonder in New Orleans' and twelve other minor gems. Various producers.

### TONY CAREY
**Tony Carey** (Rocshire)
New US middle-of-the-road rock vocalist

---

soul/funk from our American cousins. Produced by Brick and Phil Benton.

### THE BROTHERS JOHNSON
**Blast!** (A&M)
Unspectacular disco fare with bite and gloss but lacking that little extra ingredient that spells magic to the dancing shoes. Produced by the Brothers Johnson and Quincy Jones (one side apiece).

### SHEREE BROWN
**The Music** (Capitol)
New American black vocalist and guitarist with pleasant blend of mellow, swinging soul. Acolytes galore: Patrick Rushen, Larry Williams and Stevie Wonder. Pizzazz to spare. Produced by Andre Fischer, Alexander Thomas and Sheree Brown.

### PEABO BRYSON
**Don't Play With Fire** (Capitol)
Elegantly suave black performer with mostly self-penned material. Oozes sensuality and assurance. Almost perfect for the ladies of the night. Also pleasing by day. Produced by Peabo Bryson.

### BUDGIE
**Deliver Us From Evil** (RCA)
Workmanlike hot-pot of fast rock with

---

heavy metal suspicions. Well done if a trifle anonymous and samey. Produced by Don Smith.

### ROCKY BURNETTE
**Heart Stopper** (Goods)
Innocuous rockabilly outing by a genre expert now on a smaller, regional label. Chuggles along quietly but never catches fire. Amiable at best. Produced by Bill House and Jim Seiter.

### THE BUSHWACKERS
**Beneath The Southern Cross** (CBS)
Weak mixture of rock, country and Australian folk (!) from down-under outfit who are reputedly big in their homeland.

### JERRY BUTLER
**Ice 'n' Hot** (Fountain)
Welcome comeback for a polished black soul performer. Distinctive dusky tones and romantic material blend effortlessly. Produced by Jerry Butler and Lawrence Hanks.

### BUXX
**Knickers Down** (Panther)
Six-track independent release hailing from Buffalo, N.Y. Adequate pomp rock with pretensions and no circumstance.

recorded in Germany. Pleasant but bland medium-paced rockers with gentle melodies. Produced by Peter Hauke.

## DON CARLOS
**Day To Day Living** (Greensleeves)
Former lead singer for Black Uhuru on solo reggae outing. Backed by Roots Radics, he shows fine form and voice in a seductively sweet collection of songs. Produced by Henry 'Junjo' Lawes.

## CARL CARLTON
**The Bad Carl Carlton** (RCA)
Polished disco dance and soul effort by a quality black performer. Material by David Rubinson and a fiery cover of the Four Tops' 'Baby I Need Your Loving'. Produced by Narada Michael Walden.

## A CERTAIN RATIO
**I'd Like To See You Again** (Factory)
Patchy album of experimental rock/jazz doomy atmospherics. Well done but never tickles the heartstrings. Welcome intrusion of funk elements livens up matters somewhat but overall a disappointment from a British band once much loved by progressive critics. Too many dirges, not enough cerebral fun.

## CHAMELEON
**Techno-Color** (USA Platinum)
Second album from a Minneapolis quintet. Plodding stuff with upfront keyboards dominating a semi-heavy metal din. Produced by Yanni.

## CHANNEL 3
**I've Got A Gun** (No Future)
Debut album for an American punk outfit not unlike the Dead Kennedys but without the verve and wit. Indifferent (and badly recorded) thrash.

## CHARGE
**Perfection** (Kamera)
Amateurish progressive punk from an ambitious British group. Desolation rock in full flight and desperately short of ideas, inspiration or melodies. Rather pitiful.

## CHARLENE
**Used To Be** (Motown)
Title track duet with Stevie Wonder adds a touch of needed class to this generally mediocre album of re-heated soul ballads. No great shakes. Produced by Ron Miller.

## SONNY CHARLES
**The Sun Still Shines** (Highrise)
Unspectacular but easy-going dollops of soul, coated with luscious arrangements from Gene Page. Effective if quiet. Produced by Bobby Paris.

## CHAS AND DAVE
**Job Lot** (Rockney)
Jolly singalongs for the North London cockney crowd from the fun duo. Not much else you can really say about it; all so predictable and hollow. Produced by Chas and Dave.

## CLIFTON CHENIER AND HIS RED HOT LOUISIANA BAND
**I'm Here** (Alligator)
The veteran zydeco expert now in a bluesier mood following some serious health problems. Happy-go-lucky set of party material. Produced by Sam Charters.

## CHIC
**Tongue In Chic** (Atlantic)

Partly a return to form for the Edwards-Rodgers outfit but the album never fully recaptures the polished magic of a few years back. Impeccably arranged disco rhythms and one sure-fire classic, 'Hangin' ', with all the tantalising joy of past successes but the rest of the songs just appear to be going through the motions. But what groovy motions! Produced by Nile Rodgers and Bernard Edwards.

## CHICAGO
**If You Leave Me Now** (CBS)
Retrospective album on past label for Chicago who have since marched on to a revitalisation of sorts on the Warners roster. Pleasant memories of the brassy '25 or 6 to 4' or 'If You Leave Me Now'. Produced by James William Guercio, Phil Ramone and Tom Dowd.

## CHILLIWACK
**Opus X** (Millenium)
Reliable Southern rock from a long-standing band only now beginning to break through to the bigger time in the USA. A melodic trio with careful arrangements with little left to chance; mechanical and professional, leaves no lasting memory. Produced by Bill Henderson, Brian MacLeod and Ab Bryant.

## ALEX CHILTON
**Live In London** (Aura)
Shambolic souvenir of a gig at Dingwalls by the quasi-legendary Boxtops and Big Star singer. Tepid rockers performed with little rehearsal will add little to the (crumbling) legend. Produced by Aaron Sixx.

## CHINA CRISIS
**Difficult Shapes And Passive Rhythms** (Virgin)

Debut by new British band. Nice arty dance stuff about which there's little to say. Tastefully done (as is the Peter Saville cover) but going nowhere. Produced by the group and Gil Norton.

## THE CHIPMUNKS
**The Chipmunks Go Hollywood** (RCA)
The usual pleasant parody of over-inflated hits. 'Eye of the Tiger', 'Chariots of Fire', 'Arthur's Theme', 'Fame' and others come in for the treatment. Worth a few chuckles. Produced by Janice Karman and Ross Bagdasarian.

## ANNE CLARK
**The Sitting Room** (Red Flame)
Mini-LP debut for a London poet. Recitation of slight, surreal pieces over a doom-laden musical background. Bleak but well done.

## ROY CLARK
**Turned Loose** (Churchill)
Patchy country with many a dry, nay arid patch among the high grass and twanging notes. Produced by Roy Clark.

## GEORGE CLINTON
**Computer Games** (Capitol)
Urban funk from the Funkadelic mastermind. Big sound and a strong dose of mischievous humour make this an enjoyable set of disco dancers. Includes hit single 'Loopzilla'. Produced by George Clinton.

## CODE OF HONOR/SICK PLEASURE
**Fight Or Die/Dolls Under Control** (Subterranean)
One side each for these two new US punk bands from the West Coast. Eight songs

apiece. Loud, anonymous thrash. In one ear and out the other with no lasting effect.

### JOE COHEN
**Writings On My Wall** (Friendship Store)
Chicago-based singer-songwriter with a set of introspective ballads with primarily acoustic backing. Has its charms, but in small doses. Produced by Joe Cohen.

### NATALIE COLE
**The Natalie Cole Collection** (Capitol)
Classy, middle-of-the-road soul hits compilation. Produced by Chuck Jackson and Marvin Yancy.

### NAT KING COLE
**Greatest Love Songs** (Capitol)
Classic smooth ditties of yesteryear by a master of the form. Packaged for television direct sales.

### PHIL COLLINS
**Hello, I Must Be Going!** (Virgin/Atlantic)

| | |
|---|---|
| I Don't Care Anymore | It Don't Matter To Me |
| I Cannot Believe It's True | Thru These Walls |
| Like China | Don't Let Him Steal Your Heart Away |
| Do You Know, Do You Care | The West Side |
| You Can't Hurry Love | Why Can't It Wait Til Morning |

Collins' second album out of the Genesis fold is as strong as his first. An assured blend of up-tempo soul ballads with drums and emotions to the fore. Earth, Wind and Fire brass section punctuate the impeccable production work with bursts of fire. Almost perfect, but this time around there's a lack of surprise. Fave tracks are 'I Don't Care Anymore' in the footsteps of 'In The Air Tonight', and the finger-snappin' revival of 'You Can't Hurry Love'. Never puts a foot wrong. Might well be rock for middle-aged critics but I'll take this any time in exchange for most punk

or art-rock experiments that don't come off. Produced by Phil Collins.

### COMMODORES
**All The Great Hits** (Motown)
Yet another compilation of past glories already aired on similar albums time and time again. There's no denying the quality of the past hit material, particularly the Lionel Richie ballads, but how many combinations can the songs sustain and still keep on selling to the fans? Produced by The Commodores and James Anthony Carmichael.

### CON FUNK SHUN
**To The Max** (Polygram)
Synthesiser funk with fire and toe-tapping verve. Recommended, within its own narrow parameters. Produced by Con Funk Shun.

### ALICE COOPER
**Zipper Catches Skin** (Warners)
Fun trash from a veteran purveyor of good dirty fun. Not quite in his classic mode but always enjoyable, if intensely minor stuff. The usual American flirtation with heavy metal dominates but it'll do for now.

### JOHNNY COPELAND
**Make My Home Where I Hang My Hat** (Demon/Rounder)
Stripped-down 12 bar blues in a tough, no-nonsense vein. Texas funk with a vengeance from one of the more vital black musicians around. Basic but nigh perfect. Produced by Dan Doyle.

### CRASH CRADOCK
**The New Will Never Wear Off Of You** (Capitol)
Simple, boisterous country fare. Clean, uncluttered arrangements and a healthy genre reverence. Produced by Dale Morris, Buddy Killen and Joel Diamond.

### CRASH STREET KIDS
**Little Girls** (Fat City)
Invigorating new trio from Minneapolis in the footsteps of power pop luminaries like Big Star, the Raspberries or the Plimsouls. Simple, unaffected, no-frills rock and roll with youth and energy to spare. Produced by Melvin James, Crash Street Kids and Bruce Henzel.

### JOHN CRITCHINSON
**Summer Afternoon** (Code)
Contemporary jazz piano from British ranks with Morrissey Mullen keyboard player helped out by Claire Hammill on occasional vocals (whatever happened to Claire Hammill?). Lightweight but pleasant. Produced by Dennis Weinrich and John Critchinson.

### J. D. CROWE & THE NEW SOUTH
**Somewhere Between** (Rounder)
Reliable country set by old troopers. A bit on the bland side. Produced by J. D. Crowe.

### CRYSIS
**Hard As Rock** (Long St)
Independent, Oregon-based release and production for a local band in the American heavy metal mould. Riffs galore and highly imitative of so many other stadium rock outfits. Some good slide guitar work here and there comes as a minor redeeming factor.

### CULTURAL ROOTS
**Drift Away From Evil** (Germain)
First-class reggae album, the second from Cultural Roots. One of Jamaica's great vocal units, they are here ably assisted by the ever-present Sly and Robbie alias the Revolutionaries this time around and horn arrangements by Clive Hunt and Dean Fraser. Progressive, smooth and dynamic. Produced by D. Germain.

### CULTURE (FEATURING JOSEPH HILL)
**Lion Rock** (Sonic Sounds/Cultural Foundation)
Rhythmic reggae from one of the better bands around. Gospel-tinged vocals with pointed political lyrics full of protest and social commentary. Produced by Joseph Hill

### CULTURE CLUB
**Kissing To Be Clever** (Virgin/Epic)

| | |
|---|---|
| White Boy | Boy, Boy |
| You Know I'm Not Crazy | I'm Afraid Of Me |
| I'll Tumble 4 Ya | White Boys Can't Control It |
| Take Control | Do You Really |
| Love Twist | Want to Hurt Me |

White boy reggae and gentle lilting soul from a racially-mixed British band headed by the ambiguous Boy George. 'Do You Really Want To Hurt Me' was a major hit single worldwide but the follow up ('Time'

CULTURE CLUB

not included here) was the true gem. Nothing approaches it on this first, assured, easy-to-dance-to album. A polished blend of genteel rhythms, understated vocals and general good-time funk have made it a popular album with buyers and critics alike. Lacks fire, methinks. Produced by Steve Levine.

### HOLGER CZUKAY
**Canaxis** (Spoon)

Czukay's first solo album released in 1968 in an edition of only 500 copies. Serene eastern influences already permeate the Can man's cut-up techniques and formless melodies. The interleaving of radio voices that was to prove so seminal in his future work is already present, blending in with shimmering, ethereal sounds of great beauty and seduction. Listen to this one carefully; it's no antique.

# D

### THE DAMNED
**Live Shepperton 1980** (Big Beat)
Two-year-old live recording disowned by the band. Bears witness to the Damned's earlier shambolic punk line-up and inclinations and their public lack of togetherness. One for the fans only.

### DANA
**Magic** (Creole)
Bubbly, workmanlike pop by a much-overrated lady loved by TV producers judging by her uncommon number of appearances on the magic box. Forgettable MOR standards. Produced by Peter Moss.

### THE DANCING DID
**And Did Those Feet** (Kamera)
Idiosyncratic, new British band from Worcestershire with a quirky assemblage of experimental dance material with the most unusual subject matter at times. Minimal instrumentation and heavily passionate vocals underline the tongue-in-cheek element (or is it?) and make this an interesting debut that also sounds much like an artistic cul-de-sac. Where to now, Dancing Did? Produced by the group.

### MAC DAVIS
**Forty 82** (Casablanca)
A pleasant set from an old country stalwart, with a clever choice of more contemporary material (including Rodney

Crowell's modern classic-in-the-making 'Shame On The Moon') and expert assistance from the Muscles Shoals rhythm section. Produced by Rick Hall.

### MILES DAVIS
**Live At The Plugged Nickel** (Columbia)
Yet another Miles Davis live double set. This one harks back to 1965 (and was previously available in Japan only) with the line-up including Wayne Shorter, Herbie Hancock, Ron Carter and Tony Williams. Produced by Teo Macero.

### THE DAZZ BAND
**Keep It Alive** (Motown)
Large screen, soul/disco production with a carefully calculated mix of uptempo dance numbers and low-light smoochers. Effective and very similar to Earth, Wind and Fire.

### THE DEAD KENNEDYS
**Plastic Surgery Disasters** (Statik/Alternative Tentacles)
Relentless and witty second album by the premier US band that still retains its roots and anger in punk but nevertheless strives forward with surprising articulacy and slipshod musicianship. A nightmarish dose of extreme punkabilly with Jello Biafra conducting the 1984ish proceedings with glee and abandon. Listen at your own risk: this is dangerous stuff, indeed.

### CHRIS DE BURGH
**The Getaway** (A&M)

CHRIS DE BURGH

Verbose art-rock with lotsa good intentions but redundant results from this prolific British singer-songwriter. Rupert Hine's production with its shimmering wall of electronics and cutting rhythms improves De Burgh's songs a helluva lot. But give this one a miss.

**THE DEFECTS**
**Defective Breakdown** (WXYZ)
Brainless, rabble-rousing punk anthems in a familiar mode. Guitar hero posturings break through the awful din and confer some semblance of musicianship. Produced by Tony Spath.

**DEUTSCH AMERIKANISCHE FREUNDSCHAFT**
**Fur Immer** (Virgin)

DEUTSCH AMERIKANISCHE FREUNDSCHAFT

DIAMOND HEAD

The final album from the quirky, robotic German duo now each going their own ways. The relentless manic formula as before, a triumph of dour style over seduction which has had many critics foaming at the mouth. Leaves me rather indifferent but one must admire the consistency and solid, perverse beat. Produced by Conny Plank.

**DEVO**
**Oh No! It's Devo** (Virgin/Warners)
Oddball art rock now running out of steam and with the hackneyed (would-be) humour becoming less and less funny. Quirky electro-pop with a mechanistic beat but no soul. Incredibly hollow. The same as before should you ever have been attracted to Devo's idiosyncratic dance stance. Produced by Roy Thomas Baker.

**BUCK DHARMA**
**Flat Out** (Portrait)
Solo album by a member of Blue Oyster Cult. Dharma handles all the vocals, in-

struments and sundry noises on a solid outing into power pop with strong shades of heavy metal lurking around every riff. Produced by Donald Roeser.

**NEIL DIAMOND**
**Heartlight** (CBS/Columbia)
Seven tracks in collaboration with Burt Bacharach and Carole Bayer Sager situate the heavy MOR orientation of Neil Diamond's latest album. Easy-listening stuff supreme and rather soporofic at that. Seldom exploits Diamond's vibrant tones as they should be employed. A dearth of romance and strings. Various producers.

**DIAMOND HEAD**
**Living On Borrowed Time** (MCA)
Heavy metal by numbers. All the ingredients are present: fiery guitar riffs going amok, bravado vocals, staccato rhythms and drum-beat. But originality is missing with this workmanlike Birmingham group. Produced by Mike Hedges.

**BARBARA DICKSON**
**Here We Go** (Epic)
Live, easy-listening album from a singer

BARBARA DICKSON

who once indulged in folkish areas but is now a staple diet for the telly, stay-at-home audiences. Lotsa hits, tasteful but oh so boring.

## DIRE STRAITS
### Love Over Gold (Vertigo/Warners)

| | |
|---|---|
| Telegraph Road | Industrial Disease |
| Private | Love Over Gold |
| Investigations | It Never Rains |

DIRE STRAITS

Wide-screen rock without the pomp but featuring plotlines, atmospherics and a genuine touch of star quality on Dire Straits' fourth album. Eschewing autobiographical preoccupations, Mark Knopfler has changed his subject matter to the twilight zone of Italian westerns and film noir; sparse lyrics, brooding, building atmosphere all combine successfully to make a track like 'Telegraph Road' a mini-epic (with shades of Ennio Morricone). The guitar work is as fluid as ever and makes it sound all too easy when, in fact, a hell of a lot of work must have gone into this record. Deceptive but entrancing. Produced by Mark Knopfler.

## DIZ AND THE DOORMEN
### Bluecoat Man (Ace)
Reverent recreation by contemporary British musicians of the rolling New Orleans rock popularised by the likes of Fats Domino. Good time fun with horns galore.

## DOA
### War On 45 (Alternative Tentacles)
A mini-album from a Canadian punk die-hard formation. Heavy, nasty and primeval and handpicked by Jello Biafra of the Dead Kennedys. Obscene but pleasing parody of Chris Montez' 'Let's Dance'.

## DOCTOR ROCKIT LIVE!
### Great Big Fun (Perfect Circle)
Live debut for a boisterous and joyful septet from Houston with classic rockers played in a good time atmosphere. Infectious nonsense played with verve and gusto. Mostly revamps but none the

worse for wear and tear. Produced by John Moran and Rock Romano.

## TYMON DOGG
### Battle Of Wills (Y)
Eccentric British fiddle player, erstwhile collaborator with the Clash, with his first proper album. Surrounded by percussion, this is an unclassifiable but disturbing album. Instrumentals, songs, rants and protests coalesce without ever giving up their secrets. A tremulous voice, one moment angry, another plaintive. A decided oddity. Should find its market, but will take time.

## THE DOGS
### Too Much Class For The Neighbourhood (Epic)
Belated UK release for French outfit The Dogs' third album. Assured contemporary rock with venom and strong melodies; very American in style and influences but none the worse for that. Worth discovering.

## DOLLAR
### The Dollar Album (WEA)
An unnecessary album by a duo whose singles sometimes reach near perfection (thanks in great part to the production work by Trevor Horn). At 33 1/3rd Dollar's appeal is so much more contrived and lacks the peppish bounce and fizzle. All the hit singles are here, but the overall effect is cloying. Stick to the singles; for once, they're better value for money. Produced by Dollar and Trevor Horn.

## DOLL BY DOLL
### Grand Passion (Magnet)

Intense stuff by the incandescent Jackie Leven. Heartfelt soul rockers, ballads and inspirational anthems. New singing partner Helen Stewart's voice conveys smouldering passions and blends in well on the tantalising melodies. Full of good intentions but the whole is never up to the sum of the parts. Worth a detour, though; Leven will break through one day. Produced by Tom Newman and Jackie Leven.

## BIG AL DOWNING
**Big Al Downing** (Team 2001)
Anthology of a popular country performer including older and recent hits. Produced by Tony Bongiovi, Lance Quinn and Harold Wheeler.

## DREAD AT THE CONTROLS
**Jungle Signal** (Dread)
Reggae instrumental album orchestrated by the ubiquitous Mikey Dread with the help of Rico, Tan Tan and major Jamaica session men. Vital dub mixes with a heartening sting in the tail. Produced by Mikey Dread.

## THE DREAM SYNDICATE
**The Days Of Wine And Roses** (Ruby)
Earnest modern pop from Los Angeles. Singer Steve Wynn sounds a lot like Lou Reed and, in fact, the influence of the Velvet Underground comes through most strongly on this emotion-laden album. A despairing set of songs from a promising new line-up. Not party music, but worth persevering with.

## DR FEELGOOD
**Fast Women And Slow Horses** (Chiswick)
Boozy pub music from past innovators now stuck in the same groove and incapable of changing their ways, despite regular line-up changes. No surprises, a bit like industrially-brewed beer. No real ale, this.

## DR JOHN
**Dr John Plays Mac Rebennack** (Demon)
Funky solo piano playing, New Orleans style. Elegant boogie-struttin' stuff with a lone vocal on a Hoagy Carmichael piece 'The Nearness of You'. Assured, masterful return to the roots of swing. Lotsa passion too!

## DUFFO
**Lexicon** (PVK)
Madcap Australian Bowie imitator in an anonymous set of lame duck tunes with no redeeming features whatsoever. A waste of plastic.

## GEORGE DUKE
**The 1976 Solo Keyboard Album** (Epic)
The keyboard fusion player before his soul flirtations with a solo piano set of great jazz elegance. Produced by George Duke.

## DUNN AND BRUCE STREET
**Official Business** (Devaki)
Black duo of Dunn Pearson and Bruce Gray travel through a professional soul/funk set with soaring vocals and harmonies. Produced by Dunn Pearson Jr. and Bruce Gray.

## DYNASTY
**Right Back At Cha!** (Solar)
Clean-cut soul outing by an excellent funk outfit. Fresh and invigorating dance floor go-getters. Produced by Leon F. Sylvers.

# E

## THE EAGLES
**Greatest Hits Vol. 2** (Asylum)
Six years already since the Eagles' first greatest hits consumer package. However there have only been two studio albums since and many of the (familiar) tracks are already available on their double live set making this compilation somewhat redundant. Still, it does have all the soaring harmonies of 'Hotel California', 'Life In The Fast Lane', 'Heartache Tonight' and others. Produced by Bill Szymczyk.

## ELECTRONIC ART ENSEMBLE
**Inquietudes** (Gramavision)
Ambitious electronic failure. Cascades of meaningless sounds sorely lacking in melody and structure. Produced by the group.

## ENCHANTMENT
**Enchanted Lady** (FC)
Energetic New York soul and dance outfit fronted by the strong vocals of William Anderson. Equally at ease on dance-floor ravers and silken ballads. Produced by William Anderson and Raymond Reid.

## ERAZERHEAD
**The Rumble Of The East** (Flicknife)
London-based punk quartet debut album. Heavy-metal-edged, basic rock. One for the fans, but adequate for once. Produced by the group and Frenchy Gloder.

## DAVID ESSEX
**The Very Best Of David Essex** (TV)
TV compilation of already-forgotten hits by a past contender now recycled in TV-land.

## THE EVERLY BROTHERS
**Love Hurts** (K-Tel)
Yet another TV-advertised, plunder-from-the-vaults effort. At any rate, the material is still wondrously alive.

## EXPLAINER
**Man From The Ghetto** (Sun Burst)
Music from Trinidad. *Not* reggae. Winston Smith is a pleasant calypso artist with strong political leanings which come over well under a welter of cross-rhythms and infectious musical patterns. Nice one.

## EXPOSURE
**Out Of The Dark . . . Into The Light** (Abstract)
Contrived but lightweight experimentation from a London-based trio. Early punk touches but no genius on show.

# F

## THE FABULOUS THUNDERBIRDS
**T-Bird Rhythm** (Chrysalis)
Fourth amiable outing for the American rhythm and blues revivalists. Good-humoured, uptempo rockers done to a tee, but lacking that elusive sparkle that might propel the band into the big time. Produced by Nick Lowe.

## FAD GADGET
**Under The Flag** (Mute)

Another great British eccentric, Frank Tovey alias Fad Gadget plays with voice and electronics, upstaging his rather incomplete voice with the help of quirks galore in the song structures and often daft subject matter. This is already his third album and it's the familiar mixture again. Seductive, if gloomy mutant pop for 1982.

## DONALD FAGEN
**The Nightfly** (Warners)

| I.G.Y. | New Frontier |
| Green Flower | The Nightfly |
|   Street | The Goodbye Look |
| Ruby Baby | Walk Between |
| Maxine | Raindrops |

A stunning debut from the lone survivor of Steely Dan whose touch is never so evident as here. Swinging, graceful blend of pop and rock styles with just the right degree of wit and detachment. Every single track is a mini-epic of cool, romantic proportions, a slice of quaintly-distilled Americana with memories for everyone (even Brits). Superb musicianship with the best L.A. players that fame and money can buy, a delightfully reverent version of 'Ruby Baby'. In short, a mini-masterpiece. Produced by Garry Katz.

### FEAR OF STRANGERS
**Fear Of Strangers** (Faulty)
An upstate New York band formerly called the Units with their initial album, Fear of Strangers are deliberately modern and political with the fashionable female vocals of Val Haynes upfront. Seductive. A name to remember. Produced by the group.

### JOSÉ FELICIANO
**Escenas de Amor** (Motown)
Latin standards in an unusual departure for the almost-forgotten Feliciano. Help from Carlos Santana. Cringe version of Rodrigo's guitar concerto . . . with vocals. For the strong of heart and only if you don't understand Spanish. Produced by Leonard Schultz and José Feliciano.

### RICHARD 'DIMPLES' FIELDS
**Give Everybody Some** (Epic)
Smooth and funky disco material straight from the factory line. New and aseptic. Produced by Richard 'Dimples' Fields and Belinda Wilson.

### FIREFALL
**Break Of Dawn** (Atlantic)
Soft rock ballads for the American radio hinterland. Sleepy and undistinguished; might sound better on a tinny car radio, though. Produced by Ron Albert and Howard Albert.

### FIRST LOVE
**Love At First Sight** (Chicago International)
Four-girl, black vocal ensemble in standard soul and funk form. Produced by Donald Burnside.

### PATRIK FITZGERALD
**Gifts And Telegrams** (Red Flame)
Droning pseudo-poetry against mournful rock backing from a young British neo-punk poet. Naive, amateur endeavours with Casio doodles the most interesting feature of the whole thing.

### EDI FITZROY
**Youthman Penitentiary** (Alligator)
Workmanlike reggae by a new Jamaican performer of whom much is expected in some circles. This set doesn't truly deliver. Produced by Trevor Elliott.

### FLASH IN THE PAN
**Headlines** (Epic)
Danceable, quirky electro-pop with strong pop sensibility and a touch of pomp from the reliable consoles and pens of ex-Easybeats Vanda and Young, who also produced.

### THE FLIRTS
**10 Cents A Dance** (O)
First release by an all-girl trio adept at bouncy rock and roll dance tunes. Teenage music like in the old girl group days with a gloss of modernism. Pleasing. Produced by Bobby Orlando.

### THE FLYING PICKETS
**Live At The Albany Empire** (AVM)
Doo-wop acapella from a British vocal group. Both reverent and humourous, this album is a small gem of invention and, dare I say, originality. 'Oklahoma', 'Da Doo Ron Ron', 'Memories Are Made Of This' and countless others as you'll never hear them again. Great fun.

### DAN FOGELBERG
**Greatest Hits** (Full Moon)
Festive compilation of ultra-wimp mega-platinum hits. This is why California will, one day, just drift out to sea and never even notice the fact. Soporific but ever so tasteful. All your somniferous favourites are probably here if this is your cup of ginseng tea. Various producers.

### FOGHAT
**In The Mood For Something Rude** (Bearsville)
12th album by a grizzly band of veteran musicians. This time around, original material is left on the doorstep and the whole platter is made up of cover versions of old (and beloved) material by James Brown, Marvin Gaye, Delbert McClinton, Rodney Crowell and others. Unusual mixture of soul standards and country ballads, but some tunes are barely recognisable after the passage of Foghat's sledgehammer style. Missing this won't harm you. Produced by Nick Jameson and Tony Outeda.

### FOREIGNER
**Records** (Atlantic)

| | |
|---|---|
| Cold As Ice | Urgent |
| Double Vision | Dirty White Boy |
| Hard Games | Juke Box Hero |
| Waiting For A Girl Like You | Long, Long Way From Home |
| Feels Like The First Time | Hot Blooded |

Car-radio masterpieces from a band who, year after year, keep on churning out solid platinum hits despite changes in line-up

and a welter of producers. This is hard melodic rock at its most polished. All hits, all quasi-perfect three-minute rock epics. Various producers.

### FORTNOX
**Fortnox** (Epic)
Average American stadium rock with pomp and riffs firing away in all directions. Produced by Chris Tsangarides.

### THE 49 AMERICANS
**We Know Nonsense** (Choo Choo Train)
Anonymous American rock in between musical chairs, ranging from hippy meanderings to soul disco pretensions.

### FOURTEEN KARAT SOUL AND BEN HALLEY
**Sister Suzie Cinema and The Gospel At Colonus** (Burning)
A black New Jersey quintet, Fourteen Karat Soul are another, masterful, doo-wop acapella revivalist formation with a strong difference. They perform soul opera (a modern version of 'Oedipus') in a most unique fashion. Soaring harmonies with solos at both end of the scales, this is doo-wop like you've never envisaged it before. If all musical soundtracks were this way!

### RODNEY FRANKLIN
**Learning To Love** (Columbia)
Sophisticated soul-jazz-pop blend with a veneer of class and hot rhythms. Franklin excels on keyboards and emotive vocals. Produced by Stanley Clarke.

### FREE
**Absolutely Free** (Island)
Yet another Free repackaging job with the obligatory 'It's Alright Now'. A seminal band, no doubt, but surely we already have these tracks somewhere in our vinyl horde?

### JANIE FRICKE
**It Ain't Easy** (CBS/Columbia)
A veteran country female vocalist with

possibly her best set so far, nodding strongly towards cross-over acceptance. Uncluttered arrangements and less cliched material do the trick and Janie's distinctive voice does the rest. Lots of heartfelt emotion on display. Produced by Bob Montgomery.

### EDGAR FROESE
**Original Soundtrack – Kamikaze 1989** (Virgin)
Swirling synthesiser melodies and drum machine beat punctuate a lively, atmospheric soundtrack for the German film by Wolf Fremm featuring the late Rainer Werner Fassbinder. Reliable stuff from the Tangerine Dream keyboard mastermind. Makes you want to see the film. Can't say more than that. Produced by Edgar Froese.

# G

### JERRY GARCIA
**Run For The Roses** (Arista)
Languid, relaxed set by the grizzly-bearded guitarist for the Grateful Dead. Derivative of songs by the group and generally pleasant but highly innocuous, despite covers of Beatles and Dylan songs. Produced by Jerry Garcia and John Kahn.

### NICK GARVEY
**Blue Skies** (Virgin)

Solid, unspectacular rock by a member of the late Motors. Very much in an American mould. Pleasing but not very original. Produced by Nick Garvey.

### LARRY GATLIN AND THE GATLIN BROTHERS BAND
**Sure Feels Like Love** (Columbia)
Safe country and western fare from a known quantity. Nothing flash, but reliable harmonies and male tales of woe and wanton women. Produced by Jerry Crutchfield and Larry Gatlin.

### MARVIN GAYE
**Midnight Love** (CBS/Columbia)

| | |
|---|---|
| Midnight Lady | Turn On Some |
| Sexual Healing | Music |
| Rockin' After | Third World Girl |
| Midnight | Joy |
| 'Til Tomorrow | My Love Is |
| | Waiting |

Recorded in Europe, this is Marvin Gaye's first album for a new label and offers a strongly rejuvenated singer no longer grappling with the uncertainties of the heart in a blue funk. Exuberant and swinging, albeit with a light touch of healthy cynicism, Gaye's new set of songs see him at his best for a long, long time. Fluid,

MARVIN GAYE

quality soul with a pronounced lack of artifice and a helluva lot of warm talent. 'Sexual Healing' is the hit single, of course, but the rest is as entrancing. Produced by Marvin Gaye.

## CRYSTAL GAYLE
**Collection** (CBS)
Familiar hits compilation from Gayle's past label now garnering all its golden eggs in one basket.

## CRYSTAL GAYLE
**True Love** (Elektra)
Debut for Elektra sees Crystal Gayle in a more contemporary groove, cleverly moving away from her Nashville country roots with more varied material and arrangements. Gentle rockers and silky ballads mix well. All very safe but catchy. A good career move. Produced by Allen Reynolds and Jimmy Bowen.

## GLORIA GAYNOR
**Gloria Gaynor** (Atlantic)
Workmanlike black soul which never recaptures earlier magic, like 'I Will Survive'. Dull and sincere threnodies of love. Various producers.

## J. GEILS BAND
**Showtime!** (EMI)
Live album recorded in Detroit follows up the band's chart-topping previous album. Strong basic boogie, lively vocals and a welcome rediscovery of the J. Geils' bunch past catalogue, overlooked until their recent, unexpected success. A good introduction to the band. Produced by Seth Justman.

## GENERAL CAINE
**Girls** (Tabu)
Clever funk work-out at mid-tempo by a number of Funkadelic cohorts.

## DANA GILLESPIE
**Blue Job** (Ace)
Sluggish, middle-of-the-road rock from a forgotten personality of the 1970s. Strong blues feel. Produced by Dana Gillespie.

## THE GLADIATORS
**Back To Roots** (L'Escargot)
Sweet reggae tunes with an obnoxiously repetitive Rasta message throughout. Heavy, man.

## GOLDEN EARRING
**Cut** (21)
The Dutch hard rock outfit with more of the same. Catchy melodies with a lack of depth and emotion. Produced by Shell Schellekens.

## GOOMBAY DANCE BAND
**Born to Win** (Epic)
More bouncy Euro-dreck. Yecchhh. . . Produced by Jochen Petersen.

## GRANDMASTER FLASH AND THE FURIOUS FIVE
**The Message** (Sugarhill)

Includes possibly the best rap track of the year, 'The Message', a vibrant, articulate paean about revolutionary aspirations and urban plight. Unfortunately most of the rest of the album is taken up by mediocre soul and disco pieces. Very much filler material. Get the single instead. Produced by Sylvia Robinson.

## EDDY GRANT
**Killer On The Rampage** (Ice)
Simple, gentle melodies with a thin veneer of reggae rhythms. Eclectic rock from a master craftsman who was rewarded by the enormous success of 'I Don't Wanna Dance', although most of the tracks on the album could be successful singles in their own right. Produced by Eddy Grant.

## JOHN GREAVES
**Accident** (Europa)
Solo album from the keyboards player from National Health. British art-jazz rock par excellence, gently melodic but not too original in the long run. Produced by John Greaves and Armand Frydman.

## AL GREEN
**Precious Lord** (Hi-Cream)
Highly devotional gospel album by a one-time great of soul. Predictable even down to the addition of country strains, but the message is just too heavy. Produced by Al Green.

## ZAINE GRIFF
**Figvres** (Polydor)
Pretentious and particularly unsuccessful wallow in neo-romantic, glitter art-rock. Sounds like parodies but is, I gather, highly serious. Derivative nonsense.

## WINSTON GROOVY
**African Girl** (Top Ranking)
Elegant, soulful reggae, including a Lionel Richie tune. Has its charms. Produced by Winston Groovy.

# H

## SAMMY HAGAR
**Rematch** (Capitol)
Best of Sammy Hagar in ten tracks culled from his Capitol output. Needless to say, Hagar is now on another label! Tedious anthem rock that shouldn't make history. Produced by Carter, Sammy Hagar and Geoff Workman.

## SAMMY HAGAR
**Three Lock Box** (Geffen)
Predictable riff rock with Hagar's usually strong melodic sense and appreciation of dynamics. Standard rock 'n' roll fare guaranteed not to disappoint. Produced by Keith Olsen.

## SAMMY HAGAR
**The Very Best** (Capitol)
Another best of Hagar's Capitol years. Familiar, riff-infected material. Might have been a bit more representative with some older Montrose material.

## MERLE HAGGARD
**Going Where The Lonely Go** (Epic)
Mournful country set by a genre veteran. A melancholy mood dominates which doesn't suit Haggard too well over the distance of a whole album. Willie Nelson cover version and a new rendering of the eternal 'Nobody's Darlin' But Mine'. Produced by Merle Haggard, Lewis Talley and Ray Baker.

## LANI HALL
**Albany Park** (A&M)
Set of mixed rock and ballads from a veteran singer from the jazz fold. Nothing special but no catastrophes. Interesting rendition of the seldom-covered 'Rio' by Mike Nesmith. Produced by George Tobin.

## HALL AND OATES
**H₂O** (RCA)
Perfectly-tailored blue-eyed soul from

master craftsmen. Synthesiser washes colour the infectious dance music with a dash of modernism that keeps the brew from sounding too familiar. 'Maneater' is the obvious single, a fiery guitar-powered bouncer with a strong touch of misogyny, while 'Family Man' achieves the rare feat of making one dance to a Mike Oldfield tune! Produced by Daryl Hall and John Oates.

## PETER HAMMILL
### Enter K (Naive)

The usual tortured meanderings from the ex-Vandergraaf Generator lead personality. Visions of doom and existential despair, every song a mini-epic exploding in all directions. One can't really call Hammill an eccentric, but he nevertheless remains a true original on the British musical scene, impervious to fashion and outside influences and meticulously weaving a malevolent spell all around him. This is far from his best album (there are so many) but proves fascinating at times. Produced by Peter Hammill.

## HANOI ROCKS
### Self Destructive Blues (Johanna)
Third album for the flamboyant glitter heavy metal bunch. No new material per se, but a motley assemblage of past singles, EPs and demo tracks previously issued only in Scandinavia. Sleazy, titillating stuff with a nice self-deprecating wit.

## THE HAPPY FAMILY
### The Man On Your Street (4AD)
Dreary concept album from a Scottish band, an offshoot of Josef K. Simplistic, contrived and formula-laden. Avoid.

## ROY HARPER BAND
### Work Of Heart (Public Recordings)
Eclectic ballads in Harper's customary concerned style. Classy backing from his usual battery of friends (Dick Morrissey, Charlie Morgan). Protest, nostalgia and sheer Englishness as ever, but disappointing comeback effort after a few years

away from the music business, as Harper still appears stuck in a past groove and seems unable to modify his style and attitudes. For the Harper fans only, I fear. Produced by Roy Harper and David Lord.

## EMMYLOU HARRIS
### Last Date (Warners)

A live album from the grey-haired princess of contemporary country. Pleasing blend of immaculately-played music with surprisingly varied inputs, from the purer country strains of Gram Parsons ('Grievous Angel'), rockabilly ('Restless') and even Springsteen. Immaculate introduction to Emmylou if you don't know (and appreciate) her already. Produced by Brian Ahern.

## GEORGE HARRISON
### Gone Troppo (Dark Horse)
Quiet and relatively tepid album from Harrison, very much a forgotten man these days despite the general revival of interest in all things Beatleish. Breezy and laid-back, this utterly lacks ambition and betrays Harrison's peace of mind to the detriment of the music. Produced by George Harrison, Ray Cooper and Phil McDonald.

## JON HASSELL
### Vernal Equinox (Lovely)
Six-year-old ethnic jazz improvisations in

advance of their now fashionable time from a trumpeter since patroned by Brian Eno. Entrancing swirls of sound. Recommended.

## SCREAMIN' JAY HAWKINS
### Frenzy (Edsel)
Interesting compilation of the legendary, eccentric American bluesman, includes his near-immortal 'I Put A Spell On You' and other tracks in a similar vein.

## HAWKWIND
### Choose Your Masques (RCA)
Science fiction fans call the genre SF; neophytes and ignorant hacks generally use the expression 'sci-fi' alias skiffy. Well, this nth Hawkwind album with yet another revamp of 'Silver Machine' is old-style skiffy rock at its worst. Produced by the group.

## HEATWAVE
### Power Cuts (Epic)
Greatest hits package of 12 from a minor league black funk outfit. Rod Temperton wrote 11 of the tracks included here, amongst which 'Boogie Nights' is the most memorable. Formula stuff but well done.

## HEAVEN
### Bent (Columbia)
Australian heavy metal outfit with a potent dose of fiery hard rock along AC/DC lines. Twin guitars ignite the mixture quite effectively. Produced by John Bee.

## HEAVEN
### Twilight Of Mischief (RCA)
More AC/DC riff rock supreme from down under.

## HELLCATS
### Hellcats (Radio)
Five-track mini album of virulent heavy metal from a new American bunch, led by two ex-members of Starz, Michael Lee Smith and Richie Ranno. Strong, dynamic sense and clean-cut dramatics. Not bad.

## HERE AND NOW
### Fantasy Shift (Chick)
Placid white reggae from a young British band. Has a go at Bowie's 'Man Who Sold The World'. E for Effort, F for Failure.

## HERITAGE
### Remorse Code (Rondolet)
Indifferent lower division power pop of indeterminate British origin. Came and went. A bargain bin natural.

## HIGH INERGY
### So Right (Motown)
Dubious black vocal trio retreading Motown properties and standards in a tepid manner. Not a new Supremes. Far from it. Various producers.

STIX HOOPER

rock from one of Britain's most under-rated hit combinations. Includes 'Girl Crazy', 'Are You Getting Enough Happiness' and others. A pleasing experience. Pop as it should always be. Produced by Mickie Most.

## THE (HYPOTHETICAL) PROPHETS
### Around The World With The Prophets (Hypothetical)
Anonymous, experimental effort from the UK. Electronic twiddling of the console knobs, voice cut-ups and haphazard jottings make this tiresome on the ears and attention. Not quite Laurie Anderson.

## JULIO IGLESIAS
### The 24 Greatest Songs (CBS)
All Spanish songs on this double set from the Spanish crooner and purveyor of safe romance to the Mills and Boon set. Available in the US on Columbia as a single album. Smooth, smooth. . .

## IN EMBRACE
### Passion Fruit Pastels (Glass)
Nice title for an unfortunately fey duo of British angst popsters with more lurid dirges for bedsit land. No thanks.

## DAVID HINE
### Raucous Roll Us (PBS)
Super-laid-back, US Steely Dan imitation. Stick to the real thing. It's safer (and so much better).

## JOHN HOLT
### Gold (Creole)
Blandish cross-over reggae. Smooth and immaculately-produced but lacking in individuality. Produced by Henry 'Junjo' Lawes.

## JOHN HOLT
### Just The Two Of Us (CSA)
Gentle, lilting reggae with obligatory (almost) Roots Radics backing. Mostly new interpretations with Jamaican rhythms of many soul standards from the likes of Grover Washington, Stevie Wonder and others. A mixed bag.

## STIX HOOPER
### Touch The Feeling (MCA)
Polished but fireless jazz funk cocktail by the drummer from the Crusaders. Jerry Butler takes vocals on 'Let's Talk It Out'. Produced by Stix Hooper, Felder and Sample.

## HOT CHOCOLATE
### Mystery (EMI)
American compilation of clever, funky pop

JULIO IGLESIAS

## INNER LIFE
**Inner Life II** (Salsoul)
A showcase group for black singer Jocelyn Brown. Competent funk in a minor league. Produced by Stan Lucas.

## NEIL INNES
**Off The Records** (MMC)
Double set of comedy tunes, parodies and convincing music from the Bonzo Dog and Monty Python camp. All music from his reasonably funny 'Innes Book of Records' television series.

## INTENSIVE HEAT
**Intensive Heat** (My Disc)
Exciting, fourth gear soul dance pieces with upfront trio of vocalists. Assured and toe-tapping stuff. Produced by Raymond Reid and William Anderson.

## INVESTIGATORS
**First Class** (Ice Music)
Debut reggae album from a North London outfit. Straightforward, quality dance rhythms par excellence.

## DONNIE IRIS
**The High And The Mighty** (MCA)
Third album of pleasant, mid-tempo rockers for Iris and his band the Cruisers. Nothing too innovative but always tasteful. Cover version of Dave Clark's classic 'Glad All Over'. Produced by Mark Avsec.

## GREGORY ISAACS
**Lover's Book** (Charisma)
Double set regrouping two earlier albums by the suave reggae apostle: 'The Lonely Lover' and 'More Gregory'. Cool reggae ballads and sparse, intelligent arrangements. Sly and Robbie and Roots Radics provide the backing for this set of warm, intimate songs. Produced by Gregory Isaacs.

# J

## CARL JACKSON
**Song Of The South** (Sugar Hill)
Strong traditional country bluegrass singer with distinctive mellifluous vocals and intonations. Great banjo and verve and help from a myriad of friends: Emmylou Harris, Mary Stuart, Jerry Douglas, Jesse McReynolds and Blaine Sprouse. Produced by Carl Jackson.

## JANET JACKSON
**Janet Jackson** (A&M)
Debut album for a relative of the Jackson 5. Soulful and slick ballad work with all the fancy trimmings. Various producers.

MICHAEL JACKSON AND JOE 'KING' CARASCO

## MICHAEL JACKSON
**Thrillers** (Epic)
The slow-in-coming successor to the phenomenally successful 'Off the Wall' album. A safe blend of diverse, but highly commercial elements, big-sound Rod Temperton ballads, a rap track (featuring, of all people, Vincent Price), a duet with Paul McCartney ('The Girl Is Mine'), reggae, there's something here for everybody even if Michael Jackson's soul roots are in the process of being diluted. Will sell by the ton, but could have been so much more adventurous. Produced by Quincy Jones.

## MILLIE JACKSON
**Hard Times** (Polydor/Spring)
Raunchy soul set from one of today's more spectacular live performers. Only one lengthy rap on this album with a healthier majority of polished blues and soul numbers. Produced by Brad Shapiro and Millie Jackson.

## RONALD SHANNON JACKSON AND THE DECODING SOCIETY
**Mandance** (Antilles)
Impressionistic mixture of free jazz elements and dance floor funk. Closer to Booker T than Jackson's old masters Cecil Taylor or Ornette Coleman. Imaginative and great fun. Produced by David Breskin and Ronald Shannon Jackson.

## THE JAM
**Dig The New Breed** (Polydor)
A parting shot from the now defunct critics' darlings in the form of a live album serving as a documentary of their past career; definitely not just a greatest hits package. Tracks come from a variety of places and years between 1977 and 1982.

Rough but spontaneous sound conveys what The Jam meant to say. Produced by Peter Wilson.

## SONNY JAMES
**I'm Looking Over The Rainbow** (Dimension)
Seasoned country performer with his first album for a while. Depressingly familiar, but that's what his audiences want. Ricky Skaggs and the White sisters help out. Produced by Sonny James, Ken Stilts and Brian Fisher.

## JAN AND DEAN
**One Summer Night/Live** (Rhino)
Double album recapturing the sound of Jan and Dean at a reunion concert 12 years after the near-fatal car crash which almost cost Jan Berry's life. Patchy but chock-full of nostalgia and memories of better, insouciant summer days. All the old hits by J & D and the Beach Boys are present, of course. Produced by Alan Shapiro.

## KEITH JARRETT
**Concerts** (ECM)
Alternately available as a three-record boxed set or a single (edited) album. Digital recording of a piano improvisation concert of the jazz artist in Bregenz and Munich in 1981. Melodic, hearty, meaty, ethereal, seductive, hypnotic, Jarrett's piano solos are all this in turn. Do not be deceived by the jazz label, this is contemporary, eternal music. Produced by Manfred Eicher.

## JEFFERSON STARSHIP
**Winds of Change** (Grunt)
Lacklustre album reuniting Grace Slick with her former cohorts. Predominant

hard rock in an anonymous format dominates and steals any magic reminiscent of older (idealistic) days. A sad piece of work, full of recycled pap. Produced by Kevin Beamish.

## WAYLON JENNINGS AND WILLIE NELSON
**WWII** (RCA)

Belated follow-up to the platinum 1978 duet album by the rough and sentimental country rockers. Five duets this time around and seven solo Jennings pieces. Perfect for the fans of this engaging duo of grizzly, melancholy, barrel-house villains. Produced by Chips Moman.

## JOAN JETT
**Bad Reputation** (Epic/Boardwalk)

Reissue of an earlier album from the new American queen of acceptable punk and roll. Passable thrashings about with Gary Glitter covers and minor Sex Pistols involvement. Produced by Kenny Laguna and Ritchie Cordell.

## JIMMI AND THE MUSTANGS
**Hey Little Girl** (Vanity)

Gentle rockabilly bash from a young Orange County band. Raw but full of life. Produced by Tom Camache and Richard Kaplan.

## ELTON JOHN
**Love Songs** (TV)

TV-promoted set of older, sentimental Elton John tracks. Includes 'Song For Guy', 'Blue Eyes', 'Little Jeannie' and others.

## JOHN'S CHILDREN
**Orgasm** (Cherry Red)

Dated and rather pathetic re-issue of only album from so-called legendary mid-60s outfit, featuring the pre-T-Rex Marc Bolan, then Markie Field. For desperate historians only.

## HOWARD JOHNSON
**Keepin' Love New** (A&M)

Belated UK release for a quality set of dance tunes from a talented black performer equally at ease in soul and disco.

## GRACE JONES
**Living My Life** (Island)

Disco chanteuse with class and mucho pretentions, Grace Jones always promises more than she in fact delivers. This latest album is no different featuring immaculately-produced soul and reggae ditties which leave no lasting impression. Style is of the essence and all the Sly and Robbie and Compass Point studio chief session men won't change matters much. A star with little inside the hollow shell. Produced by Chris Blackwell and Alex Sadkin.

# K

## AMY KANTER
**The Other Girl** (Atlantic)

Gentle, good girl rock, self-penned material with a galaxy of name helpers like Elliott Randall, Teresa Brewer, Alan Lanier. . . Undistinctive and tepid. Produced by Earl McGrath and Robert Thiele Jr.

## MICK KARN
**Titles** (Virgin)

Solo album by the striking bass player from Japan. Ethnic influences abound but

GRACE JONES

despite great bass sound, the ultimate lack of melodies brings this down to earth with a resounding thud. Too clever by half. Just another (pointless) exercise in style. Produced by Mick Karn, Colin Fairley and Rick Wilde.

## CHAKA KHAN
**Chaka Khan** (Warners)
Powerful slice of red-hot soul by one of the best black performers in the business. Oozes sex-appeal and funk through every pore. A cast of many soul luminaries includes Rick James and Robbie Buchanan but Chaka Khan, multitracked throughout, steals the show. A dance classic. Produced by Arif Mardin.

## KHEMISTRY
**Khemistry** (Columbia)
Pleasing black trio on up-front vocals and tight musicianship backing them up. Produced by Willie Lester and Rodney Brown.

## THE KIDS FROM FAME
**The Kid From Fame Again** (RCA)

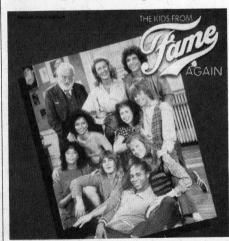

More musical spin-offs from the television series spin-off of the Alan Parker movie. Teeny-bopper stuff. Produced by Barry Fasman.

## KILLING JOKE
**Ha – Killing Joke Live** (EG)
A 10-inch album souvenir of the shambolic demon punk rockers in concert in Canada. Six tracks, some previously not available on previous studio albums, all bear witness to the malevolent strength of the British band. Rough and ready but has dark charms. Produced by the Group and Conny Plank.

## JONATHAN KING
**King Size King** (PRT)
16 tracks by or produced by King in his many past guises. A whiff of quickly disposable nostalgia from a mini-master of the novelty pop hit. Produced by Jonathan King.

## KING TUBBY
**King At The Control** (Tads)
Hard rhythm-charged dub reggae from one of its foremost exponents.

## KISS
**Creatures Of The Night** (Casablanca)

Return to form by the dictators of the glitter/heavy metal kingdom. Simple but effective and powerful stuff to be played loud or not at all. Basic soundtrack for the coming apocalypse. Produced by Michael James Jackson, Paul Stanley and Gene Simmons.

## KITSYKE WILL
**Kitsyke Will** (Highway)
Pleasant new arrangements of traditional folk tunes. All instrumental. Produced by the group and Bill Leader.

## KLYMAXX
**Girls Will Be Girls** (Solar)
Eight-strong American black girl group with an assured touch of funk and danceability. Fun stuff, not to be taken too seriously. Produced by Otis Stokes, James Jam III, Terry Lewis, Stephen Shockley and William Shelby.

## PAUL KOSSOFF
**Leaves In The Wind** (Street Tunes)
A motley collection of old tracks, some previously unreleased, by the late guitarist from Free. Dated.

## ROBERT KRAFT
**Retro Active** (RCA)
Assured jazz pop tunes from a pleasing singer and pianist. Strong, bluesy influence adds a smokey touch of romance. Produced by Larry Carlton.

## ROBBIE KRIEGER
**Versions** (Passport)
Fourth solo album from Robbie Krieger since the demise of the Doors. Partly instrumentals with a strong guitar predominance and covers of more contemporary material like the Pretenders' 'Tattooed Love Boys' and a reggae version of the Doors' own 'Crystal Ship'. Produced by Robbie Krieger.

## KRIS KRISTOFFERSON
**Songs of Kristofferson** (Monument)
12 cut anthology' from the eternally gravel-voiced Kristofferson. Includes all his best (and earlier) songs like 'Me And Bobby McGee', 'Sunday Mornin' Coming Down', etc. . . Produced by Fred Foster and David Anderle.

# L

## SLEEPY LaBEEF
**Electricity** (Rounder)
Blues and gospel performer comes up with a vintage rockabilly set, full of drive and joy. Basic but energetic boogie-woogie strains. Produced by Scott Billington.

## CRISTY LANE
**Here's To Us** (Liberty)
Fey, understated country ballads by a female singer with a sure touch in delicacy and affectation. Well-done but breaks no new ground. Produced by Ron Oates.

## ELOISE LAWS
**All In Time** (Capitol)
Pop-jazz excursions very much in a family mood with Ronnie Laws on sax, Hubert Laws on flute and sister Debra on backing vocals. Pleasant, mellow pieces in a black-radio format. Produced by Ronnie Laws and William Jeffrey.

## RODNEY LAY AND THE WILD WEST
**Heartbreak** (Churchill)
Flat and indifferent country set from a singer who often plays with Roy Clark. Produced by Roy Clark.

## LED ZEPPELIN
**Coda** (Swan Song)
After-the-fact, live album from the giants of power rock. Eight tracks recorded between 1969 and 1978. The studio tracks are usually left-overs of no special quality and although this will sell it adds little to the legend. Dire drum solo by the late John Bonham 'Bonzo's Montreux' is the nadir of the set. Undistinguished. Produced by Jimmy Page.

## ALBERT LEE
**Albert Lee** (Polydor)
Tuneful, good taste, modern country rock by the adopted English guitarist of the genre, a veteran of Emmylous Harris' Hot Band. Lightweight voice but good production and arrangements. Produced by Rodney Crowell.

## JOHNNY LEE
**Sounds Like Love** (Full Moon)
Unspectacular set of standard country love songs. All sounds very familiar – journeying where a thousand pedal steel guitars have been before. Produced by Jim Ed Norman.

## LEMON KITTENS
**The Big Dentist** (Illuminated)
Dreamy, impressionist musings in an experimental mood by the Anglo-French duo of Danielle Dax and Karl Blake. Subdued but never offensive as their past efforts often have been.

## JOHN LENNON
**The John Lennon Collection** (EMI/Geffen)

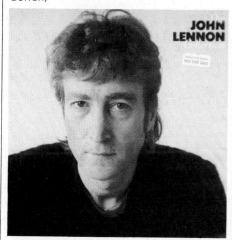

JOHN LENNON

15-track compilation mostly culled from Lennon's few solo albums and Plastic Ono Band efforts. The lack of Beatles material provides a lopsided view of Lennon's career. Still some gems ('Imagine', 'Jealous Guy', etc. . .) though. Various producers.

## DAVID LINDLEY
**Win This Record** (Asylum)
Simple unassuming rock and roll (with

JOHN LENNON

133

many incursions into other forms like reggae, country, Tex-Mex, blues). Although Lindley has a mostly unappealing voice, his instrumental virtuosity and the easy-going garage band sound win the day. A happy record. Produced by David Lindley and Greg Ladanyi.

### LITTLE RIVER BAND
**Greatest Hits** (Capitol)
A retrospective anthology of hits from the low-profile but big success Australian band who have recently changed lead vocalists (from Glenn Shorrock to John Farnham). Catchy, punchy stuff, ideal party music with a bounce. Produced by John Boylan, Glenn Wheatley, George Martin, Ernie Rose and the group.

### LITTLE STEVEN AND THE DISCIPLES OF SOUL
**Men Without Women** (EMI)

Springsteen inseparable Steve Van Zandt, also the brain behind the unlucky Ashbury Dukes, now out on his own with a patchwork band made up by members of the E Street bunch as well as various others (even a Plasmatics!). The passion and fire of the Boss is present and the tunes are very similar without being too derivative, but Van Zandt just hasn't got the right voice to put this into the big league. Great

fun, I'll play it again and again but it'll never be art rock. Produced by Miami Steve.

### JIM LORD
**Inside Out** (Inlet)
Assured folk rock album by a new, unknown American artist. Ever tasteful, sometimes bland, but has its quiet, effective moments. Produced by Ken Pine.

### LENE LOVICH
**No Man's Land** (Stiff/Epic)

Eclectic bunch of quirky, passionless rockers from Ms Lovich. Lots of bounce but overall an unmemorable set of songs in dire need of sparkle and further inspiration. Not a successful comeback from one who's been on the sidelines for some time. Produced by Lene Lovich and Les Chappell.

# M

### RICK JAMES PRESENTS BOBBY M
**Blow** (Gordy)
Showcase for alto sax virtuoso Bobby Militello. Adequate blend of pop, funk and soul disco. Abetted by Motown's Rick James and studio vocalists Jean Carn and Keely Curtis. Produced by Lenny White and Bobby Militello.

### JACK MACK AND THE HEART ATTACK
**Cardiac Party** (Full Moon)
10-piece Los Angeles band made up of veteran session men and playing diverting good-time music with no other purpose than getting those dancing shoes bopping and the booze flowing. A constant homage to the old Stax tunes, although all the material is surprisingly enough original. Produced by Glenn Frey and Allan Blazek.

### MADNESS
**Rise And Fall** (Stiff)
Sombre album from the Madness funsters of past days. If the nuttiness is gone, the

band are now emerging as more mature and a track like 'Our House' is a less frantic, more measured hit. Less immediate impact overall than previous efforts, but an album that will probably linger longer in your mind. A commendable effort in progression and growing up. Produced by Clive Langer and Alan Winstanley.

### MAD PROFESSOR
**Beyond The Realms Of Dub** (Ariswa)
Dub reggae from one of the genre's almost legendary figures. Potent and bass heavy. Produced by Neil Fraser.

### MAJOR ACCIDENT
**Massacred Melodies** (Step Forward)
Progressive punk with strong musical velleities (guitar solos and innovative sound structures). A new North of England group who appear to have broken out of the punk straight-jacket, although they still have a long way to go.

### STEPHEN MALLINDER
**Pow-Wow** (Fetish)
Solo effect by the singer and bass-player for Sheffield electronic doom rockers Cabaret Voltaire. Paranoiac and dense syncopations akin to Stockhausen without the clarity. 'Modernist chamber music' (*NME*).

### MAMA'S BOYS
**Plug It In** (Albion)
Heavy metal rock and roll from a new Irish band fronted by the three McManus brothers. Formula stuff but performed with undeniable gusto, clichés and all.

### MANDINGO GRIOT SOCIETY
**Mighty Rhythm** (Flying Fish)
Chicago-based American black band with a strong yearning for their original roots, although most of the musicians involved come from the progressive jazz scene, soul and reggae. Uneven but fascinating blend of black cultural influences: Afro-American, Cuba, Caribbean and others. Worth a lengthy detour.

### LOUISE MANDRELL AND R. C. BANNON
**(You're) My Superwoman, (You're) My Incredible Man** (RCA)
Lush, cute country ballads by indifferent performers who in fact fare slightly better when solo. Produced by Eddie Kilroy.

### MANDRILL
**Eversize** (Montage)
Black, big sound funk from the four Wilson Brothers and their band. Produced by the group.

### BARRY MANILOW
**Here Comes The Night** (Arista)
(titled **I Wanna Do It With You** in the UK)
The usual schmaltz from the darling of the

MADNESS

younger blue-rinse set. Safe mix of emotive ballads from the past and present (including 'Memory' from 'Cats') and revamped rockers 'Some Girls', 'I'm Gonna Sit Right Down And Write Myself A Letter', etc. . . Produced by Barry Manilow.

## MARC AND THE MAMBAS
**Untitled** (Some Bizzare)

Double set (although one album plays at 45 rpm) by Marc Almond outside of the Soft Cell camp. Not quite a solo as he uses other musicians quite extensively, particularly pianist Ann Hogan and Matt Johnson alias The The. Self-indulgent but never less than seductive set of personal favourites including Lou Reed and Jacques Brel songs pared down to minimalist but emotional extremes. Almond has a most distinctive voice and carries off (just) what could have been a perilous exercise in diversification. A bit long, though.

## RITA MARLEY
**Harambe** (Shanachie)

Soft and mellow second album by the female reggae vocalist and inheritor of the Marley flame. Produced by Ricky Walters, Grub Cooper and Steve Golding.

## MATCHBOX
**Crossed Line** (Magnet)

Indifferent British rockabilly with a leering eye on the pop charts. Produced by Brian Hodgson.

## MATERIAL
**One Down** (Elektra)

A sell-out, disco album from a jazz funk band with an impeccable pedigree. Beat, choruses and swing are all here but it sounds strained and artificial. Guest appearances by Chic, Archie Shepp, Oliver Lake, Nona Hendryx and Fred Frith show the esteem in which Bill Laswell's men are held, but overall a major disappointment. Produced by Material.

## MATUMBI
**Testify** (Solid Groove)

Sluggish British soul-cum-reggae collection. Thin production doesn't help. Devotional tunes and social protest. Unconvincing.

## MAXIMUM JOY
**Station MXJY** (Y)

Uneven, British, would-be funky outfit with extended brass work-outs and derivative material at best. Produced by Adrian Sherwood.

## CURTIS MAYFIELD
**Honesty** (Boardwalk)

A tasty return to past form by one of the more reliable soul performers in the business. Has suffered a bit of an eclipse in popularity but this new set shows him at his most fluent and entrancing. Quality funk.

## GWEN McCRAE
**On My Way** (Atlantic)

Sophisticated and emotional slice of funk from a powerful black singer; danceable toe-tapping songs dominate. Produced by Webster Lewis.

## RONNY McDOWELL
**Greatest Hits** (Epic)

Mc who? is the first thought that arises. In fact, McDowell is yet another from the great American country-singer production line. Gruff voice, dobros, women, sex, booze and love. Conway Twitty makes a guest appearance. Workmanlike. Produced by Buddy Killen.

## FREDDIE McGREGOR
**Love At First Sight** (Joe Gibbs Music)

Seductive reggae album from the man behind last year's 'Big Ship'. Strong on love songs and less rasta than usual make this a good cross-over bet. Produced by Erroll Thompson.

## McGUFFEY LANE
**Let The Hard Times Roll** (Atco)

Third album by a country sextet. Basic medium-paced rock blending self-penned material with some standards. Par for the prairie course. Produced by Marshall Morgan and Paul Worley.

## MDC
**Millions Of Dead Cops** (Alternative Tentacles)

Deafening din from a hardcore US punk group sponsored by Jello Biafra's new enterprising label. Strong stuff with primary politics reeking of naivety and likely to be unpopular with MacDonald's, the ghost of John Wayne and other revered US institutions.

## BILL MEDLEY
**Right Here And Now** (Planet)

Seductive, polished pop by the ex-Righteous Brother. Material by Barry Mann and Cynthia Weill and Michael McDonald, production by Richard Perry. Everything that money can buy. Tolerable in small doses.

## THE MEKONS
**The Mekons Story** (CNT)

A redundant, non-chronological compilation of a bizarre little British band spanning the years of punk and electro-pop and falling/failing in between. A curio, no more.

## THE MEMBERS
**Uprhythm, Downbeat** (Arista)

American debut album for the revived British band who now boast a couple of horn players to make their sound even meatier. Upbeat, toe-tapping tunes with funk and reggae prominent behind the cheeky vocals of ebullient Nicky Tesco. Produced by Dave Allen, Martin Rushent and the Group.

## MENTAL AS ANYTHING
**If You Leave Me, Can I Come Too?** (A&M)

Good-time rock with a deft touch of wit from a now-established Australian band. Easy-going attitude cleverly conceals well-crafted tunes with strong melodic touches. An impressive album altogether. Produced by Bruce Brown and Russell Dunlop.

## MEN WITHOUT HATS
**Rhythm Of Youth** (Statik)

A little gem in the electro-pop league from a surprising band out of Quebec! Owing something to Kraftwerk and others, they quickly transcend the dreary synthesiser trap with infectious, bristling melodics and

a genuine sense of joy (and sometimes mischief) in their playing. Modern pop at its best (despite the monotonous vocals which could be improved on next time). Produced by Marc Durand.

## MERCYFUL HATE
**Mercyful Hate** (Rave On)

Twin-guitar, heavy rock with the standard themes of devil and malevolence. Distasteful turmoil at best.

## MESSENDGER
**Messendger** (Jab)

Powerful hard rock from a new Georgia band on a local label. Guitarist Brady Sayre cops all the honours with virtuoso riffing on mostly original material; the covers are, on the other hand, far from original: 'Hang On Sloopy' and 'Be Bop A Lula'. Produced by Messendger.

## PAUL METSERS
**Momentum (Highway)**

Average British modern folk performer with cross-over possibilities. Produced by John Gill.

## MILKSHAKES
**14 Rhythm and Beat Greats** (Wall City)

Sixties beat revival done with enthusiasm and application. Basic, clean-cut fun from a new British outfit led by one Wild Billy Childish.

## SUGAR MINOTT
**Bitter Sweet** (BMD)

Laidback reggae from a regular on the rasta turn-tables. Lazy, sunny set of tunes.

## MISSING PERSONS
**Spring Mission M** (Capitol)

After the success of their indie mini-album, Capitol have taken Missing Persons under their wing and are marketing the group as next year's answer to Blondie or The Cars in the new wave acceptability stakes. Effervescent vocals from ex-Playboy pin-up Dale Bozzio and quirky key-

board work from husband Terry (a Zappa alumni) keep the mixture fizzy and lightweight. All very contrived. Produced by Ken Scott.

## JONI MITCHELL
**Wild Things Run Fast** (Geffen)

| | |
|---|---|
| Chinese Café | Be Cool |
| Unchained Melody | (You're So Square) |
| Wild Things Run | Baby, I Don't Care |
| Fast | You Dream Flat |
| Ladies' Man | Tires |
| Moon At The | Man To Man |
| Window | Underneath The |
| Solid Love | Streetlight |
| | Love |

After a few years off, smarting from the muted response to her jazz album 'Mingus', Mitchell now returns with a bittersweet collection of songs which hark back to easier days. A straight rock 'n' roll version of the Leiber/Stoller 'You're So Square' and strains of 'Unchained Melody' signal the nostalgic feel of the album, a gentle meditation on what it's like to be a rock star at 40. I'm personally seduced through and through, but then I've always been a sucker for the lady. Grows on you fast, even when you have some minor reservations which it would be ungallant to even mention here. Take that, objectivity! Produced by Joni Mitchell.

### T. S. MONK
**T. S. Monk** (Human Mirage)
Sophisticated funk dance action with speed and flash but samey throughout. Never moves into higher quality gear. Produced by Eric Mercury.

### THE MONKEES
**Monkee Business** (Rhino)
One for the faithful fans. Picture disc compilation of generally more obscure tracks, including an Italian version of the Monkee's TV theme song and various B-cuts. Various producers.

### GARY MOORE
**Corridors Of Power** (Virgin)
Riff-infested guitar work-out album by Moore, better known for his group contributions to Skid Row, Thin Lizzy and other minor British rockers. Predictable but well done; help from familiar names like Ian Paice, Neil Murray, Jack Bruce and Tommy Eyre. Workmanlike British rock. Produced by Jeff Glixman.

### MELBA MOORE
**The Other Side Of The Rainbow** (Capitol)
Disco funk in overdrive and great enjoyment from a class black performer wrestling with hits galore. Various producers.

### MOVING PICTURES
**Days Of Innocence** (Network)
Six-piece band from Australia with strong, horn-driven rhythms. Quality pop with mucho power and gusto led by vocalist Alex Smith. Produced by Charles Fisher.

### JUNIOR MURVIN
**Badman Possie** (Dread At The Controls)
Soulful reggae collection from the author of the Clash's 'Police and Thieves'. A majority of dullish ballads mute the appeal of this album, lacking in rhythm and drive.

### MUSICAL YOUTH
**Youth Of Today** (MCA)

Junior reggae with a cute touch which certainly touched the great British public with the overwhelmingly successful 'Pass the Dutchie'. Unceasingly pleasant jingle-jangle rhythms but a whole album of Musical Youth is like ice-cream indigestion. A slight political edge is welcome and however minor, it at least helps to break down musical barriers and make reggae more generally accepted. Produced by Peter Collins.

### MUTANTS
**Fun Terminal** (MSI/Quality)
Seven-piece, new San Francisco band with female vocalist and strong, percussive elements. Quirky songs in a progressive manner but easy on the ear and the senses. Produced by Snakefinger and the group.

# N

### NASH THE SLASH
**And You Thought You Were Normal** (Cut-throat/PVC)
A return to the independent fold for Canadian one-man band Nash the Slash after his UK Virgin/Dindisc experiences. Engaging electro-pop with electric violin to the fore. One side is instrumental. The acceptable face of experimentalism. Produced by Nash the Slash.

### THE NEATS
**The Monkey's Head In The Corner Of The Room** (Ace Of Hearts)
Seven song mini-album from a Boston independent. Nifty beat pop hooks and melodies with a nice touch of modernism in the surrounding atmospherics. Worth looking out for in the bargain bins.

### BILL NELSON
**Flaming Desire And Other Passions** (PVC)
US compilation of tracks available in different packages in the UK. Clever, if a little contrived electro-pop with Nelson here taking all instrumental chores. Derivative at worst, pleasing at best. No great shakes overall, lacks the conviction of many other synthesiser rockers. Produced by Bill Nelson.

### NEU
**Black Forest Gateau** (Cherry Red)
Uneasy compilation of up to ten-year-old tracks from the seminal German band who spawned Michael Rother and others. Stark electronics and percussion well ahead of its time. Lacks humour, though.

### NEW BIRTH
**I'm Back** (RCA)
Somewhat dated mixture of black funk and slower ballads reminiscent of the Chambers Brothers. Modest and mildly entertaining. Produced by James Baker and Bright Lights Productions.

MUSICAL YOUTH

## OLIVIA NEWTON-JOHN
**Greatest Hits Vol. 2** (MCA)

Ten odd tracks from the back catalogue, half of which are from Livvy's two films ('Xanadu' and 'Grease'). Produced by John Farrar and Jeff Lynne.

## OLIVIA NEWTON-JOHN
**Greatest Hits** (EMI)
British compilation with 20 tracks spanning her whole career from 'The Banks of the Ohio' to 'Physical', including the film songs. Produced by John Farrar, Bruce Welch and Jeff Wayne.

## PAPA KEEBLE ALIAS NICODEMUS JR.
**Snakes And Ladders** (Carousel)
Another reggae rising star with Sly and Robbie providing the rhythm power house. Competent. Produced by K. C. White.

## MAXINE NIGHTINGALE
**It's A Beautiful Thing** (Highrise)
Strong soul outing often reminiscent of the early days of the black girl groups. A duet with Jimmy Ruffin is the main feature of the album. Snappy throughout, though. Produced by Sam Brown III.

## THE NIGHTINGALES
**Pigs On Purpose** (Cherry Red)
Debut by a five-man Birmingham (England) group. Murky, punkist tales of urban woe with strong self-deprecating humour, particularly from singer Robert Lloyd. Very basic musicianship and rough production, but still a freak minor success. Produced by Richard Strange.

## NITRO
**Lethal** (Red Dog)
Five-track, ten-inch mini-album from a bunch of heavy metal screechers and creatures from Philadelphia. Blues boogie in overdrive, school of Van Halen, is the dish of the day.

OLIVIA NEWTON-JOHN

## NO GUITARS
**No Guitars** (CMI Music)
Inventive, four-man rock band eschewing guitars and with leads played by violin and keyboards. Good vocal harmonies by all involved in addition make this an interesting and innovative rock excursion. Produced by Michael Levine.

## THE NOLANS
**Altogether** (Epic)
A greatest hits compilation by any other name, including as it does all the insipid hits by the Nolan sisters. Produced by Nicky Graham.

## NU-CLEAR ENERGY
**Ground Zero** (J. P. Productions)
A white reggae band from Brooklyn! Why not. Basic but fun. Produced by Dave Elliott and John Pergamo.

## ODYSSEY
**The Magic Touch** (Telstar)
TV-advertised compilation of soul and disco hits by Odyssey (who?).

## OK JIVE
**Live At The Blue Chonjo Sky Day And Night Club** (Epic)

White rock band plays African music and rhythms. Warm and bright touches make this less contrived than it initially sounds. Good to dance to but lacks basic excitement. Produced by Bavon Wayne Wayne.

## ONE WAY
**Wild Night** (MCA)
Highly danceable black funk and soul from the hitmakers of 'Cutie Pie'. Dynamic Detroit sound and lots of energy to spare. Produced by Irene Perkins.

## YOKO ONO
**It's Alright** (Polydor)
More Ono doodles. More melodic than her early vinyl efforts but, to my eyes, calculating and manipulative stuff (with a repugnant back cover photo of Yoko and Sean Lennon overshadowed by a shadowy shot of John in the background, like a benevolent ghost). Not my cup of tea. Also bloody pretentious. Produced by Yoko Ono.

## ORANGE JUICE
**Rip It Up** (Polydor)
An improvement on their first effort, with stronger rhythm and vocals courtesy of new member Zeke Manyika. Addition of brass also tightens up the sound, but once more the material is so minor and derivative that it negates all other Orange Juice assets. Sentimental ditherings in a very minor key. Produced by Martin Hayles.

## ROY ORBISON
**The All-Time Greatest Hits Of Roy Orbison** (Monument)
Lavishly-packaged, two-record set regrouping everything you've ever heard (and more) by Orbison. Ranging chronologically from the days of 'Only The Lonely' to more recent country-oriented material, this is a class sampler put together with a lot of care. Produced by Fred Foster.

## OZZY OSBOURNE
**Talk Of The Devil** (Jet)
Live orgy of the raging Osbourne on public display blending material from his two rip-roaring solo albums as well as material going back to his Black Sabbath days. A double set recorded in New York, this is strictly for the fans . . . and there are scores. Produced by Max Norman.

## GILBERT O'SULLIVAN
**Life And Rhymes** (CBS)
Distinctive ballads no better, no worse than before. All in all, pretty boring. To think, O'Sullivan was once a ray of hope for British pop. How the mighty fall. Produced by Graham Gouldman.

## OUR DAUGHTER'S WEDDING
**Moving Windows** (EMI)

New York synthesiser band specialising in consumer futurism. Has nowhere near like the punch and melodiousness of many similar British bands, although a touch of funk and r&b glimmers under the thin surface. Back to the drawing board. Produced by David Spradley, Frank Simon and the group.

## THE OUTCASTS
**Blood And Thunder** (Abstract)
More guts and blood, neo-British punk with anger and venom to spare and little musical capabilities to show for it. Even a cover of Gary Glitter!

## OUTLAWS
**Greatest Hits Of The Outlaws: High Tides Forever** (Arista)
Worthy compilation of material culled from the Outlaws' first eight albums. Courageously, new versions or live renditions are sometimes preferred to established tracks, including 'Riders in the Sky' and 'You Are The Show'. Amiable mid-tempo rock, guaranteed not to offend. Various producers.

# P

## AUGUSTUS PABLO
**Earth Rightful Ruler** (Rocker)
First class set of Jamaican reggae dominated by Pablo's sonorous vocals. One of the better reggae albums of the year with

GILBERT O'SULLIVAN

the obligatory complement of Taxi and Roots Radics personnel beating the rhythm away in the background.

## PALAIS SCHAUMBURG
**Lupa** (Phonogram)

Already the second album for the quirky, jazz-oriented German band. Both intense and sleazy, this fails the language barrier test but has insidious rewards if you can spare the time. Produced by Andy Hernandez.

## TRISTON PALMA
**Joker Smoker** (Greensleeves)
Limpid collection of reggae tunes, most of which conceal clear-cut references to the happiness herb. Produced by Nkrumah Jah Thomas.

## TRISTON PALMA
**Touch Me, Take Me** (Echo)
A new name in the reggae field but an assured album all the same, jingle-jangle beat and mellifluous vocals to the fore.

## PAPA MICHIGAN AND GENERAL SMILEY
**Downpression** (Greensleeves)
Second album of deejay ranting by this Jamaican pair; less of a humourous streak than others and more of a bitter commentary on the state of affairs with strong anti-feminist stance. Produced by Henry 'Junjo' Lawes.

## THE PARAGONS
**Now** (Starlight)
Ordinary set of reggae from the band who provided Blondie with a hit single (not included here).

## RAY PARKER Jr.
**Greatest Hits** (Arista)
Artificial 'Greatest Hits' compilation as only four of the tracks were released by Ray Parker. The remaining six were in fact penned by Parker for his band Raydio. Nevertheless, this is sophisticated rock with strong soul inflections. Includes 'The

TOM PETTY AND THE HEARTBREAKERS

Other Woman' and 'Jack and Jill'. Produced by Ray Parker Jr.

## PASSPORT
**Earthborn** (Atlantic)
Stodgy, mainstream jazz rock; mostly instrumentals although keyboard player Hermann Weindorf does take a few, unconvincing vocals. Lots of pomp and little heart. Produced by Klaus Doldinger.

## PASTOURELLE
**Pastourelle** (RCA)
Folk songs from an operatic performer with valuable assistance from Rod Argent, Ray Cooper, Julian Lloyd-Webber and others. Barbara Courtney-King has a strong voice but displays too much rigor for a folk mode. No more than a curiosity.

## HENRY PAUL
**Henry Paul** (Atlantic)
American anonymous power rock with a bite in the tail and lotsa hooks. Passes the time of day but in one ear and out the other. Produced by Peter Solley.

## PERFECT ZEBRAS
**Mixing With Wildlife** (Focus)
Unfocused art rock experimentation with a strong, fatal dose of naivety and misplaced whimsy. Eminently dispensable.

## LEE 'SCRATCH' PERRY
**Heart Of The Ark** (Seven Leaves)
Re-release of past studio out-takes by a reggae master producer. Radical subject matters allied with sparse, simple rhythms and instrumentation make it a rare pleasure to rediscover rock steady, as reggae was once called.

## PETER AND THE TEST TUBE BABIES
**Pissed And Proud** (No Future)
Irreverent punk rock recorded live – insults, jibes, awful musicianship, warts and all. The surprise is that it somehow works. A matter of bad taste winning out, I suppose. Will cause a few frowns and smiles; doesn't aspire to much more.

## TOM PETTY AND THE HEARTBREAKERS
**Long After Dark** (MCA/Backstreet)

Okay but conservative new album by Petty. Strictly safe formula stuff: moody vocals, tense guitar breaks, tight percussion and a general lack of excitement. Although Bob Tench's keyboards assume a more important role, Petty's melodies are tired and unmemorable. Still. he does it better than most of his other mainstream American rockers still practising their power chords in empty garages or elsewhere. Produced by Tom Petty and Jimmy Iovine.

## PHAROAH
### Point of Entry (Scarab)
Faceless Southern rock with the boogie element on a slow burner. A new name with straight commercial vocation and ambitions. Produced by Sam and Joe Locricchio.

## PICTURE
### Diamond Dreamer (Backdoor)
Heavy metal vaguely reminiscent of Deep Purple in their heyday courtesy of a hirsute bunch of Dutch bozos. Not bad, I suppose.

## THE PINKEES
### The Pinkees (Creole)
Bland pseudo-Beatles imitations by a young British band. Crisp mid-sixties ditties which add little to the state of things.

## PLASMATICS
### Coup D'Etat (Capitol)
Gross heavy metal orgy by the infamous band now under the wings of a major label. The same din as before; without the spectacular live theatrics and Wendy O' Williams' mammaries, this doesn't quite work on record. Produced by Dieter Dierks.

## POCO
### Ghost Town (Atlantic)
Indigent country rock by a band who should have given up the ghost long ago (and I say this as one who loved their early years and albums). Mid-tempo dirges by Rusty Young, Paul Cotton and the other

quasi-anonymous members of the band; replete with tired harmonies. Produced by the group and John Mills.

## POINTER SISTERS
### Greatest Hits (Planet)
Safe anthology of outstanding material from the Pointer Sisters' new lease of life under the umbrella of Richard Perry's Planet Records. Smooth, sophisticated soul and pop, includes 'Fire' by Bruce Springsteen, 'He's So Shy', 'Slow Hand' and others. Produced by Richard Perry.

## POISON GIRLS
### Where's The Pleasure (XNTRIX)
Politically-committed punk band struggling with the contradictions of life in England under Thatcher. Sincere but ineffectual. Produced by Simaen Scholfield, Stuart James and the group.

## POWER PLAY
### Avanti (Epic)
Dutch trio with crisp, assured mid-tempo rockers tailored with precision for the great American radio public. Equally at ease in all genres. Could do well, if somewhat soulless. Produced by Hans Vermeullen.

## PRELUDE
### After Hours (AFT)
Languid, middle-of-the-road crooning by a one-hit British vocal group of indistinct talent.

## ELVIS PRESLEY
### The Elvis Medley (RCA)
Reaching the bottom of the Presley barrel, RCA are now reduced to organising a hooked-on type medley with computerized drums and new instrumentation to revive old Elvis hits. True fans will avoid. Produced by David Briggs.

## BILLY PRESTON
### The Best (A&M)
Memorable back catalogue material including 'You Are So Beautiful' and other ballads, funky instrumentals and Preston's ebullient pre-Motown pop. Produced by Billy Preston and George Martin.

## BILLY PRESTON
### Pressin' On (Motown)
Pedestrian soul and funk from the keyboard player who seems to survive every new passing fashion. Produced by Billy Preston, Ralph Benatar and Galen Senogle.

## CHARLEY PRIDE
### Live (RCA)
15 familiar tracks crammed into one album of country delights. Easy-going stuff. Produced by Norro Wilson.

## PRINCE
### 1999 (Warners)

Fourth (and double) album for the cheeky, Minneapolis prince of sexy, macho funk. Artfully-arranged synthesiser pop with all the right bravado and naive political faith in the powers of unbridled sensuality mix well with the more customary rhythm and blues and disco soul. But the overall feeling is of stylistic stagnation as nothing on this set reaches the height of Prince's previous, innovative efforts since so heavily imitated elsewhere (Time, Vanity 6, etc. . .). Still an important (and danceable) statement. Produced by Prince.

## PRINCE JAMMYS AND SLY 'N' ROBBIE
### Black Uhuru In Dub (CSA)
Dub dissection of the first Black Uhuru album ('Black Sounds of Freedom' aka 'Love Crisis') by expert manipulators of the dread controls. A bit unnecessary, as the original music stands up well enough on its own.

## THE PROMENADERS
### The Promenaders (Y)
Awful busker versions of non-rock standards. A fine mess, with no hint of fun either. As *Music Week* aptly puts it: 'GBH: grievous busking harm'.

## PROPER LITTLE MADAMS
### Proper Little Madams (Starward)
Witty, would-be contemporary folk inspired, no doubt, by the Roches. Left-wing political bias dominates. Patchy. Produced by Proper Little Madams and Mark Tibenham.

## PSYCHIC TV
### Force The Hand Of Chance (Some Bizzare)
Old Throbbing Gristlers Genesis P Orridge and Peter Christopherson on the road to mass acceptance with a surprising set of almost lush disco material with a zest of tasteful electronics. Weird elements abound to put off the casual mainstream

buyer but, overall, an interesting and accessible piece of work. Produced by Psychic TV and Ken Thomas.

# Q

## SUZI QUATRO
**Main Attraction** (Polydor)
Workmanlike power pop from an old hand. Professional but highly unremarkable set of mostly new (self-penned by Quatro and hubby Len Tuckey) material. Nothing offensive, but nothing immortal either. Bargain bin filler. Produced by Chris Andrews and Len Tuckey.

# R

## EDDIE RABBITT
**Radio Romance** (Elektra)
Tepid country cross-over rock. 'You and I', a lachrymose duet with Crystal Gayle, typifies the overall mellow, almost soporific mood of the set. Produced by David Malloy.

## RANK AND FILE
**Sundown** (Slash)
Country-tinged rock and roll in an uncluttered fashion from a new young American band. Amiable. Produced by David Kahne.

## LOU RAWLS AND DESIREE GOYETTE
**Here Comes Garfield** (Epic)
Upbeat pop songs derived from the American TV show, itself inspired by the Garfield cat books. Cute but unlikeable. Produced by Lee Mendelson.

## HARRY RAY
**It's Good To Be Home** (Sugar Hill)
Mellow and soulful debut platter for the former member of the Moments. Falsetto ballads for black radio and, maybe, just beyond. Innocuous. Various producers.

## RAY, GOODMAN AND BROWN
**Open Up** (Polydor)
Soul goes pop with strong inspirational vocals. Lots of unbounded energy. Black dance floor tunes done with fire and gusto. Produced by Vincent Castellano.

## JERRY REED
**The Bird** (RCA)
Good-natured country fare by a veteran picker and singer who, over the last few years, seemed lost to the movies. Solid, reliable tunes with the usual virtuoso guitar work. Produced by Rick Hall.

## R.E.M.
**Chronic Town** (IRS)
Five-song mini-album by new American progressive outfit with strong guitar emphasis. Passable debut.

## RENATO
**Save Your Love** (Lifestyle)

Not quite the comedy album of the year, but not far from it. Following on the surprising success of schmaltzy ballad 'Save Your Love' (included here), more standards ('Danny Boy', 'Granada', 'Ave Maria', and more of that irksome ilk) by the pot-bellied Italian waiter.

## JOHN RENBOURN GROUP
**Live In America** (Flying Fish)
Double live set from the Pentangle avatar featuring both Renbourn's baroque and ornate guitar work and Jacqui McShee's crystal vocals. Gentle, unassuming British folk. Grows on you, fast. Produced by Mitch Greenhill.

## RESURRECTION BAND
**DMZ** (Elektra)
Hard rock with a strong Christian vein running through the songs' lyrics. Alternate male and female vocals from Glenn and Wendi Kaiser sound all too familiar and the whole shebang is mucho contrived. Leave the message at home, boys and girls! Produced by Resurrection Band.

## R. J. RICE
**R. J.'s Latest Arrival** (Zoo York)
Dance funk from the Detroit club scene. Effective in an unspectacular way. Produced by R. J. Rice.

## LIONEL RICHIE
**Lionel Richie** (Motown)
Long-awaited solo debut by the smooth-voiced singer of the Commodores, and partner to Diana Ross for romantic duets like 'Endless Love'. A master of the syrupy ballad, Richie comes across like sheer velvet on the slow numbers while faster pieces navigate through a gentle dance

groove. Maybe too subdued and lacking some soul and fire, but all very sincere. Produced by Lionel Richie and James Anthony Carmichael.

## RIDERS IN THE SKY
**Prairie Serenade** (Rounder)
Gentle, traditional country and western with elegant fiddle and guitar playing. A mite nostalgic and full of evocative ballads. Produced by Fred LaBour and Woody Paul.

## LEE RITENOUR
**Rit 2** (Elektra)
Jazz fusion guitarist in a complete cross-over to rock. Fluid contemporary pop songs featuring Eric Tagg on mellifluous vocals. The instrumentals are a better showcase for Ritenour's talents, though. Safe and comfortable. Produced by Harvey Mason and Lee Ritenour.

## ERIC ROBINSON
**Walk In The Light** (RCA)
Newcomer with a hybrid album of progressive black funk and roll with touches of gospel. Has its moments although coyness intrudes with the presence of a children's chorus on some tracks. Patchy. Produced by Allen Zentz and Eric Robinson.

## TOM ROBINSON
**Cabaret '79** (Panic)
Now three years old live recording by the gay protest rocker, updating popular Noel Coward and other camp material with lots of humour. Produced by Tom Robinson.

## THE ROCHES
**Keep On Doing** (Warners)

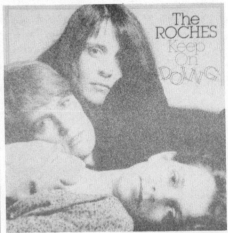

Third album for the coy US vocal trio now back in primarily acoustic territory. Mannered, too clever by half but nevertheless charming with its polished harmonies, quirky songs and tongue-in-cheek wit. Familiar but endearing. Produced by Robert Fripp.

## LINDA RONSTADT
**Get Closer** (Asylum)

Excellent return to the record scene by Ronstadt after a lengthy break in theatre, Gilbert & Sullivan and film. A careful selection of old and contemporary material which suits her voice (stronger than ever) to perfection. A duet with James Taylor, a trio with Emmylou Harris and Dolly Parton, covers of Lee Dorsey's, 'Lies', Jimmy Webb, Joe South. . . The lady is still an undeniable force for all that she's out of fashion. Produced by Peter Asher.

## ROSE TATTOO
**Scarred For Life** (Carrere/Mirage)
No frills heavy metal in fifth gear by a new Australian powerhouse of a band who sound as if they've been touring and breaking up joints for a decade already. No subtlety but a lot of guts and sweat in evidence. Produced by Vanda and Young.

## DIANA ROSS
**Love Songs** (K-Tel)
TV-advertised compilation from the extensive Diana Ross catalogue of ballads and torch songs, drawn from the Motown years through to 'Endless Love'.

## DIANA ROSS
**Silk Electric** (RCA)
Most eclectic second album by Diana Ross for RCA. 'Muscles' was the hit single in answer to Olivia's 'Physical', no doubt, and was penned by Michael Jackson. Elsewhere, Ross uses quality new songs by Barry Blue, Luther Vandross and herself, switching with consummate ease from sleek ballads to soul extravaganzas and non-stop rockers. All the gloss and charm that money can buy and used well. An almost perfect commercial album. Produced by Diana Ross and Michael Jackson.

## ROUGH TRADE
**For Those Who Think Young**
(Boardwalk)
Interesting new Canadian art-rock duo

DIANA ROSS

with female vocalist Carole Pope to the fore (multi-instrumentalist Kevan Staples is the other half). Theatrical, sometimes contrived but always intriguing, could go far if given half a chance. Investigate if it comes your way. Produced by Gene Martynec and Kevan Staples.

## THE ROYAL PHILHARMONIC ORCHESTRA
**Plays The Queen Collection** (EMI)
It was bad enough when Freddie Mercury sang, but why, oh why foist such an inane record upon us? Queen's songs are sufficiently pompous as it is without bearing the full weight of a symphony orchestra in a slumming mood. Produced by Brian B. Culverhouse.

## RUBBER RODEO
**Rubber Rodeo** (Eat)
Providence, Rhode Island sextet cleverly

blending new wave echoes with more traditional country strains. Idiosyncratic but enticing, with a lot of humour to boot. Produced by John Doelp.

# S

## SAGA
**Worlds Apart** (Portrait)
Versatile American band who switch easily from hard rockers to more gentle electronic ballads. Lead vocalist and keyboards player Michael Sadler is the main personality in this five-man group. Produced by Rupert Hine.

## SAMSON
**Before The Storm** (Polydor)
Thunderous heavy metal with energy and watts to spare; a first album for a major

company for a band once tarnished with a mighty bad reputation. Tidy riffing and ranting to suit the headbanging aficionados. Produced by Jo Julian.

### SANDII AND THE SUNSETZ
**Immigrants** (Sire)

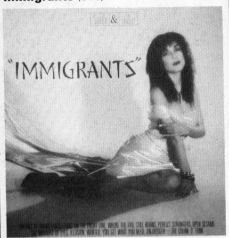

Attractive set of Japanese pop (mostly sung in English) with just a hint of synthesiser washes. Sandii's vocals veer from Kate Bush to Blondie and back again and the album is lightweight. The Oriental touch comes through strongly and salvages this from being just another girl vocalist new wave group; David Sylvian guests on one track. Produced by Makoto Kubota.

### SANTERS
**Mayday** (Ready)
Four-track EP of Canadian heavy metal, half studio endeavours and half live in concert souvenir. Uninspired formula stuff.

### SANTERS
**Racing Time** (Heavy Metal)
A quick second album already for the Canadian heavy metal group. A massive improvement on the preceding 'Mayday' with which it shares a track, 'Mistreatin' Heart', now changed beyond recognition. Hard-hitting, frenzied power pop in the best of traditions. Produced by Jack Richardson.

### LARRY SANTOS
**Interplay** (Casablanca)
Collection of smooth, effortless r&b ballads, some of which have already appeared on previous albums by Santos. Various producers.

### MICHAEL SCHENKER GROUP
**Assault Attack** (Chrysalis)
Featuring the short-lived presence of Graham Bonnet on vocals, a tight and fiery album of quality heavy metal by the German guitar virtuoso. Produced by Martin Birch.

### IRMIN SCHMIDT
**Filmmusik Vol. 2** (Spoon)

Atmospheric background music and innovative instrumentals for this further collection of soundtracks for modern German movies by the Can veteran. Produced by Irmin Schmidt.

### KLAUS SCHULZE
**Trancefer** (DJM)
Indifferent synthesiser doodles and cosmic swirls by an old hat at this mug's game, school of early Tangerine Dream (they've improved since – he hasn't). Produced by Klaus Schulze.

### THE SCORPIONS
**Lonesome Crow** (Heavy Metal)
First release in England of a 10-year old-album featuring both the Schenker brothers (Michael was then barely 16. . .). Crisp old-fashioned heavy metal which stands the test of time well.

### BOB SEGER AND THE SILVER BULLET BAND
**The Distance** (Capitol)
Immaculate new album from the Detroit romantic blending uptempo, burning rockers with the most attractive, reflective and sentimental ballads possible. Seger both mellows and gets tougher with age. It's

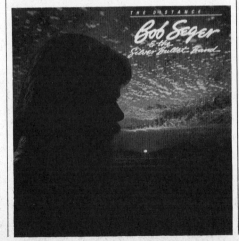

formula stuff but impossible to criticise, what with songs by Rodney Crowell, crisp boogie and lots of rasping, contemplative slow numbers. A must for any collection. Produced by Jimmy Iovine.

### SHAKATAK
**Invitations** (Polydor)
Basically instrumental British dance hall jazz fusion tunes with minor female vocals to pep matters up. A thin veneer of sophistication but overall a lightweight, forgettable album. Produced by Nigel Wright.

### SHAKIN' STEVENS
**Give Me Your Heart Tonight** (Epic)
Packed with his infamous hit singles, this is a major album for Stevens as with the help of famous session musicians he tries to impose his own personality with some self-penned tunes. However the results are both predictable and dire. Minor pop at best. Includes the immortal 'Que Sera Sera'; Shaky in the footsteps of Doris Day? God forbid. Produced by Stuart Colman.

### MARLENA SHAW
**Let Me In Your Life** (South Bay)
West coast soul with a cast of many for this vocal outing. slick and easy, if not particularly memorable. Produced by Johnny Bristol and Webster Lewis.

### T. G. SHEPPARD
**Perfect Stranger** (Warners)
Manly country singer with cross-over touches. Nice duet with Karen Brooks on 'Faking Love'. Easy listening in a deceptive manner. Produced by Buddy Killen.

### SHIVA
**Firedance** (Heavy Metal)
British three-man heavy metal band based in Bristol. Lots of fire and conviction, but all the usual tired riffs and clichés. Produced by Shiva and Andy Allan.

### ALFIE SILAS
**Alfie** (RCA)
Sophisticated black dance debut by a new performer (though most of the material is written by his producers). Catchy disco rhythms and strong melodies. Produced by Lewis Parker and Brian Potter.

### SILVER CITY
**Silver City** (Baldwin)
Clean-cut modern rock from a Pennsylvania group. Most of the material is about baseball heroics and angst! Produced by Silver City and Dave Still.

### SIOUXSIE AND THE BANSHEES
**A Kiss In The Dreamhouse** (Polydor)
One of the British punk new wave's most improved bands. Already their fourth album and the sound of the Banshees be-

comes a veritable swirl of atmospherics, assured jangling guitar and eerie, evocative vocals as Siouxsie grows in stature. Idiosyncratic mood pieces and melodic landscapes of ice and mist dominate the album. A gratifying set which confirms their enhanced status in today's rock pantheon.

## PETER SKELLERN
### String Of Pearls (Mercury)

Pre-World War Two chestnuts sung with Noel Coward-like sophistication by a young British refugee from the pop crossroads. Amusing but contrived. No more versions of 'Stormy Weather' please! Produced by Peter Skellern.

## SLADE
### On Stage (RCA)
Old troupers never die, they keep on recording live in Newcastle, presenting grateful audiences with their hard-as-rock, ebullient pop of well-worn ditties. Safe and reliable. All the old hits are present (and unchanged). Produced by Slade.

## SLAPP HAPPY/HENRY COW
### Desperate Straights (Recommended)
Art rock in the European mood re-released for reasons I cannot fathom. Featuring Anthony More who has since progressed beyond this random lunacy. Was fun in its day, but no longer means much.

## MICHAEL SMITH
### Mi Cyaan Believe It (Island)
Debut by a Jamaican dub poet of great promise. Whether singing to a classy reggae background or unaccompanied, this is meaty stuff, social anthems and observations with a vengeance. One of the best reggae albums of the year. Produced by Linton Kwesi Johnson and Dennis Bovell.

## SNEAKER
### Loose In The World (Handshake)
Second album of confident mainstream American pop. Easy-listening stuff including a surf-tinged instrumental 'Pour It Out'. Produced by Jeffrey Baxter.

## THE S.O.S. BAND
### S.O.S. III (Tabu)
Poppish funk with female vocalist Mary Davis in good form. Dance floor muzak with lotsa gloss. Produced by Ricky Sylvers and Gene Dozier.

## THE SOUND
### All Fall Down (WEA)
Third album of British doom rock. Strong backbeat and emotional vocals but a lack of ideas and the impossibility of moving into higher gear make this a dreary record to listen to.

## SOUNDTRACK
### Atomic Café (Rounder)
From the disturbing montage film about past nuclear civil defence propaganda, a collection of pro-nuclear ditties by non-entities from all walks of life and music (country, r&b, ballads, rock, etc...). Fun in a perverted sort of way.

## SOUNDTRACK
### Honky Tonk Man (Warners)
Varied country tracks for the new Clint Eastwood movie even features the man himself on two tracks and an ensemble rendering of 'In The Jailhouse Now'. Also in evidence are country stalwarts John Anderson, Frizzell and West, Porter Wagoner, Ray Price, Johnny Gimble, Marty

PETER SKELLERN

Robbins and the incandescent Linda Hopkins. Produced by Snuff Garrett.

## SOUNDTRACK
### An Officer And A Gentleman
(Island)
Music from the Taylor Hackford movie featuring Richard Gere and sultry Debra Winger which has proved one of the surprise successes of the year in the USA. This soundtrack has, of course, spawned the chart-topping 'Up Where We Belong' duo by Joe Cocker and Jennifer Warnes. The rest of the record is a safe compendium of well-known tracks by the likes of Dire Straits, Pat Benatar, Z. Z. Top, Sir Douglas Quintet and Lee Ritenour. Various producers.

## SOUNDTRACK
### One From The Heart (Columbia)
Music from the ill-fated Francis Ford Coppola movie with Nastassia Kinski and Frederic Forrest. The music is by Tom Waits and is both bitter-sweet and atmospheric. Waits shares vocal duties on smokey ballads with Crystal Gayle. Produced by Bones Howe.

## SOUNDTRACK
### Party Party (A&M)

Uneven anthology of well-known British artists tackling generally unfamiliar material for the movie of the same name. Elvis Costello with a jaunty title track and Sting with a sincere if slightly misplaced blues (done better years ago by Christine Perfect, now McVie with Fleetwood Mac) come out best. Also present are Bad Manners, Midge Ure, Madness, Dave Edmunds, Altered Images (a dire 'Little Town Flirt'), etc. . . Various producers.

## SOUNDTRACK
### Vortex (Neutral)
New wave minimalist material for the Beth and Scott B 16mm Lower East Side tongue-in-cheek private eye caper featuring Lydia Lunch and other semi-underground New York personalities. Patchy and useless outside of the film's context. Music by Lunch herself, Adele Bertei, Richard Edson and Kristian Hoffman. Produced by Beth and Scott B.

## SPECIAL DUTIES
### '77 in '82 (Rondolet)
Retrospective look at a minor punk band from 1977. Social protest and one chord wonder solos on guitar make this just one more in a dreary series.

## SPIDER
### Rock 'N' Roll Gypsies (RCA)
Minor league heavy metal with headbanging, clichés and lots of indistinctive riffs. Another one bites the dust.

## THE SPINNERS
### Grand Slam (Atlantic)
Everlasting black vocal group with soul and talent to spare. Increasingly sophisticated production and arrangements suit them well. Par for the course and likely to be very popular. Produced by Freddie Perren.

## SPLODGE
### In Search of the 7 Golden Gussetts
(Razor)
22 tracks (on a single album!) of irreverent punk humour at the expense of Spandau Ballet and other less deserving targets by the idiosyncratic main man from the overlooked Splodgenessabounds. Strong country strains throughout. OK in small doses.

## SPOONS
### Arias and Symphonies (A&M)
Four-piece, Canadian progressive rock formation with art school leanings. A bit pretentious and full of glittering pomp but well done overall. Produced by John Punter.

## DUSTY SPRINGFIELD
### White Heat (Casablanca)
Yet another comeback attempt by the once-great British soul singer. Fast-buck try at modernism with use of synthesiser throughout and new wave material (the acceptable part of it, that is) by Elvis Costello and Sting. Second-rate. Produced by Howard Steele and Dusty Springfield.

## RICK SPRINGFIELD
### Wait For Night (RCA)
Re-issue of a six-year-old album, from before the heart-throb days. Fluffy pop. Hasn't changed that much during the intervening years, anyway. Produced by Mark K. Smith.

## SPYROGYRA
### Incognito (MCA)
Fluent, wall-paper music in a jazz fusion mood. Mostly played by New York and Los Angeles session hacks. Tasteful and a bit pointless. Produced by A Beckenstein and Richard Calandra.

RICK SPRINGFIELD

146

WALTER STEDING

keep-fit set to the accompaniment of familiar pop hits and the chirpy tones of the Scottish folk singer turned TV personality.

### WALTER STEDING
**Dancing In Heaven** (Animal)

New York avant-garde scene violin player's surprisingly accessible set of songs in a quirky, progressive rock frame. Danceable. Produced by Walter Stedding.

### STEEL BREEZE
**Steel Breeze** (RCA)
Middle-of-the-road, pleasantish mainstream American rock. Guaranteed not to offend and with a minor hit single to boot.

### IRA STEIN/RUSSEL WALDER
**Elements** (Windham Hill)
Soft-focus jazz duo with a delicate, almost ethereal feel. Combination of piano and oboe evokes chamber music comparisons. Gentle and unassuming. Produced by William Ackerman.

### DIDI STEWART
**Begin Here** (Kirshner)
Assured, contemporary pop from a new artist with large, traditional audience in mind, abetted by Steve Perry on lead guitar. Quite distinctive; yet another Stewart whose name might soon become more familiar. Produced by Stephan Galfas.

### SQUEEZE
**Singles 45s and Under** (A&M)
Almost a requiem for the group, this select choice of past hits, each a minor little pop masterpiece: 'Take Me I'm Yours', 'Cool For Cats', 'Up The Junction', 'Another Nail In My Heart', etc. . . An unlucky band who were constantly on the verge of greater acceptance and, possibly, broke up too early. Various producers.

### STAMPEDE
**The Official Bootleg** (Polydor)
Live heavy metal from a band with second division status. Loud, derivative and familiar as soon as the first track bursts out through the speakers. Heard it all before (well-known tune. . .).

### JOE STAMPLEY
**Backslidin'** (Epic)
Solid mixture of country categories by an habitual hit maker. Lotsa barrel-house dance numbers. Raucous and fun. Produced by Ray Baker.

### THE MICHAEL STANLEY BAND
**MSB** (EMI)
Polished mainstream rock with a touch of Springsteen street-sassiness from an experienced American group with a track record as long as my arm. Guitar-oriented songs, with a zest of heavy metal sympathies from past efforts; just perfect for the US airwave nation. Workmanlike, honest music.

### STARGAZERS
**Watch This Space** (Epic)
Reverential rockabilly revival from a faithful band of British musicians who treat the originals well but add little. Useless curiosity. Produced by Pete Brown and Stargazers.

### STATUS QUO
**F.T.M.O.** (Vertigo)
Metal box set for the collectors of the supreme British headbanging masters, includes three compilation albums (two greatest hits and one live). An impressive legacy although bloody boring to listen to all the way through. . .

### ISLA ST CLAIR
**Shape Up And Dance Vol. 3**
(Lifestyle)
More calisthenics and aerobics for the

147

## ERIC STEWART
**Frooty Rooties** (Mercury)

Solo album by the 10CC man, which sounds just like another 10CC album, albeit a rather tired one. Well-crafted, catchy, frothy but in the long run rather lifeless. Moderately enjoyable, geriatric rock in the McCartney style. Produced by Eric Stewart.

## BILLY STEWART
**The Greatest Sides** (Chess)
14-track compilation of classic 60s tracks from the hallowed Chess vaults of soul. Produced by Marshall Chess and Tomie Swan.

## ROD STEWART
**Absolutely Live** (Riva/Warners)
Double live album with all Stewart's fam-iliar past hits and two new tracks including a cover of the Platters' 'The Great Pretender'. Which almost epitomises what Stewart has become today, a shadow of his former innovative self. Duets with Kim Carnes and Tina Turner, but a dispiriting lot it all is. Produced by Rod Stewart.

## THE STRINGS
**Yum Yum** (Parsley)
Mini-album of mainstream, new wavish pop from a new Belgian band. Hmmm. Produced by J. M. Aerts.

## ANDY SUMMERS AND ROBERT FRIPP
**I Advance Masked** (A&M)

Scintillating album of duetting electric guitars. Although the sound always remains a Fripp/early King Crimson one, Summers' contribution mellows the aggressivity of the set. Evocative, atmospheric compositions, virtuoso, shimmering twin solos. A minor masterpiece. Produced by Robert Fripp.

## BILL SUMMERS AND SUMMERS HEAT
**Seventeen** (MCA)
Average black funk and soul set. Good brass contributions. Produced by Bill Summers, Larry Batiste and Claytoven Richardson.

## SUNFIRE
**Sunfire** (Warners)
Average black dance album, strong on the funk with a touch of the bouncing discoes. Not very original. Produced by Reggie Lucas.

## SUNS OF ARQUA
**Return Of The Mozabites** (Rock Steady)
Odd reggae album from Manchester, blending incongruous Indian tablas, Spanish castanets and Irish jigs with the more familiar Jamaican rhythms. Still quite coherent, though. Worth looking out for! Produced by Michael Ward.

## SUPERTRAMP
**'. . . famous last words. . .'** (A&M)

Crazy
Put On Your Old
 Brown Shoes
It's Raining Again
Bonnie
Know Who You
 Are
My Kind Of Lady
C'Est Le Bon
Waiting So Long
Don't Leave Me
 Now

New album from the British California residents after a three-year lay-off. Laid-back melodies with craft and care, a trifle lachrymose at times. Spacey sound and imagery captured in full digital splendour but another annoying so-called French track 'C'Est Le Bon' which means nothing whatsoever. Massive arrangements and little ambition. The fans will love it; I have reservations. Produced by Supertramp and Peter Henderson.

ANDY SUMMERS AND ROBERT FRIPP

SUPERTRAMP

### SURVIVOR
**Premonition** (Scotti)
Tepid, mainstream American rock. This time around, Survivor haven't even the alibi of a film-influenced hit single (This is an earlier album, though, released after 'Rocky III' in England). Instant oblivion. Produced by Jim Peterik and Frankie Sullivan.

### SWAMP CHILDREN
**So Hot** (Factory)

Fascinating debut for a new band from the Factory stable which never ceases to surprise. Martin Morscrop of A Certain Ratio is the only known quantity (on drums) but the five other members of the band including vital vocalist Ann Quigley are new to me. Emotional jazz funk with a difference, this sizzles and sparkles. Swamp Children: a name for tomorrow.

### RACHEL SWEET
**Blame It On Love** (CBS/Columbia)
Fourth album already by the former jail-bait country rocker who first emerged on

the dubious but legendary Akron compilation. No rough edges now, just a placid set of mid-tempo rockers with lots of session men vibrating away in the background to keep things clean and polished. So-so. Produced by Rachel Sweet and Larry Gottlieb.

# T

### TANK
**Power Of The Hunter** (Kamaflage)
Tough, gravel-voiced British heavy metal rock. Confident high octane thrash. Produced by Nigel Gray.

### JOHNNIE TAYLOR
**Just Ain't Good Enough** (Beverly Glen)
Smooth soul package with equal share of ballads and up-tempo numbers from a mature performer. Produced by Patrick Moten and Otis Smith.

### TOT TAYLOR AND HIS ORCHESTRA
**Playtime** (Easy Listener's Series)
From the man behind the success of the hard-working but revolting Mari Wilson. Customary kitsch 60s mood with night club pianos, movie soundtrack strings and dubious trumpet solos. Doesn't even work as nostalgia.

### TECHNO ORCHESTRA
**Casualtease** (Techno)
Alias the Techno Twins plus friends. Cabaret version of the electro-pop fashion. Indulgent, hollow dance music.

### GLEN EDWARD THOMAS
**Take Love** (Capitol)
Intense and seductive debut from a polished new American black performer whose tones are sometimes reminiscent of Stevie Wonder. Oozing charm and gentle rhythms, Thomas appears to be eclectic in his tastes and material which augurs well for his future. Produced by Don Cornelius.

### THROBBING GRISTLE
**The Psychick Sacrifice** (Illuminated Karnage)
Yet another live souvenir of Throbbing Gristle's experimentations with sound and aural textures. Collectors only.

### JOHNNY THUNDER AND THE HEARTBREAKERS
**D.T.K – Live At The Speakeasy** (Jungle)
Slapdash rock and roll of dubious historical value by a US new wave band whose sole claim to fame lies in its drug excesses. Untidy and tasteless.

### TOP SECRET
**Another Crazy Day** (Cheapskate)
Lightweight musical humour which is more embarrassing then entertaining.

### TOYAH
**Warrior Rock** (Safari)
Live double album for the British singer. Her material comes off so much better in a performance context, carried along by a fanatical audience at London's Hammersmith Odeon. Flair and theatrics, all the hits, enough to convert the unconvinced.

### TRANSLATOR
**Heartbeats and Triggers** (CBS/Columbia/415)
New Wave California band in a 60s British beat groove. Preppy music at its most derivative, but an overall strength in melodies and inconsequential lyrics keeps this palatable.

### PAT TRAVERS
**Black Pearl** (Polydor)
Stylish heavy metal by the Canadian rock

star now living in England. Hard rock with the occasional attempt at something different; here, Beethoven's Fifth Symphony (!) and a gentle Bob Marley tune. Produced by Pat Travers.

### KATHY TROCCOLI
**Stubborn Love** (Reunion)
Contemporary country from a new US performer whose husky tones tackle ballads and up-tempo rockers with equal ease. Worth looking out for. Produced by Brown Bannister.

### TONY TROUTMAN
**Your Man Is Home Tonight** (T-Main)
Black Atlanta singer-songwriter steps out from family activities with a polished solo album. Strong melodies reminiscent of Otis Redding done with much taste. Produced by Tony Troutman.

### MASAMI TSUCHIYA
**Rice Music** (Epic)

Japanese guitar player who has appeared in England with Japan (!). Part of Ippu-Do, Tsuchiya is helped out on this solo album by Mick Karn and Steve Jansen of J. the group, Bill Nelson, Riuichi Sakamoto of YMO, etc. . . A fluid slice of electro-pop with Oriental influences cutting through the atmospheric blanket of synthesisers. Slithery. Produced by Masami Tsuchiya.

### TOMMY TUCKER
**The Rock Is My Pillow And The Cold Ground Is My Bed** (Red Lightnin)
Last album from the recently-deceased veteran rhythm and blues performer who will long be remembered for his pioneering 'High Heel Sneakers'. A fine, powerful album that deserves a listen.

### TONY TUFF
**Tuff Selection** (Island)
Safe reggae with a keen eye on the blander white market, what with a Bob Marley cover and cautious use of Aswad musicians and horns. Dirge-like.

### THE TURTLES
**Greatest Hits** (Rhino)
All the familiar mid-60s hits from a happy-go-lucky band who haven't dated too much over the passing years. Still fun. Various producers.

### THE TWINKLE BROTHERS
**Underground** (Twinkle)
Now independent, the Twinkle Brothers led by Norman Grant on a tasteful set of reggae tunes, mixed by the Mad Professor. Produced by Norman Grant.

### JUDIE TZUKE
**Road Noise** (Chrysalis)

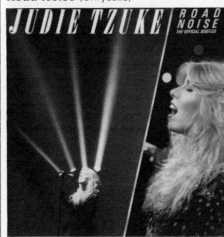

This obligatory double live set continues the trend towards hard rock begun on gentle Judie Tzuke's last studio album. Strong voice and solid, hard-driving backing by her band see her disposing of her 'English rose' image in favour of a more rounded, seasoned pop performance. A set with a few surprises. Welcome ones, at that. Produced by Paul Muggleton.

# U

### UK SUBS
**UK Subs** (Recorded 1979–1981) (Abstract)
Exhaustive and exhausting compilation reflecting the life and times of the epitome of British loser punk groups. Main virtue of the set is the value for money aspect of its 20 tracks. Predictable, boring riff rock and shattered vocals school of DHSS.

### ULLANDA
**Watching You Watching Me** (Atlantic)
Smooth, sophisticated black singer Ullanda McCullough is a promising newcomer in the soul ballad stakes and acquits herself well. Pleasing. Produced by Bert deCoteaux.

### JAMES BLOOD ULMER
**Black Rock** (CBS/Columbia)

Ex-Ornette Coleman jazz sidekick now in a strong funk mood in a similar, free improvisatory format. A guitarist of strong pedigree now taking bows in the direction of Jimi Hendrix, Ulmer interplays quirky leads with the intricate rhythms laid on by his musicians and the whole patchwork erupts into life at surprising intervals. Raw vocals are a black mark, though.

### ULTRAVOX
**Quartet** (Chrysalis)

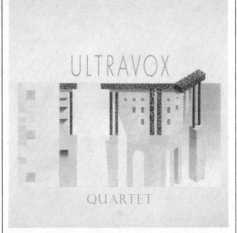

And now the music of the videos. . . As Ultravox progress along the road to pomp electro-rock blandness, style appears to be gaining the upper hand. While the melodies remain strong (and 'Reap The Wild Wind' is excellent in this respect), the passion that was once present is slowly draining away. Immaculate, anaemic rock for the connoisseur of icey beauty. Sterile album. Produced by George Martin.

### UNIPOP
**Unilove** (Kat Family)
Abba-clones done with taste and full-blown melodies. Comes from Atlanta and could well fool some into mistaking it for the real thing. Clever. Produced by Sonny Limbo and Scott McLellan.

ULTRAVOX

### UXA
**Illusions of Grandeur** (PBS)
American new wave with a lead singer called De De Detroit; it's a she, in fact, and the sound is akin to early Penetration – i.e. lots of good ideas badly harnessed, strident guitar work and a patchwork of various feelings.

# V

### VANDENBERG
**Vandenberg** (Atlantic)
Dutch heavy metal band with a good knack for (loud) melodies. Burns with power and conviction and more imagination than most. An improvement on the average headbanger fare. Produced by Vandenberg.

### LUTHER VANDROSS
**Forever, For Always, For Love** (Epic)
Second solo album of sweet soul crooning. Revivals of Sam Cooke and Temptations songs come as a homage to past values but mid-tempo romantic gems dominate the few bouncy dance numbers. Accomplished slice of vulnerable, mellow melodies. Produced by Luther Vandross.

### THE VANDYKES
**No Man Is An Island** (Solid Smoke)
Rediscovery of an American black vocal group from the Texas of way back in the early 60s. Inspired by The Impressions and sporting similar falsetto lead vocals. Sweet, heartbreaking ballads as they just don't sing them anymore. Great stuff.

### VARIOUS
**Aces International** (Greensleeves)
A Jamaican dance hall experience courtesy of 'Junjo' featuring the best in Kingston deejays: Buro, Welton Irie, Yellow Peril, Super Mouse, etc. . . Produced by Henry 'Junjo' Lawes.

### VARIOUS
**American Youth Report** (Bomp)
Compilation of 16 hardcore Los Angeles bands. Unremitting doom and despair colour these visions but the emotional commitment remains generally overpowering. Includes Black Flag, Social Distortion, 45 Grave, 100 Flowers, Minutemen, Legal Weapon, Lost Cause, Rhino 39, Channel 3, Red Kross. . .

### VARIOUS
**Beat The Streets** (Prelude)
Six extended disco tracks from the CBS stable, featuring Sharon Redd, D Train, The Strikers, Nick Straker Band. . . Produced by François Kevotkian.

### VARIOUS
**The Best Of Great Gildersleeves** (Gilded)
Studio sessions by 11 bands who have appeared at the above-named Bowery club. Mostly anonymous heavy metal rock with little in the way of individuality or redeeming features. Avoid. Produced by Tim Finnegan and John Morales.

### VARIOUS
**Best Of Ralph** (Ralph)
A tantalising compilation showcasing the multifarious and weird talents present on the roster of America's most idiosyncratic label. Boasts the quirky likes of the Residents, Snakefinger, Tuxedo Moon, Wild Man Fischer. A double set arrived at by popular votes as well as staff choices. Various producers.

### VARIOUS
**Birth Of The Y** (Y)
Label compilation by the independent London company with a smart eye for jazz and experimental talents. Includes Disconnection, Pigbag, Maximum Joy, Shriekback and the Sun Ra Arkestra.

### VARIOUS
**Bullshit Detector Vol. 2** (Crass)
Anarchist collective compilation of newer bands, most in the punkish metal sphere. Names on random display of 24 bands: The Omega Tribe, The Suspects, The Deformed, Kronstadt Uprising, Polemic Attack, Naked, Anthrax, Total Chaos, Metro Youth, Youth in Asia, Riot Squad, The Destructors, The Bored, Chumbawamba. Double set.

### VARIOUS
**Burning Ambitions – A History of Punk** (Cherry Red)

An interesting attempt to document the rise, fall and stagnation of punk on a double album. Licencing tracks by major name bands like the Clash or the Sex Pistols and Siouxsie having proved a problem, there are obvious gaps, but the selection is nevertheless a worthy one. Includes Boomtown Rats, Adam Ant, Dead Kennedys, the Buzzcocks, the 101ers, Heartbreakers, the Lurkers, the Adverts, Attila the Stockbroker amongst the 38 cuts. Recommended for a sense of historical perspective.

## VARIOUS
**Casino Lights** (Warners)
A live sampling of the 1981 Montreux jazz festival with a majority of fusion-dance numbers and performers: Randy Crawford, Al Jarreau, Yellow-jackets, David Sanborn, Neil Larsen, Buzzy Feiten, Robben Ford, Mike Mainieri, etc. . . Innovative and accessible compilation. Produced by Tommy LiPuma.

## VARIOUS
**A Christmas Record** (Ze)

Is the Ze Xmas platter to become the Spector Xmas disc of the 80s? This is its second release with small modifications bringing in the Waitresses, a new Cristina track and the already-available in the earlier version Darnell, Was Not Was, Davitt Sigerson and other flamboyant contributions. Witty but no more re-releases with extra tracks, please. Various producers.

## VARIOUS
**Crucial Reggae Driven By Sly And Robbie** (Taxi/Island)
Compilation of reggae artists aided and abetted by the ever-present Sly and Robbie rhythm section: The Mighty Diamonds, Yellowman, Jimmy Riley, etc. . .

## VARIOUS
**Dangerous Dance Music** (Jive)
Sampler of snappy dance-oriented tracks and performers by this eclectic label: A Flock of Seagulls, Whodini, Zinc, Impi, Q-Feel, Robert Jon Smith and others.

## VARIOUS
**A Dee-Jay Explosion** (Heartbeat)
Another Jamaican dance hall celebration with innovative deejays at the controls: Eek-A-Mouse, Ringo, Sister Nancy, Jamaica, Gemini Disco, Welton Itie, Brigadier Jerry, etc. . . 11 tracks in all.

## VARIOUS
**Die Neue Deutsche Welle Ist Da Da Da** (Phonogram)

Compilation featuring the best of the so-called German new wave: Trio, Palais Schaumburg, Yello are better known outside of the Teutonic borders but it's an interesting package proving that much is happening beyond our linguistic ken. Investigate.

## VARIOUS
**Euro-Wave For Rednecks** (Parsley)
Enterprising compilation from a small Belgian independent label. Includes much local talent as well as Briton G. T. Moore on dub reggae posturings. Produced by Paul Evrard.

## VARIOUS
**15 Florida Bands – The Land That Time Forgot** (Open)
Garage music in the best do-it-yourself American tradition from a whole assortment of regional no-hopers. Names you'll never come across again include The Eat, Rubber Thongs, The Vulgar Boatmen, The Breathers and 11 others.

## VARIOUS
**For The Good Times** (Epic)
Decent if distinctly familiar set of country greats: Willie Nelson, Marty Robbins, Tammy Wynette, Janie Fricke, Charlie Rich, Johnny Cash, etc. . .

## VARIOUS
**Ghosts Of Christmas Past** (Remake) (Crepuscule)
Seasonal compilation from the innovative Belgian label with a keen eye for experimental and progressive rock. Bands featured here include The Pale Fountains, Cabaret Voltaire, Durutti Column, Tuxedo Moon and others.

## VARIOUS
**Guitar Wars** (Columbia)
Major label guitar-oriented compilation featuring tracks by Loverboy (live), Blue Oyster Cult (also live), Journey, Joe Perry, Frank Marino, Billy Burnette, Judas Priest and Santana. Safe.

## VARIOUS
**Heavy Metal Heroes Vol. 2** (Heavy Metal)
12 second division, British heavy metal pretenders, featuring Witchfinder General and Shiva. Various producers.

## VARIOUS
**Heroes And Villains** (Dakota)
Live memento of 60s revival show staged for charity in London and featuring such faves from the past as Sandie Shaw, Billy Fury, The Swinging Blue Jeans, Dave Berry, Junior Campbell, Chris Farlowe, etc. . .

## VARIOUS
**Hundreds And Thousands** (Native)
12-track compilation with no apparent theme or unity. Veers from heavy metal to melodic pop with 12 unknown bands, including City, Mirage, The Fuse and other nonentities.

## VARIOUS
**Journey Without Maps** (101)
24-track, double-album compilation full of British hopefuls: One Hand Clapping, Binky Baker, Disposable Pop, Man Ray, Two Minds Crack, the Fix, 23 Jewels, The Outsiders, etc. . . Varied quality; take your pick for tomorrow.

## VARIOUS
**Junjo Presents A Live Session With. . .** (Greensleeves)
Reggae dance hall session recorded in Jamaica featuring Yellowman, Eek-A-Mouse, Fathead, Toyan, Welton Irie and Little John.

## VARIOUS
**Just When You Thought It Was Quiet** (JWY. . .)
Primitive British punk school of rants and protests against the system compilation. Stand accused: The Troops, Urban Dogs, Knox, Blurt, Method Actors, Half Japanese, Headhunters, Sex Gang Children, Mxyztplk. Some odd choices intrude like a sore thumb, but mine is not to reason why.

## VARIOUS
**Laser Reggae Hits** (Blue Moon)
Good reggae compilation: Althea and Donna, Dennis Brown, Me and You, Culture, Prince Mohammed and Errol Thompson. A collection of easy-going, poppish, rasta fare. Various producers.

## VARIOUS
**Maximum Rock 'N' Roll Presents Not So Quiet On The Western Front** (Alternative Tentacles)
State of the art, Northern California,

present-day punk on a double-set featuring 47 bands on the Dead Kennedy's label.

**VARIOUS**
**Methods Of Dance Vol. 2** (Virgin)
A second dance-oriented sampler culled from the mighty Virgin modern romance roster: Simple Minds, Japan, Culture Club, DAF, Rip Rig and Panic, BEF, etc. . .

**VARIOUS**
**Move Groove and Night-Clubbing** (Move)
Extended dance mixes of famous hits for the disco market: Irene Cara, Visage, Shakatak, the Jam, Kandidate, Metro, etc. . .

**VARIOUS**
**Pillows And Prayers** (Cherry Red)
A loss-leader priced compilation from what is probably the best small independent British label with a policy of both innovation and eclecticism. 17 tracks from most of the roster, among which jostle: Kevin Coyne, the Monochrome Set, Attila the Stockbroker, the Misunderstood, Eyeless in Gaza, Quentin Crisp, Tracey Thorn, the Nightingales. A venture worth encouraging.

**VARIOUS**
**Platinum High School** (Magnum Force)
Early tracks by latter-day rockers like Shakin' Stevens, The Jets, Johnny Storm. A feast of simple, basic rockabilly.

**VARIOUS**
**Raiders Of The Pop Charts Vol. 1 and 2** (Ronco)
Strong double set of recent British chart hits: Modern Romance, Culture Club, Japan, Kid Creole, The Beat, Shakin' Stevens, Madness, UB 40, Yazoo, Kids From Fame, Simple Minds, Pretenders, Haircut 100, etc. . .

**VARIOUS**
**Rapped Uptight** (Sugarhill)
A rap anthology from the specialist label in the field. Features a bevy of top US performers: Grandmaster Flash, Candi Staton, the Sugarhill Gang, Sequence, Wayne and Charlie, the Funky Four. . . The crème de la crème.

**VARIOUS**
**Reading Rock Vol. 1** (Mean)
Big names in the heavy metal field recorded over the years at the traditional Reading Festival bash. Untidy sound but many big names like Whitesnake, UFO, Budgie, Michael Schenker, Marillion, Spider, Bernie Marsden, Twisted Sister, Jackie Lynton, Randy California, Grand Prix and other lesser luminaries.

**VARIOUS**
**Salsoul's Greatest 12" Hits Vol. 1** (Salsoul)
Extended dance versions of four minor hits for the label: Loleatta Holloway's 'Hit And Run', Double Exposure's 'Ten Percent', First Choice's 'Doctor Love' and the Salsoul Orchestra's 'Magic Bird Of Fire'. Various producers.

**VARIOUS**
**The Secret Life Of Punks** (Secret)
Run-of-the-mill, and a trifle pedestrian, British punk compilation with the disreputable likes of The Exploited, Infa-Riot, The Business, Blitz, Peter and the Test Tube Babies, the 4-Skins, Chron-Gen, The Last Resort, The Partisans, the Gonads. . .

**VARIOUS**
**State Of The Union** (Zoar)
Experimental package featuring 34 groups of musicians each with more or less one minute to express his thoughts on the state of the arts. Patchy, of course, but a few nuggets here and there. Includes all US names: Adele Bertei, Tuli Kupferberg, John Lurie, etc. . . Produced by Elliott Sharp and L.A.M.G.F.

**VARIOUS**
**Streetnoise Vol. 1** (Epic)
Anthology of well-worn disco material from the Epic tape vaults.

**VARIOUS**
**Total Anarchy** (Anarchy)
14-track compilation of second-rate British no-hopers in the punk/heavy metal stakes: names you'll never hear again in all likelihood, such as One Way System, Chaotic Youth, Uproar, the Fits, External Menace, Antisocial and Death Sentence.

**VARIOUS**
**Touchdown** (Fontana)

touchdown

The best of the new Phonogram British signings: a healthy diversity of styles and many promising artists and bands among The Higsons, Farmer's Boys, Animal

Magic, Popular Voice, Maximum Joy, Vital Excursions, Dislocation Dance, Design for Living, Pinski Zoo. Many already have their first albums; this is an ideal sampler of their wares.

**VARIOUS**
**The Winning Hand** (Monument)

A modern country bonanza featuring a whole selection of duets with Dolly Parton, Kris Kristofferson, Willie Nelson and Brenda Lee in various combinations. Most of the collaborations involving Kristofferson come off best but overall the effect is most impressive and make this more than just a star-studded novelty set. Produced by Fred Foster.

**VARIOUS**
**Wonder Women: The History Of The Girl Group Sound, Vol. 1, 1961–1964** (Rhino)
Impeccable anthology including (among many others): the Shangri-Las, the Chiffons, the Jaynetts, the Dixie Cups. All of them undeniable hits which bring yesterday back with a whiff of joy and nostalgia. Various producers.

**VARIOUS**
**The Young And The Free** (Luna)
10-inch coloured vinyl sampler with scratch and sniff sleeve. What a load of gimmicks to introduce four tentative new British bands: Vietnamese Rose, Experiments with Ice, Stranger Comforts and Active Restraint. Did I hear the word 'psychedelia'? Produced by John Taylor.

**VELVET UNDERGROUND**
**(And So On)** (Plastic Individuals)
Australian import of semi-bootleg Velvet Underground memorabilia and rare-cum-demo tracks. Strictly for collectors of historical trivia.

**VELVET UNDERGROUND**
**Everything You've Ever Heard About. . .** (VU)
Triple boxed set of Velvet Underground

EVERYTHING YOU'VE EVER HEARD ABOUT.......
THE VELVET UNDERGROUND

rarities; includes pre-VU cuts by various bands with Lou Reed involvement (or even, in one case, suspected involvement), flexi-disc giveaways, out-takes of studio and live recordings. . . The power of Velvet Underground shines through on some tracks despite the atrocious sound quality, but three albums is really too much. The treasures could have been kept to two sides and proved more effective.

## VENOM
**Black Metal** (Neat)
Barbaric set of high-speed heavy metal. Disquieting rampage with nothing spared from the cliché and loudness artillery formation. For headbangers with terminal brain damage only.

## THE COUNT JOSEPH A. VIGLIONE
**Love & Flame** (New Rose)
Boston independent with an assured blend of melodic rockers with a gentle touch of early psychedelia. Various producers.

## EDDIE 'CLEANHEAD' VINSON
**Back In Town** (Charly)
Jazz and rhythm and blues of the 40s and 50s from a veteran swinger.

## VIRGIN PRUNES
**If I Die, I Die** (Rough Trade)
Debut independent album from a flamboyant Irish band mining the unending streak of British, 1984, doom rock. Tries unsuccessfully to be mind-expanding but remains dutifully earth-bound at all times. Anthems and dirges and little to say. Produced by Colin Newman.

## VOICE OF PROGRESS
**Mini Bus Driver** (Negus Roots)
Harsh, roots reggae from Junior Reid's group. An assured debut, in the same class as, say, Black Uhuru.

# W

## WAH!
**The Maverick Years 80–81** (Wah!)
Greatest (mostly) unreleased hits by the Liverpool band who, unlike Teardrop Explodes or Echo and the Bunnymen, garner all the Kudos but can't manage to sell any decent quantities of product. A cult band par excellence, Pete Wylie's Wah! are the missing link between psychedelia, Jim Morrison and the more contemporary British pop sensibility epitomised by Joy Division: a must buy for the cultured disc collector.

## THE WALL
**Day Tripper** (No Future)
Patchy British rock with Beatles cover, rocked-up version of the marriage vows ('Ceremonies'), Slade cover and other inconsequential musical oddities. Goes nowhere fast.

## WAR
**The Best Of The Music Band** (MCA)
Rapid compilation culled from War's only two (weaker) MCA albums. A trifle premature collection of lukewarm funk. Produced by Jerry Goldstein, Lonnie Jordan and Howard Scott.

## STEVE WARINER
**Steve Wariner** (RCA)
First album for a quality country guitar player sponsored by Chet Atkins. Smooth, effortless mid-tempo ballads at times reminiscent of the early Glen Campbell. Produced by Tom Collins.

## DIONNE WARWICK
**Heartbreaker** (Arista)
Dionne meets the Bee Gees and enjoys chart success again (with the title track). Rich production, languid vocals, a duet with Barry Gibb and a pleasant romantic excursion for the listener. Produced by Barry Gibb, Karl Richardson and Alby Galuten.

## MUDDY WATERS
**Rolling Stone** (Chess)
14 familiar but ever-pleasant r&b chestnuts by a master of the form, includes an alternate take of 'Rolling Stone'. Great company with Otis Spann, Jimmy Rogers, Little Walter, Willie Dixon and James Cotton all present and reelin'. Produced by Marshall Chess and Tomie Swan.

## WAVELENGTH
**Hurry Home** (Ariola)
Middle-of-the-road British pop, bouncy and empty. Not likely to be remembered long. Produced by Christopher Neil.

## WEEKEND
**La Variété** (Rough Trade)

la Varieté     by Weekend

The new band featuring Alison Statton of the lamented Young Marble Giants. Soft focus music drawing on African and Latin American rhythms and feels, this is a tasteful but ultimately disappointing album done with exquisite crispness but lacking in personality. Veers dangerously towards cocktail lounge, semi-exotic muzak (Astrid Gilberto music?). Could have been so much better. Produced by Robin Miller.

## WHITESNAKE
**Saints 'n' Sinners** (Liberty)
Harder sound for the veteran heavy metal and blues group with Cozy Powell now on drums. Crisp British power rock in the Deep Purple lineage with David Coverdale on vocals. Produced by Martin Birch.

## THE WIBBLEY BROTHERS
**Go Weird** (Rondolet)
Dubious satirical pop from a Midlands band. Flounders in its own puns.

## IRIS WILLIAMS
**You Belong To me** (EMI)
British soul singer with a safe choice of mouldy golden oldies for the slippers and cocoa set.

## CRIS WILLIAMSON
**Blue Rider** (Olivia)
Sixth album for an unassuming but always pleasing American folk-singer with feminist overtones. Produced by Cris Williamson and Tret Fure.

## PRECIOUS WILSON
**Light** (Epic)
Tasteful black soul singer who's big in Germany (land of Boney M?). Stylish and boring. Produced by Frank Farian.

## GARY WINDO
**Dogface** (Europa)
British saxophone player with a long list of jazz and experimental rock credentials on

solo outing, crossing over into diverse genres with his wife, Pam Windo and members of NRBQ. Often self-indulgent. Produced by Hal Willmer and Gary Windo.

### GEORGE WINSTON
**December** (Windham Hill)
Third solo piano effort from Winston on what is probably this year's jazz label (stealing honours from the perennially excellent but samey ECM) is a collection of improvisations on the theme of Xmas, going from carols to classical themes (Bach, Pachelbel). Nowhere as nauseating as you may think. Give it a try. Produced by George Winston and William Ackerman.

### ROBERT WINTERS AND FALL
**L-o-v-e** (Casablanca)
Traditional soul strong on vocals and harmonies. Al Green's title track stands out forcefully but the choice of material is consistent and a mighty dance feeling dominates throughout. Produced by Jimmy Bee and Morey Alexander.

### WISHBONE ASH
**Twin Barrels Burning** (AVM)
Now no longer on a major label, Wishbone Ash hit hard times on their own label. The usual outdated formula of roaring twin guitars and redundant power rock. No worse than before, its just that music has changed in the last ten years or so and this kind was always minor entertainment anyway. Produced by Ashley Howe, Stuart Epps and Wishbone Ash.

### WITCHFINDER GENERAL
**Death Penalty** (Heavy Metal)
Dispiriting heavy metal with an old-fashioned nod to devils and the occult. British, lacklustre and marred by a dubious sleeve. Produced by Pete Hinton.

### BILL WOLFER
**Wolf** (Constellation)
Blue-eyed, pop funk under the twin influences of Stevie Wonder and the Doobie Brothers. Pleasant if a bit samey and derivative at times. Wonder himself as well as Michael Jackson provide the good soul brand of approval with backing vocals. Produced by Bill Wolfer.

### STEVIE WOODS
**The Woman In My Life** (Cotillion)
Big sound, lachrymose ballads to keep those ladies emoting. Insincere attempt to cash in on the Bary Manilow effect. Produced by Jack White.

### WRIGHT BROTHERS
**Made In The USA** (Warners)
American country and western trio with a strong patriotic bent in their song lyrics ('Made in the USA', 'All American Girl').

WISHBONE ASH

Crisp harmonies and a tasteful album. Produced by Gary Klein.

### TAMMY WYNETTE
**Good Love And Heartbreak** (Epic)
Par for the course menu of plaintive country melodies and mildewed ballads with strings pouring out of every tremolo by the lady who does it best. Produced by George Richey.

# X

### XTC
**Waxworks/Beeswax** (Virgin)

Two albums initially packaged together regrouping past band efforts. 'Waxworks' regroups all the quirky, poppish singles ('This Is Pop', 'Making Plans for Nigel',

'Generals and Majors', 'Sgt Rock', 'Senses Working Overtime' etc. . .) while 'Beeswax' is a similar compilation of B-sides. Amusing concept but stretching matters a bit thin despite the catchy humour and sarcasm of Andy Partridge and cohorts. Various producers.

# Y

### YELLOWMAN AND FATHEAD
**Bad Boy Skanking** (Greensleeves)
Top ranking, reggae deejay fare with two of the best Jamaican stars combining forces. Lots of humour. Produced by Henry 'Junjo' Lawes.

### YOU'VE GOT FOETUS ON YOUR BREATH
**Ache** (Self-Immolation)
Alias Frank Zappa's San Francisco imitator Frank Want. Already a second album of angry, experimental rantings. Patchy humour amongst the musical collage. Will never make decent elevator muzak.

# Z

### ZIGGURAT
**Melodic Scandal** (Robox)
Second album by a group from Atlanta. Standard Southern rock fare done with professional élan. Two covers of Byrds material reflect the nostalgic roots of the band. Produced by Eddy Offord.

# The Best of the Best

## *Melody Maker's* records of the year

Although *Melody Maker*'s record of the year as featured in their end-of-year issue of 18/12/1982 is THE ASSOCIATES' Sulk, a closer tabulation of the individual choices submitted by 28 of their writers and photographers show this to be a particularly undemocratic choice. The following is a more accurate reflection of *MM*'s staff preferences:

1  **SIMPLE MINDS** New Gold Dreams (81–82–83–84)
2  **ABC** The Lexicon Of Love
3  **ELVIS COSTELLO** Imperial Bedroom
4  **SQUEEZE** Singles – 45s and Under
   **YAZOO** Upstairs At Eric's
   **DEXY'S MIDNIGHT RUNNERS** Too-Rye-Ay
7  **THE ASSOCIATES** Sulk
   **DURAN DURAN** Rio
   **MARVIN GAYE** Midnight Love
10 **SIOUXSIE AND THE BANSHEES** A Kiss In The Dreamhouse

Runners-up were FASHION (Fabrique), KID CREOLE AND THE COCONUTS (Tropical Gangsters), ORANGE JUICE (You Can't Hide Your Love Forever) and SHALAMAR (Friends).

*MELODY MAKER*'s contributors selected a total of 158 different albums.

## The *Guardian's* top 20 albums

Robin Denselow is the rock reviewer for the *Guardian*. These are, according to him, the best 20 albums of the year.

**GRACE JONES** Living My Life
**GRANDMASTER FLASH AND THE FURIOUS 5** The Message
**KID CREOLE AND THE COCONUTS** Tropical Gangsters
**THE JAM** The Gift
**KING SUNNY ADE AND HIS AFRICAN BEATS** JuJu Music
**ORCHESTRA MAKASSY** Agwaya
**BRUCE SPRINGSTEEN** Nebraska
**BLANCMANGE** Happy Families
**HAIRCUT 100** Pelican West
**ABC** The Lexicon Of Love
**YAZOO** Upstairs at Eric's
**RICHARD AND LINDA THOMPSON** Shoot Out The Lights
**DONALD FAGEN** The Nightfly
**MARVIN GAYE** Midnight Love
**JUNIOR** Ji
**SCRITTI POLITTI** Songs To Remember
**THE BEAT** Special Beat Service
**JIMMY CLIFF** Special
**DON HENLEY** I Can't Stand Still
**MADNESS** The Rise And Fall

Nine of the above 20 records do not appear in the list of 158 records nominated by *Melody Maker* contributors. Nor does it include 7 of *MM*'s top 10 (including 'both' winners)!

## The *NME* top twenty albums plus three

32 *New Musical Express* contributors, artists and staff got together and the following emerged as their choice for the albums of 1982.

1  **MARVIN GAYE** Midnight Love
2  **ELVIS COSTELLO** Imperial Bedroom
3  **ABC** The Lexicon Of Love
4  **THE CLASH** Combat Rock
5  **DEXY'S MIDNIGHT RUNNERS** Too-Rye-Ay
6  **YAZOO** Upstairs At Eric's
7  **DONALD FAGEN** The Nightfly
8  **KING SUNNY ADE AND HIS AFRICAN BEATS** JuJu Music
9  **SHALAMAR** Friends
10 **GREGORY ISAACS** Night Nurse
11 **SIOUXSIE AND THE BANSHEES** A Kiss In The Dreamhouse
12 **KID CREOLE AND THE COCONUTS** Tropical Gangsters
13 **VAN MORRISON** Beautiful Vision
14 **GRANDMASTER FLASH** The Message
15 **CURTIS MAYFIELD** Honesty
16 **ROBERT WYATT** Nothing Can Stop Us Now
17 **BOBBY WOMACK** The Poet
18 **THE ASSOCIATES** Sulk
19 **ROXY MUSIC** Avalon
20 **CULTURE CLUB** Kissing To Be Clever

Compilation albums were voted on separately and the following three came out tops:

1  **MADNESS** Complete Madness
2  **SQUEEZE** The Singles – 45s and Under
3  **VARIOUS ARTISTS** Sounds d'Afrique Vol. 2

## The *Smash Hits* readers' top twenty albums of 1982

*Smash Hits* is the most popular music magazine in the UK. The following poll results were featured in the 23rd December issue.

1  **DURAN DURAN** Rio
2  **THE KIDS FROM FAME** The Kids From Fame
3  **ABC** The Lexicon Of Love
4  **YAZOO** Upstairs At Eric's
5  **ADAM ANT** Friend or Foe
6  **THE JAM** The Gift
7  **DEXY'S MIDNIGHT RUNNERS** Too-Rye-Ay
8  **HAIRCUT ONE HUNDRED** Pelican West
9  **CULTURE CLUB** Kissing To Be Clever
10 **MADNESS** Complete Madness
11 **DEPECHE MODE** A Broken Fame
12 **ULTRAVOX** Quartet
13 **SIMPLE MINDS** New Gold Dream (81–82–83–84)
14 **GARY NUMAN** I, Assassin
15 **TOYAH** The Changeling

16 **KID CREOLE AND THE COCONUTS** Tropical Gangsters
17 **THE CLASH** Combat Rock
18 **SHALAMAR** Friends
19 **PAUL McCARTNEY** Tug Of War
   **ROXY MUSIC** Avalon

## *Time* magazine's best of 1982

**RY COODER** The Border
**GREG COPELAND** Revenge Will Come
**ELVIS COSTELLO AND THE ATTRACTIONS** Imperial Bedroom
**BILLY JOEL** The Nylon Curtain
**DAVID JOHANSEN** Live It Up
**LITTLE STEVEN AND THE DISCIPLES OF SOUL** Men Without Women
**PAUL McCARTNEY** Tug Of War
**BRUCE SPRINGSTEEN** Nebraska
**RICHARD AND LINDA THOMPSON** Shoot Out The Lights

## and finally . . . Jakubowski's choice for 1982

Faithful to my aggravating habits, this is a highly personal and idiosyncratic list of my own 25 fave albums – not necessarily the best but those I enjoyed most and will still be playing more often than they perhaps deserve over the coming years. The order is alphabetical – damned if I could rate them individually!

**ABC** The Lexicon Of Love
**LAURIE ANDERSON** Big Science
**BLANCMANGE** Happy Families
**T-BONE BURNETT** Trap Door
**JOHN CALE** Music For A New Society
**ROSANNE CASH** Somewhere In The Stars
**GREG COPELAND** Revenge Will Come
**FELT** Crumbling The Antiseptic Beauty
**A FLOCK OF SEAGULLS** A Flock of Seagulls
**PETER GABRIEL** Peter Gabriel 4
**HI-FI** Mood For Mallards
**RUPERT HINE** Waving Not Drowning
**ROBERT HUNTER** Promontory Rider
**KING CRIMSON** Beat

**JONI MITCHELL** Wild Things Run Fast
**NEW ORDER** Movement
**RICHARD PINHAS** L'Ethique
**LOU REED** The Blue Mask
**ROXY MUSIC** Avalon
**SIMPLE MINDS** New Gold Dream (81–82–83–84)
**SOUNDTRACK** Cat People
**BRUCE SPRINGSTEEN** Nebraska
**TALKING HEADS** The Name Of This Band Is Talking Heads
**RICHARD AND LINDA THOMPSON** Shoot Out The Lights
**ROBERT WYATT** Nothing Can Stop Us Now

But then, a number of worthy albums missed out by very little – a question of mood, what I ate for breakfast or hazy aural memories. Still in no order, these are the next 25 which stand out for me from the vinyl jungle. Call it an alternative top 25!

**KING SUNNY ADE AND HIS AFRICAN BEATS** JuJu Music
**CARLA BLEY** Live!
**DAVID BOWIE** Baal
**CAPTAIN BEEFHEART** Ice-Cream For The Crows
**PHIL COLLINS** Hello, I Must Be Going
**COMSAT ANGELS** Fiction
**DONALD FAGEN** The Nightfly
**JOHNNY G.** Water Into Wine
**MARVIN GAYE** Midnight Love
**JOE JACKSON** Night And Day
**DAVID JOHANSEN** Live It Up
**GREG KIHN BAND** Kihntinued
**MEN WITHOUT HATS** Rhythm Of Youth
**IGGY POP** Zombie Birdhouse
**PSYCHEDELIC FURS** Forever Now
**THE RECORDS** Music From Both Sides
**SNIFF 'N' THE TEARS** Ride The Blue Divide
**THE SHOES** Boomerang
**PETE TOWNSHEND** Even Cowboys Have Chinese Eyes
**TUXEDO MOON** Divine
**VARIOUS ARTISTS** Music And Rhythm
**JENNIFER WARNES** The Best of Jennifer Warnes
**X** Under The Big Black Sun
**YAZOO** Upstairs at Eric's
**WARREN ZEVON** The Envoy

And one more for the road, which rightfully belongs in either of the above selections but gets a solo mention as a rather unusual box of 3 albums of improvisatory piano music: KEITH JARRETT's Concerts.

# Index